YUGOSLAVIA

TISZA RIVER

Y

R O U M A N I A

MURESUL RIVER

čka Topola
OVINA
ja
ad
Petrovaradin
Sremski Karlovici
Zemun
BELGRADE
acla
Senaja
Ub
Darosava
Mladenovac
Arandjelovac
Topola
Grošnica
Knić
Kragujevac
rad
će
Čačak
Z. MORAVA
MORAVA R.
Nova Varoš

OLTUL R.

DANUBE RIVER

B U L G A R I A

J. MORAVA

Slivnica

Sofia

Scoplje

Dračevo

A L B A N I A

Tirana

VARDAR R.

STRUMA R.

CAREV
DVOR

G R E E C E

Salonika

PALACIOS

The Silent People Speak

THE
SILENT PEOPLE
SPEAK

Robert St. John

GARDEN CITY, N.Y.
Doubleday & Company, Inc.
1948

The lines from "Thanks" by Arthur Johnston & Sam Coslow are copyrighted, 1933, by Famous Music Corporation.

To the Orphan of Goražde Who May Not Live;
To the Moslem Who Was Killed But Didn't Die;
To the People of Bosnia Turning Yellow from Too Much Corn;
To Jacqueline, David, Anita, and Other Seekers-after-the-Truth;
But Especially to Those Silent People Now Learning to Speak

THIS BOOK IS HUMBLY DEDICATED

Contents

Part Four
THESE ARE THE DALMATIANS

Part Five
THESE ARE THE MONTENEGRINS

Part Six
THESE ARE THE CROATIANS

Part Seven
THIS IS THE VOJVODINA

Part Eight
THESE ARE THE SERBS

Part Nine
THIS IS GREECE

Part Ten
THESE ARE THE MACEDONIANS

Part Eleven
THIS IS YUGOSLAVIA'S YOUTH

Foreword

Peace TODAY is that little curly-haired girl who once lay in the hospital at Argos, Greece, whimpering in the dark all night because her right arm hung in blackened tatters and she wanted her mother, who was dead. Today she lives with foster parents in a village high in the hills. Today she's hungry because the government of her country has decided to starve people in the hills, for certain political reasons which the little girl with only one arm is still too young to begin to understand.

Peace today is crowds of singing people in Belgrade's public square called Terazzia, where dead bodies once lay by the hundreds because they rushed out to see what that crazy noise in the sky meant. Today the people singing in Terazzia are students, professors, bank clerks, and office workers, giving their time voluntarily to push wheelbarrows and handle shovels, to make a new city.

Peace today is a lot of American soldiers in a lot of places like Greece wondering why they are there.

Peace today is thousands of people in America clapping approval when some politician, trying to outdo some other politician, shouts that we must start atomizing the rest of humanity without further provocation.

But peace today is other people, millions and millions of them, not only in America but all over the world, impatient with their politicians and silently angry when they are told that there must be another world war.

Peace today is smells. Good smells. The smell of fresh-cut pine from the mountains being hauled down into the valleys to rebuild houses and hospitals and schools. The smell of good earth being plowed again for the first time in many a year. The smell of apple blossoms, new-mown hay, and clover. But there are people who still remember the smells of war. The smell of burning villages. And the smell of roasting human flesh.

Peace today is noises. Good noises. The noise of hammers and saws; thrashing machines and reapers. The shouts of young people building a new railroad. But there are people who still remember the noises of war. The noise of a Stuka when it screams down in a dive right at your head with the wind making the sirens go round and round like mad. And the thick, heavy noise of a bomb when it falls. And the noise when the glass breaks and the walls crumble. And the noise of silence which holds all eternity in its grasp for a split second and then lets go, quickly. And the noises people then make. Hopeless, scared, soul-seared people who scream and moan, or just whimper. In Europe they still remember those noises of war. Peace today is the fear that those noises will soon return.

You can forget what you see. And what you smell. But you can never forget noises. They beat through your head years later. They make you see Belgrade when you're way off in New York. They make you smell burning human flesh when you return and revisit a peaceful town where you once saw Stukas dive-bomb a hospital train and set thirty cars full of wounded soldiers on fire. The noises of war won't let you sleep, even years later. You think you know about noises? Wait until you hear the noises of war and then you will understand why Europe looks to the United States and cries:

"Why?"

I know about the little girl with the arm that hung in blackened tatters because I lay beside her in a hospital all one night while she whimpered. I know about war because I was there and saw things and smelled things and heard things. I know about the sights and the sounds and the smells of peace, too, because I have come back to see and to hear and to smell once more. But I may not be able to put it down so it will make any sense to you. I don't know any of the answers, so don't expect me to figure them out for you. I'm just an observer of the human comedy, only it begins to look more than ever like the human tragedy.

If I were on somebody's pay roll in Moscow I could tell you things that would either make you hate certain American leaders, or say I was on somebody's pay roll in Moscow.

If I were on somebody's pay roll in New York I could tell you things which would either make you hate the Russians, or say I was on somebody's pay roll in New York.

And it would all be the truth, either way. Or part of the truth, anyway. You can see what you wish to see and think what you wish to think in times of peace, just as in times of war. And you can make it all fit into any pattern you wish, if you have a pattern already. But you can't change the facts. It's easy to be a propaganda dispenser or a propaganda consumer. Everything fits in so perfectly. But I'm just telling you what I saw and heard and smelled. If it makes any sense to you, all right. If it fits into your pattern, fine. If it doesn't, just skip it. Then you will be able to forget. And that will be fine too—for you—maybe.

Bohinjska-Bistrica-Jezero,
Yugoslavia.
September, 1947.

PART ONE

This Is Anyman's Land

Chapter One

LIGHTS AND SHADOWS

ON DECEMBER the twentieth the S.S. *Drottningholm* sailed from her berth at the foot of Fifty-seventh Street, Manhattan, for the port of Göteborg, Sweden. Any schoolchild knows that that's an odd route to follow to get from New York to Yugoslavia. But the *Drottningholm* was the only ship sailing that particular week. And she had plenty of vacant cabins because few people wanted to be at sea on Christmas Day.

On the night of December the twenty-fourth I stood at the deck rail staring off into the black of the sea. Sky and water were one. No line of demarcation. Just deep, deep black. Except for the white foam created by the ship. It's a spiritual experience, standing on a ship's deck at midnight looking at . . . nothing . . . and thinking of . . . everything. Behind me the purser quietly tacked a typewritten sheet of paper onto the *Drottningholm's* bulletin board. A summary of news received over the ship's radio.

In Indo-China French troops were in open warfare with troops of the native republic. Martial law had been declared. In Louisville fire broke out in a hotel. People panicked. Disaster was narrowly averted. In London a British M.P. declared that head-hunting in Borneo had been resumed on a heavy scale. In Washington the United States Army announced revolutionary changes in the size and armament of the American infantry and tank corps. Washington said this would greatly increase fire power, shock, and maneuverability. In Bombay six persons were killed in riots. In New York City a banker's wife jumped out of the fifth-story window of her hotel. Funeral services would be held Sunday. In London Ernest Bevin took part in a debate over whether it would be possible for Russia and Great Britain to get along. In Indiana a man killed a number of people with a knife. From China correspondents reported their opinion that a full-scale civil war was now inevitable. In Washington they were arguing about how to outlaw strikes.

Everywhere men, feeble little men, fighting and feuding and making a mess of trying to get along. But here on the Atlantic, where sky and sea merged in a blackness so subtle no eye could see the line, the great waves rolled on and on. Back and forth. Up and down. Endlessly. Unceasingly. With the rhythm of nature. Defiantly. Incontrovertibly. Back and forth. Up and down. In and out. With the rhythm of nature. Nature has a great mystic purpose. But man founders. Man has yet to understand his place in the scheme of things.

Civil war in China. Riots in Bombay. Plans for war in Washington. And plans for breaking strikes. A near-riot in Kentucky and a man gone berserk with a knife in Indiana.

Man out of tune with nature. Man who has neither become reconciled to letting nature be the master nor has succeeded in conquering nature. Man out of rhythm. Man, the one discordant note in the Symphony of Life. Man, the violinist playing E-minor when the score calls for C-major. Man who can split an atom and make a piece of steel fly through the air faster than the speed of sound. But still he can't figure out how to stop a civil war in China. Or strikes in the U.S.A. Or a near riot in Kentucky. Or killings in Indiana.

You stand at the rail of a ship at midnight and look at the place where sky ought to meet the sea. But there is no line of demarcation. Nature has blended her colors so well that it's all a black fugue. A symphony of color and sound in which there's no discordant note.

The ship stays afloat as long as it does not try to oppose the rhythm of the sea. It rolls and tosses. To the rhythm of the sea. But man has no rhythm. Man takes two steps forward, one backward. Two forward, three backward. One forward, one back. And there is no rhythm. The sea moves with a majestic beat. And the sky blends in with the water. Nature has her moods, calm and severe. But she seems always to move with a rhythm and a purpose, which *is* a purpose, although its purpose may be its very lack of purpose.

PART TWO

This Is Belgrade

Chapter Two

THE CHASE OF THE WILL-O'-THE-WISP BEGINS

THE *wagon-lit* conductor woke us at eight-thirty. I stuck my nose out from under the covers and then rolled over again. I lay there thinking that I was really warm for the first time in many days. Through the frosted window I could see that snow was falling outside. It might be a long time before I'd be warm again. And so I lay there until the train got almost into the city, enjoying the warmth. I lay there telling myself:

Now the test really begins. This is the Balkans. And it's midwinter. They're short of fuel all over the country. Things will be grim in many ways. The Balkans aren't like New York or Chicago or San Francisco. This is the edge of the Orient, even if it doesn't look like it on a map. Just existing here, the way Americans like to exist, is a job. A man hunting for the truth would have other problems.

I thought these things as the Simplon-Orient Express wormed its way through the snow-packed approaches of Belgrade on the morning of January the thirtieth. We were getting into the capital city of the Yugoslavs. Here truth would probably take a great deal of hunting. Here, if Truth were found at all, she would be hiding behind frightening camouflage. Strong forces on either side would be trying to conceal her from anyone's view. And if she were captured and photographed and fingerprinted and put on display there would be skeptics, of course, who would say:

"How do you know? How do you know she's not an impostor? How can we be sure that this is the Real Thing? She doesn't look a bit like I was told she would look. How do you know this is the right one? Have you got her birth certificate? Have you talked to her mother? When was she born? Who was her father? Have you got witnesses? What does the Embassy say? Let's talk to Mister Marshall, and Truman, and Churchill."

They'll twist her and pull her apart. They'll take off an arm and hold it up and say to the crowd:

"Does this look like Truth to you?"

And the crowd will laugh.

Outside it was fairyland. The snow lay deep on the ground. The trees were tinseled with hoarfrost as delicately as if it had been put there during the night by the hands of angels. Outside there was no sign of human or animal life. Yugoslavia was in the grip of bitter winter.

We crossed the Sava and entered the ancient capital of the Serbs. At the station I pushed my steamer trunk, two suitcases, a typewriter, and two coats through the window to a porter. He didn't understand sign language very well but he did get me through the depot without any inspection of my luggage. Each city in Yugoslavia maintains its own controls. Bundles, parcels, suitcases, and trunks are searched as passengers enter or leave a railroad depot to prevent the transportation of goods which might be sold in the Black Market. It's annoying and it's bureaucracy. But after a sample, in France, of what happens to a country when the disease of the Black Market starts working on its inners, no one can be very critical of what a country does in the way of controls. Yet it is an annoyance having to open every parcel and piece of luggage each time you go through a railroad station.

In front of the depot the porter made a noise in his throat which bore a faint resemblance to the English word "automobile," so I answered him with the first Slavic words I'd ever learned:

"*Da da.*"

But there were no automobiles in front of the depot. Just hundreds and hundreds of sleds and sleighs. Some were pulled by scrawny horses. Most of them were pulled by panting human beings. All the horse-drawn vehicles were grabbed up immediately. A man who might have been a taxi starter if this had been America and if there had been any taxicabs made a long speech with sweeping gestures. I remembered back six years and realized that most of the words were numbers. He obviously was trying to tell me that it was only x minutes or x miles or x kilometers to the center of town. So I hailed a man with a contraption on runners about twice the length and width of a child's sled and engaged him. He loaded the trunk, two suitcases, and typewriter onto the sled. Then he took off two coats he was wearing and put them on top of the luggage. I didn't understand, because it was bitter cold here in Belgrade. An icy wind was blowing from across the Sava. But as soon as he hitched himself into the harness and we started I did understand. It was uphill most of the way and the hill was steep. In a few minutes perspiration was running down his nose, his forehead, his neck. The snow was piled high on either side of the street. Horsedrawn sleds were trying to pass us. And sleighs with tinkling bells. Farther along we got involved in traffic tangles of American-made jeeps and big American trucks. Some had the letters "UNRRA" on their hoods. Others were marked "Red Cross." All of them were driven by Yugoslavs who swerved in and out and around each other in typical Balkan style. Finally my perspiring human horse got tired and showed me how I could help by getting into harness too. I don't suppose it's more than a mile from the railroad station to the center of town, but it seemed a dozen times that distance, going uphill all the way. I hadn't had any breakfast yet. Not even a cup of something hot. But we finally made it. The Majestic is a hotel I couldn't forget. It was in the Majestic on the night of March 26, 1941, that many members of the pro-Nazi Cvetković-Cinco-Marković Government were living. The night of March the twenty-sixth was when Air Force General Simović pulled off the *coup d'état* that led to the invasion of Yugoslavia by the Germans. It was the Majestic I was trying to get into at two-thirty the next morning when General Simović's tanks moved into the city. I was to meet Ray Brock of the New York *Times* at the Majestic and exchange bits of information about what was happening. But instead they threw me into a miniature concentration camp in a park for several hours. When I finally got free the Majestic was surrounded by enough guards to prevent the entrance or exit of a mouse or an army.

This time the Majestic was guarded only by great mounds of white snow. The sled puller took my luggage into the lobby. I changed a twenty-dollar bill at the desk. I felt sorry for him so I tried to figure out what a generous fee would be. On the train someone had told me that an important government official here in Yugoslavia gets four thousand dinar a month. That's one hundred and thirty-three dinar per day. Or about two dollars and sixty-six cents. At that rate . . .

But I was saved the trouble of showing my appreciation. The little man told the clerk his fee for the twenty minutes of work was one hundred and twenty dinar. Almost the income of an important government official for a full day. So I paid and stopped feeling sorry for him.

The desk clerk in a mixture of Russian, German, English, and Serbo-Croat said there were no vacant rooms. There wouldn't be any for many days. And he didn't think there was a vacant room in any other hotel in the city. I was hungry and tired but housing was the prime problem. So I left the luggage in the Majestic lobby and started on foot for the American Embassy.

Chapter Three

WHO SAID THE DEAD DON'T CRY?

To GET from the Majestic Hotel to the American Embassy it's necessary to go through the square called Terazzia. Terazzia is dominated by a large white structure called the Albania Building. It's Belgrade's only skyscraper. Nicky used to have an apartment on the top floor. Nicky was a handsome young Serb who held an important job in the State Senate in the old days. From one of the windows of his apartment on March 27, 1941, I covered the coup d'état celebration. From up there I watched hysterical crowds breaking the windows of German and Italian travel agencies, stamping their feet on pictures of Hitler and Mussolini, and cheering each new display of British and American flags. Before the day was over someone draped a big American flag from a window near the top of the Albania. I still remember how attractive it looked against the white stone of the building.

I also remember the morning of Bloody Sunday. How we went through Terazzia with a milk wagon loaded with what luggage we'd managed to save from our rooms at the Srpski Kralj, after the hotel had been bombed and set on fire. We'd been surprised that the German pilots had missed the Albania because they came down low with hardly any opposition from guns or fighter planes. But that Palm Sunday morning after the German raids were over the Albania Building stood intact except for a few broken windows. On another Sunday, four years later to the week, American planes unloaded onto Terazzia. They weren't able to fly low, but their bombs were bigger and their pin-pointing was almost as accurate as if they, too, had been flying at chimney height. Yet here was the Albania Building. White and chrome. As glistening as ever. Even though there were now a lot of vacant lots in the neighborhood. Even though the buildings clustered at the Albania's feet hadn't fared so well.

Terazzia six years later.

Today the square was heaped high with snow. Someone said the snow had been falling for five days. They said most of the country was completely snowbound. But traffic was flowing through Terazzia as if it were a summer day. Hundreds of men were loading the snow into trucks. They were all American trucks. I wondered whether the workmen knew they were American trucks.

Walking through Terazzia I remembered the railroad station at Milan, Italy, forty-eight hours before. The train shed. A thousand men with wooden shovels small enough for children to use. And it was cold there too. Yet we noticed that the average man, by stop-watch timing, moved one shovelful every minute and thirty seconds. Here in Belgrade there was no leaning on shovels. These men in Terazzia were going at it as if they really wanted to get the streets clear of snow. Could it be the difference between the temperament of Italians and Slavs? One might think so if one hadn't been here years ago. In those days Belgrade was just like Milan. Perhaps more so.

Then memories began to crowd in again. This shop we're passing now. Six years ago it was a jewelry store. On Bloody Sunday morning at this very spot I kicked a cardboard box on the sidewalk. I kicked it because it was one small way I could express my feelings about what the Nazis had done here in the previous few hours. The box was full of diamond rings and watches and other glittering baubles. They went flying into the street. But no one stopped to pick them up. Everyone was more interested in saving his neck than he was in loot.

Today this same shop is a *kafana*. A place to buy food and drink. A stream of humanity pours through the doors. Today at this same spot people are primarily interested in getting a little nourishment and bodily warmth.

That trolley car going by. It isn't like the trolleys we had in Belgrade six years ago. The old ones were beautiful things. They glided along as if they were on rubber tires. Six years ago there was one right here in Terazzia lying on its side. During the war they were all either destroyed or sent north by the Germans. The ones they have now are relics. And they don't sound as if they had rubber tires.

In Terazzia I saw a man slip on a piece of ice and fall flat on his back. For a split second he lay there without moving. Then a young Yugoslav army officer gave him a hand and they both laughed and the man who had slipped got up and went on.

On Bloody Sunday this same sidewalk was covered with bodies that lay still for longer than a split second. They lay still because they were dead. But there was no blood on them. There were no more signs of wounds and death than on this man who had just slipped. This man's face was bluish-white because of the cold. Those faces were bluish-white too. As if some master make-up artist had just finished preparing them for ghost roles. I remember that I turned one of the corpses over to see what had caused death. It apparently was just the repercussion from the bombs that had landed out in the street. That day six years ago we were almost alone in Terazzia. Except for the dead and dying. Today Terazzia is jammed with humanity. At least half the men are in army uniforms.

In the old days under the monarchy Belgrade was a man's city. Just as New York has always been a woman's city. Here the male was the peacock. I once made a survey and compiled some statistics. I found four and a half men's shops in Belgrade to every establishment dealing in things for women. Looking around Terazzia today that situation doesn't seem to have changed. There are many officers in gray and gold, with heavy greatcoats almost touching the ground. They're dazzling to look at, so tall and erect, so handsome, and so perfectly groomed. Their wives and sweethearts who tag along beside them, willing to shine in their reflected glory, have shawls over their heads and shoes on their feet not fit for this kind of weather, and the wraps over their shoulders are pathetically insufficient for the sort of winter Belgrade is having.

At the American Embassy a reception clerk said she was sorry but Ambassador Patterson was not in the country. He was somewhere in America writing a book, she said, or delivering some lectures. So I talked to Mrs. Bogogević, the Embassy's housing expert. In between making phone calls for me she said she had been right here in Belgrade since I last saw her six years ago. I mentioned what a freak it was that the German pilots hadn't hit the Albania Building on Bloody Sunday. She smiled strangely and said:

"You thought Bloody Sunday was something, didn't you? It was a children's picnic compared with that other Sunday four years later when your American planes came. The Germans dropped little bombs. Really big ones hadn't been invented yet. But in 1945, on Easter Sunday . . . I shall never live to forget it! It was so terrible! There isn't a word in your language or ours either to say it. And you missed the Albania too. You didn't knock it into the street. But one of your bombs did come down in a slanting direction like this"—she cut a diagonal swish through the air with her hand—"and it hit the side of the building near the bottom. That was one bomb we were glad about."

I could tell she was by the way she smiled.

"You see, the Germans were using the Albania for their offices. Down in the cellar they had an air-raid shelter. The best in the city. Whenever the bombs started dropping the rest of us were very jealous of those Germans down in their deep shelter. How could anything happen to them?

"Down there with them they were allowed to take their girls. The girls who worked in their offices and . . . well, their girls . . . the girls who worked for them in other ways. Anyway, that Easter Sunday the Albania shelter was full of them when the American bomb came slanting down this way."

She went through the gesture again. She seemed to like pretending her right hand was that American bomb.

"I know all about it because one of the girls was a Yugoslav who rented my apartment from me. She was one of them killed. One hundred and twenty German officers and girls were *morte* . . . dead. But now"—and she sighed—"now they have it all fixed up so hardly anyone who wasn't here will ever believe the story."

Mrs. Bogogević found me a room in a place in Terazzia called the Grande Hotel Kasina. On the ground floor there was a dirty *kafana* packed all day and late into the night with an odd assortment of people. They lingered a long time, probably because the place was so warm with so much concentrated body heat. The smells which floated up through the hotel rooms made the stale-beer odor of a cheap waterfront saloon seem like sweet perfume by comparison.

The clerk said I had Suite 504, top floor. It consisted of two bare rooms and a bath. There was one blanket on each of the two narrow beds. Both faucets in the bathtub turned out water cold enough to use in a highball without ice. The roof of the building was apparently flat and it apparently was piled high with snow. And the roof obviously leaked. When I arrived the water was just beginning to trickle through the ceiling. By night the trickle was a river and the water stood several inches deep in the bedroom, living room, and bath. I went to the manager and tried to explain. He didn't understand so I took him by the hand upstairs. He stood there shaking his head. Then he cluck-clucked several times with his tongue and left. The water continued to pour in. I never saw the manager again.

The only reason I'm positive the temperature in the room was above 32 degrees Fahrenheit is because the water on the floor never froze. But it was close to 32. I'm sure of that. There were three radiators in the three rooms and 15 per cent was added to the rent for *chauffage*. But I couldn't put my hand on any of the radiators they were so cold to the touch.

After I got my bags settled in my new home I went out looking for a doctor. I laughed at myself as I limped along. It was the left leg that got banged up in Cicero, Illinois, when some of Scarface Al Capone's friends took me for a ride a great many years ago. Then in Greece, after getting safely out of Yugoslavia in '41, it was the right leg that stopped a few machine-gun bullets from a Nazi plane. And now it was the left leg again. It had happened at Venice, on the way from Paris to Belgrade. The Simplon-Orient Express had gone off without me while I was in the railroad station trying to get some water to put into a thermos bottle that belonged to a diplomat's wife. In trying to catch the train I'd met with an accident which left an ugly hole in my left leg.

Myrtis Colthorp, the Red Cross nurse at the American Embassy, said there was a scarcity of doctors in Belgrade so she'd look at it. She said the gash should have had some stitches taken in it. But it was too late for that. Now the danger was infection.

"We wouldn't want to have to amputate."

I asked her why medical people always seem to have such a grim sense of humor. She just laughed.

It was dark by the time I returned to the Grande Hotel Kasina and I wanted to get to work at the typewriter. But the only electric-light bulb in the three rooms had a power of twenty watts and was up near the ceiling. So I interviewed the concierge. His knowledge of English was very limited. So was the supply of electric-light bulbs in Yugoslavia. I understood that much. Back in No. 504 I found I could no longer get into the bathroom because of the stream of water pouring through the ceiling. It made a pleasant sound and it put me to sleep, although I dreamed all night of going over Niagara Falls in a barrel. By morning most of the accumulated water had drained off into the rooms below.

Chapter Four

IF THERE'S NO SPARK, MAKE ONE

IN THE SPRING OF 1941 there were often as many as twenty or thirty British and American reporters making their headquarters at the Srpski Kralj Hotel. All three American news agencies were represented by full-time correspondents. Also the three American radio networks and the important American newspapers. The two largest American news agencies also had "stringers" in at least three or four other Yugoslav cities who reported every day to the bureau chief in Belgrade by telephone. The four veterans of this Anglo-American press colony had been in the country a total of thirty or forty years. They spoke the language like natives. They knew the country as well as you know your own back yard. They could sing the native songs, dance the native dances, and tell you all about the sectional customs and costumes. One of them had the largest private collection of books on Yugoslav art in existence. Two had married Yugoslav girls. A third had lived with a Yugoslav mistress so long that they were accepted as husband and wife.

Today only one American newspaper and one American news agency have full-time staff correspondents in Belgrade. And there are no "stringers" in the rest of the country. The only permanent full-time British correspondent is the representative of the Reuters agency.

All three of the Anglo-American reporters are young and inexperienced in European reporting. One is a German refugee who became an American citizen in 1940, worked for a year on a New York paper, and then went into the Army. The second was a New York press agent before he became an army public relations officer. The third had a brief experience at foreign reporting in Palestine before being sent to Belgrade.

All three are married. The wives of two of these three men have learned about journalism watching their husbands at work. One of them sends an average of one or two cables a week to the second largest American agency. The other writes occasional newspaper and magazine articles on a free-lance basis. All five of these young correspondents suffer from inadequate salaries in a country where there is no Black Market, where the penalty for changing money at anything but the legal rate is execution, and where the cost of living is extremely high.

American agencies and papers are so worried about being beaten a few minutes on a story by some other agency or paper that the Belgrade reporters don't dare leave home base to find out what's happening in the rest of the country. So they remain most of the time within a few hundred yards of Terazzia being barraged by propaganda from both sides. All five of them have tried to keep their heads. They told me that they put up a running fight with editors at home and diplomats on the spot in their effort to tell the truth as they see it. They said they were principally handicapped by the demand of their editors for sensations which will make headlines that will sell more papers. They said that they rarely have an opportunity to engage in what Victor Lawson, one-time publisher of the Chicago *Daily News,* called "constructive journalism." If there's an airplane shooting, a riot, or some other development which appears to put Yugoslavia in a bad light, there's hardly any limit, they said, to the number of words they can cable. But if any one of them tries to send a dispatch which tells how the people are building a new railroad, or increasing their own food supply, or overcoming illiteracy, back comes the "hold-down" order.

Messages from their editors, which they showed me, kept them constantly aware that they were in a highly competitive business in which the rewards often go to the man who can find some way to steal the headlines away from his competitors.

I watched them for months fighting with the Yugoslav Press Department over various matters. But they agreed fully with the Yugoslav Press Department on one thing. That the most twisted reporting about Yugoslavia came from the typewriters of what they called the "Hit-Run Reporters." Papers and agencies which do not wish to bear the expense of covering Yugoslavia between sensations send roving correspondents in at frequent intervals. They stay in a capital city just long enough to pick up the latest collection of diplomatic rumors. They don't have time to check them thoroughly. Nor the contacts either. They steal the headlines away from the permanent correspondents and make life difficult for Anglo-American reporters who follow them.

When I got to Belgrade the press colony was still talking about the last Hit-Runner who had gone through. She was young and they said she was beautiful. She had come from New York to gather material for some magazine articles. She was having her first fling at foreign reporting and she liked it. It had been a long time since the foreign colony of Belgrade had seen a new American feminine face, so the young lady from New York was wined and dined. She was rushed from one cocktail party to another. The permanent correspondents said she hardly got out of the area bounded by the British Embassy, the Majestic Hotel, and the Moskva. But after a visit of a few days she wrote some fine articles on "What I Found Out about Yugoslavia."

One day soon after I reached Belgrade Osgood Crowthers, the Associated Press correspondent, showed me something his New York office had sent him without comment. It was a statement made at a meeting of managing editors in Los Angeles by a New York State publisher. It was a criticism of foreign reporting. It said no American could know another country simply by reading press dispatches from abroad in his daily paper. Then it said:

"In reporting on relations with other nations, too much emphasis is put upon our conflicts with them, ideological and otherwise. If a spark is there we tend to blow it into a flame. If the spark is not there, we break out our flint and strike one."

Crowthers was encouraged when he read it. He'd seen many sparks kindled by many Hit-Run reporters. But he didn't look very happy when I met him a few days later. He had just received some clippings from America. They were clippings of a dispatch he had written about the trial of a Croatian bishop on a charge of collaborating with the enemy during the war. Crowthers had tried to be objective and impartial. He had tried to give equal space to the government's charges and the arguments of the defense. But somewhere along the line, probably on the copy desks of the individual papers, the paragraphs giving the government's side of the story had been cut out, leaving only the bishop's defense. That made the dispatch sound very one-sided. Crowthers said:

"What's a man to do? How can you get the truth in print even if you try?"

I talked to all the permanent and non-permanent correspondents I met in Belgrade about the Iron Curtain which is supposed to keep America from getting the truth about what is going on in Yugoslavia.

Before the war Yugoslavia and practically every other country in this part of Europe had a strict censorship. We used to talk slang over the phone to our offices in Switzerland for twenty or thirty minutes at a stretch trying to get one small piece of news out of the country over a censor's objection. I remember one time when we couldn't get a word out of Belgrade for fifty-six hours because of censors. How about censorship now?

They all agreed on the answer. Today there is no censorship in Yugoslavia in any form, hidden or otherwise. A man writes out his dispatch, takes it to a cable office, and within a few hours it is received in London or New York as sent.

Arthur Brandell of the *Times* did have one complaint.

"They go farther than that, darn them. If you make a few typographical mistakes in your dispatch and cross out the words with x's, the cable company won't accept it unless you count the crossed-out places and sign a statement that you yourself crossed out exactly that number of words. I suppose it's a good idea because then nobody can accuse them of crossing out the words, but it's a hell of a bother."

How about letters?

Mary Brandell, Arthur's wife, who writes dispatches occasionally for the United Press, laughed and said:

"There is no censorship of mail either. In fact if you drop a letter that's going abroad into a mailbox unsealed they'll send it back to you and ask you to seal it. When that happens of course someone screams that it's 'The Terror.'"

How about traveling around the country? Had they ever been prohibited from going where they wanted to go?

Peter Furst of Reuters said:

"The government press office is always trying to get us to go places. They keep telling us that Belgrade isn't Yugoslavia; that we ought to see the country and what people are doing. But that's one thing you can verify yourself. You're lucky. You don't have to sit here in Terazzia worrying about being beaten three minutes on some manufactured sensation."

Chapter Five

ANGELS ON THE CEILING

THE American Embassy in Belgrade is housed in a bank building on the main street called Ulica Maršala Tita. The consul, who hands out visas and passports, sits with his two secretaries and an assistant in what used to be the meeting room of the bank directors. The ceiling of that room is covered with a mural, or whatever it is you call a mural when it's on a ceiling. The painting shows four satyrs pursuing or being pursued by eighteen beautiful young women technically known as Lorelei. Nine sailors look on with curiosity. The Lorelei appear to be in their early twenties. They're dressed in extremely transparent veils. As you sit in the consul's office with your neck bent back, the dancing girls actually appear to be dancing. And their veils seem to blow in the breeze from the open window. Many a Yugoslav who has come to beg for a visa to America has had his mind temporarily taken off the country of skyscrapers and factories by the girls with the veils.

In many of the offices of the American Embassy in Belgrade there are copies of a calendar put out by the State Department for use in such places as embassies and legations. The leaves of the calendar are covered with pieces of the Benjamin Franklin type of wisdom in short sentences which can be easily memorized. Some of the slogans for 1947 read:

ONE TODAY IS WORTH TWO TOMORROWS

ACTIONS SPEAK LOUDER THAN WORDS

CONFIDENCE BEGETS CONFIDENCE

BETTER ASK THAN TO GO ASTRAY

In European countries where there is wild inflation the value of the native currency is constantly dropping. In neighboring Hungary the *pengö*, once worth as much as a prewar French franc, finally acquired the value of a fraction of one trillionth of an American penny. When something like that happens to a currency, people naturally try to change what money they have into sound currency like pounds and dollars. People who are trying to get their money out of a country also try to buy foreign currency to smuggle out. The present Yugoslav government since it came to power has taken drastic steps to avoid inflation and to prevent its money from going into a catastrophic nose dive. One law makes it a capital offense to buy or sell foreign currency except at a branch of the national bank.

For more than a year the American Embassy in Belgrade paid its staff members their living allowance in dollar bills. Most of them lived exclusively (some did it exclusively in two senses of the word) on this part of their income and had their salaries deposited in banks back home in America. This was possible because of what happened to those dollar bills. The banknotes were turned over to a certain Mister X on the Embassy staff. He sent them by messenger to a certain Mister Y. The messenger was often an American soldier. Mister Y was a Yugoslav Black Bourse operator. He gave dinar for the dollar bills at two or three times the legal rate. Once the rate went up to six times what the bank would have given.

Somehow the Yugoslav Government heard about the illegal dealings and trailed the G.I. and arrested him in the process of exchanging the money. The G.I. was not prosecuted but a note was sent to the American Embassy suggesting that it might be well in the future for official representatives of the United States Government to obey the law of the land in which they were living. There were two incidents like this before the Embassy finally realized that the Yugoslavs meant business. In neither case was the American money-changer executed, as he might have been under the law. In both cases he was set free. What happened to the two Yugoslavs involved I never was able to find out. The American Embassy didn't know the names of the two men, so I couldn't trace their court records.

There was one execution. Everyone in Belgrade knew about the case. The man was Milan Stefanović. He was an interpreter for an assistant commercial attaché at the American Embassy named Eric Pridanoff. One day Pridanoff suddenly resigned, went home to America, and wrote a series of articles for a newspaper syndicate which were widely syndicated. The articles contained what the Belgrade correspondents who saw them called "glaring inaccuracies and gross distortion of facts." Stefanović was arrested. At his trial the prosecutor produced a mass of evidence to substantiate the government's charge that he was engaged in widespread counterrevolutionary activities. He was accused of supplying enemies of the state with secret military information. And misinformation. He was found guilty of sedition and attempting to bring about the downfall of his own country. He was given the death penalty. Mr. Pridanoff was last reported to be still in America.

When Belgrade fell in April of '41 Radio Belgrade went off the air. But the Germans soon got the station working again. In 1944 Partisan soldiers in the mountains often used to sit around their camp fires listening over portable receiving sets to a soft female voice broadcasting German propaganda over Radio Belgrade. They nicknamed her Axis Sally after her counterpart in other countries. They often speculated about who she was. Under the laws of nearly any country, ours as well as Yugoslavia, she was a traitor and subject to the death penalty if ever caught. It wasn't until 1946 that the new Yugoslav Government located her. She was working as a clerk in the American Embassy in Belgrade.

In the past two years there have been many arrests of Yugoslav employees of the American Embassy in Belgrade. Some of them have been tried and found guilty of treason. Several of them have paid for that crime, as they would have under American law, by execution.

It is probable that the State Department, through its Belgrade representatives, employed some of these people without knowing who they were. Without knowing of their records. In the United States a prospective employee of the State Department is subjected to an examination by the F.B.I. into religion, political connections, social activities, attitude toward minority groups, and even family background for two or three generations. Apparently State Department employees abroad are sometimes hired without any investigation of their friendship for Nazis and Fascists. As one staff member pointed out, if the Embassy maintained even slightly cordial relations with the local government, it would be easy to check the past record of any prospective employee.

Some come begging for jobs because they hope that by working under the aegis of the American Embassy they will somehow escape detection and punishment for past crimes.

One of the correspondents kept a small notebook of remarks he overheard Embassy employees making as he walked through the corridors of that large stone building with the nude ladies on the ceiling. He said that looking over what he had jotted down in his notebook, he wondered if an anti-Yugoslav phobia wasn't one of the requirements for a job there.

Shortly before I arrived in Belgrade the Yugoslav Government ordered cessation of all activity by the United States Information Service. This was done on the ground that the United States Information Service in Belgrade was circulating inflammatory material designed to induce the people of Yugoslavia to overthrow their government by force. An investigation disclosed that copies of an article or speech made in America against the Tito regime actually had been turned out on the mimeograph machine in the United States Information Service office and were then distributed by someone around Belgrade. The American press and cultural attaché then in charge said that someone must have used the machine without his knowledge.

Chapter Six

SHE CALLED THEM "MY PEOPLE"

SOMEONE told me about Jacqueline the day I arrived in Belgrade. They said she was a member of a good New England family, had gone to conservative Bryn Mawr College, and that she was one person in the American Embassy who "had her feet on the ground." That's the way my informant put it. "Had her feet on the ground." The story of how she had come to Belgrade was like a bit of fiction. Reading books, in college courses, she found out about Yugoslavia. Something about its history and its strangely mixed people. She decided that of all the countries she had ever heard about this was the one she would like to visit and study and live in for a while. But she knew that she was not very well prepared to find out anything, even if she could get to Yugoslavia. So she did two things. She began to take lessons in Serbo-Croat so she could talk to the people. And then, fresh from college, she applied for a job with one of the Yugoslav relief organizations in New York. Learning this Slav language was no easy matter. Jacqueline had had years of French. But French doesn't help much. And there was no Slav blood in her veins. But she kept at it. In New York she sought out all the Yugoslavs she could find and asked them an endless series of questions. She went to Yugoslav recitals. She learned Yugoslav songs. She studied Yugoslav poetry. Finally she decided she was ready. But in those days one didn't just buy a steamship ticket for Yugoslavia. There was the matter of passport and visas. She had to produce a reason for coming which would make more sense to hard-headed people than a mere interest in a country and its population. So Jacqueline applied to the State Department for a position, passed all the screenings and tests, and finally was given a job behind a typewriter at the Embassy in Belgrade.

She sounded to me like an interesting person so I asked Harriett Scantland, United States Information Service librarian, to try to arrange a date. She did, and the next night Harriett, Jake Hoptner of the American Red Cross and I went around to pick up Jacqueline for dinner. The home of her "family," as she called the Yugoslavs with whom she lived, was a quarter of a mile from Terazzia on a hill looking out over the Sava River. It was one of the few buildings in the center of the city which still bore evidence of a direct bomb hit. The rest had all been repaired. Half the building had been blown away. Winter had stopped reconstruction work so the place was festooned with scaffolding and ladders. Poking our way through the mess was like going through freshly made bomb ruins. As we climbed the stairs to the third floor Harriett said that if you make a misstep you'll walk right off into thin air because the wall by the stairway is missing.

When we rang the bell a small, soft voice invited us to come in and climb another flight.

Jacqueline is somewhere in her twenties. Like Antoine de St. Exupéry's Little Prince, she hates mathematical questions so I never found out just where in her twenties. She entertained us in the "family's" sitting room. We had dinner in one of the "accepted" restaurants called the *Dva Ribara,* or Two Fishermen. Then the other two members of the party had to leave. With the eagerness of a small child Jacqueline said:

"Have you ever walked across the Sava? Across one of the bridges, I mean?"

I was glad I was able to say that I never had because she clapped her small hands together and said:

"Would you walk across with me? Now? Tonight?"

So Jacqueline went home and put on some boots and wrapped a white scarf around her head that made her look like a Madonna and we started out.

It was bitter cold but neither of us paid much attention to the weather. We talked excitedly about many things. Except that back in my hotel room later I realized that Jacqueline's talk had been principally questions. She was like a child that way too. And she seldom answered any question I asked her. I couldn't figure out that night whether she was just shy, or suspicious that perhaps I was an investigator from the State Department in disguise trying to trap her into making some committal statements.

In all the time I knew her I never discovered what her political ideas were, if she had any. Perhaps she was too young to have any deep convictions. But one thing I do know. We had in common a deep interest in truth. And also in people. She loved to be taken to out-of-the-way *kafanas* and to sit in a corner watching people. She always called the Yugoslavs "my people." That was her affectionate compliment to them.

We never did get across the Sava that night. In the bombings and in the final retreat of the Germans all the bridges over the river were destroyed. Except for the railroad bridge only one had been rebuilt and we couldn't seem to find it. Perhaps it was the snow that blew in our faces and blinded us. But we did walk for hours. And the snow in our faces felt good. Suddenly I stopped, looked straight ahead at a vacant space, and announced:

"There, Jacqueline, is the Srpski Kralj Hotel!"

A small, soft voice said:

"I don't see anything."

"I mean, that is where the Srpski Kralj Hotel used to be."

For the next five minutes I'm afraid I ignored the bundled-up child beside me. We walked around the corner of the snow-filled street and I half closed my eyes. Yes, this was it. On this large vacant lot now covered with a white blanket to hide even the slightest trace of what had been here there once stood the Number-One hotel of Belgrade. Over the telephone lines which ran into that building I'd reported a great deal of history. The signing of the Axis Pact. The start of the coup d'état. The flight of Prince Paul. Preparations for the invasion.

It didn't take much imagination at that hour of the morning to picture the great stone hotel standing there just as it was this same time on the morning of Sunday, April 6, 1941. It was about this same hour that I made my last telephone call to the A.P. office in Berne, Switzerland, with a prediction that war for Yugoslavia would probably arrive before the day was over.

It was about two hours later than this, sitting in Ray Brock's room, right up there, that we heard Von Ribbentrop's voice over a little radio reading the marching orders to the Wehrmacht. The orders to invade.

The balcony on which Brock and I had had our breakfast at dawn that morning used to hang out over the sidewalk a little. This sidewalk here. We'd been up there with field glasses, squinting into the morning sun, when the first planes came into sight.

The Srpski Kralj dining room with its great glass windows used to be right along here. And the piano was over there. We hid under that piano when the bombs started dropping on the roof.

Jacqueline came over and said:

"What is it you're looking at? What do you see?"

But her voice, as gentle as a spring breeze, couldn't break the spell. I said:

"I see fire, running in little rivers, from the sixth floor down to the fifth. I see hysterical people. Guests and waiters and maids. And I can hear . . . I can hear that damn-fool countess. I think she was in room 504. She got angry because we broke into her room to tell her the hotel was on fire and that she'd better get the hell out of the place in a hurry. I can hear the way she screamed. I can see her trying to hide her skinny bare legs with a bath towel. I can hear the way she slammed the door in our faces and locked it again. I'm just wondering who won, the fire or the countess.

"Room 225 was over here. That was my room. I left a lot of things in that room I'm sorry I lost. But I wonder what happened to Milutin. Milutin was the chief porter of the Srpski Kralj. He could speak Serbo-Croat, German, Russian, French, English, Italian, and half-a-dozen minor languages. He was one of the handsomest Serbs I ever knew. And that's saying a lot, for they turn out the best-looking men in the world here, as you probably know.

"That morning of the bombing I gave about seventy books to one of the porters. I think it was to Milutin. I've often worried whether those books got him into trouble when the Germans arrived, because one of them was *How to Recognize German Planes* and another was called *Inside Germany,* which said a lot of things about Hitler which Nazi soldiers wouldn't have liked.

"But it couldn't have been Milutin, because I remember him going off into the army a few days after the coup d'état. We all bought him drinks and wished him well. We said:

"'God help the Nazis when you get into action, Milutin!' and we meant it, too, because he was a giant of a man, and in his uniform he made one of those Superior Race blonds look like a patient in a consumptive home by comparison.

"Yes, I wonder what ever happened to old Milutin!

"And then there was Milan. Milan was the little Srpski Kralj barman. The bar used to be right over here, where that mound of snow is. Milan was called up about the same time. He was a happy little character. But when he came around to the hotel to say good-by, we felt sorry for him. His uniform fitted him badly, and he was a good thirty years too old to be a soldier. Milan didn't have the cockiness that Milutin had. Milan told us:

"'I've fought in two wars already and I've got some bayonet wounds from the last one, if you want to see them. But I don't like this business. We're all going to catch hell!' (Milan had mixed enough drinks for Americans to know the vernacular.)

"Then he said:

"'We Serbs are brave, but what can we do with bayonets against those bastard Germans with their planes and their tanks?'

"Poor little Milan. He probably didn't get far with his bayonet. But I'll wager that Milutin made out all right. He probably became a big officer in the Partisans before it was all over."

Then I walked across the street into Kalemegdon Park. Jacqueline trailed helplessly along.

"There is the very air-raid shelter in which we hid while the second wave of planes came over. Under the snow somewhere here must be something to mark that other shelter, just a couple of hundred feet away, which got a direct hit, with a hundred people inside. They didn't have to bury those bodies. The bomb did it for them. But they must have put up a stone of some kind.

"It was right here that we stopped a peasant with a horse and a milk wagon and bribed him, with a fistful of dinar, to haul our baggage to the American Legation. It was a legation in those days, you know, Jacqueline.

"I wonder what ever happened to the Minister of the Netherlands, who got so angry, first because we wouldn't take his luggage along, too, and then because a hatbox which he said was full of valuable diplomatic documents got buried under all our unimportant things."

Memories crowding in on memories!

But it was nearly 3 A.M., and how could one expect a child fresh out of Bryn Mawr to understand? Jacqueline had probably never seen a dead body, and of course she had never heard the noise that a bomb makes when it falls, and the noise people make, like those hundred people in that air-raid shelter right over there: The noises of death.

So I took Jacqueline by the hand and we plodded our way home through the snow. We didn't talk much, on the way home, but once Jacqueline interrupted the silence.

"That Minister of the Netherlands you were talking about. He's back here again. I haven't talked to him, but I have heard people say that he's very anxious to see you. He hopes your paths cross again sometime. He knows that passage from your book by heart; that passage in which you mention him and his hatbox. Only he says now that what he didn't tell you at the time was that the hatbox was full of the crown jewels of Holland. That's what somebody told me he said."

Chapter Seven

PROVING THAT YOU CAN'T ALWAYS TELL

THERE are three hotels in Belgrade, unless you count the Grande Hotel Kasina, which I refuse to do. All three are on or very close to Terazzia. The Majestic, the Moskva, and the Balkan. Correspondents and diplomats who haven't had the good fortune to find apartments live in one or another of them.

One day I went into the Balkan to call on Arthur Brandell and his wife, Mary. When I asked the desk clerk the number of their room, he didn't answer right away. He just stared at me. Finally, rather pathetically, he said:

"Don't you remember me?"

He said it in the voice of a small child who had been terribly hurt and was showing it.

I wanted very much to remember him. I could tell that it was going to mean a great deal to him whether I remembered or not. He stood behind the hotel desk waiting. I looked him over quickly.

He was a tall, gaunt man. It was hard to tell his age. He looked quite old. His eyes were deep sunk in his face. They didn't have a trace of softness or good humor about them. They were bitter eyes and for some reason, which I couldn't explain even to myself, I didn't like to look into them. His whole face was sad and empty looking. His shoulders were stooped and he leaned heavily on a cane. He came from behind the desk out into the lobby. I could see that he walked with difficulty. He wore the remnants of a uniform. A pair of army boots and a khaki jacket.

Then he asked the question a little differently.

"Surely you remember me, don't you?"

He was begging me to remember and God knows I tried. I'd never seen him before. I was positive. Yet I couldn't hurt him. And so, suddenly, as if everything had all at once become clear, I took several steps to his side, threw one arm around his shoulders, and with as much enthusiasm as possible I said:

"Well, of course! How stupid of me! Of course I remember! How are you? How have you been? I hope things are going all right with you. It's been a long time, hasn't it?"

But I didn't fool him. He didn't even reply. Not for a full minute. He just looked down at me with an expression in his eyes I shall never forget. There was hatred in his eyes now. But I didn't know whom it was he was hating. There was fear in his eyes. But I didn't know what it was he was fearing. There was hopelessness too. And I thought I also saw a trace of contempt. Contempt for me and the rest of the world. Finally the voice which belonged to those eyes spoke. The voice was still half that of a hurt child. But it was also something else. It was bitter and hard. It was soft and whimpering. Bitter and soft, hard and whimpering. All at the same time. The Voice said:

"I didn't think you would ever forget the Srpski Kralj Hotel and old Milutin, the head porter. I was your friend."

How could I tell him why I hadn't recognized him? Milutin! Tall, handsome Milutin, with the bearing of a king. Milutin, who had been the quintessence of all the fine qualities of the Serbs. Strength, health, defiance, the will to live. How could I tell him that I hadn't recognized him because the Milutin to whom I had said good-by six years ago in the Srpski Kralj Hotel had been a full head taller, with great broad shoulders without a sag to them, and with the fire of mountain people in his eyes? Would I dare say to him, now, that I remembered as if it were one hour ago how he had gone off with his head held high and his soul full of determination to "show those damned Nazis a thing or two"? What could I say to Milutin now? I had to say something. And quickly, too, because those eyes were beginning to bore through me again. So I gave him a pale smile and said as cheerfully and nonchalantly as I could:

"Well, of course I remember, Milutin. I told you I did. How could I ever forget! I walked by where the Srpski Kralj used to be just the other night with a friend and I was telling her all about you. I was telling her about that day you went marching away. The day we all bought you drinks and . . ."

If I had only looked at him while I was talking I would have stopped sooner. Milutin, too, was thinking back. His eyes wandered off into space. There was a new look in them now. Softer, a bit. But I could tell that his mind as well as his body was near the breaking point. Talk like this might be the straw.

The elevator was three feet away. And the door was open. The easy thing to do would be to jump across those three feet, get into the elevator, and go. That's what part of me wanted to do. The coward part of me. But I won that battle and stayed. I stayed and tried to get the monosyllabic conversation going again. In a new direction. I pointed to the leg on which he obviously couldn't stand and said:

"How did you get it, Milutin?"

He answered in one word. But in that one word he put all the feelings and emotions I had seen in his eyes.

"Dachau."

It's an ugly little word, said by anyone, under any conditions. But the way Milutin the Porter said it, it wasn't a word at all. It was the entire Nuremberg Indictment. It was even more than that. It was a wholesale condemnation of civilization.

"Dachau. Eighteen months in Dachau!"

There isn't much you can say to a man who's spent eighteen months in Dachau. You can't ask him how he liked it. You can't ask what happened to him there. You can't say:

"How did they treat you?"

You don't have to. You can tell all those things just by looking into the face of a man who's spent eighteen months in Dachau. And listening to what's in his voice.

The Golden Age of Literature will finally arrive when some writer comes along who can put into words what the eyes say and the voice says of a man who's spent eighteen months in Dachau. Then a real art will be born.

Anyway, I finally asked him:

"What are you doing now, Milutin?"

"There isn't much that I can do. This leg . . . I may have to lose it."

Then he explained that the Balkan is one of the hotels which the government has nationalized. That's how he got his job behind the desk. The government gave him the job as . . . well, as a bit of a reward for what he'd been through. Tomorrow he was going to start working nights. He didn't like working nights. Most everyone went to bed at midnight and from then on it was . . .

Suddenly he stopped, put a hand on my arm, looked down into my face, and said:

"Listen! Come around and see me some night, won't you? Come and sit with me, eh?"

He said it pleadingly, the way a child talks when it's asking its mother please not to turn out the bedroom light and leave it alone in the dark.

I promised Milutin I would.

Chapter Eight

ALSO PROVING THAT YOU CAN'T ALWAYS TELL

ONE night, sitting with Milutin, I mentioned Milan the Barman and said I wondered what ever happened to him.

"Didn't you know? He's back too. They gave him a job behind the bar of the Majestic. That's a government hotel like this one."

So I drifted one evening into the Majestic and there he was. He hadn't changed so much as Milutin had. But he'd changed all right. For the better. Milan seemed to have grown as much taller as Milutin had grown shorter. I'm sure that if I could put them side by side they would, today, be of an almost equal height. And Milan had grown younger looking too. His shoulders were squarer. He stood more erect. There was a fire in his eyes which had never been there before.

We didn't have much of a chance to talk, because Milan was very busy. In the old Srpski Kralj days a drink cost us about nine cents, and Milan was never stingy with the amount of liquor he put in the bottom of a glass. But it's different now. There is no *šljivovica* these days because "slivo," as we used to call it, the national drink, is made from plums. And for the past two years Yugoslavia has been the victim of a killing drought. So there were no plums and there is no šljivovica. Instead, the Yugoslavs drink what they call *rakia*. Rakia can be made from almost anything, but these days it's generally made by distilling grapes, after the juice has all been squeezed out of them for wine. Rakia is not a very palatable beverage, and so most foreigners who can afford it insist on whisky or gin. Enough whisky or gin, at the Majestic bar, to cover the bottom of a glass and that's about all, costs a dollar and a half. But the patrons of the Majestic bar are mostly diplomats with sizable living allowances to take care of just such expenses, and so Milan is always busy.

But I did find out that the frightened little man who went off to war so worried about what was going to happen wound up in the mountains with the Partisans, became an officer, distinguished himself in action, and now . . . now he was happier and younger looking than he was six years ago when it all began.

So, you can't always tell.

Chapter Nine

"THE TERROR"

PETER FURST of Reuters and I used to patronize a trafika in Terazzia which carried a complete stock of English newspapers and magazines. It also sold publications in French and other languages.

I never made any mental notes about the proprietor, but Peter and I used to discuss a man who always seemed to be loitering around the place. He was about thirty-five years old and very unhappy looking. Each time we went in he'd eye us. He always seemed on the verge of speaking.

One day he did speak. He went up to Peter and said, loud enough for all the other people in the shop to hear:

"I know that you are an American. That's right, isn't it? Well then, you are just the man I wish to talk to. You must help me get out of this country to America."

He spoke English stumblingly.

Peter said:

"Yes, I am an American, but I don't run a steamship company. How can I get you to America?"

Then, excitedly, the little man explained. He had been to the American Embassy. The American Embassy said that the first step was to get some American to sign a statement of financial responsibility, guaranteeing that the immigrant, if he got to America, would not become a public charge.

Peter did not reach immediately for his fountain pen. Instead, he asked:

"Why do you wish to leave your own country?"

That started it. For the next fifteen minutes the little man, in a voice loud enough to be heard out in Terazzia, told what he thought of the New Yugoslavia. And it wasn't much. He got so excited that half the time he was talking in Serbian and half the time in his broken English.

He spoke a great deal about Osna. He talked of "The Terror." He said no man's life was safe. People were always getting arrested, and then disappearing. Prices were high. There weren't enough homes for everyone. The rakia was no good. Trains didn't run on time. There were no freedoms in Yugoslavia. All you read in the newspapers was about Youth Railroads, and competitions between factory workers, and speeches by Tito.

Did we know that the regime had killed three hundred and fifty thousand good Yugoslavs up near the Rumanian frontier.

Peter pricked up his ears at that one.

"How were three hundred and fifty thousand Yugoslavs killed up near the Rumanian frontier?"

What he was referring to, the little man said, was the three hundred and fifty thousand people killed up there during the war. Battle casualties.

"That was just as bad as if the government had shot them all, making them fight the Germans!

"Life here in Belgrade was better under the Nazis than it is today. For me, I prefer Fascism to what we have now."

Peter said:

"I remember seeing photographs of the Nazis hanging Yugoslavs from lampposts right out there in Terazzia. At least they don't do that now."

The little man replied in a stage whisper which still could be heard by everyone in the shop.

"No, because now they kill them *under* Terazzia. Didn't you know that? They have secret chambers down there where they kill them!"

Had he ever seen these chambers? Had he ever seen anyone being taken down there? How did he know about such things?

"People have told me."

He kept talking about "The Terror" and how no Yugoslav could even think his own thoughts, let alone express himself these days. Everyone lived in terror of being picked up by Osna and thrown into a death chamber.

Peter winked at me and said:

"There are six people besides us in this shop right now. Some of them probably understand English. And you have been talking half the time in Serbian too. If this terror is as bad as you say it is; if a man can't even think, let alone speak his feelings, how is it that you dare, here in public, so close to those death chambers you mentioned, to talk like this? Aren't you afraid someone will report you? Aren't you afraid that you will be picked up by Osna?"

The little man was silent for a full fifteen seconds. Then he suddenly found the answer. He brightened up, got excited again, and said:

"Ah, but you don't understand. These people"—and he waved his hand toward the others in the shop, including two women who had just come in—"these people wouldn't report me, because they all feel the same as I do. They agree with me."

Peter asked him if he knew all these people. If he didn't, how was he so sure that they all agreed with him? Did he even include the army officer in the corner, who wore an emblem indicating that he was a "1941 Partisan" and had fought for four years in the hills?

The little man sighed and spread his hands out in a helpless gesture.

"You Americans don't seem to understand. You don't understand that *all* Yugoslavs feel the same way I do!"

At this point a woman who had just purchased a London newspaper gave the little man a cold stare and walked out, slamming the door.

Then Peter said:

"But you don't know anything about me. Maybe I am an Osna agent."

"No," said the little man, "I know that you are my friend and that you will sign the paper so I can get to America."

When we started to leave, Peter's new acquaintance said:

"I may see you here again tomorrow to get your answer. But if I am not here, it will mean that they got me too. If that happens, I shall at least go to my death knowing that I have talked with a friend!"

Months later, when I finally left Belgrade, I paid a last visit to the trafika in Terazzia that sells foreign publications. The unhappy little man who wanted to get to America was still there. "The Terror" hadn't gotten him yet.

Chapter Ten

FREEDOM—TO WANDER

THERE were four British correspondents in Belgrade when I was here before. Between them they knew almost all there was to know about this country whose tragedy has been, as a wit once put it, that she had had altogether too much history.

When I returned I knew that I was not going to encounter one of the four. I knew what had happened to Terence Atherton. I knew that his body lay buried on a hillside not far from the Dalmatian coast.

The second, "Harry" Harrison, had been in and out of Yugoslavia several times in the past two years and had written some excellent objective dispatches.

The third, Kenneth Syres, was here in Belgrade now and I made a date to meet him.

The fourth, Lovett Edwards, was a question mark in my notebook. He was the dean of them all. He had lived for fifteen years in Yugoslavia and had "gone native." He spoke the language perfectly. He had a Yugoslav wife, Duka, whom we all liked. They lived in an apartment across the street from the British Embassy—an apartment bulging with Yugoslav books and Yugoslav works of art.

The last time I saw Edwards was in Sarajevo on Easter Sunday in '41. Somehow he and Duka had worked their way down from Belgrade to the Bosnian capital. But they had no way to get any farther and they knew, as we all did, that any day the Germans would arrive and it would be all over. So they begged us to take them in the automobile we had. We couldn't. We were already crowded to the roof with human beings and cans of gasoline. If we left the cans of gasoline behind, in order to crowd Lovett and Duka in, no one would get anywhere.

So we said good-by, in front of the Europa Hotel in Sarajevo, and that was the last I ever saw of him.

Often, in the years that followed, when I met some Englishman in some odd part of the world, or when I got to London, I inquired about him. But no one ever knew what had happened to Lovett Edwards.

That's why I almost dropped the receiver one day soon after I'd returned to Belgrade when a soft scholarly voice said:

"Hello, Bob. How about a cup of tea? This is Lovett—Lovett Edwards. I'm in room 301 in the Balkan. Drop over in half an hour."

So the old rascal had lived through it! It would be good to see him again. Perhaps Duka was with him too!

I noticed, when he opened the door of Room 301, that his hair was snow white. What little there was left of it. He was thin, and he looked permanently tired. But otherwise he was the same quiet character who was always much more interested in Yugoslav poetry than he ever was, despite the fact that he was a newspaper correspondent, in the intricacies of Yugoslav political maneuverings.

"Come in," he said, and then he added in a whisper, "My wife is in there. But don't be surprised that it isn't Duka. This is a new wife. I'll tell you about Duka later."

In the next room I met Bosa. She was tall and lithe. At least two heads taller than Lovett. Very young and very beautiful. She appeared less than half Lovett's age. As we talked, I picked up odd bits of information about her. Her father had been one of the leading citizens of Belgrade in the old regime. Or at least one of the most wealthy. During the war and the change-over to the new regime he had lost most of his fortune. Now the family, although they still had a large apartment in the center of town next to the Majestic, were fallen from their previous state. They were living in fear of what might happen next.

Bosa, by virtue of her marriage to Lovett, had automatically acquired British citizenship and a British passport. In some countries it's possible to give up your citizenship voluntarily as easily as you renounce your party affiliations. But over here it's different. Here citizenship is considered a duty and an obligation, as well as a right to be cast aside whenever you choose. Bosa said she had had to fill out a lot of papers and forms, and it took many months. But at last she had her heart's desire. She was no longer a Yugoslav. She was British! She had even learned to talk English with a bit of an Oxford accent.

Lovett filled me in on what had happened to him. Somehow, somewhere, he and Duka had separated. That part he didn't make clear. But Lovett had teamed up with Seagrue and with him had tried to get to the north.

Seagrue was the oldest of all the correspondents in southeastern Europe. He was the "dean" up in Budapest. He had lived there as long as Edwards had lived in Belgrade. Maybe longer. He had a Hungarian wife and he loved Hungary with a great passion. And they loved him in Budapest too. He was sure that he didn't have an enemy in the country. He was sure that if he could get back to Budapest his friends there would see that no ill befell him and his aged wife. Others argued with him, but he always went back to his prime consideration:

"If I get out myself, what about my wife?"

And so he and Edwards together started for the north. Seagrue never did get back to Budapest. He never saw his wife again. The Germans got him and killed him. A helpless, harmless old man, whose only crime in sixty-five years or more was that he loved that city up on the Danube, and he loved his wife.

Edwards fared better. He was captured by the Italians. Years later, documents were found in Berlin which showed that Edwards was high up on the Nazi Black List. The Gestapo had ordered his execution if he ever was caught. But the left hand didn't know what the right hand was doing. His captors called him "just another damn-fool Englishman" and they kept him in prison, alive.

He was shunted from camp to camp, first in Italy and then in Germany itself. In prison he wrote poetry while his body got thinner and thinner. Finally his latest camp was liberated by the Americans. As soon as he could, Edwards started back for Yugoslavia.

One of the first things he did was to try to trace Duka. He found her. After their separation, she had joined the Partisans and had fought with them for years in the mountains. Now she was no longer willing to be the background wife of a scholarly British correspondent. She was a woman of action now. There was other work still to be done. She was interested in the reconstruction, now that the liberation had been accomplished. And so they were divorced.

And then Edwards met Bosa, the daughter of wealth-confiscated. They were married a short time later.

Just as we do in America, the Yugoslavs give a foreigner what they call a *permis de sejour*—a permit which allows you to stay in the country a certain length of time. The customary time is two months, but when that period expires you just send a messenger boy around to the proper government office and get a renewal for another two months.

Edwards's permis de sejour read "Good for two months" and so did the one they issued to Bosa the day the Yugoslav Government gave her the right to renounce her Yugoslav citizenship.

A few days before I arrived Edwards sent both permis to the proper government office to have them renewed. His came back with a renewal. But Bosa was given an exit visa instead—an exit visa allowing her to leave the country within two months.

Edwards went roaring to the press office. What did this mean?

He was informed that the proper authorities had decided it would be best for everyone concerned if Mr. and Mrs. Lovett Edwards found happier hunting grounds elsewhere. There had been frequent reports that his wife was exerting an undue reactionary influence on him, and that he was passing on this undue reactionary influence to other correspondents, in conversation, in translating the newspapers for them, and in rumors and reports he circulated among them.

"And so," said Lovett, spreading his hands out in a helpless gesture, "I guess we'll be leaving one of these days."

I asked if it wasn't really for the best. After all, isn't that just what Bosa wanted and had wanted all the time?

"Yes," said Edwards, "but it will mean that she will probably never return to her native country, which will be sad, because her family are all here."

At that point Bosa, who had been silent most of the time, spoke up quickly and said:

"That—that really isn't so important. I do want to leave. The sooner the better!"

Then we changed the subject and Edwards told me how bitter he felt when he returned to Belgrade and found that the Germans had stolen every picture, every book, every statue, every rug, every article of value he'd left locked in his apartment, being naïvely sure that such things wouldn't appeal to drunken Nazi soldiers on the loot.

Some months later I saw Lovett and Bosa again. It was in Athens on Orthodox Easter Sunday. They were coming into the Grand Bretagne Hotel hand in hand. They had just returned from climbing the Acropolis and Lovett was out of breath. Bosa clapped her hands when she saw me and started to tell me all the places they had been. She talked so rapidly and excitedly that I'm not sure that I got it right. But I think they had been in Hungary, Austria, Switzerland, Italy, France, and I don't know how many other countries. Lovett, with a little worry in his voice, said:

"My paper assigned me to Ankara, Turkey. I should have been there weeks ago."

"But what does it matter, Lovett? We're having a wonderful time, aren't we?"

And then the graying husband asked me about Belgrade. I had an engagement down the street and I was in a hurry. But he kept me there asking a whole string of questions. When I finally got away I said to myself:

"I think Lovett Edwards is going to miss Yugoslavia, despite his new wife's political ideas. I think he's going to miss Yugoslavia terribly!"

Chapter Eleven

THE MAN WHO WOULD NOT BE KING

PRINCE MICHAEL PETROVIĆ-NJEGOSH was the second son of the man who was king of Montenegro in the days when that area of black mountains was a kingdom all by itself, before it was made part of Yugoslavia. Prince Michael Petrović-Njegosh is also a nephew of Queen Helena of Italy, who is now enjoying the hospitality of certain foreign countries because of certain incidents in Italy which make kings and queens no longer welcome there. When the Germans came into Paris in 1940 Prince Michael Petrović-Njegosh fell into their hands. They treated him well, at the start, because they thought they might have a good use for him later. They didn't say anything to the prince about it at the time. They sprang it on him the next year, after the fall of Yugoslavia. They asked him how he would like to be King of the Montenegrins. The prince was second in line for a throne which no longer existed. But the Germans were going to restore the throne and make Montenegro a kingdom again. To do so they needed a king and they thought they could make some attractive terms to the young prince, even though he was not next in line. For example, he could have . . .

But the prince turned the offer down cold. As a price for his stubbornness he was sent to a concentration camp. Not a special concentration camp for royalty. Just an ordinary concentration camp for common people. He was kept in internment for two or three years. He didn't really breathe free air again until after Paris was liberated.

Today Prince Michael Petrović-Njegosh is back in Yugoslavia. He lives at the Moskva Hotel. Osgood Crowthers, the A.P. correspondent, lives in the same place and that's how Crowthers bumped into him one night and got the story. Then Crowthers introduced him to me.

The prince is tall and handsome in that masculine way that all men of the Montenegrin mountains are handsome, only unlike most of the rest of them he had no long flowing mustachios and no trace of a beard. His French-born wife, Genevieve, is a blonde and attractive in a Parisian way. They live together at the Moskva in a single room which several American correspondents had turned down on the ground that it was too small for comfort.

Some months ago in Paris Michael and Genevieve received a cable from Belgrade. I think it was from Tito himself. It said that Yugoslavia had need of all the man power and brain power she could lay her hands on. The Ministry of Foreign Affairs, for example, was in need of men who could talk foreign languages. The job they would give him would not, perhaps, be so important a job as a man of his lineage and education might feel he deserved. But after he had acquired a little experience he might get a promotion. Anyway, his country was calling him and Belgrade hoped he would hear and answer. So Michael and Genevieve packed up and left Paris and all their friends and all that life in Paris means, to come to this pint-sized capital city, and live in a single room in a modest hotel.

"I have no politics," the prince told me. "I just came back as a patriot believing that the real history of Yugoslavia lies in the future."

One little matter about the future he would like to discuss.

"Germany and Italy and Japan," he said, "all went to war because they were crowded countries. Because they wanted what Hitler called *Lebensraum*. Now that all three have been defeated, it is inconceivable that there can be another great war in our time. It is inconceivable that there should be a war over religious, ideological, or political differences. It is inconceivable, to me, that Russia and America should go to war. After all, they are both self-sufficient nations. Neither has any real need. And I am sure that the people of both those nations sincerely want peace."

How did the prince, accustomed to the pleasures of gay Paris, spend his spare time here in Belgrade?

The prince smiled. I could see that he was a bit embarrassed.

"As you know, I speak perfect English. And fluent French and Italian too. I can also speak the Scottish dialects, because I was brought up by a Scottish nurse. But it happens that I speak no Serbo-Croat at all. That's because I never lived in my own country. And so, with all the spare time that I have, I am studying my own language. The language of the Yugoslavs.

"The only thing that worries me, working for the Ministry of Foreign Affairs, is that maybe they'll send me to London or Washington because they know I speak English. For me that would be a tragedy. Now at last I am in my own country. And I'd like to stay here awhile."

Chapter Twelve

"SYMPATIČNA"

WHEN I started out from New York I had a blind faith that somehow, somewhere I would be able to find Sonia. In Rome. In Paris. In Belgrade. Somewhere. I also had a blind faith she would say:

"I'm delighted that you came back. When do we start on that automobile ride?"

I met Sonia just before the bombing of Belgrade. One evening we had dinner in the big open-faced dining room of the Srpski Kralj Hotel. Suddenly the sirens went off and the lights went out. Sonia reached under the table and grabbed my fingers and said please hold her hand tightly. No, tighter than that! She was terrified. I held her hand tightly in Belgrade, in Bosnia, in Montenegro, in Dalmatia every time a plane came over. I tried to keep her calm through a dozen raids. Sonia had been principally responsible for several of us getting out of Yugoslavia alive. It was Sonia who begged gasoline for us down through Bosnia and Montenegro. It was Sonia who stole the keys to a room in the Europa Hotel of Sarajevo. It was Sonia, one day when we were so hungry it hurt, who gave a man her leather jacket, which she needed because it was cold, in return for a ten-cent can of cherries, which we gobbled down in less time than it takes to tell about it. When I said good-by to her on a hill overlooking the harbor of Kotor, because three other men thought she was a spy and wouldn't let her go out onto the Adriatic with us, I made Sonia a promise.

"Swear to me," she had said, "that someday you will come back and take me for another automobile trip when there aren't any bombs or planes in the sky."

I swore.

For six years I had carried with me the last picture I had of her standing in the middle of the road in the foothills of the Dalmatian mountains waving a small red handkerchief. Once in those six years I had heard from her. The letter came from Rome. It said she was all right. How was I? And had I remembered the promise? But she gave no address. Only a telephone number. And in those days it was impossible to call Rome from New York.

But passing through London on the way to Belgrade I found that I could call Rome from there. So I did. When a girl's voice answered in Rome I said as casually as I could:

"I'm in London on my way to Yugoslavia. There aren't any bombs or planes in the sky, so how about that automobile ride we were going to take together?"

Then I realized I wasn't talking to Sonia at all. The voice that came over the wire spoke pure Oxfordian English and wanted to know what on earth I was talking about. And who was I anyway? I must have the wrong number. Of course it wasn't Sonia. Sonia spoke with a delightfully broken accent and her English was much more American than Oxford. But it was Sonia. For some years she had been working for the Red Cross and with UNRRA. Her friends were mostly British. She was very, very sorry, but a trip to Yugoslavia right now was out of the question. She had an important position. And besides . . . There was much else to tell. If I could get to Rome sometime . . . If not, have a good trip. Maybe our paths will cross another day.

When I got to Belgrade I learned a little more about what had happened to her from some of her friends. They said that from Kotor, where I left her, she went to Zagreb where her family lived. There the Gestapo got on her trail because she had had Anglo-American connections. So one day she had to leave Zagreb quickly. She worked her way to Belgrade. The Gestapo in Belgrade didn't like her either. So she went to the Dalmatian coast. No one was quite sure about the next chapter of her life. They said she met an Italian army officer who took her to Rome. She married the Italian, they said, and was still living in Rome. That's all they knew about her in Belgrade.

Now the problem was to find someone else to go on a trip down through Yugoslavia. I wanted to retrace the route of that old flight for many reasons. Not just sentimental reasons either. But it would be difficult. In a country where they speak three different native languages and many dialects there is always the problem of language. For example, the people in Slovenia in the north can understand little of the conversation of the people of Macedonia, in the far south. And so I had great need of an interpreter.

On the way from London to Belgrade I made a mental list of the qualifications an interpreter should have. Youth was important because this was one of the worst winters Europe had known in a long time. We would be roughing it. We'd travel third-class to get away from foreigners and close to the people of the country. We'd be staying in third-class hotels in a country where first-class hotels are sometimes named the Grande Hotel Kasina. We'd be bitten by bedbugs and fleas. Getting enough to eat would also be a problem. The mere business of existing would test the physical stamina of anyone who came along.

I should try to find someone with an open mind. Neither a violent opponent nor a blind proponent of the present Yugoslav regime.

My interpreter should be a sensitive person with a good feeling about people. Otherwise I would never be able to explain to him the kind of material I was after.

It would be better not to take along a Yugoslav. Objectivity would be difficult for a Yugoslav. An American would be better if I could find an American with all the other qualifications.

But my interpreter should know something about Europe and Europeans. Otherwise the ways of peasants would confuse him. Otherwise he'd expect Yugoslav peasants to be like American farmers.

And finally there was the matter of congeniality. We'd be spending all but our sleeping hours together for months. And that's something even husbands and wives don't do. Sixteen or eighteen hours a day for months. Living under primitive conditions. Traveling in cold, dirty trains. Eating sparse meals in strange places. Scratching fleabites and hunting bedbugs. Trying to work out problems of transportation. Arguing with officials. Trying to persuade people to talk who might be afraid to talk. Yes, the person would have to be what the Yugoslavs call *sympatična*. Very *sympatična!*

I scoured Belgrade looking for such a person. If I could find someone with only four or five of the six requirements it would be all right. Then I cut it down to three of the six. And then to two. After ten days of hunting I would have been willing to settle for someone who spoke Serbo-Croat passably well and to hell with the other qualifications.

Jacqueline would have been perfect in many of the six ways. But Jacqueline couldn't have roughed it. And besides, she had a State Department position. In desperation I went to Vladimir Baum. Vladimir Baum was in charge of the foreign section of the government press department. The job he had was one to wear down the physique of a Samson, the mental endurance of a Job, and the forgiveness of a Christ. All day long correspondents speaking half-a-dozen different languages paraded into his office and dumped their problems, complaints, and difficulties of life into his lap. I even heard one American correspondent asking Baum one day what to do about his wife. So I took my problem to Baum. He said maybe he could produce a student from a Belgrade *lyceum* who knew enough English to do the job. He was very honest about it. He said:

"Many of our best people were killed during the war. You know about that. Also, before the war if a person spoke foreign languages it generally meant he had gone to the university and had traveled. Before the war few people were able to go to the university or travel unless they came from one of the wealthy families. Today most families of wealth are opposed to the regime. They've either gone out of Yugoslavia or they're lying low and not helping us. But perhaps I can get a young student for you."

I knew a young student wouldn't measure up to many of my six requirements. And then I thought of all the stories I had heard about "The Terror." So far I hadn't found any evidence that any terror existed. But maybe it did. If there was a "Terror" the person I took on a trip might become a victim of it. He'd be blamed for anything unfavorable I wrote. If the Belgrade gossip were true, dreadful things might happen to him.

I wasn't very happy when I went to bed that night. But the winter sun was bright the next morning and the next morning while Peter Furst and I were talking about something else he mentioned Anita. What he said about her gave me an idea that she might be the person I was looking for. She'd been born in Russia. Her father had been a factory owner. A minor capitalist. During the revolution he packed up his wife and children and fled the country. Eventually various members of his family got to the United States and became American citizens. Anita was still a small child when she reached New York. She learned Serbo-Croat in the States. She came to Yugoslavia for the first time just a few weeks ago to attend the All-Slav Congress.

"Of course," Peter said, "if we can't find her there are some other American delegates to the Congress still around. There's a fruit grower from California, and a bartender from some place or other, and there's even a Republican state senator from Wisconsin."

I didn't want a state senator, or a bartender, or a California fruit grower. I wanted to meet Anita. Did Peter know where she could be found? He said she was traveling around the country on her own, trying to see things and meet people. He thought maybe he knew how to get in touch with her.

Five days later Anita was found. We met her in the apartment of a friend at eight o'clock one evening. Anita was probably in her early thirties but she was small, and a small girl's age isn't easy to guess. She wore a blue tam on her brown hair at a jaunty angle. You could tell she was of Russian origin. She had a serious intensity and moved across the room as if she were going somewhere and knew exactly where she were going. We got down to business right away. I said I couldn't promise anything except that we wouldn't return to Belgrade until we had seen every corner of the country. Not until we had met and talked to hundreds of Bosnians, Macedonians, Montenegrins, Dalmatians, Croats, Slovenes, Moslems, Serbs. And the people of the Vojvodina too.

Anita said she'd think about it and give an answer tomorrow. She wanted to go very much. The idea appealed to her. She wanted to answer for herself some of the riddles of the New Yugoslavia. But . . .

At luncheon the next day the truth came out. It was a contest between Mind and Heart. Back in New York there was an impatient young man whom she had promised to marry as soon as she returned. He was already sending lovesick cables asking her to hurry back. But she was going to compromise. She would come along for a month. Well . . . maybe it could be stretched into two. Let's not make too definite a timetable. Let's just start out and see. When would we go? Did I have maps? We would need maps showing railroads as well as highways. And about food. We ought to take some food with us. Canned goods. Maybe the Fursts would lend us a thermos bottle. On a trip like this a thermos bottle would be very important. She'd bring a camera. Did I know where I could get some canned heat? But we must travel light. She'd bring just one small suitcase. Did I have clothes that were really warm? And how about overshoes? There would be a lot of snow and maybe mud, too, before we got back. And could I get some DDT powder from someone? She didn't smoke so I wouldn't have to worry about that. She didn't drink either, in case I was interested. Hated the stuff. All except a certain kind of Yugoslav wine called *Fruškagorski Biser*. It was bubbly. Like champagne. But it cost only fifty dinar a bottle, and that's only a dollar. But of course we couldn't carry things like that with us. She had some cakes of soap. But for heaven's sake don't forget the DDT! And now, if there was nothing else, Anita must hurry off to send a cable to a young man in New York.

As I watched her small, vibrant figure weaving through the tables toward the door I thought that maybe she would even meet Qualification Number Six.

Chapter Thirteen

GOOD-BY TO ALL THAT

JAKE HOPTNER, who was head of the American Red Cross in Yugoslavia, gave us two cardboard boxes of food. He said he'd done some traveling around the country himself. When we got into the "wilds" we'd be glad we had them along. They weighed fifteen pounds apiece and together they measured one foot by one foot by one foot. That wasn't my idea of traveling light. But the boxes were packed with coffee, tea, sugar, butter, cheese, chocolate, oatmeal, raisins, and other items I knew we wouldn't see again until we got back home to America someday.

Anita found a collection of six maps. They were two feet square apiece. Together they covered all Yugoslavia and showed every small stream, every narrow-gauge railroad, every excuse for a road.

The press department gave us a travel pass covering all the places we said we might go and a lot of others besides. The list of republics, counties, cities, towns and villages on that pass read like a page from a geography book.

Warrant Officer René LaPlante in the military attaché's office loaned me two United States Army knapsacks after I signed two or three copies of a very official-looking document.

Myrtis Colthorp, the Red Cross nurse from Texas, said we ought to take some sulfa pills in case we ran into the G.I.'s. While she counted them out I told her that we used to have much more interesting names for the ailment, depending on where it caught up with us. In Egypt we called it "Gippy Tummy." It was also known as the Zagreb Quickstep, Bucharest Belly, Balkan Blight, Athens Adventure, Sofia Shuffle, and the Istanbul Impudence. Miss Colthorp gave us some other sulfa pills "just in case you get pneumonia or something more serious." I didn't have a chance to thank her for her cheerfulness and optimism because just then she had to rush away on a queer assignment. Someone had left a baby wrapped in blankets on the doorstep of the United States military attaché's office. The unwed Yugoslav mother had pinned a note to the blanket. It was up to the American Government to support the child because "the father is one of your soldiers."

We took one change of clothes apiece, a Boy Scout knife, six cans of DDT, a pencil sharpener, and a considerable quantity of paper. By this time I was living in the Majestic. In New York the Majestice would be classed as a second-rate hotel. But a single room at the Majestic cost considerably more than a fancy suite at the Waldorf-Astoria in New York.

And there wasn't anything you could do about it except what I did. I decided that if we were going to travel light and if we were going to take millions of words of notes, the weight of the notes might ultimately be a problem. So what could be better than a stack of neatly folded pieces of very thin paper? Besides, it would be a subtle way of getting back at the Majestic for its exorbitant rates. So for weeks I'd been stocking up.

I don't remember what else we jammed into the two musette bags and Anita's suitcase, but all three were full to the bursting point. Besides, we had the thirty pounds of food, a typewriter, a parka with a fur hood, and a vest lined with the fluff of some animal which was a farewell gift from a friend in New York.

The night before we started I tried to figure out what I'd learned so far about Yugoslavia. The weeks in Belgrade had been like standing in no-man's land getting shot at from both sides. But I'd learned one thing. I'd learned that you can't find out much about a country in the capital city. It's true whether you're in Washington, Bucharest, or Istanbul. Under present conditions it was especially true here. In Belgrade nearly everyone you met fell into one of two camps. Either the group which argued that here the best of all possible worlds was in formation. Or the other group which would have liked the power to press a button and wipe Yugoslavia off the map in one blinding flash, providing of course that they could get out first.

Belgrade was a depressing place for other reasons. The streets were always full of soldiers. All public buildings were under guard. You needed passes to get into most of them. This military atmosphere in time of peace bothered all Americans, whatever they thought of the system. Yugoslavs would point out that there always were soldiers on their streets. That public buildings in this part of the world always were under guard. They would say not to forget that they just recently went through a bloody revolution and that after every revolution it is incumbent upon the side which wins to take enough security measures to make certain that a counterrevolution doesn't break out. They would say we should remember that there are powerful forces abroad that would like to see a counter-revolution break out. They would say that America and France both took security precautions after their revolutions. But still it was disturbing. Especially to people not used to the ways of the Balkans. Especially to Americans who "don't like to be shoved around."

There were other disturbing things in Belgrade. Wherever you turned you stared into the face of Marshal Tito. Cabinet ministers had original oil paintings of him on the walls of their offices. Little storekeepers had reproductions of those paintings in their shop windows. Instead of pastoral scenes in hotel rooms, the interior decoration centered around pictures of the marshal. Tito pictures hung in the windows of homes. Tito pictures appeared almost daily in the papers. Tito pictures were everywhere you looked. Few men in history have been painted and photographed so much in so short a time. The fact that the head of the Yugoslav state has a strong face and is handsome didn't relieve the feeling of being faced by him at every turn.

The Yugoslavs argued that during the war Tito became a hero of great dimensions to a large portion of the Yugoslav public. In war he offered them what Winston Churchill called "blood, sweat, and tears." He offered them the almost certain destruction of their homes, the probable killing of their families, and for themselves years of hardship in the mountains possibly topped off with death. But he somehow inspired them with a belief in the ideals and principles he expounded to them. The sacrifices they made proved it. Now that the war was over he was offering them a better way of life than most of them had ever known or even dreamed about, at the cost of hard work and patience. He offered them now sweat, song, and running water. First they had to tighten their belts and reconstruct the damages of war. But enough material rewards of their industry were filtering down to them already to give them a preview of what might be in store for them later. This was possible, in spite of all the war damage and the complete dislocation of the national economy, because past regimes had never made any attempt to give the people anything. That's what I was told in Belgrade. And they said that it was only natural for the people to want to display pictures of the leader who was inspiring them in peace as he had inspired them in war. They asked if shops and homes in America hadn't displayed pictures of Franklin Delano Roosevelt at one time. They asked is it wrong to revere a man while he is still alive, or must they wait and build stone monuments to him after he is dead? Opponents of the regime answered that it was fear and intimidation that were responsible for the Tito displays. Whether it was love or fear no poll could ever establish. If it was fear and intimidation it was bad and no argument. If it was hero worship, that also seemed bad to many people. Even to people who were reminded that the United States of America is one of the greatest hero-worshiping nations in the world.

It was also depressing to find all the newspapers saying the same thing at the same time in almost the same way. It was depressing to see bookshop windows full of volumes which all followed the same line.

But what was almost frightening was the fever and earnestness of the people. Even if one is in complete agreement with the ideals of a missionary, fanaticism can be frightening. Even if one wears BVD's and a derby hat and likes them, it's frightening to see some earnest soul trying to force BVD's and derby hats on all the natives of a South Sea island. It's even frightening if all the natives wind up liking BVD's and derby hats, and wearing them.

Casual observers, hit-run correspondents, and diplomats talking for a purpose often pictured the Yugoslavs as victims of oppression and terror. They often argued that the will of the few was being forced upon the many by brutal means. So far there had been little evidence that this was true. Instead, it seemed to be an almost fanatical majority of the people who were imposing their ideas for the future on the country over the bitter but generally silent opposition of a small minority. Mouthpieces of the New Yugoslavia argued that this is democracy. They argued that there is nothing wrong with a way of life in which the oppressed are the few. Especially if the few being oppressed are the ones who in the past were the oppressors of the many.

But oppression and fanaticism can be frightening even if they come from the many. Even if they come from the 90 per cent. No one in Belgrade ever argued that there were real happiness and complete freedom here for the 100 per cent. Their defense of the oppression of the few was that under any other system which might be substituted for the present system the few would again turn to the oppressing of the many. And they had plenty of incontrovertible evidence about the past oppressions on the part of people now bitter against the new regime.

One foreign diplomat, neither Russian nor American, put it this way: "Your reactionary observers are doing their own cause a great disservice when they give your people back home a picture of Yugoslavia as a country in which the great mass of the people are having something forced down their throats that they don't like by a small group of evil dictators. Even if your reactionaries are planning to fight this way of life, either with atom bombs or with diplomatic weapons, it's important that they know what they are fighting. If 90 per cent of the people are fanatical followers of the new regime, then it's an entirely different problem than if the 90 per cent are just waiting for an opportunity to overthrow their government."

What the percentage of ardent followers might be no one could say for certain. No poll, however honest, could fix the figure. But it took only a few weeks in Belgrade to make certain of these facts:

Enemies of the regime who take active steps to bring about a violent change in the way of life of Yugoslavia are considered traitors. It doesn't matter whether they are Axis Sallies or men who feed misinformation to American diplomats. They are treated as traitors and face the punishment which all states reserve for traitors.

Opponents of the present way of life who are passive in their resistance live in a state of nervousness, which becomes a fever, which in turn permeates the air and infects other people who engage in frequent association with them. The result is a tension in Belgrade which is not pleasant. This tension is nothing new. It existed here under nearly all the past regimes, for Yugoslavia is a Balkan country, and the Balkans for centuries have had a tradition of changing their governments by force.

Would it be like this in the rest of the country? Or did such tension exist only in Belgrade? That would be one thing to find out. Anyway, the sooner we got out of the capital the better. In Belgrade one spent too much time listening to rumors, trying to trace them down, getting a new batch of wild reports as fast as the last ones were checked. Here in Belgrade everything was secondhand. Here it was impossible to come to grip with facts. Here Truth, if she were ever found, was so battered and bruised that she was not very interesting to look upon. Rumors. Statistics. Cold little claims of fact. And denials. It was time to get out and see for ourselves.

PART THREE

These Are the Bosnians

Chapter Fourteen

WELCOME TO SARAJEVO

ANITA and I pored over maps and decided to hit first for the valley of the Drina River in eastern Bosnia because some of the fiercest fighting of the war had taken place there and some of the worst destruction. There in the Drina Valley we ought to be able to see the New Yugoslavia being built on the ash piles of the old.

The train for Sarajevo was due to leave at eleven forty-five. Just before midnight. I asked Anita to meet me in the lobby of the Balkan Hotel at ten. I knew how long in advance people in this part of the world start flocking into trains. A few minutes after ten I arrived at the Balkan festooned with enough equipment for an Arctic expedition. Anita appeared at eleven with two suitcases instead of one and with a leaking thermos bottle. She was full of apologies. She'd had trouble heating water for tea and the thermos she'd borrowed from the Fursts turned out to be minus a cork. We reached the railroad station fifteen minutes before traintime. The depot was jammed with ill-smelling humanity. Most of the peasant women were so exhausted from a day in the big city that they'd fallen asleep on top of bundles of food and clothing. Their children clustered around them, filling the station with the noise of their crying.

The third-class coaches were jammed to the doors but we finally wedged ourselves and all our luggage into the corridor of one of them. But there wasn't even room enough for us to sit on the suitcases. And it was going to take nineteen hours to get to Sarajevo. It didn't make the trip seem any shorter for Anita to remark that a plane can make it in one hour.

Before the train even started Anita struck up a conversation with a young Yugoslav lieutenant who was traveling to the town of Laikovac. She translated every word he said to her and every word she spoke in reply. Even including some remarks about what he thought of her figure and couldn't they meet alone somewhere sometime. The lieutenant was very much interested in Anglo-American politics. He said everyone in Yugoslavia knew about the help the Western allies had given his country during the struggle and also during the past two years. He said the people of Yugoslavia had a great affection and respect for Britishers and Americans. But they were bothered by our foreign policy. He asked why we supported Franco and "the Fascists in Greece." His particular hate was Winston Churchill. He could quote the Fulton, Missouri, speech almost word for word.

There were no lights in the car. The odors were strong. Most of the time someone in the car was chewing on an onion or eating garlic sausage. The wooden seats were hard. The night was bitter cold. Three quarters of the passengers were standing, jammed so close together that they could hardly breathe. And yet they sang all night long. The tunes of most Yugoslav songs are simple. There is much repetition of words. Most of the songs were born in the war. Most of them were about the Partisans. The one they repeated the most was the song of the 1946 Youth Railroad. A typical song that Anita translated to me was about a mother trying to call her dead son back from the grave. Another contained the line:

"America and Britain will be proletarian lands someday too."

When the lieutenant left the train Anita sat down on her suitcase. At least on the half of the suitcase that wasn't already occupied by a twenty-three-year-old boy who was bursting with questions about America. Do the people of America really want war? If not, then why do we let our leaders foment a war? Isn't America a democracy? Do young people in America sing on trains like this? Do they have dances like the *kolo*? Do they have youth projects like the Youth Railroad? How do they spend their leisure time? Do they do any voluntary work for the government without pay?

At four-thirty we found two seats in a crowded compartment. First traces of morning were in the sky. Our compartment companions were three soldiers and an old woman who kept to her corner until Anita started drawing her out in conversation. Anita was earning her way this first night. The old woman warmed up to me a little when Anita told her I was in Belgrade for the first German bombing. That seemed to make me "belong." The old woman said she lived in the village of Medjedje in Bosnia. The whole place was wiped out in the war. She was in an Italian prison camp in Albania. That was where the Italians put out her left eye.

"See!" she said, pointing to an empty eye socket.

Her thirteen-year-old daughter was killed by a mine. Her two sons were in the Partisans. She dug into a greasy pocketbook and pulled out a photograph of herself taken just before the German attack on Yugoslavia. In the picture she looked very attractive. And not more than forty. Now she looked at least sixty-five. She was a simple peasant woman but under Anita's prompting she gradually became articulate. She said it was true, wasn't it, that England and America were under the influence of an evil ruling class. She'd read about it. She'd heard people talk who knew. There can never be any peace in the world until the American and British people let their governments know they want peace.

Another peasant with a burlap sack over her shoulder came through the car selling small pock-marked apples. The Old Lady from Medjedje pulled a ten-dinar bill from her pocket and bought five apples and passed them around. As she bit into the one she saved for herself she started cursing the last king of the Yugoslavs, young Peter.

"While we were spilling our blood he was . . ."

Anita blushed. She said she was sorry, but she would rather not try to translate the rest of the sentence. The old lady had used very down-to-earth language. The three soldiers were laughing. Anita finally gave me a cleaned-up translation:

". . . he was making love to a Greek princess."

Night gradually blended into day. Our narrow-gauge train, looking like something out of a Disney film, was puffing its way around and around the curves of the Bosnian mountains. For one hour just after dawn the train was quiet. But then everyone began singing again. The three soldiers stopped only long enough, occasionally, to point out some spot on the landscape where "my brother was killed" or "we fought a great battle with the Chetniks" or "the Ustaši killed many of our people." Anita said:

"Something new has entered into the Yugoslav people's appreciation of the natural beauties of their own country, now that so many spots have been stained with blood. To us foreigners this place we're going by may be attractive simply because of its post-card sort of beauty. But under that snow there are graves. And bones. And ruins. Those things have given new meaning to the landscape. These three soldiers in our compartment.

I know from talking with them that they see the beauty of the countryside as much as we do. But now they see something else. Something we will never really be able to understand."

There was no diner on the train, and we didn't stop long enough anywhere to buy anything. Already we were grateful for Jake's two boxes of food. We shared some of it with the other four. Then the Old Lady from Medjedje gave us each a piece of peasant cake she said she baked herself. She apologized for it with a long face. In the days when they had butter and eggs and sugar and cream the cakes she baked were really good.

All day long we went through the wreckage of what once were villages. We rarely saw a house with its four walls and roof intact. In one village the only structure rebuilt so far was the church. We couldn't get the name of the village because the railroad station had been destroyed.

The Belgrade–Sarajevo line goes over hundreds of bridges of all sizes and shapes. I told Anita I'd give her a prize if she spotted a bridge which looked as if it hadn't been destroyed and rebuilt again. The soldiers laughed and told her not to bother. There weren't any. In most places we could see in the river bed the pieces of twisted steel which had been the old bridges. At various points along the right of way ditches at the side of the tracks were filled with the wreckage of railroad trains. They'd been blown up during the night by Partisan soldiers in their fight to destroy German communication lines. To clear the tracks the Germans had just tipped them off into the ravine. Or rolled them down the hillside into a gully. The Yugoslavs hadn't had time yet to salvage many of them.

There is probably no railroad line in the world with more tunnels per hundred miles than this one. Most of the tunnels were "blown" by the Partisans during the war. Since the war, we were told, millions of man hours of labor had gone into clearing them again. In many cases the same men who blocked them up had to remove the debris.

Several hours before Sarajevo a pleasant Bosnian wedged his way into our compartment. He told us he would show us a trick to get to the Europa Hotel quickly. We must get off with him at the stop before Sarajevo. Then all we had to do was to walk a mile down a steep hill and there we were.

It was dark as we approached the capital of the Republic of Bosnia and Herzegovina. Dark of the next night. Our train circled the rim of this city-in-a-cup. Then we started down into the center of the cup. For the first time I noticed that the cup was really the shape of a crescent. That was appropriate, for the crescent is to Turkey what the eagle is to the United States, and Sarajevo has the reputation even today of being the most Turkish city in the world. More Turkish than Istanbul itself. This city below us with her twinkling lights was once the favorite of the sultans. Their window-dressing spot. They tried to make of Sarajevo a glowing example of what a foreign city under Turkish domination could be like. Life in Sarajevo in those days was rich and beautiful. It was a city of craftsmen who were famous the world over. Buyers flocked here from every corner of the globe to select pieces of embroidered silk, rugs, and jewelry turned out on the twisting thoroughfare called The Street of the Filigree Workers. Tonight a soft snow was falling. Tonight Sarajevo looked like a scene from light opera. Memories again. There was nothing light opera about Sarajevo the last time I passed through the city.

Several hundred peasants got off at the same stop we did. Control officers stood at the depot exit to inspect baggage and *legitimacije*. Anita said:

"I suppose some of our friends back in Belgrade would call this 'The Terror' too."

We showed our passports. They didn't even look into our bags. We noticed that they did inspect all the Yugoslavs' identity papers very carefully. The Bosnian who was going to show us the way said that's because some men who have been charged by the War Crimes Commission with committing atrocities during the fighting haven't been rounded up yet. The check is also made to prevent the circulation of any enemies of the regime who may have sneaked across the frontiers from Italy and Austria with the idea of trying to foment an armed uprising against the State.

It was a long walk down the winding hillside road but it was a good place to get a first view of Sarajevo. Slender white minarets were silhouetted against the dark sky. Hundreds of them, it seemed. Anita and I agreed that no school of architecture has ever developed anything more beautiful than the minaret of a mosque.

Finally the Europa Hotel. The last time I saw it bombs were dropping in the streets outside. The city was full of panicky people. But tonight Sarajevo is calm and quiet. Except for the inevitable singing of several groups of young people making their way home from gatherings of some kind. The hotel lobby looks different than it did six years ago. The hotel must have been considerably damaged in that Easter-Sunday raid I saw commencing here, because a major job of reconstruction is going on. On the way upstairs we passed Room 201.

"That," I blurted out to Anita, "that was where . . ."

Memories came floating back. That was the room Sonia got us, by the simple expedient of stealing a key someone had foolishly left in his door on Easter eve when there wasn't a room to be had in all Sarajevo. Not for a king's ransom. That was the room that belonged to a British major who had to spend the night out in the cold because Sonia was such a Machiavellian creature.

After nearly twenty-four hours on a dirty train our rooms at the Europa looked like Paradise Regained. Mine had a bath attached. But there was no water. Neither hot nor cold. So Anita went down and argued. She argued them into violating a rigid rule about no water after dark, in order to conserve fuel and power. We took turns at the bathroom and then had food which was not out of a can. This was our first taste of what the people of Yugoslavia, away from Belgrade's foreign colony, were eating. We had a choice between two kinds of dried or smoked meat. Beans or potatoes. Potato or bean salad. No dessert. No coffee. No soup. Not a **very** tantalizing meal. But it was food and it was hot. And it was good to be clean and warm again.

After dinner we tramped through the snow looking for the mosque in which some of us tried to hide when the Germans came over in planes. I told Anita how we got into trouble that day because in our excitement we forgot to take off our shoes before entering the holy place. The keeper of the mosque didn't like it. We found the street of little stalls and oriental shops called the bazaar. But we couldn't find the mosque. On our way home we heard music coming from a wooden shack about as large as your bathroom. Anita said:

"Let's go in and join the party."

As we pushed open the door, three or four characters inside took one look at us and then scampered out and vanished in the dark. They all acted terrified. One man was left. He had an accordion across his knees which had kept him from running. He kicked the door shut and we were alone again in the street. While we were wondering what it was all about one of the men came back down the street. We could tell he was drunk by the way he walked. He said that if we were foreigners he wanted to talk to us. He said he spoke "every language." What languages? All languages. Hungarian, Turkish, French, German, Spanish, Serbo-Croat. All languages. Apparently he didn't think English was much of a language because he didn't even mention it. Anita tried him first in German. He knew only three or four words. I spoke to him in French. He didn't know any French. Then I tried a few phrases of Hungarian that I remembered from my Budapest days. He didn't react at all. So Anita talked to him in Serbo-Croat. He did know the language of the Yugoslavs. He said he was a Croat. He'd fought as a Croatian pilot in the Luftwaffe. He was sent down here in 1943 by the Germans. He escaped and joined the Partisans. Now he was a tailor again, as he had been before the war. Anita and I both decided his story was a figment of a drunken imagination. He was obviously a simple peasant. He could no more have been the pilot of a plane than Anita could have been a general. He said his wages now came to three thousand five hundred dinar a month, which is seventy dollars. Anita asked him how he liked the present regime. He hesitated. Then with a deep breath, as if he were about to make a long speech, he said it was all right except the "speed up." Anita and I already knew about the Yugoslav speed up. In America the speed up is fought by labor unions on the ground that it forces factory people to do more and more work per hour for the same amount of money. In Yugoslavia the idea of the speed up is to increase the total industrial output of the country at a time when the country is in great need of manufactured goods it cannot obtain from abroad. In Belgrade they'd told me that the speed up is essential if slow-going Balkan peasant people are ever to be transformed into an industrialized race, and that it is especially essential in the southern half of the country which developed shiftless habits during the centuries of Turkish domination, when industrial sabotage was one of the weapons they used against their occupier. But our friend the drunken tailor didn't like the speed up. He didn't want the State or anyone else telling him he had to do more work per day. We asked him if he made as much in the old days as he was making now. It took him three or four minutes to decide. Finally he said no. We asked him if his standard of living were higher or lower now. He said:

"Maybe it is a little higher. Maybe I can buy more with my wages. But you've got to see the people in charge and make them stop pushing us. We don't like to do so much work every day. We like to sing and take it slow and easy. You tell that to the people in charge."

When he finally left us, Anita said:

"I'm sure he thinks we're members of some kind of an investigating commission. But right now the only thing I'm interested in investigating is a soft-looking bed back in my room at the Europa Hotel."

Chapter Fifteen

IT ALL DEPENDS ON THE POINT OF VIEW

IN 1930 Dushan Pilja went to work for a Sarajevo newspaper. He was twenty years old and had had a better-than-average education. After a few years of experience he became an excellent journalist. When the war started he was one of the editors of his paper. He was making fifteen hundred dinar a month, which in those days would buy about what twenty-five dollars will in America today.

Dushan Pilja had a difficult time making ends meet. He still remembers the day the roof of his house began to leak and he had no money to pay for a repair job. So he went to the publisher of his newspaper who was also a local merchant and asked for a small loan. Or for an advance on his salary. He explained what it was for. He would need the equivalent of four or five dollars.

Dushan Pilja says he will never forget the answer he got. His employer explained that he was a businessman. Every dinar he had, had to work for him. If he advanced Dushan the sum he would have to take it out of his business where it was making money for him. No. He was sorry. But the idea was out of the question.

Today Dushan Pilja is editor in chief of Sarajevo's one daily newspaper. He was the first person I interviewed in the Bosnian capital. Newspapermen the world over talk the same language. Even if they have to do it through an interpreter. I thought the Sarajevo editor might be able to give us some tips on where to go and what to see. He did. But in talking about the trip he gave us something else.

Dushan Pilja is now thirty-seven years old. What he went through during the war added a good ten years to his appearance. He's slight and wiry and is rapidly growing bald. He isn't a *Front Page* type of editor, but he does have a phone which rings constantly and he himself moves like a jack-in-the-box.

Dushan was called into the army at the start of the war. When the army collapsed he came home. A few weeks later he heard that the Ustaši were looking for him. He knew what that meant. The Ustaši were members of a Croatian terror organization formed before the war with Italian backing. They set out to eliminate the Serbian race. Dushan was a Serb. So he fled to the hills. He was captured, escaped, joined the Partisans, and fought in Tito's army for the rest of the war. Now he was back where he'd started from. An intellectual again instead of a mountain fighter. Back on the same paper. Only now he was the editor in chief and the paper was owned by the government.

As he talked to Anita in Serbo-Croat I studied a crayon sketch over his desk. It showed a Partisan warrior in long-flowing Moslem robes on horseback on a windswept mountaintop. You could almost feel the wind blowing through the white robes and hear the crunch of ice under the horse's hoofs.

After we discussed the trip I told him that our greatest criticism in America of the New Yugoslavia was that we understood there was a complete lack here of any of the freedoms we value so highly. For example, what about freedom of the press?

It took *Gospodin* Pilja one hour and twenty-seven minutes to answer the question. In that one hour and twenty-seven minutes Anita translated every word he said, and I took every word down on neatly folded pieces of tissue paper. Here is a condensation of what he said:

"Our press is free today. It is free because it writes in the spirit of the people. Those who think our press is not free are those reactionaries who object because we do not write from their point of view, the way your American press writes. Our press represents the big majority of our population, just as your press speaks for the small minority. Look at the difference between our press now and under the old regime. Under so-called democracy in Yugoslavia, which wasn't democracy at all.

"What did we write about formerly? On the first page was some big political article of intrigue. About how some government somewhere was about to fall. About political machinations. The rest of the paper was about scandals and sensations. We wrote about fancy-dress balls and parties and fashions which in no way concerned the lives of the majority of the people. Stories about expeditions to the North Pole and diplomatic cocktail parties. Foreign affairs were presented in a sensational way. That is the press on which our people were brought up.

"I worked on the old press. I started as a police reporter. When a well-known person was murdered, I went out and spent days finding out all I could about the person's private life. The gossip. The sensations. And then I tried to steal pictures of the dead person and members of his family. I went back to my office and wrote pages and pages of sensations. We worked in such an unresponsible manner that I could reveal all the inner secrets of the family. And I was accountable to no one. I could blacken the reputation of a whole family.

"The thing always was to create one great sensation. If there were bandits in the hills the story was written in such a way as to romanticize the crimes of those bandits, rather than to try to drive them out of existence.

"And then our papers carried novels with no literary value whatsoever. Just more sensations.

"It was well known that our ministers in the old Yugoslavia were mostly thieves. Perhaps you've heard that a British journalist once said that Yugoslavia must be almost the richest country in the world, because everyone steals, and still she is rich.

"There was a minister of transportation who stole eighty-two million dinar (nearly two million dollars) and he was never called to answer for it."

At this point a little man came in with three cups of Turkish coffee. While Dushan officiated at the coffee ceremony, Anita translated a printed motto on the wall which read:

"Freedom of the press in our country means freedom to write the truth and expose lies."

We sipped the thick sugary liquid, and then Dushan went on.

"When the war minister would prepare his budget, he would ask for so many million dinar. He never listed how the money was to be spent. There was graft and corruption in every department.

"Today all is different. Today we write of the problems of the people. We write news which concerns every human being in Yugoslavia. We tell them the government plans. We write of the reconstruction of our devastated land. Let us look at today's issue of my paper.

"The lead article is about a meeting of railroad workers. They have assembled to discuss their own problems. Let me tell you about the life of the railroad worker before the war. He lived miserably. No one ever asked him how he felt about anything. Today the manager of an enterprise such as a railroad comes into a meeting of the workers and explains what the enterprise is trying to do. The workers themselves say whether it can be done or not. Or whether they can accomplish more than the plan says.

"Put it this way. Our land is in the process of reconstruction. Workers know that. Workers in an industry often raise the norm without ever asking how much additional pay it will mean for them, because they know that even if there is not any additional pay, the sooner the land is reconstructed, the better their standard of living.

"We in the press do not give the picture of the directors of the railroad but of the plans which the workers themselves have drawn up. In the New Yugoslavia we are interested that each person develops as much as he is intellectually able. We have training courses in every field of activity.

"For example, during the war many of our most able and most talented people were killed, so we are badly lacking in leadership in certain fields. We need good engineers. To get them we are starting short engineering courses all over the country.

"In Bosnia we had the greatest illiteracy in the country. This winter we will practically do away with illiteracy. There is not a town, however small, which does not have a literacy course.

"Our press today carries news like that. It does not carry news of crimes. That is not because there are no crimes. Of course there are. But today we are attempting to rehabilitate criminals. We treat them as sick people. We are working hard on juvenile delinquency. We do not wish to ruin the lives of people. We wish to cure them. News of crimes does not act as a deterrent to crime.

"We carry little news from abroad, because there is so much to write about at home. Our papers must be mirrors of what the people are doing and trying to do and hoping to do. Later we may be able to devote more space to activities in other countries."

I interrupted to ask if they couldn't carry more constructive news about America. Dushan replied:

"We should like to have more news about America, but if we get it from your own newspapers or news agencies it is mostly about crimes and sensations and troubles, in which we are not interested."

Wouldn't the literacy campaign greatly increase the circulation of his newspaper?

"Yes, it has begun already. You see, after one or two months of classes the students, who are sometimes very old men and women, organize themselves into reading groups. They read pamphlets, poetry, and newspapers. They take turns reading.

"For the Moslems we still have separate courses for men and women. But already the women have begun to put aside their veils and when the older generation dies off there will be no veils any more. But already things are different. Before the war if a Christian boy took a Moslem girl home from a party he would be beaten up. No associations were allowed. Today there have been mixed marriages right on the staff of my own paper."

While Dushan was talking, his associate editor had slipped into the room. He'd sat in silence up to this point, but now he wanted to say something.

"You Americans may not know it, but we have already achieved the first goal of the peace. We have convinced the people of Yugoslavia that they are brothers. Of course there are still a few old pepole who can't grasp this idea. They had sons and daughters killed by the Ustaši, for example. The Ustaši were Croats. So these people today hate all Croat people."

Dushan nodded and continued himself.

"We are a young country. The foundation of the New Yugoslavia is our youth. As our youth grows so will our country. Our youth is our strength. You can't expect us to create the Perfect Life out of chaos all at once. Reactionary forces are already using this against us. Already they are saying:

" 'Look! The Perfect Life has not been created in Yugoslavia.'

"But let them wait another five years. One of our first aims is the industrialization and electrification of our country. For that we need steel. But to make steel we must have coal. We have plenty of coal hidden in the mountains of Bosnia. But to get it out we need railroads. The first thing after the liberation we mapped out one new railroad. The best engineers said it would take two years to build it, if we had plenty of mechanical tools. We had no mechanical tools and no trained railroad builders. So last summer the job was turned over to our youth. Last summer, in one hundred and sixty-four days, sixty-four thousand young people built that railroad. The railroad the experts said would take two years."

At this point we got Dushan to tell us the story of his life. He wound it up by saying:

"I told you how I once worked as a sub-editor for fifteen hundred dinar a month. Well, today the members of my staff earn from four thousand to six thousand per month. The top is soon to be advanced to nine thousand. That's quite a difference, isn't it?"

Finally he said he couldn't give us any more time because he had an editorial conference. He wanted to tell us, though, about that.

"We hold a conference every day at the same hour. All members of the staff attend. The editor merely suggests ideas for stories for the next day. He *suggests* that this or that story in yesterday's paper was good or bad. The editor can *suggest* that this or that man be hired or fired. But all final action on any matter is taken by the staff, not by the editor. Quite a change from the old days when the editor was a tyrant!"

From the editor's office Anita and I went shopping. Despite our load of luggage, Anita said there were other things we would need. We had tea and coffee but nothing to boil water in. We had a canned-heat stove but no canned heat. We had butter but no bread. We had cans of meat but no can opener.

Back at the Europa dining room we discovered something about the menu. There were always two choices. If you ordered Item No. One you got smoked or dried meat, potatoes, and a bean salad. If you ordered Item No. Two you got smoked or dried meat, beans, and a potato salad. Whichever it was, you got smoked or dried meat, beans, and potatoes. And the menu never changed.

Chapter Sixteen

THE DANCE OF DEATH

THERE's a great mountain in one corner of Bosnia called the Kozara. It rises to a height of nearly six thousand feet. On the top of that mountain, in 1942, a considerable number of Partisan soldiers one night discovered that they were surrounded. Escape was impossible. In the morning the whole unit would probably be wiped out. The way they spent what did turn out to be the final night of their lives for many of them is something no one could understand who didn't understand the type of men these Partisans were. They spent the night in song and dance. They danced all the *kolos* they knew. They sang the songs they loved the best. And then they invented a new kolo and put it to music. And they wrote words for it too. One of the men who escaped from the mountaintop the next morning was responsible for perpetuating what all Yugoslavia today calls *The Kozara Kolo*.

A kolo is a dance. It differs from a fox trot, a waltz, or most dances we know about first because it takes a whole crowd of people to do it. It isn't done in pairs. Girls and men form a circle and join hands. Just how the hands are joined is important. It varies according to which kolo you're doing. In the Kozara Kolo you hold the hands not of the people on either side of you, but the two people beyond them. In that way there are two people's arms crossed in front of your body.

The music of the Kozara Kolo is wild and full of fire. There's a great rhythm to it. The music breathes savage defiance. As you hear it you can close your eyes and see that circle of men on the top of the mountain in the light of their camp fires. You can almost feel their reckless abandon. Their laughing at death. The Nazis had encircled them, had they? The slaughter would commence at dawn? Long live the Partisan Army; the slaughter will commence at dawn. Death to Fascism; freedom for the people. That's the Partisan motto. *Let* the slaughter commence at dawn! Did those Nazis down below think they were afraid up here on the mountaintop? If they did, let them listen! So the slaughter commences at dawn, does it? Get your guns and your knives ready, you down below, for many a Nazi will fall, too, when the slaughter begins at dawn. We Partisans are fighting for some ideals which you down below couldn't possibly understand. So come on at dawn, and see! Come on and see men who are not afraid of the slaughter, which you say will commence at dawn!

The music gets wilder and wilder. You can hear it shouting defiance to the encircling Germans below. A man from Timbuctoo who didn't know a bit of the history of it would understand. The beat of the rhythm. The stomp of the feet.

The step of the Kozara Kolo is actually quite simple to learn. It probably had to be a simple step, because the feet of those men on the mountaintop were probably close to frozen already. The ballad they sing while they dance is simple too. It's about how Partisans never, never shall be slaves.

I'd heard about the Kozara Kolo but I had never seen it danced until we wandered into what the poster Anita spotted in a shop window that afternoon in Sarajevo called a "Youth Cultural Evening."

The young people were waiting for a jazz orchestra to get its instruments unpacked. And as they often do they suddenly got into the middle of the floor, formed a circle, locked hands across each other's waists, and started weaving around and around while they sang the words of the ballad.

I don't know whether Anita felt as I did or not. For me, it was a great spiritual experience, listening to that wild music and watching them dance. It was just the music of those young people's voices, accentuated by the stomp of their feet. But it was music nevertheless. It was music that was in their blood.

Listening and watching, I suddenly understood a great many things. I suddenly understood how a handful of men in the mountains could pit themselves against the mightiest military machine the world had ever known. I understood how they could steal all the weapons they needed to fight that machine for several years from the machine itself. I understood how they could go cold and thirsty and hungry for weeks and still continue what some people called their "insane, nonsensical" fight. I suddenly understood many things including what they had done that night on the top of a mountain called *Kozara*. And I could understand, too, the story Louis Adamic once told, which I had repeated many times over the radio and to lecture audiences without ever really understanding it myself. The story of a Partisan girl who, when the enemy surrounded a hospital she had in a cave in the mountains, took a gun and shot each one of her twenty Partisan soldier patients through the head at their own request and then, clutching the rifle to her breasts, jumped over a cliff to her own death.

Everything seemed clear as I listened to the music and watched the dance. They were intoxicated, all of them. Not with the cheap kind of an intoxicant one buys in a bottle. Or smokes in a pipe. They were intoxicated with an overwhelming belief in the rightness of what it was all about. In their own deep-rooted principles and ideals. They were all of them intoxicated. The girl who jumped over the cliff. The twenty patients who asked her to shoot them. Those men on the top of Kozara. And these dancers here in Sarajevo too. Some of them may have lost members of their families at the end of the night the dance had its birth. Anyway, the intoxication had been somehow passed on to them. An intoxication born in war was carrying over into the reconstruction and the peace. It explained many things. It explained how sixty-four thousand youngsters could build in one hundred and sixty days, almost with their bare hands, a railroad which experts had said would take two years to finish. It explained how they could put up with discomforts which some of the rest of us would call unbearable. It explained many things we had not yet seen but which I suspected we would see. New villages and towns rising out of hopeless ruins and debris. It explained all those new wooden bridges we'd seen over rivers and streams. It explained the spirit of the New Yugoslavia.

And then suddenly I noticed something else. At first it seemed incongruous. Like seeing the figure of a white angel in the black smoke pouring from a locomotive funnel. Then it didn't seem incongruous at all. It was part of the Kozara Kolo and properly so.

In the center of the circle of dancers a young boy and a girl were fluttering around like butterflies. They started off facing each other about ten feet apart with their arms spread out like wings. And then, to the rhythm of the music, they jumped up and down in the air. "Jumping up and down" doesn't really describe it. That sounds ridiculous. Actually they seemed to float in the air for a moment. Then they touched the floor and were up in the air again. It was the most graceful thing I had seen since Pavlova in her Swan Dance. When one dancer got tired another stepped into the circle and went on where the other left off without breaking the rhythm. The two in the center of the circle always faced each other. The whole thing had something of the element of a contest until finally one of the fluttering butterflies called quits. Then the entire kolo ended.

It was a delicate, almost unearthly touch to the wild mountaintop dance. It made the Kozara Kolo combine the spiritual and the mundane.

This all happened on a Saturday night in Sarajevo. Saturday night in Sarajevo is what Saturday night is in most of America. The night before the morning when you can sleep late. The Youth Cultural Evening began about eight. The posters said there would be a dance preceded by an hour of "culture." The word "culture" in America is generally associated with some nice old lady reading a poem out of a book by Browning, or a piano recital by an unhappy-looking young woman who makes a living giving lessons. But in Yugoslavia the word has no stigma attached to it. It doesn't frighten people away. We saw proof. The hall was packed by eight o'clock with young people waiting for the "culture." Half boys, half girls. Half Moslems and half Christians. You could tell by the clothes they wore.

The program was dull and stupid from an American's point of view. Everything was too obvious. But Anita, sitting beside me in the darkened balcony, leaned over and whispered:

"Be tolerant. Remember this is not being put on for people like you and me. The audience seems to be enjoying it and that's what really counts."

Later we saw some Bosnian dances which had been kept alive for five hundred years until the liberation from the Turks in 1918. Kept alive despite every attempt by the Turks to stamp out all trace of native culture in the Bosnian hills.

During the dancing part Anita went off on her own to entertain and be entertained by some young army officers. I got into conversation with a Yugoslav air-force boy who spoke French. He looked very young. I was sure he must have just won his wings. So I started telling him about the Royal Yugoslav Air Force in 1941. How it wasn't much of an air force. How I had seen, the day of the first German bombardment, what feeble resistance they put up. The flier looked hurt. The reason was soon apparent. He was in the Royal Yugoslav Air Force in 1941. He was flying a bomber. That first day they bombed Hungary and Austria four times. On the fifth mission he was shot down and spent four years in prison camps. He said that when he returned after the liberation he was amazed at the new spirit of the country. He was "all for it." We were by ourselves and we were talking a language no one else understood. But he had nothing to say in criticism of the regime.

To make up for my unkind remarks about his air force I went to the refreshment stand to get him a bottle of beer. I was having difficulty making myself understood when a voice behind me said:

"Can I help you? You seem to be having trouble."

It was the first English I'd heard since leaving Belgrade, except from Anita. The voice belonged to a young Jew. There was no more beer, so we stood and talked for a few minutes. He said there had been twelve thousand Jews in Sarajevo before the war. Now there were no more than five hundred. His father was one of those killed when the Germans came in. He said there was a story in what happened to the Jews of Sarajevo. He was sorry he didn't have time to tell me. There was someone waiting for him. And now if I would excuse him:

"Good night to you."

Chapter Seventeen

"A SEA OF INK AND THE SKY FOR MY PAPER"

ON A SMALL HILL in Sarajevo there's a dirty alley in which Jews and Moslems and Serbs have lived side by side, peacefully, for centuries. At the end of the alley there's a gray deserted temple. It's surrounded by the gleaming minarets of Turkish mosques. It stands there in odd contrast to the magnificence of a Greek Orthodox Church not far away at the bottom of the hill.

The windows of the temple were once filled with panes of bright-colored glass. The windows told the story of Moses and Jeremiah and the other prophets. The windows today are covered with wooden boards on which words have been written which don't bear repeating. The walls of the temple are pock-marked with holes made by rifle bullets fired at close range. The metal doors of the temple are yellow with rust. Spiders have built their webs over the handles. A small side door is half open. It obviously has been half open for a long time because the snow underfoot is untrampled. The ceiling above is naked. But if you kick around in the debris at your feet you'll find bits of glass which were once part of a cut-crystal chandelier that hung right up there, from the center of the ceiling. Water drips through the roof from the melting snow because the roof is now made of ill-matched boards. There is no trace of the metal roof which was once over the building.

It's quiet here now. Not a whisper. But if you knew the story of what once happened here you'd hear a thousand voices. Not pleasant voices either. Hysterical voices. Voices chanting the Lamentations of Jeremiah. Voices praying, out loud, to their Hebraic god.

When they held services here in the old days the rabbi read from a sacred book called the Torah. Its pages were yellowed with age for it was an ancient holy book. The Jews of Sarajevo were very proud of their Torah, although there was some difference of opinion as to exactly how old it was.

Down this small alley which hugs the side of the synagogue there's a family that knows the whole story of what happened here. They live in a place that hardly looks like a house at all. You have to bend low going through the door. It's only two or three miniature-sized rooms. It's little different from the other houses in the alley. The cobbled yard. The outside toilet. The perpetually running outside faucet. Here the family Abenum has lived for all of eighteen years. Before the war the family consisted of the old mother, her four daughters and three sons, and the wife and two children of her eldest son. They were eleven of the twelve thousand Jews who called Sarajevo their home before the Nazis arrived. The twelve thousand were shopkeepers, factory owners, intellectuals, and workers. They were the kind of Jews you found in most any European city before the war.

The family Abenum came to Yugoslavia from Spain four hundred and fifty years ago. They considered themselves Yugoslavs first; Jews, second. But they attended, regularly, all the services which were held in the temple next door. They had a deep feeling for that holy place. They liked to watch the evening sun stream through the stained-glass windows, making strange figures on the walls and the floor. They felt a certain reverential excitement when a beam of light would play on the cut crystal of the chandelier. But especially they liked to hear the rabbi read from that ancient book called the Torah.

Their lives were not happy in those days before the war. Just having a Jewish name was often enough to cause trouble. The oldest son worked as a tailor. The pittance he and his brothers and sisters brought home barely kept the family going. He often dreamed of the Dalmatian coast of Yugoslavia and how, people said, you could have a wonderful vacation over there, for a whole week, for a few thousand dinar. But he had never seen a few thousand dinar, all at one time, in his life.

Yet they were happy, in their own way. And it was good to go into the temple and watch the sunlight come through the stained-glass windows and see the chandelier which sparkled and almost seemed to dance when the light struck it, and to hear the old rabbi reading from the Torah.

Then came April of 1941.

With April came the Nazis.

Every Jewish home in Sarajevo was looted. Everything of the tiniest value was carted away. They even searched this little hovel, in an alley on a hill.

With the Germans came the Ustaši from the north. Together, one day, they turned their attention to the temple. Stones and bullets went crashing through the stained-glass windows until not a piece one square inch in size was left.

Then they played a game, seeing who could hit the chandelier with rocks. Everyone won. The chandelier was soon only something in the memory of the Jews in the alley who hid and put their hands across their ears, somehow hoping that if they didn't hear it, it wouldn't happen.

And then they started rounding up the Jews of Sarajevo, to ship them to places few people in the world had heard of then. Places bearing names like Dachau and Buchenwald.

With a nice sense of etiquette they gave their attention first to women and to children.

What they left of the desecrated temple was used as a marshaling yard— a place to store the Jews until transportation arrived. But transportation was slow in coming. Jews could wait. Food and ammunition first, for the Nordic followers of Adolf Hitler!

They packed them into that small wooden building until the walls themselves groaned with the agony of it. They packed them in until there wasn't one square foot of standing space left. Then they packed in some more.

For twenty-one days and twenty-one long nights they kept them there. When they begged for food the Germans said they weren't aware that Jews had to eat. When they cried for water the Germans laughed and told them to drink their tears. When they began to die the Germans remarked that they'd need fewer trucks to cart the rest away. Even in death the Jews of Sarajevo couldn't lie down. There wasn't room enough. The four daughters of the family Abenum were in there. And the wife of the oldest son. And his two children. The other two sons had already been shot and killed.

And then what happened?

At the end of the twenty-one days they shipped those who were still alive away. Few of them ever returned. But one did. She was sitting in a dark corner of the hovel down the alley when Anita and I came in. Her name was Ančika, they told us. Now she's ten, which means that in '41 she was only four. Ančika is the daughter of the oldest son who somehow also escaped. That's him over by the window. He says:

"Yes, my four sisters all died, or were killed, and my two brothers, and my wife, and my son. But I still have little Ančika." He called the child from the dark corner. She climbed eagerly into his lap.

What happened to Ančika? How did she escape?

It turned out to be a long story. She and her mother and brother were taken to a concentration camp in the north of the country. It was so crowded that they had to "sleep on top of each other." That was the way Ančika herself put it. They "drank the snow." They were infested with bugs and lice. They were given no food, except that occasionally Jews from a nearby village tossed packages over the fence to them.

What happened to the mother and brother?

Ančika's father didn't answer at once. He waited until his small daughter looked out the window at something. While her back was turned he made the gesture of drawing a knife across his throat.

Tiny Ančika was taken from the camp by the wife of a Zagreb cantor who bribed the guards to give her the child. A few months later she paid for that "crime." The Gestapo picked her up and killed her. But before it happened Ančika was secretly passed on to another Jewish woman in Zagreb. She was also put to death. The story finally had its happy ending, for eventually the child was restored to her father in Sarajevo, and here she was now, sitting on his knee in a shack down an alley on a small hill near the remains of the temple.

Anita and I studied the face of this child who had seen her mother and brother killed; who had lost two uncles and four aunts, and was alive to-day only because two Jewish women in Zagreb had gone to their own death for her. By now all physical traces of the experience were gone. She smiled as she looked out the window watching a cat at play. Her body had bounced back to normal. What had happened to her mind we had no way of telling.

But about the temple?

Oh yes, the temple. After the women and children were carted away the Nazis turned the place into a store. They looted foodstuff from the peasants in the villages, brought it into the city, and sold it to the people of Sarajevo. They had no wrapping material so they ripped sheets of yellowed paper from the ancient book called the Torah and used them to wrap up grapes, dried prunes, and other foodstuff. They tore off the tin roof of the temple and made pots and pans which they sold to the Jews who remained.

There was silence for a moment in the little home down the alley, and then from a far corner of the room where it was dark there came the voice of a woman saying:

"I can tell you things about those Nazi camps. I was there. They killed my father, my mother, and my grandmother. I was in one of those places for two years. Finally, when the mass killings began, I lost my mind. For many months I don't remember anything. They said, later, I was completely insane.

"But then my wits returned to me and I escaped. I located a Partisan band in the hills and I joined up. I served with the Partisans the rest of the war."

How, we asked this voice which belonged to someone we couldn't even see, how were they living now, under the new regime?

The voice said:

"Dobro!" which is the Serbo-Croat word for "good—fine."

And from all around the room came an echo of that word:

"Dobro! Dobro!"

The voice added:

"I can use my own name now, without fear of what will happen to me, just because it's a Jewish name."

Then a man in the room said:

"I went to a dance last night here in Sarajevo. I saw you two there. I didn't get home until late. Before, in the old days, I had to lock myself in my house by six—by the time it began to get dark."

The girl who had gone temporarily insane volunteered:

"And I have a career now. While I was in the Partisans I learned a trade. I learned to be a telephone operator, and now I have a job at the Sarajevo postoffice exchange."

How did Ančika's father find life under the new regime?

He was eager to tell. He leaned across the table and answered with great intensity, anxious for us to understand every word:

"We are all living 100 per cent better than we ever lived before.

"As soon as the enemy was driven out of Yugoslavia, some of us opened a co-operative tailor shop. Then we turned the shop over to the government. Now it has three hundred employees.

"This year all of us are getting a fifteen-day vacation with pay. And fifteen days more, if we want to take it without pay. It will be the first vacation I have ever enjoyed. And so, this summer, I am going to take Ančika to the seaside for fifteen wonderful days."

As he announced his plan the child looked up at him, smiled, and took his hand.

The Girl Who Had Been Insane said:

"There's an old Spanish song which says, 'I would like to write my remembrances, but I would need a sea of ink and a sky for the paper.' We sang that song while we were in exile. While we were in those camps. Each one of us could write a long book, but we would need a seaful of ink and a skyful of paper."

Anita said to them:

"It's going to be difficult to make America understand what you people have gone through to lay the foundations for a new life."

The Girl Who Had Been Insane, with an intensity which was now almost insane, said:

"Tell them I saw the Sava River run red with blood, because it was covered with dead bodies. Tell them I saw soldiers stab little babies in the neck with their knives. Tell them I was seventeen years old when they took me. When I escaped from the camp I weighed eighty-two pounds. During my year and a half with the Partisans I gained back thirty-three pounds. There were many of us Jews in the Partisans, and that's something the Partisans have never forgotten."

Anita said:

"Do any of you have any desire to leave Yugoslavia? Tell us frankly. We're Americans and we'll not get you into trouble for telling the truth."

The answer came in a chorus from all over the room:

"Neh! Neh! Yugoslavia dobro! Neh!"

And then Ančika's father said he had something more he wanted to say.

"If you have any way to reach the Jews who escaped from Yugoslavia when our land was occupied, tell them, please tell them, that they should now return, because only here and in Russia is the Jew really free.

"For example, here the law provides (the law of the land) that if any Jew wishes to celebrate the Sabbath on Saturday, he may take the day off and work, instead, on Sunday. In what other country in all the world do they have a law like that? In what other country in the world is it possible for a Jew who works in a factory, an office, or a shop to take Saturday off and work on Sunday?"

And then we asked about the dozens of photographs and pictures on the walls. That was a mistake. It took a full hour for them to explain. This person died at Dachau. This person was dead when she was taken out of the temple. This man was shot right in the alley. These were photographs of the four daughters. This was the youngest son.

There were twelve thousand Jews in Sarajevo.

There are five hundred left.

Chapter Eighteen

WEALTHIER THAN A SULTAN—ONCE

THERE are twelve stories to the Albania Building at the head of Terazzia in Belgrade. That makes it the tallest building in Yugoslavia. But on the main street of Sarajevo they'll be finishing work any day now on an office building which pokes its way thirteen stories up into the blue of the Bosnian sky. That will make it the tallest building in all of southeastern Europe. And I don't remember seeing a taller in London or Paris either. Nor in Turkey. Nor anywhere in Africa.

But that doesn't mean Sarajevo is a modern-looking city like Kingsport, Tennessee, or St. Paul, Minnesota. At certain intervals during the day in Sarajevo you can hear the wailing of the muezzins as they walk slowly around the platforms which encircle the minarets. That's the way they call Moslem people to prayer. Half the women you see in the streets wear thick black squares of cloth over their faces, despite the government's campaign to get them to forget religious custom and expose their eyes. Moslem women's dresses are long, flowing affairs of dull, somber colors. Some wear pantaloons tied tightly at the ankles. The men wear Turkish fezzes. Generally red.

Down the street, not an eighth of a mile from that new skyscraper, there's the bazaar. In Istanbul the bazaar is colorless and uninteresting by comparison with Sarajevo's. Here, in this Bosnian capital, there is more left of the Old Turkey than anywhere in Turkey itself since the days of Kemal Ataturk and the Great Reform.

The bazaar is a number of twisting streets lined with what we would call shacks. Each shack contains a shop, and in mild weather the front is taken away, exposing the inside to full view.

In these shops, if you know your way around, you can find many rare items of oriental design. Some have come from the East itself, transported on the backs of camels. Others were made right here in Sarajevo by craftsmen who know something about art.

The largest and most famous of these shops is one which had been owned for generations by the family called Ćićo. It isn't any larger than a good-sized hotel room, but generations of tourists know about it. There you can buy the best oriental rugs anywhere in these parts. Rare antiques are hidden in boxes and cartons all over the place. Of course the old man who ran the shop didn't show his prize pieces to everyone. For the common, garden variety of tourist, some of that modern filigreed silver stuff was good enough.

The Ćićos also had a shop by the edge of the sea, in a walled city on the Adriatic called Dubrovnik. That was a fancier place. Modern too. More in the Fifth Avenue manner. Designed for the elegant people of the Mayfair crowd who never got farther away from home than the so-called "civilized" part of the Balkans.

Old Man Ćićo spent most of his time in the musty shop in the Sarajevo bazaar. He let his son and his daughter and his daughter's husband take care of the fancy place by the sea. They liked to meet the important people who came to Dubrovnik. But the father didn't. He didn't like their manners and their airs.

If you'd asked anyone in Sarajevo, in those days, what the Ćićos were worth, their eyes would have opened wide. Then they would have spread their hands out in a gesture which said as well as words:

"Who knows?"

But everyone did know that they were wealthy. Probably as wealthy as many a sultan once was.

Just before the war the daughter, Fatima, lost her husband, after a long illness. Then, about the time bombs were falling all around Sarajevo and its fragile bazaar, the Old Man died. Then the only remaining male of the family, Fatima's brother, disappeared. That was more than five years ago and nothing has been heard from him since.

After the liberation, when the government began its policy of nationalization, appraisers were sent to Sarajevo and to Dubrovnik to set a price on what the State would give for the two Ćićo establishments. Now they are both government stores.

Anita met Fatima when the two of them were going in opposite directions through Dubrovnik. They took a fancy to each other and when they separated, Fatima gave Anita her Sarajevo address and said:

"If you ever get there, be sure to call."

Anita dug the address out of her handbag that Sunday afternoon we were being "social" in Sarajevo and said:

"If you're looking for an enemy of the regime, I'd suggest Fatima Ćićo. I'm sure she's not very happy, after what's happened to her. And besides, it might be fun to see the inside of a real Turkish home."

So we walked several miles to the edge of the city and called on the Ćićos. Madame Fatima is as tall as I am. About six feet. She weighs almost twice as much. A good two hundred and seventy or eighty. The weight is well distributed around her bulky frame. She would be one of the most beautiful women in Europe if she could find a way to lose a hundred pounds or more. And if Yugoslav dentists since the war, because of the non-availability of porcelain, weren't forced to make all false teeth of silver. Every tooth we could see in Fatima's mouth was of highly polished silver. I said later to Anita that after seeing thousands of Yugoslav mouths full of tens of thousands of silver teeth, if a man could still love silver then he must have a consuming passion for it.

Fatima has lovely eyes, a beautiful complexion, and a charming smile, if you can just avoid looking at her teeth. Her home from the outside looks little different from any well-built, fairly expensive suburban home in America. Say in Westchester County, or Wilmette, Illinois. Inside it's quite oriental. Deep divans draped with oriental rugs. Rugs on the floor. Rugs over the furniture. Rugs on the walls. I even looked up expecting to see rugs fastened to the ceiling.

Fatima apologized and said we wouldn't mind sitting in the kitchen would we, because that was the only room they had fuel enough to heat. She still hadn't heard from her brother. He may have been killed, but she lived in the hope that he had escaped to some foreign country and eventually would turn up alive.

Then Fatima's daughter appeared. A bubbling, effervescent child in her middle teens. Dika wore her arm in a sling. Her mother explained about the ski accident. Dika could stay with us just a little while because she had schoolwork to do. She was a student in the *gymnasium*. Like an American high school. She wanted to graduate at the head of her class and probably would.

We spent a whole evening with Fatima and Dika. We tried to get the mother to talk about how she felt toward the present regime. She'd just shrug her shoulders. But in that gesture we could see that she wasn't happy about life. She had lost her father, her brother, her husband, and now the two businesses were gone.

Once during the evening there was an exchange of words between mother and daughter which revealed a great deal. Dika was telling us that after her graduation she was going to study metallurgy and become the best metallurgist in all Yugoslavia. She said it with sparkling eyes. We sensed that she had the ambition and brains which probably would enable her to do it. Then Fatima spoke up.

"Dika, why does it have to be metallurgy? Why don't you just plan to get married to some nice boy and settle down?"

The way Dika ignored what her mother said indicated that this was no new divergence of opinion. And then the child began to bubble again.

"I've just about decided to do my studying, after I get through with the gymnasium, at a university in Moscow."

Fatima turned to Anita and me with a hopeless look on her face.

"She keeps insisting that she's going to Moscow because she says they have such a good metallurgy school there. I tell her why not London or Paris. Some respectable place. Even some city in America. Oh, Dika, why does it have to be Moscow?"

The tension in the kitchen was broken when Fatima asked us if we'd like coffee. We made our great error when we said yes. Fatima first produced a large sack of coffee beans, pure white. She put a handful of them in a saucepan, stirred up the wood fire in the cooking stove, and then for exactly thirty-seven minutes she stood there wiggling the pan the way you do a popcorn shaker, while the beans slowly turned brown. The aroma was good. But by this time Anita and I were weary and we knew we had to be off early in the morning on the great adventure over the mountains. Then the beans were put in a long brass cylinder with a handle and were ground. Only the handle was broken and it took thirteen minutes to grind those few tablespoons of beans to a powder. By this time the fire had almost died. There was no more wood. It took an eternity for the water to boil. Finally we had our two ounces apiece of thick, sugary Turkish coffee. On the way home to the Europa Anita said:

"That was interesting. We saw the Old Yugoslavia and the New together in the same house, didn't we?"

I said that the New Yugoslavia seemed to be passing Fatima by. And men were passing her by too. If she only had white teeth and a waist somewhat approaching a perfect thirty-six!

Chapter Nineteen

NOW THEY'RE JUST BANDITS

ROMANIJA is a beautiful word. It's beautiful enough to be a girl's name if you say it the way the people of The Romanija do. The "j" is silent. You roll the "r" a bit with your tongue. You accent the third syllable, pronouncing it as if it were spelled "knee."

Romanija is the name of a great mountain that you can see far off to the east from Sarajevo. The peak is one thousand six hundred and twenty-nine meters high. That means five thousand three hundred feet.

When you put a "the" in front of Romanija it means all the villages up and down the mountain slopes, and the villages in the valleys at the foot. The Romanija is therefore a small section, of one district, in the eastern part of Bosnia, which in turn is one of the republics that make up Yugoslavia. It is hundreds of miles removed from the country called Rumania and there is no connection.

To get to the Drina Valley from Sarajevo it is necessary to travel by highway. The towns of Sokolac and Rogatica, two places we especially wanted to visit, are not on any railroad line. The highway from Sarajevo to Sokolac and Rogatica winds its way almost up to the top of Romanija and then through a mountain pass which at this time of the year, they told us, fills deep with snow. In Sarajevo they said not to try The Romanija now. Go to the Dalmatian coast first. Come back here to Bosnia and The Romanija in the spring. Bosnia is lovely in the spring. The late spring. Wait until April or May. Of course June would be better. I had been over Romanija Pass once before. Then it was April. Forsythia bushes were flowering back in Belgrade. Along the way fruit trees were in blossom. Once, somewhere, someone stopped and picked a bunch of violets as a gesture of defiance of the planes overhead. That other time we were part of a caravan of automobiles. We were trying to catch up with the Royal Yugoslav Government before the ministers and their king reached an airport and found planes to carry them away. That was six years ago. But I'd never forgotten the icy roads and the snow-filled mountain pass called Romanija. We skidded around curves at such a speed that many cars went plunging over ravines, burst into flames at the bottom, and that was the end of flight for another half-dozen people. Many times we had to get out and help twenty or thirty other men push one car after another up inclines too icy for the wheels themselves to manage. That was in April. Now it was February.

In Sarajevo they did everything they could to talk me out of my idea.

But a hunch told me that the story I was really looking for lay beyond that mountain pass called Romanija. And what they didn't know in Sarajevo was that my perfect interpreter had promised to remain with me only until the middle of March. After that the call of the heart might get too insistent to be ignored any longer.

So we arranged for a jeep and a driver. Dushan Pilja, the editor, said he had a reporter on his staff who knew the area we were going to like a book. If we wanted him . . . Of course we could go alone if we preferred, but Dushan thought his reporter could be a great deal of help. There aren't many hotels in the Drina Valley. He could find us places to stay. He could help us with our transportation problems. He could make himself useful in many ways. So we agreed to take him. With four of us in a jeep we knew we'd have to travel light. Really light this time. So Anita left one of her suitcases in the Europa. I left my typewriter, one box of food, and one duffel bag of miscellaneous items most of which we were sorry we didn't have with us before the trip was over. But we did take some "civilized" things like toilet paper, medicines, heavy clothing, and a few cans of DDT.

I put the fur-lined parka over my overcoat. Anita put on the down-filled vest. Dressed like that we had to attend a suddenly arranged coffee party in the private office of the Prime Minister of Bosnia and Herzegovina. The secretary to the Prime Minister had heard we were in town. She wanted to pass on to us, very formally, the Prime Minister's regrets that he himself couldn't see us. He was in Paris attending the peace conference. But . . . wouldn't we have another glass of *rakia* and more cups of Turkish coffee? When we left her she raised her glass and said *"Srećan put!"* They're nice words. They mean "Happy journey and may the gods who watch over travelers get you to your destination safely."

We had prayed earnestly that the jeep would be of the closed-in variety. Or at least that it would have side curtains. Those prayers were not answered. Anita and I consoled ourselves by whispering to each other that at least there wouldn't be any ventilation problem. It wouldn't matter now whether the reporter ate garlic until he reeked of it, as so many Yugoslavs do.

When the jeep driver saw Anita he refused to let her get into the car. At first I thought he must have an aversion to women. It wasn't that. He insisted she go back to the hotel and put on some "more sensible clothing." He had just had a weather report from the Pass. It was doubtful whether we could get over the mountain. No car had been over in days. It was below zero up there. We might get stuck. He himself was going back home to put on two or three more suits of underwear. We should do likewise. He would meet us at the Europa in half an hour. Neither Anita nor I had two or three extra suits of underwear. But she did change into some corduroy slacks and a couple of sweaters. When the jeep returned the driver had on a woolen helmet that covered his whole face except his eyes. I gave Anita a fur cap and pulled the hood of the parka over my head.

The reporter was dressed as if for a stroll down the Champs Elysées in May. But Anita whispered:

"He has more surplus weight than Fatima. Don't worry about him."

And so we started. It was noon already and we had to make Rogatica by night.

If you want to test the low gear of your automobile take it up Romanija Mountain in February when the snow is deep. I don't think we got out of first gear for a couple of hours. The higher we circled the deeper the snow got. Deeper and deeper. The wind howled through the open jeep with a vengeance. The only track in the snow had been made by a truck with an oversized wheelbase. That meant that if we got our right wheels in the right-hand track the left wheels were in no rut at all and the jeep was tipped at a crazy angle. So we kept bouncing from rut to rut. Even the reporter sitting in the back seat with the luggage began to get nervous. At most spots the mountain rose on the left side straight up from the road. On the right side there was a drop, from the edge of the road down into the valley, of hundreds then thousands of feet. There were no guard rails along the road. Not even an occasional block of stone to keep a car from going over. Anita and I were nervously exhausted by the time we reached the top. But getting to the top was worth it. Up there we went into the clouds. The driver didn't like it because it was as bad as driving in a London fog. But Anita and I just stared at the landscape. The clouds were filled with frost which they deposited on the branches of every tree with the skill of a great artist. Most of the trees were giant spruces. The tallest trees I've ever seen in my life . . . except when I saw these same trees looking just like this six years before. It was beauty such as man never achieves by himself. Nature, seldom.

As Anita and I in the front seat were gasping at this primeval splendor the reporter behind us suddenly barked out three or four short words in Serbian. The driver slammed on his brakes. The jeep did some contortions which no self-respecting car is supposed to do. I looked down and picked out the rocks I was sure I was going to land on. Two wheels of the car, on my side, were so close to the edge that if the ground hadn't been frozen we would have been down on those rocks already.

Anita translated the quick little dialogue that was going on. The reporter had seen three figures with guns. They ran from the forest toward our car as it approached. Then they apparently changed their minds and went back into the woods again. The reporter and the driver agreed that they must be Chetniks. No one but a Chetnik would be going around in Romanija Mountain on a day like this with a gun. Anita and I knew that there were a few followers of Mihailović who were still in hiding. Twice the government had issued amnesty offers. The government agreed that any Chetnik who came out of hiding would be given all his rights as a citizen and would not be punished in any way, as long as he personally had not burned houses, killed women and children, or engaged in any other maniacal activity. He would be excused even if he did those things if he could prove that he had merely taken orders from higher up. Thousands had come out of the hills in answer to those offers. But we were told that there were a few hundred, perhaps a few thousand, still in hiding. In every remote community, they told us, we'd hear tales of these hunted men. How they come out at night and loot a home and steal food and in some cases even commit murders in their determination to avoid capture and keep alive. One of their favorite tricks was to prey on automobiles that they held up in lonely places. And this was surely a lonely place. We hadn't passed a house in a dozen miles.

The reporter and the driver each had a pistol. They took them out of their pockets and started on foot back down the road. I looked around for a weapon for myself. I couldn't find anything more lethal than Peter Furst's thermos bottle. Then the two men came back and argued about turning the jeep around. I was all for witnessing a battle. But the idea of trying to turn the jeep around on a road not much wider than a dining-room table frightened me. There are pleasanter ways of dying than dropping off into space. Anita and I were relieved when they decided to go on and send a searching party back from the first village we came to.

Now the cold began to get really bitter. I dug an extra pair of gloves out of my pocket. The driver's woolen helmet was covered with hoarfrost just like the trees. Anita, sitting between us, said she was quite warm, thank you. The reporter in the back seat began to drink himself into a state of intoxicated warmth. He had a bottle of vile-tasting *rakia*. His system was to pass the bottle up to the front seat after each third drink he took himself. Then it became after each fourth drink. Finally he finished the bottle himself.

At two o'clock we started down the far side of Romanija. And that's how we got to Sokolac.

Chapter Twenty

THERE ARE NO PLOVIĆS ANY MORE

WHEN I tell you that Sokolac is a county seat don't close your eyes and think of some county seat you know in Iowa, Kansas, or Massachusetts. If you have ever stepped on an anthill or stood beside a hive of bees coming and going it will make it easier for me to describe what Sokolac was really like. It looked to us more like a lumber operation than a town. Hundreds of horses, mules, and oxen were hauling logs from the mountains down the icy roads to a sawmill. These were some of the great spruces of The Romanija on their way to becoming houses, churches, schools. The mill itself was obviously postwar. Its walls and roof were of lumber which neither time nor weather had yet stained. Close by there was another frame structure, about the size of a construction office on a building project. From the insignia nailed over the door we could tell that this was head-quarters for the People's Government of the county of Sokolac.

We were more cold and more hungry than we were eager for information. So we took our brown cardboard box of food inside and got permission to use the desk of the president of the People's County Council for a table. Anita dug a can of solidified heat from the musette bag and began to boil water for tea. Corned beef from a can tasted better than I thought corned beef could ever taste. The reporter, city man though he was, made his meal from chunks of dark bread he pulled from one pocket and slivers of uncooked smoked meat he cut from a greasy slab of the stuff he fished out of another pocket. As we ate, the room began to fill up. Word had apparently spread through this lumber camp they called a town that strangers were here. It was cold in that small room at first. Almost as bitter as the out of doors. But before long the amount of body heat raised the temperature a bit.

My first impression of Sokolac was that of a logging camp in the Far West. It wasn't just the sawmill and the animals and the fallen trees. It was the pioneer spirit of the place. The appearance of the people. The primitiveness of the scene.

We stayed in that one small room for more than an hour. Before we got through we talked with many people. At first they were hesitant. Diffident. But soon their timidity wore off and before we left they were pouring out their life stories to us as if we were long-lost kin. But especially they wanted to talk about their village of Sokolac. And the county named Sokolac too. They wanted to tell us how this place had just been named a county seat because of the role it played in the resistance.

The first person to become really articulate was Mirka Kostić. He'd been secretary of the People's Council for about a year. Except for the language he spoke he might have been an American college boy. He was still in school when war hit Yugoslavia. He joined the Partisans. He'd had his share of adventures. While we were talking to him another young man came into the room. On his breast pocket over his heart he wore a large silver medal with slender shafts of gold streaking out from the center like rays of the sun. He said in Serbian it's called a *Spomenica,* which means "reminder." It's worn by everyone who was in the Partisans as far back as 1941. It reminded me of President Roosevelt's inner-circle club of men and women who had supported him before the 1932 Chicago convention. The general idea was the same. Mirka said wearers of the Spomenica have many privileges. They're entitled to one free airplane ride a year anywhere in Yugoslavia, to treatment in any hospital or sanitarium at the State's expense, to a 50 per cent reduction in railroad fare, to an extra two weeks' summer vacation with the government footing the bill up to one hundred and twenty dollars, and finally to a free funeral "corresponding with the social position of the man." Mirka said that that meant that this man and Marshal Tito would both be buried free by the State, but of course the Marshal would get the better funeral. The man with the medal turned out to be Mihail Obranović, president of the People's County Council. He had fought through most of the war here in The Romanija. He had fought back and forth through this very village many times. His home, like most others, was destroyed. His brother and three other close relatives were killed. After his return from the army he married a village girl named Persa who had done secret work for the Partisans during the occupation. Mihail, like everyone else we interviewed, looked old for his years. He was still in his early twenties but he was already slightly bald. He hadn't lost his enthusiasm though. With flashing eyes he told us how "the new democracy" works. Seven men are elected to the County Council. Their job is to interpret and put into action the laws passed in Sarajevo, the capital of the republic. They have a lot of local discretion. They also have plenty of problems. "But we're doing all right." The president told us that just last night an attack was made on a home in a deserted mountain area by some hungry Chetniks. Maybe they were the same men we saw. A searching party would be sent out after them immediately.

Then the earnest young president gave us a picture of his town. Sokolac before the war had three hundred houses. About eight hundred population. Every one of those three hundred houses was destroyed. Most of them were made of wood from Romanija trees. They were burned first by the Ustaši, then by the Chetniks, and the few that were left by the Germans. This was part of the enemy's effort to discourage the people of the Romanija from joining Tito's army. The first houses burned were those inhabited by families of men who had gone off with the Partisans. The president said he had never heard of Lidice. In 1942 the Partisans captured the ruins of the village and were able to hold on here for six months. Then they were driven out by the enemy.

In the county before the war there were two thousand houses. Practically all of them were destroyed. In the past summer eight hundred, not quite half of them, were rebuilt. The rest would have been rebuilt by the first fall of snow—that was the plan—except that nature played a trick on the people of Sokolac. A forest fire broke out on Romanija. It burned for most of the summer and destroyed millions of dinar worth of trees. It also destroyed twenty-five of the newly built homes. But that wasn't the worst of it. The worst was that thousands of men who should have been at work on reconstruction jobs had to fight the fire. Mihail looked over our heads into space as if he were actually seeing the burning forest. "We got help all the way from Sarajevo. But it was a hard fight. As hard, in some ways, as whipping the Germans, the Chetniks, and the Ustaši."

Then he suddenly looked straight into my face.

"I hadn't thought of it before, but they were alike a little, the enemy we had last summer and the enemies we had during the war. They were all of them evil. And all of them destroyed, with just as little sense and reason. I hadn't thought of it before."

Then he leaned back in his chair, puffed out his chest slightly, and added:

"But we beat them. All of them!"

There was still another enemy he wanted to tell us about. The drought. Of course it was two summers of drought that made the forest fire so bad. The drought ruined the crops and cut down the food supply. They'd had everything to contend with during the first two years of peace. Everything!

"Would you like some figures?"

Seven schools in the county had been reconstructed. Six more would be finished this coming summer. For the first time in history the county was going to have a hospital. "A real hospital!" I asked when it would be completed. "Our plan calls for it to be finished by autumn. That means it will be finished—by autumn." The other men in the room wagged their heads in solemn agreement. The plan also calls for a modern county building, a warehouse large enough to store seventy-two carloads of grain, a creamery, two dormitories for government workers now sleeping on desks here in the temporary county building, a new sawmill, and hundreds of additional houses.

I asked Anita to find out how work like this is financed. Mihail answered that the federal government contributed three million dinar worth of supplies, paid the cost of cutting, hauling, and milling the timber, and also sent in quantities of brick. The government also paid some of the labor costs. Then Mihail interrupted himself. His eyes sparkled again.

"You understand, don't you, that a lot of this labor is voluntary? Last summer, when the fire was going, all the men who went up in the mountain to fight it gave their time without any pay. The government just sent them food. That's all."

I wanted to know something more specific.

"Let's say I'm an old lady. My husband's dead. My sons were killed in the fighting. When I came back to Sokolac I found my house in ruins. What happens to me?"

"It doesn't matter how your sons were killed. Even if they were in the Chetniks or Ustaši. You just make out an application to us. To the County Council. Then we ask for voluntary labor to cut trees, haul in the logs, and mill them. The government supplies you with nails, hardware, bricks, and things like that. And then . . ."

Mihail made a gesture with his hands to indicate that that's all there was to it. I had a new home, free.

Someone over in the corner wanted to know whether we had heard about the Plovićs. Everyone in the room wanted to tell us about the Plovićs. From the confusion of sounds we gathered that there were ten families in the county by the name of Plović. Every member of every one of the ten families was killed. In the silence that followed a single voice spoke out.

"How about the Abozovićs. There were eight families of them. I know. One of them lived near me. Everyone in all eight families aren't any more."

Then the Pušhanes. There were six families of them. All killed. President Mihail held up his hand for silence.

"This could go on for a long time. You have enough to get the idea."

There was a lull then, while Anita brewed tea for as many as we had cups to serve. During the lull a girl came in and whispered something to the county president. He brought her over and introduced her. Her name was Koprivica. She had just arrived from a village called Bandine Odzak, seven kilometers away. There had been thirty houses over there. Not one of them was standing today. The girl had come to see the council about having houses built for those who hadn't been killed.

We looked at our watches and said we had to be on our way if we were to get to Rogatica by night. But President Mihail said there was one more story we must stay to hear because it would give us a human picture of what really happened here. We must listen to the story of Radmilla, the Partisan fighter. So we stayed and heard the story of Radmilla.

Chapter Twenty-One

GOOD STEEL DOESN'T BREAK

BIALOCKOVIC was a pleasant mountainside village before the war. It was typical of many communities of The Romanija. Several hundred humans. Two or three times that many animals. Mostly sheep and goats. A large percentage of the adults were illiterate. Families were large. The village school provided only four years of education and there were some children who didn't get even that.

The Pialovs were a typical Bialockovic family. Except that there weren't so many of them. Just the father and mother; two sons, Lubo who was seven and Mirko, eight; a daughter, Radmilla, fifteen; then Father Pialov's brother and his wife and six children. That made thirteen in all. Thirteen turned out to be a very unlucky number for the Pialovs.

When the Wehrmacht thundered down the snow-filled road into the village of Bialockovic, two Yugoslavs accompanied them. One was a Chetnik. The other was a member of the Ustaši. These two men went from house to house marking a white cross with chalk on each place to which they wanted the Germans to give "special attention." At least one person was taken from each chalk-marked house to the village square. But for some reason they gave extra "special attention" to the Pialov home. All thirteen were taken.

There wasn't much ceremony about what they did in the village square. They just placed everyone in a circle and began to fire at them with rifles and machine guns. Of course there was great confusion. In that confusion a number of people escaped into the woods. It was not difficult because the edge of the woods came right down to the edge of the village. And the peasants of Bialockovic knew those woods as well as they knew the insides of their cottages. The Germans were a little reluctant to follow them into the woods because of reports about Partisan snipers there.

Among those who did not get into the woods because they were killed by the first shots were Mother and Father Pialov, the father's brother and his wife, one of their children who was only two years old, and the younger Pialov boy named Lubo who was seven. Four of the children who escaped remained together for a long time. Radmilla, her brother Mirko, and two of their cousins. Because Radmilla was the eldest she became the leader of the party. She told us:

"The first night was the worst. We were very cold. That was because the Germans didn't let us put on any overthings. Any coats or mittens. I guess they didn't know we were going to need them up on the mountain.

The first night was the worst because of what we saw happening down in Bialockovic. From the side of the mountain we watched them burning our houses. It must have been very warm down in Bialockovic that night but we were very cold up on the mountain."

In the days and nights that followed the four youngsters had hard going. They had no destination. They were just wandering in circles. Even that was difficult because now enemy forces were beating through the woods trying to locate the Partisan snipers. The children could tell a German soldier at a good distance because of his uniform and his helmet. But it was difficult to spot Chetniks and Ustaši. After all they were Yugoslavs too. And many of them wore civilian clothes. This was something Mirko couldn't understand. He said many times to Radmilla that first night:

"Why do they want us to be killed? They're our own people, aren't they, Radmilla?"

Radmilla didn't try to explain. She herself, even though she was fifteen and the head of a family now and had finished four years of school, didn't quite understand.

Often during the night when they huddled together on the mountainside trying to keep warm they'd talk about the rest of the family. Mirko had seen his father and mother fall dead, but he kept saying:

"Radmilla, don't you think maybe Lubo got away? Don't you think maybe he's here in the woods too? Can't we try to find him?"

It was many weeks before Radmilla told her brother Mirko the truth. She waited until the life of a wild animal he was living had transformed him from a timid child of eight into a hardened man. She told him the day he killed a wolf with a club he had made from a branch of a tree. That day she told him that Lubo was dead. What she still didn't tell him was that she was certain because she had seen him fall. Because she had seen what happens to a little boy's head if the man who is aiming a machine gun at the little boy's head fires from a distance of only ten feet.

Radmilla didn't remember how long it was before they found a Partisan unit. Maybe it was six days. Maybe two weeks. Dates and time become very unimportant under certain conditions. Anyway they did find the Partisans. The Partisans wanted to know what had happened in the village of Bialockovic. The other children broke down and cried when they tried to tell. But Radmilla gave the Partisans the whole story. And she begged the Partisan leader to "do something" to the men who had done that to the village of Bialockovic. It was Radmilla who led a small unit of the Partisan army back through the woods to Bialockovic. On the way they found three of their young cousins hiding in a cave, blue with cold and almost starved to death.

What they saw when they finally got back to Bialockovic made them realize why the light in the sky had been so bright that first night they were on the mountain. There wasn't a single house left. There was no occupying army in Bialockovic because there was nothing left to occupy.

Just some black places where houses once stood. Black places now mostly covered with snow. And a mound in the village square also covered with snow. Radmilla knew what was under the mound. But she didn't say anything about it. She was afraid someone would want to dig some graves. There wasn't time for that if they were going to make somebody pay for what had happened in the village square.

I've read in books about people's eyes "shooting out sparks." I've always thought that that was a foolish, exaggerated expression. I always thought so until I sat in the headquarters of the People's County Council of Sokolac, Yugoslavia, and listened to Radmilla Pialov telling her story. Her eyes were like two of those sparklers we used to have on the Fourth of July when we were children. She stood through the whole recital. She said she preferred to stand. She wore a pair of dark blue trousers, a white shirt open at the throat, a blue coat, and around her neck there was a bright red scarf tied in a knot behind.

I don't know what kind of girl Radmilla was when she was fifteen and they tried to kill her. Now that she was almost twenty she had all the qualities of one of those two-edged swords I used to watch Old Tom making in the Wilkinson sword factory on the edge of London. She was a piece of finely tempered steel. The sharp way she talked, not wasting a word, reminded me of the needle point of a good sword. The fact that life had bent her almost double but had not broken her reminded me of the way Old Tom used to take one of his swords and make the point almost touch the handle. But it always went back into its original shape.

Radmilla was not beautiful. Not in a Hollywood way. She never could have starred in a movie. But standing there with her feet slightly apart she seemed to me the strongest woman I had ever seen. The strongest in every way.

Then what happened?

Well, she and her small brother Mirko spent two years in the woods with the Partisans, summer and winter, rain and snow. The first thing the Partisans did was to give her a nursing course. Then she was made a nurse and treated the wounded. Even though she was a nurse she carried a rifle and a single hand grenade.

"Did you ever use the rifle?"

"Yes, once I shot and captured a German officer. The swine!"

"Were you sorry you hadn't killed him?"

She answered with her eyes. She didn't say a word. But we knew the answer from her eyes.

Then she became a youth leader with the Partisans.

"There were a great many children in our army. Like Mirko." Obviously she didn't consider herself a child, although by then she was only sixteen. "Marshal Tito gave orders that the children were to be allowed—— No, that's not the word I mean—that they were to be required to continue their education, even in winter while they were doing odd jobs for the army.

Some of them were so young they hadn't learned yet even to read and write. But we taught them. That was my job. To make them literate. Between every battle, classes were conducted wherever we were. After they had all learned to read and write we would take turns reading any books or papers we could get. Those were some of the first things we'd look for when we liberated a village. Then I would preside at meetings. At the meetings we would decide which of them in the next engagement would have charge of hauling bombs. Which would clean rifles. Which would act as message runners. Some of us became expert in camouflage. Some of us would go ahead of the army and look for camouflaged enemy gun emplacements and snipers' nests."

At twenty this child who so suddenly grew into a woman is the youth leader for Sokolac County. She directs the reconstruction and care of war orphans. She has charge of all educational and cultural activities. She travels from village to village, generally on a mule. In her spare time she goes up the mountainside with the men and cuts timber in preparation for the spring building program.

"Oh, by the way," she said as we were packing the remains of our food into the brown cardboard box. "By the way, when they started to clear away the debris of the old sawmill right out the window there, they found the bodies of fifty men, women, and children in a pile of sawdust. Did anyone tell you that?"

We all shook hands with Radmilla when we left. She shook hands like a lumberjack.

Chapter Twenty-Two

ATOM BOMBS COULD DO NO WORSE

WHEN the headlights of the jeep silhouetted Rogatica against the dark evening sky we rubbed our eyes quickly and then looked again. It was no mirage. It wasn't a painting by an impressionist artist. It was stark, horrible reality . . . those rows and rows of crumbling buildings . . . those walls without roofs . . . those narrow streets almost knee-deep with mud . . . a shadowy figure here and there hurrying, ghostlike, through the gloom.

That picture we saw of Rogatica in the headlights of our jeep could well be the final picture of all time. A scene of the last Armageddon. The end of civilization.

I don't know how long we sat there in the jeep saying nothing. Just staring. All of us apparently reacted the same way. Shocked into silence. Even the fat phlegmatic reporter in the back seat and the laconic driver at the wheel. Finally Anita whispered three words:

"Horrible, isn't it?"

All she got for an answer was the bark of a dog. Only it wasn't a bark at all. It was as unearthly a sound as what we were seeing was an unearthly sight. If Lady Macbeth's witches had suddenly come riding through the sky on broomsticks I wouldn't have been surprised. We had heard about Rogatica. We knew what had happened here. We thought we knew what it was going to be like. But we weren't prepared for this. It was night now. There were only two or three flickering lights in the entire ghost city. How large Rogatica was, or had been, we couldn't be sure because off in the distance, only faintly illuminated by our headlights, the black wreckage of buildings blended in with the black of the backdrop. The black of the hills. But we could see hundreds of houses, or what had once been houses, all in ruins. The street we were on, if you can call a churned-up strip of mud six or eight feet wide a street, was such a quagmire that the driver said he thought he'd better park the jeep right here. When conditions are too bad for an American jeep, then you can be sure that they're bad. So we got out and started to walk. I wanted to walk. I wanted to touch some of these buildings and make sure that they weren't papier-mâché. That they weren't pieces of a stage setting put there by some stage designer with an exaggerated idea of what a bombed-out city is like. Anita and I had on knee boots and we had a flashlight. The Fat Reporter sloshed along behind us.

I wondered how many bodies were still left in the ruins, two years after the shooting, the looting, and the burning had stopped. I know that corpses aren't supposed to smell in winter. But that night there was the smell of death over Rogatica. Even two years later. Rogatica was like a corpse someone had forgotten to bury. Both as to sight and as to smell. Rogatica was like a body which bore not only the wounds which had caused its death but evidence also that birds of prey had been at work. Two years of rain, snow, frost, and wind had eaten at the dead body of Rogatica.

My first reaction to this city that needed to be buried was the same reaction I always got during the war when the bombs started dropping and the wounded started screaming and walls started crumbling. A feeling of fury at the forces which could create such horrors. At the people who could unleash such forces. My second and slightly delayed reaction was that this scene, here in the heart of Yugoslavia, in a cup of the hills, should be preserved for all time just as we were seeing it, and that politicians and school children, and people who make money out of the business of war, and people who write warmongering newspaper articles and draw warmongering cartoons should be forced to spend the rest of their lives sloshing through the mud of Rogatica at dusk of a bleak winter evening, just as we were doing now.

This isn't sentiment. It isn't softness. I'd seen ruins before. I'd seen places like Hull and Coventry, and Belgrade and Corfu and Patras, and Sarajevo and Canterbury and London, when ruins were in the process of being created. I'd been a war correspondent. I'd seen what a block buster could do in one split second of its exploding. But I'd never seen anything like this. I'd tried to run from V-1's streaking through the sky. And I'd gone weak inside when a V-2 came down from the stratosphere without warning and crumbled a great building as if it were an eggshell. And I'd seen all the pictures of Hiroshima and had read every word of John Hersey. But this was different. This was a whole city, two years after war's end, still standing here, a gaunt skeleton, just as the "civilizing" forces of gun and bomb and fire had left it. Except that the carrions of death had added a few macabre touches.

Desolation. That was the word for it. Utter and complete and black desolation. As we plodded along the road toward one of the flickers of light we could see in the distance I began thinking up other words that begin with "d." Destruction. Demolition. Despair. Depravity. Desperation. Damnation. Yes, most of them could be applied to Rogatica, City of Death.

This kind of thinking was interrupted by a noise made by a man. It was encouraging to know that there was some human being here anyway. The man was a gendarme who apparently looked upon us with suspicion. And no wonder. In the light of his torch he had seen a bearded face topped off with a Daniel Boone fur cap. It was a sight which might have shaken the morale of anyone in surroundings such as this. He wanted to see our *legitimacija*. We showed him our passports and our *permis de sejour*. He didn't seem completely satisfied. But he let us continue.

The building we finally came to, with a light, turned out to be the temporary headquarters of the People's County Council. The room we entered was whitewashed and lit by a single flickering kerosene lamp. The county officials were sitting there at the end of their day's work talking things over. The president introduced himself. He was Edhem Mahmutević, a Moslem and a native of a nearby village. This was his county clerk, Momčilo Marković, or "Momock," as they all called him for short. Momock seemed just a boy. Very fresh and very alive looking. Momock turned out to be the most articulate person in the room. Within ten minutes we had him telling us his life story. We'd discovered that this was the best approach. Even class-conscious butlers in England who wouldn't dream of intimate conversation with one of their "betters" will unbend if you ask them what happened to them during the blitz. And besides, Anita and I both knew that we couldn't begin to understand the present here in Yugoslavia unless we got it into perspective with the past. What a Yugoslav does or thinks or says makes sense only if you know what he's been through the past six years.

Momock had been in the Partisans since the start. Right from the start. He was only seventeen when he joined up. A brother and sister went to the woods with him. He handled a machine gun for two years. Then the enemy caught him. The next year he escaped from a prison camp in Germany by stealing a German uniform and forging a German military pass. The boy's eyes brightened when he got to this part of the story.

"I beat my way down to the Yugoslav frontier. Right down to the edge of my own country. I thought now my troubles were over. I came to a Yugoslav guard. I whispered to him who I was. I told him where I had come from. I told him I was a Yugoslav. I told him I had been one of the liberation fighters and that I wanted to come back in again to fight those dirty sons of bitches some more." That isn't exactly what Momock called them. He used a more descriptive phrase which we don't have in English. "But the guard turned out to be a member of Nedić's army. You know who Nedić was. He was our Yugoslav Quisling. So they arrested me. One of my own people arrested me. Eleven days later I was back in the camp I had started from. Back in Germany where I'd been before. But on the way back something happened. They took me first to Vienna. I heard that Nedić was in Vienna. So I said I wanted to see him. They arranged for me to meet this great Yugoslav patriot." Momock's eyes were narrow and his lips were tight as he said that last word.

"When I saw him I made just one request. I said:

" 'I am a Serb. You are a Serb also. So maybe you will understand. I wish to be taken back to my own country. Shoot me if you wish. But I desire to be shot by a Serb. Not by a dirty swine of a Nazi.'

"Nedić didn't like my speech. Of course as it turned out I wasn't shot at all. And he was—by a Serb.

"The prison camp where they held me was liberated by an American division. I don't remember the exact number."

How did the Americans treat him?

"Okay!" Momock laughed as he said it. Then he repeated it to be sure we had noticed. "Okay!" That was one of half-a-dozen English words he had learned from his liberators. He liked the Americans. But the British! Momock's face was not pleasant to look at.

"After the liberation, while they were trying to decide what to do with me, a British officer came by one day. He saw the red star on my cap. All of us wore the red star. It was the emblem of our army. He saw the red star and got angry. He slapped me across the face with his hand. It had a ring on it. He said:

" 'You Yugoslav bastards are all god-damn communists, aren't you?'

"I've forgotten the pain of the wounds I got in the hills. I've also forgotten the cold and hunger we suffered. I've even forgotten the way Nedić looked when he said I had to go back to Germany. And the way the Nazis treated me. But I can still feel that slap I got across the face from the officer of an allied army. I've forgotten most of the things I heard during the war. And I heard plenty of things I didn't like hearing. But I can still hear that British officer calling me a bastard because he didn't think I had all the same political ideas he had. It was so wrong of him, too, because today we are not all communists. And in those days we didn't have any politics at all. We were just trying to help a lot of other soldiers, Americans, Russians, and British, win a war."

Momock paused. Nobody interrupted the silence. Then he leaned across the table and said very intently:

"And what if I had been a communist? Is that a sin in England? I thought the Communist party in England was a political party just like all the others. I thought they held conventions and voted and . . ."

Then Momock was silent again. When he continued he was off on a different subject. He apologized for having to speak through an interpreter. He said he had learned German, Polish, Czech, and a little French in the prison camp. But he hadn't had much opportunity to do anything with English. He had met one American. A soldier from Cleveland. But unfortunately in a way the man was of Yugoslav origin and so they spoke Serbian all the time. This Yugoslav-American spent hours arguing with Momock about how he should come to America as soon as they were liberated. He told him how easy life was out there in Ohio. He told Momock about running water in the houses, and about bathrooms, and electric refrigerators, and jobs that paid . . . "Yes, thirty dollars a week, and he said that's the same as fifteen hundred dinar." The man from Cleveland even went to the American commander of the camp and tried to get permission to take Momock home with him. But Momock refused. The man from Cleveland didn't seem to understand until Momock told him about his sister.

Momock's sister was only fourteen when she went into the Partisans. She was wounded eleven times. After she got home she wrote to Momock about what the enemy did to their village. Their village was Breza, right on the edge of Rogatica. Momock said:

"If you think this is bad you ought to see Breza!"

The little sister had written that there was nothing left of it but ashes. She had written that it would take all the courage and industry and fighting spirit they had shown in battle to bring order and life out of the chaos the enemy had made of Breza. That's what the Little Sister Who Was Wounded Eleven Times wrote to Momock in his prison camp in Germany. Momock tried to explain to the man from Cleveland that his work wasn't done yet. The fighting was over now. But the same men who defeated all of Yugoslavia's enemies must now whip the problem of reconstruction. What if all the Partisans emigrated to America? Momock laughed. "I answered the question myself, because I knew. I told him what would happen then would be that the people who had misruled our country for so many years would get into power again. If that happened then the whole war and everything we went through would make no sense. He was very unhappy when I said I would not go to Cleveland with him but I think he understood."

Momock took a cigarette from his pocket. He broke it into two pieces and gave one of them to the president. Then he lit the other half himself. I asked him about his sister. What could a child of fourteen do in a guerrilla army? Momock said that if it hadn't been for the fourteen- and fifteen-year-olds they wouldn't have won the war. Mostly they acted as couriers. They went into enemy-held territory, around enemy lines, through enemy-held villages delivering secret military communications.

President Edhem Mahmutević spent the next half hour telling about his war experiences. Then, without much prompting, he compared the Old and New Yugoslavia.

"I told you I'm a Moslem. In the old days no Moslem could hold any high rank in the Yugoslav Army because of his religion. He couldn't hold an important government job. Whoever was in power in Belgrade capitalized on the differences among our people. In the old days this town was 45 per cent Christians, 55 per cent Moslems. It was run by an official sent from Belgrade. That official, of course, was never a Moslem. He probably had never even been in this part of the country before. Today the town is run by a People's Council. We're all elected. I'm the president and I'm a Moslem. The other members are from all over the county. They are real representatives of the people they are supposed to represent."

Over and over Edhem repeated the phrase, "In the old days it was hatred." He said, "They always tried to stir up hatred among us. Always hatred. But today there is no hatred. Look at us in this room. We didn't know you were coming. This is the way we are all the time. Look at us. Turks and Christians. We work together. We eat together. We fought together so we understand now that we are all human beings. It doesn't make any difference about the color of our skins or our religions or our nationality or anything else. There is no hatred in Yugoslavia today. That alone is worth all the suffering we have had."

Then a third figure we'd hardly noticed spoke up. A tall, dark-mustached fellow who still wore a pair of Partisan army pants and a leather flying jacket. Shila Kvadir was twenty-four and a Moslem. Before the war he was a student and took some courses in a teacher's college. Now he's the educational officer for the county. The county of Rogatica was 80 per cent illiterate before the war. Anita and I checked back to be sure we hadn't misunderstood. He repeated: "Eighty per cent." There were nearly twenty-four thousand people who could neither read nor write. Now the percentage is down to fifty. In the past two months alone three thousand more peasants became literate. Shila is also in charge of the county cultural center. Two or three times a month a play is presented. Itinerant theatrical groups go from village to village. Every village, no matter how small, has its own cultural center. Shila also wanted to talk about hatred.

"There is still a small percentage of old people who have hatred in their hearts. But even they never exhibit it openly. The campaign against hate was an easy one to win. Once those who gained something by stirring people up against one another were gone the hate itself began to disappear.

"During the day you should sit here and look out the window. You'll see Moslems carrying on their backs pieces of lumber for some Christian to use in rebuilding his house."

But what we wanted to know about was this Ghost City. How had it happened? They all chimed in with the answer. The job was done by German, Italian, Bulgarian, Chetnik, and Ustaši soldiers. Also by German and British bombings. There were one thousand and seven homes in Rogatica. One thousand and six were destroyed. The other one was damaged. Eighteen thousand people in the county were killed. Once the Partisans held Rogatica for a short time. But when they arrived there wasn't a single house in condition to use for military headquarters.

When the Germans were here they kept their horses in the vineyards on the edge of the city. The horses were so hungry they ate the grapevines. Someday all the vineyards will have to be replanted. When the Germans evacuated Rogatica they mined the ruins. Mines were placed everywhere. Even in old ovens. Even under heaps of hay which the Partisans might use for their horses. One small boy who had watched the mines being planted remained in the village after the Germans left. When the Partisans came he showed them where each mine had been placed. His memory was very good. But the Nazis must have planted one when the boy's back was turned. He was killed by the one mine he hadn't known about. Today he is one of Rogatica's well-remembered heroes.

At this point someone suggested food. The fat reporter jumped to his feet and started for the door. Anita and I looked at our watches. It was 21:00 hours, the way Europeans reckon time. It was late anyway you reckon it. So we went to dinner.

Chapter Twenty-Three

WHY?

ALL Yugoslavia is sprinkled with government *mensas,* just as all England during the war was sprinkled with what they called British restaurants. They're very much alike. A mensa is a mess hall where engineers, government workers, lorry drivers, and others who are away from home may get their meals. Three meals a day cost a man nine hundred and sixty dinar per month, which makes it about sixty cents a day.

For supper we had thick *chorba,* a fried bread of some kind, heated-up spam, and hot corn bread. The wine was extra. Halfway through dinner Vojo Mrakić, the head of the People's Militia of Rogatica, came in and apologized for one of his soldiers stopping us in the street. He was sorry if we had been annoyed, but it was "regulations."

There were fourteen men and Anita around the mensa table. That was counting the Fat Reporter for two, which we always did because of the quantity of food he ate. The ten men of Rogatica didn't want to talk about the war, or even about Rogatica. They wanted to talk about America.

So we put off work until the next day and had a "bull session." I told Anita that after all it was part of our job to find out what was going on in the minds of people, as well as what they were doing with their hands. And so—what did they want to know?

The first man to speak said:

"Your *Gospodin* Roosevelt had a majority of the people with him all the time he was alive, yes?"

Yes.

"And now that he is dead, what leader in America most closely follows the political ideas of your Gospodin Roosevelt?"

While we hesitated the man answered the question himself.

"Henry Wallace. Yes?"

We smiled and nodded. Now he was very intense. He leaned across the table and went on.

"What we cannot understand is why your Gospodin Wallace therefore does not have the big majority of the American public with him."

Then the intellectual of the crowd, Gutal Risto, took the floor. He made little speeches rather than asking outright questions. He said:

"We Yugoslavs, you must know, shall always be appreciative of the help your country gave us in the war. We shall always say if it were not for UNRRA we might have starved these past two years. We have met some of your people. We like them. But we also know about the policies of your government. Those we do not like. We do not like them because we do not want war again. We had enough war. We are trying to rebuild our country. For that we need the peace. We are not just trying to build it up to what it was before. We are trying to make a new and better life. But the policies of your government are aimed at war. At war or world domination. We know that your people are not against our people. And they probably do not want war either, even if they do not really know what modern war is like. And now this is what we cannot understand. If that is all true, and if it is true that you have a democracy, why is it that the people cannot make their voices heard?

"Your newspapers talk about our having a dictatorship over here. I am sure you will discover before you have gone very far that our government is doing much more the will of the people than your government is. If not—if this is what your people want—then it is very sad and we have misjudged the Americans. Either way it is very sad, unless your people make their voices heard."

He said he knew so much about America because he had read a great deal. He knew all about William Randolph Hearst, for example. He said he had read all the books of Upton Sinclair, John Steinbeck, and many other American authors.

The party lasted long into the night. The cloth on the mensa table was dirty. The men who sat around on wooden benches were an odd assortment of characters. Most of them were young, except Gutal the Intellectual, and Milan the Cook who came from the kitchen after he had finished with his pots and pans. They weren't very clean, any of them, by American standards. After all, there hadn't been a single facility for bathing in Rogatica for six years! The odors of the place were not very pleasant either. The simple Yugoslav people eat a great deal of garlic and onions. The odor of garlic and onions, eaten constantly, is exuded not only by the breath but through every pore of the skin.

Yet as we sat there in the dim kerosene light, very tired and wondering occasionally where we were going to find four beds for the night in this city of ghost buildings, I thought back to another Yugoslav gathering I once attended.

It was held in Washington, D.C., in celebration of the Orthodox Christmas of 1942, at the Yugoslav Embassy. I think I was the only American there. Ambassador Fotić said he had invited me "because you are such a good friend of our people."

This was before some of us in America had learned the truth about the conflict between Chetniks and Partisans. This was before some of us in America realized that the Yugoslav Ambassador in America was a representative of the most reactionary forces in Belgrade.

Sitting now in the heart of Bosnia with a dozen simple Yugoslav people who were opening up their hearts and minds to us, I thought back five years to that other party.

There was soft candlelight. Waiters in impeccable attire moved noise-lessly around among guests in equally impeccable attire. Excellent food prepared in the best French (*sic*) manner. Five kinds of imported wine, topped off with a rare French champagne. In a corner a stringed trio played soft chamber music, and when I asked for a Yugoslav song they played it as if it were a Brahms lullaby.

I didn't eat much that night of the fancy food which had been bought with money which should have been feeding war orphans back in the home country. But I did drink a lot of wine. I drank a lot to try to forget the contrast between how Orthodox Christmas was being celebrated that night by Yugoslavs in Washington and Yugoslavs in the mountains of their own country.

Finally, having had too much of the wine, I beckoned to the Ambassador, who was circulating from one supper table to another, and said:

"Mister Ambassador, many people here have proposed toasts tonight—to your health, to the health of your boy king. May I propose a toast too?"

The Ambassador beamed and filled my glass and started to clap his hands to hush the discreet hum of conversation. But I stopped him. I said:

"First, perhaps it would be well for me to tell you the toast I would like to propose. I should like to lift my glass and say:

"*Živeli!* A toast to the men and women of Yugoslavia, your relatives and my friends, who tonight are in the forests and mountains of their country, hungry perhaps, cold perhaps, tired perhaps, but certainly un-able, tonight, to celebrate this holiday, which is theirs, too, with fancy wines and sparkling champagne and soft lights and fine food and discreet chamber music.'"

The Ambassador's face, as I finished, was worth recording on a movie film. It went through many contortions. But then he proved that he was a diplomat by raising his own glass, clinking it with mine, and saying:

"Good! That is good! But I think we drink the toast together. Just you and me."

That was the last time I was ever invited to the Yugoslav Embassy in Washington.

Anita turned to me and said:

"Why are you so quiet?"

So I had her tell them the story of the Fotić Christmas party. When she finished, Gutal Risto, the Intellectual, said:

"The money which bought that wine and champagne was from our country's gold supply abroad. We have heard many other stories of how the monarchists spent our money in Britain and America. We consider Fotić as great a war criminal as the Nazis and Ustaši and Chetniks who burned down our homes and killed our families. He has already been tried and condemned, in absentia, you know. But I suppose your country will continue to give him sanctuary."

Then Milan the cook spoke up from his far corner of the table.

"How about Jevdjević?"

I had to confess that I didn't know who Jevdjević was. About ten of them tried to explain at once. We had a time calming them down.

The man about whom they were talking was Dobrasev Jevdjević. He had been an important Chetnik, on the staff of General Draža Mihailović. This town, Rogatica, was his native spot. Yet, with an odd twist to his mind, he led the Chetnik troops who put a torch to so many of the one thousand and seven houses in Rogatica.

And it was his men, under his own direction, they told us, who had committed some of the worst atrocities of the war in the streets right outside the building we were now in.

Every man present had some additional information to add about what Jevdjević and his men had done.

"And so," I finally asked, "what about him?"

Handsome little Momock the county clerk was the one who answered. His black eyes were full of fire.

"What about him! Yes, what about him? That's what we ask you! Do you know where he is now? He is in your hands. In one of your camps over in Italy. It is two years after the war, and you have taken no step to hand him over to us, so that he can be tried for the criminal that he is.

"He lives well in Italy, they say. You Americans are treating him as if he were a royal guest. You treat him like . . . Never mind. You even allow him to edit a newspaper which he puts out every week.

"How would you like it if Adolf Hitler were in our hands and we treated him that way, and refused to give him up? But even that would not be the same. I cannot say what would be the same, because there is no man in the world you could hate so much as we hate Jevdjević. That is because there is no man in the world who has killed your women, and strangled your babies, and burned down your houses, and done to your towns what you shall see tomorrow this man did to our Rogatica."

Mahmutević, the Moslem president, broke the tension by saying:

"Well, anyway, we don't have to worry about Ćaplić."

Ragib Ćaplić, it developed, was a Moslem who came into this area to recruit other Moslems to fight Serbs. But first we must understand something, they said. We must understand the neat little system the Chetniks and Ustaši worked out. They divided southern Yugoslavia systematically; partitioned it between them. The Ustaši, who were Croats themselves, were to recruit Moslems to fight Serbs. Serbs were free game for the Croatian Ustaši. If the Ustaši went into a village, they had carte blanche to exterminate the Serbian population. But they must let the Moslems alone.

The Chetniks, on the other hand, were Serbs themselves. They were free to recruit other Serbs wherever they found them. They could pillage the homes of Moslems and kill however great a number they pleased.

The referee of the whole business was the Nazi commander of the district.

The men of Rogatica that night in the mensa told of case after case, town after town, which had been annihilated by this German "divide-and-conquer" system . . . divide and exterminate . . . brother against brother . . . neighbor against neighbor . . . Croat against Serb against Moslem.

"But," concluded Mahmutević, "we don't have to worry about Ragib Ćaplić. His body was found in one of the streets of Rogatica, after a battle. At least Ragib Ćaplić isn't able to edit a newspaper."

It was late by now and we were tired. Yet no mention had been made of where we four were to spend the night. One of the men said:

"We don't have visitors like you people very often in Rogatica. You will pardon if, maybe, we talk too much."

Of course talk was what we really wanted more than anything else. We had come thousands of miles across water and land to hear these people talk. Now we were behind what some people liked to call "The Iron Curtain." This was one of the lands where people were supposed to be too frightened to speak out. This was one of the lands, they said, where no foreigner could travel freely. Where no foreigner could see anything. Or hear anything. Where the great mass of the population lived in fear and trembling. But it was almost midnight and still the talk flowed on.

When I got so tired I couldn't take notes any more, I asked them if they would sing some of their *Sevdalinke* songs for us. Yugoslavia is a small country but every section has its own songs. In area Yugoslavia is exactly the size of Oregon. In population it isn't much larger than New York State. It's really six countries in one, Croatia, Serbia, Bosnia and Herzegovina, Slovenia, Montenegro, and Macedonia. And that's not counting the Vojvodina and Slavonia. By plane it's possible to hop from one of those sections to another as quickly as hopping from one county to another in America. Yet each section has its own songs, its own costumes, its own customs. They reflect the history of each one.

Bosnia, the land of great green mountains, was under Turkish domination for nearly five hundred years. For nearly five hundred years the sultans tried with every force at their command, and every stratagem, to obliterate the culture, the religion, the identity of the Bosnian mountaineers.

Every four years one fifth the population was seized and taken off to Constantinople. The Turks were especially interested in bright young boys between the ages of six and ten. These youngsters were educated in the manners and religion of Islam. They were sent to military schools. Legally they were the slaves of the Sultan. They were dressed in white flowing robes and were compelled to wear small white caps. They were required to take two of the three monastic vows, the vows of celibacy and obedience. Those who showed marked ability were sent to special schools where they learned to be architects, engineers, and statesmen. The rest were known as *janissaries* and were forced to bear arms for the sultans who for hundreds of years could boast that they had the largest professional army in Europe if not in the world. No one who had been born a Moslem could ever be a janissary. It was what the Turks called an army of "converted infidels." Constantinople ran a large part of Europe in those days by the *gauleiter* system. Hundreds of years before Hitler was born the Turks tried it. In one way they were smarter than Hitler. Every gauleiter was a native of the spot over which he ruled. *Vesires* was what the Turks called them. They were picked from among the healthy young males who were stolen from their mothers at an early age. They were trained for ten or fifteen years in Constantinople for the job that was to be assigned to them. Then they were sent back, thoroughly Moslemized, to serve as yeast among their own people.

Under Turkish rule the Bosnians were forbidden to ride horses, to carry or possess firearms, to dress better than their Turkish occupiers, or to build a Christian church any taller than the local mosque. The privilege of owning property was reserved for Bosnians who gave up Christianity for the Moslem religion. And converts weren't taxed quite so heavily. Thick black veils were put over the faces of the Bosnian women. Red fezzes with black tassels were put on the heads of the men. When the muezzin climbed the circular staircase inside the minaret and walked out onto the balcony of the mosque to chant his call to prayer, all Bosnia must face in the direction of Mecca and pay obeisance to the gods of Islam.

For nearly five hundred years it went on that way. But Bosnia did not die. Bosnians continued to sing their own songs even though the tunes and the words changed down through the centuries. Now they were songs of bitter almost hopeless longing. And songs of bitter almost hopeless love. Songs of the tragic plight of the women of Bosnia who lived out their existence behind veils of black. Women who were forced to dwell behind windows covered with iron bars. Women who bore children only to have them stolen away, as a farmer takes a calf for slaughter from the stall of its mother. There were songs of the longing of the women for freedom from all this slavery. And then there were the songs of men who were forced to marry women whose faces they had never seen. There were songs of women in harems. There were songs of love in the Romeo-Juliet manner. The tunes were all set in a minor key, with a touch, ironically, of Turkey and the Orient in the way the tunes played so much of the time on a single note and the half notes and quarter notes around it. They call all these songs of the Bosnian mountains Sevdalinke. So we asked our friends around the table, now that the evening was spent, if they would sing some of them for us.

The president whispered to Milan the cook. Milan disappeared. Later we found out what that was all about. Mahmutević, who was one of Bosnia's one million Moslems, wanted to make a good impression so he had sent Milan out with instructions to go through town and round up Rogatica's best voices. They drifted in during the next half hour singly and in pairs; sleepy-eyed boys, mostly in their teens or their twenties, with great over-coats over the underwear in which they had gone to bed.

They sang, first, some of the Sevdalinke songs. And then some Partisan fighting songs. Then some songs of the reconstruction. There were the songs the boys and girls made up last summer, when they were working on the Youth Railroad. Songs about the rebuilding of cities; songs about red fezzes floating on the Drina.

I don't know where the Fat Reporter and the Laconic Driver slept that night. But Momock took Anita and me home with him.

The Marković family lived on the first floor of a building which had been partly repaired. They had a single room. Off that room there was something the size and shape of a closet. In the single room there was an old-fashioned stove, a three-quarter-size bed, a cradle which contained a five-month-old baby, a wooden kitchen table, and that's about all, except a shelf on which we noticed some cans of food plainly marked "UNRRA."

In the closet there was a wooden ledge with a pillow and two blankets on it.

Momock whispered something to Anita. I noticed that she blushed. Then the two of them began to talk excitedly, looking first at the bunk and then at the family bed in which a plumpish girl was now nursing at her breast the baby she had picked up out of the crib.

Finally Anita announced that the sleeping arrangement would be that she, the mother, and the baby would sleep in the bunk. Momock and I would share the bed. I turned that one down quickly. For several reasons.

Instead, I took all the overcoats in the room and curled up on the floor under the kitchen table. Anita slept on the ledge.

The coats on the floor were not too uncomfortable, except that I put most of them under me, because Momock loaded the stove full of dry wood before climbing into bed with his wife. About 3 A.M. the fire went out. The rest of the night I spent trying to pull coats from underneath me to put on top of me. Also sleep-disturbing was the fact that the Momock infant wanted to be fed every twenty-seven minutes from 3 A.M. until dawn.

Chapter Twenty-Four

COUNTING THE DEAD ISN'T EASY

ROGATICA is on the banks of the Rakitnica River. It is surrounded by mountains which are steep and forbidding, but none so high as the peak called Romanija, which can be seen from anywhere in town, to the west, halfway to Sarajevo, which is seventy-nine kilometers. The valley, which is the town, is six kilometers from north to south by four kilometers from east to west, which means it is little more than two by three miles.

Rogatica was founded five hundred years ago. Before the Turkish occupation. It gets its name from the word *rog,* which means horn—horns of the oxen which were used to bring water down from the mountains into town.

There is a main street called Husejnbegova-Mahala for generations. There's one sign left, on a shattered store front, which still bears this name. Someday, when Rogatica is all rebuilt, new signs will go up reading: "Tito Ulica."

Tito Ulica runs from north to south, the long way of the town. It is crossed by eleven mud paths which you can call streets if you wish.

Somehow in this teacup of a community four thousand five hundred people lived before the war. About half of them were Moslems, which meant that every other man you met on the street wore a red fez, and every other woman wore a black drapery over her face. There were also sixty Jews in town. They had their own synagogue building.

In the old days, Christians and Moslems and Jews got along all right together, except during those periods when politicians tried to stir them up against one another.

Rogatica was the county center and trading place for peasants who came in from the hills to exchange grapes, wine, corn, and wheat for the simple articles which were sold in the shops along Husejnbegova-Mahala.

There was a small coal mine in the valley, which was worked by the most primitive of methods. Some of the people of the town earned a living making oriental rugs at home.

The homes were either of mud, or, the better ones, of timber cut in the mountains.

It's difficult to imagine it, walking through what is left of Rogatica today, but they say that life flowed on with a certain degree of placidity from generation to generation. Children were born; they grew up, fell in love, were married, had children, and eventually died. Of course if they fell into the bad graces of the Turkish gauleiter, who was later supplanted by an Austrian gauleiter, they might die sooner.

The standard of living, as you might expect, was shockingly low. Not only in the outlying villages, but in the town as well. Only the more prosperous merchants, the priests, the one Jewish rabbi, and a few others in town could read and write.

Rogatica was not on any railroad, and to get here from Sarajevo meant crossing through Romanija Pass. Until American jeeps and trucks appeared that was something no sane man would even dream of doing a good many months of the year.

In this isolated city of a valley people knew little of the outside world and cared less. They wished only to be let alone. That was a wish seldom granted.

There was a single telephone wire leading in and out of the valley. Over that wire, on Bloody Sunday in April of '41, came the news that the Germans, Italians, Hungarians, Bulgarians, and Rumanians had attacked Yugoslavia.

It wasn't many days later that Rogatica was taken over by the men of Ante Pavelić's Ustaši; those men who pretended to cater to the Moslems but actually hated them almost as much as they hated people who followed the Serbian religion.

If you ask the men of Rogatica how many times their town changed hands between then and the final liberation on the tenth day of March in '45 they will look at each other with some perplexity and say:

"It would take a good deal of figuring. Let's see! First the Ustaši. Then the Partisans came in and liberated us for a while. Then the Nazis. Then they withdrew and gave it back to the Ustaši. Then the Chetniks took over. They were driven out by the Partisans. Then the Germans came back. After a while they gave the town over to Ante Pavelić once more. And then . . . But really what difference does it make, after all?"

In all that fighting over one rather insignificant town in the Bosnian mountains, how many of Rogatica's forty-five hundred people were killed?

"Well, that's another difficult question. Let's see. There were at least three hundred men in the Partisans from here who never came back. And at least five hundred women and children of the town were slaughtered. And . . ."

But that's as far as Momock the County Clerk got. An argument broke out and for a few minutes they were all talking at once. Out of the confusion we finally got a co-operative, consolidated, compromise estimate of fifteen hundred in all. One out of every three inhabitants. That didn't count those who were wounded and may have died later.

They explained that counting the dead in a town like this isn't easy. Hundreds of the inhabitants were taken off to concentration camps. What happened to some of them no one ever found out. Do you count as dead those who never came back? If you do, then the figure is much larger.

We asked what it was like in those days when the town was so frequently changing hands. How were the one thousand and six buildings destroyed?

We got a chorus of explanations. When the Ustaši were driven out by the Partisans that first time, they set the torch to every building in Rogatica, hoping to leave the place a charred ruins for the enemy. A majority of the buildings did burn. To the bare four walls. The fires in other places were put out.

That happened over and over again. Some people, in between invasions, did a bit of rebuilding, only to have their homes destroyed again.

It happened over and over again until Rogatica was just a grim, blackened skeleton of what it had once been.

Each time the town passed from one army to another there was street fighting. And each time there was civil war among the handful of civilians trapped here.

The strangest periods were those brief intervals when Rogatica was left without any occupiers. Of course those periods never lasted for more than a few hours or a few days.

"It was horrible then," one man said. "It was even better when some enemy was here, because then we knew what to expect. But those hours and days of waiting, not knowing who our next guests would be; whether Ustaši, Chetniks, Germans, or Partisans! They were hours and days of frightening uncertainty. We would just hide and wait. Hide and wait!"

There was one of those periods when not a living male was left in town. Rogatica, then, was a community of mothers and babies, who set up their own self-government. They called it *Dvenska Vlada,* which means "Women's Administration."

When the Partisans finally liberated Rogatica "for keeps," in March of '45, it was an almost completely deserted place. A mere handful of families were trying to keep life going in the ruins. Mostly old people and the ill, who hadn't had the strength to go into the hills. They were disease-ridden, starving, nearly dead from the winter's cold.

But now! Now Rogatica is beginning to rise from the dead.

Looking around, you may not believe it, but already two thousand three hundred people have returned. Not really "returned," of course, because many of those now here came from other parts of the country; from other parts of Bosnia and Serbia.

Anyway, we have two thousand three hundred people now. And someday Rogatica may be back to her old population again.

But let's walk the length of the main street and see what we can see. This whole area, all of what was the Old Town, is going to be abandoned. That's why the skeletons of buildings still stand. The men of Rogatica have been so busy building new homes, in a new location, that they haven't had time for demolition work. But someday all these structures are going to be pulled down and the old business district will become a public park. Until that happens, a few merchants are trying to carry on.

Last night, in the gloom, these buildings along Tito Ulica seemed completely abandoned; just shells. But in these ruins, without doors and windows, there's a shoe shop. There's a stand where you can buy buttons and thread and a few other Woolworth items. And over there is a blacksmith, making wagon wheels. Close by each other there are three barbershops. Momock makes a joke of why three of them. He says:

"We need that many barbers to cut the beards off the Chetniks who give themselves up. Of course you know that the Chetniks nearly all wore beards. Well, you won't find many beards in Yugoslavia today."

In one of these three shops a winter sun beats down through a hole in the roof onto the bald head of a man who is getting a shave. That barber probably has to close for the day if a thunderstorm ever breaks out. The other two barbers are standing in their doors waiting for business.

Near the north end of Tito Ulica is the town's one primary school. It was one of the first buildings they reconstructed, even before they worried about fixing up homes.

The classroom on the main floor is presided over by a boy who looks young enough to be a pupil himself. It's cold in the school because like most every other place in town it's unheated, even though this is February of the bitterest winter these parts have known for a long time. The children sit huddled close together, seventy-eight of them. Ferid Felhatbegović, the teacher, stands in front of them lecturing, with a fur cap pulled down over his ears.

Ferid says he's nineteen. He had four years of primary school, four years of secondary school, and four years of teachers' college. Twelve years. The equivalent in America of a high school education.

There are nearly seven hundred children attending this one school, which means that all classes have to be as large as this one, and Ferid has to stand here, with his cap over his ears, trying to teach reading, writing, and arithmetic for eight hours at a stretch. He explains that in the old days, because of the Turkish influence, there were separate schools for boys and girls. But today . . . And he points to boys and girls sharing the same seat. Ferid is one of six teachers in town.

On the schoolroom wall there are slogans the children have made with colored crayon. Some of them read:

"Let's Be Shock Brigaders in Education and in Work."

"Learn and Work; Work and Learn."

"We Are Pioneers in the Building of a Better Future."

In Serbian most of them rhyme.

Just beyond the schoolhouse there's a barracks which was built about the same time as the school to provide living quarters for the engineers brought in from Sarajevo to supervise the construction of the New Rogatica.

Across the road there's what the invaders left of a mosque. Now it houses a co-operative commissary. Peasants from the villages sell their wheat here, when they have any wheat to sell.

Close by the school there's a newly completed, four-story hospital.

Rogatica never had a hospital before. But it's one of the most rigidly followed policies of the government that there must be a hospital for every county seat, and that it must be one of the first structures erected.

That three-story building near by is going to be the town's modern hotel. It's nearly finished already. It was built on the cellar hole of the old police barracks. Momock says that the basement was used as an execution chamber by the Nazis and the Ustaši. I didn't doubt the story but I went down to look for myself. I saw splotches of dry blood and gore on the white stone. The stains are black by now. In another few years they'll be mistaken for dirt.

Across the road there's the Catholic Church. It was built by the Austrian Army in the days when Bosnia was part of the Austro-Hungarian Empire. Nazis, Ustaši, and Chetniks wrecked it with battering ram and fire. It probably will never be rebuilt because there have been few Catholics here since the departure of the Austrians after World War I.

In back of the hospital many substantial new homes are in the process of completion. They are two-story brick buildings, in contrast to the mud, thatch, and frame abodes of the Old Rogatica. This whole area we're in is the New Rogatica. This is the part of town we were not able to see in the headlights of our jeep twelve hours ago.

Where twenty-three hundred people are living until these homes are finished it's difficult to judge, standing on this height, looking down into the bottom of the cup; looking down on those rows and rows of skeleton homes.

On the way back along Tito Ulica, Momock and the president rattle off some statistics. In the county, before the war, there were sixty-nine hundred and seventeen houses, of which five thousand were destroyed by the enemy. Five out of every seven. So far, twenty-two hundred have been rebuilt and are being lived in. This coming summer another two thousand will be built.

But that isn't all. They have a "County Plan." Under that plan, so far, an electric plant, a brickyard, a cultural center, a poultry and pig farm, and six schools have been constructed or rebuilt. During the summer the plan calls for the completion of those two thousand additional houses, a new county building, eight more schools, an entirely new business district, a veterinary center, a lumberyard, an enlarged *lyceum* or *gymnasium,* and an addition to the pig and poultry farm.

As I listened to the youthful officials talking, I watched their faces. One advantage of having an interpreter translate everything a man says is that you can study his face while he's talking without having to worry about writing down the words he's saying. You can study his face, and get the words from your translator later.

The words, in this case, were important, but of greater importance was the enthusiasm on the faces of the young county officials. They were all boys who had lived and fought in the hills for four or five years. They had seen more action than soldiers of most any other army on earth. The

battle they were fighting now, against disease, illiteracy, the natural laziness of peasant people, and against the warborn hates of various groups
of Yugoslavs for each other was not so dramatic as their life with Tito in
the mountains, but they were fighting it just as they fought Germans,
Chetniks, Italians, and Ustaši. Enthusiasm was written on their faces.
And the certainty that they were going to be able to accomplish all the
miracles demanded of them in their "Plan."

On the way back down Tito Ulica, Edhem Mahmutević said:

"Another thing you must not ignore is the fact that the women of the
New Yugoslavia have come into their own. On our County Council we
now have two women members. In the old days women had no voice in
anything but running the kitchen. It's different now. More things will
be different tomorrow, if we are just let alone to carry out our plan."

As he spoke four Moslem women in veils passed by, going in the opposite direction. We had grown accustomed to the veils, but these four
women had used cloth so thick that they couldn't see through it themselves. They nearly bumped into us as they passed. I turned around to
watch the trouble they were having just in time to see one of them run
into the back end of a mule. The mule got frightened and ran galloping
down the street. We all laughed. The president said:

"You see, we still have much to do. But give us time. Most of them in
the villages have discarded their veils. They just wear them when they
come to town."

Then two large Chevrolet trucks loaded with lumber went by.

"Good machines!" Momock said. "American machines. Without them
our reconstruction job would be taking us twice as long."

Chapter Twenty-Five

HEADLINE WRITERS WOULD CALL IT A "FOOD RIOT"

SOME had come on horseback. Some had come in carts pulled by great lumbering oxen. But mostly they had come on mules. There were already about one hundred of them milling around in front of a building on Tito Ulica. Hundreds more were streaming down the mountainsides from the villages of The Romanija. They were clogging Tito Ulica with their carts and wagons. They were churning up the mud of the roads until it was a deep, sticky mass which kept the wheels of their vehicles from turning. There were as many women as men. The women nearly all wore veils. Their dresses were mostly black. The men's clothing was nondescript except for what they wore on their heads. From the neck up each man was a peacock in his own dirty way. Each one was expressing his own individuality in what he wore on his head. Some of the material they had wrapped around their heads, to make turbans, was heavy and striped. Some looked like bed ticking. But there were other turbans of flaming pink, or brilliant green, or the crimson of blood. The turbans shouted for admiration.

The president said they were peasants from the villages. This was their marketing day. They were coming in to Rogatica to get their week's rations.

It probably was the sheaf of paper in my hand and the fact that I was poking around taking notes which caused all the trouble. They obviously thought that Anita and I were members of some kind of an investigating committee, judging by what happened.

They ignored the three or four county officials with us. They ignored the building in which their rations were stored. They forgot that they had all been in some kind of a queue. They formed a circle around us and started talking all at once.

Anita had a difficult time, at first, translating what they were trying to say. But in a way it wasn't so difficult, because all of them seemed to have a single complaint. They had been getting a ration of twenty-four pounds of corn a month. Now it had been cut to sixteen. And there were reports that it would soon be only twelve.

The first of the protesters was an old-looking woman. She said she had three children and an income of only six hundred dinar (twelve dollars) per month. Her husband had been killed by the Chetniks. Six hundred dinar was the pension she got from the government. One of her children was four; another was eight; the oldest was twelve. She must have more corn. Wouldn't we tell the proper people that they must give her more corn?

A Moslem man with a red fez shouted:

"Eight kilos isn't enough to keep a man alive. We're hungry most of the time."

We asked him what his work was. He shook his head.

"I can do no work. On eight kilos of corn I'm not strong enough to work."

A hag of a woman with most of her teeth missing spluttered:

"For twenty-five days I have had nothing but bread. How can we keep well on nothing but bread?"

Still another shouted above the confusion:

"We sowed our land for two years and for two years nothing came out of it. For two summers we have had the drought. All we have is the corn they give us and a little soup now and then. But why must they cut down the amount of the corn?"

The president took a few steps over to her side.

"In the old days, before the war, what happened if you had a drought?" She stared back blankly at him.

"Be truthful now. These people are from America. You know the answer but they don't. Be honest now and tell them whether the old government ever brought in truckloads of food and tried to feed you as we are doing?"

The old woman didn't answer. She just stared down at the ground.

But then, on the outer rim of the crowd, someone shouted:

"How about the one who died of starvation?"

While Anita tried to locate the voice, the president whispered:

"It isn't true. No one has died of starvation."

I said:

"I'd like to have some proof of that."

Now the whole crowd took up the song. Almost in chorus they began to chant:

"How about the one who died of starvation?"

The president got angry. In a loud voice he called for silence. Then he said:

"If there is anyone here who knows of anyone in the entire county who has died of starvation, let him step forward and give us the name. I would like the name. These Americans would like the name."

There was dead silence for a moment. But by now Anita had located the original voice. It belonged to a woman who was brought forward. Did she know the name? She said:

"No. But it must be true because everyone knows about it."

Where had she heard the story?

"From people. Everyone has heard it."

Then I picked a character at random from the crowd and had Anita ask her how much corn her family got.

"Twenty-five kilos for my husband and myself. That's because he's what they call a 'heavy worker' and gets an extra ration."

I looked over the heads of the crowd at all the wreckage which lay about us and got an idea. The bitterness of the winter had stopped most of the reconstruction work in the New Rogatica. But why couldn't these peasants from the villages be forced to spend their time clearing up this depressing eyesore which was the Old Rogatica? Why didn't they pass a law making the right to draw food dependent on a man's willingness to work?

The president smiled strangely and said:

"If we did that, you Americans would be the first to call it dictatorship and criticize us for capitalizing on the hunger of the population. But it isn't really as bad as these excited people would have you think. Come along with me through the back door of the co-operative and I'll show you."

As we tried to get out of the jam of peasant humanity, a woman with a fifty-pound sack of corn balanced neatly on her head, in the manner of the women of Bosnia, came galloping after us. She was waving her arms and shouting:

"Give us more corn or we'll die before spring!"

No one was paying much attention to her. But I was watching the burlap sack, balanced so precariously. Just then the sack fell to the ground, hit a stone, and broke. The yellow kernels scattered in a thousand directions. No one made a grab for the grain, which seemed to prove something. When we came from the building half an hour later the old woman was still on her hands and knees, picking up her precious corn, kernel by glittering yellow kernel.

Inside the commissary the president showed us food being doled out to the people who had been clustering around us. The monthly allotment per person was eight kilos of corn, fifteen decars of sugar and fifteen of fat, a one-pound can of South American corned beef, one pound of salt, and one small piece of soap. That was the minimum anyone got, whether he could pay for it or not. This basic ration was free for widows, the destitute, and those whose homes were so badly damaged they needed help from the State.

When they were getting twelve kilos of corn it was quite a sufficient ration for peasants accustomed to little more, even in times of plenty, the president said.

Now?

Well, with UNRRA stopping, with the United States turning a deaf ear to Yugoslavia's appeals for food, with the effects of two years of drought really beginning to be felt, there was nothing to do but cut, and to try to spread the nation's food supply out evenly. No one would starve. Plenty of people might go very hungry. But what could Yugoslavia do? She was scraping the bottom of the barrel.

For those who had the money to buy, there was also canned beef stew from Pennsylvania for thirty-six cents a can, onions for fifteen cents a pound, coffee beans (if anyone could afford them) for a dollar and a half a pound, four-ounce American chocolate bars, forty-three cents; margarine or lard, forty cents a pound; sugar, thirty-three cents.

Children under two received a chocolate bar and ten pounds of canned milk apiece per month as part of their minimum ration.

The glittering corn sold for thirty-four cents, for the eight-kilo allotment.

While Anita continued to get facts and figures for me, I went off on my own. There were some things I wanted to see.

Chapter Twenty-Six

THEN THEY ALWAYS SAY *"IZVINITE"*

By now thousands not hundreds of peasants were pouring down from the mountainsides. Tito Ulica was a seething sea of humanity, mixed with a confusion of pack mules, dwarfed ponies, and oxen with great sweeping horns.

I went to where we had parked the jeep the previous night, got some pipe tobacco out of a duffel bag, and stood there surveying Old Rogatica.

In the decaying ruins great black birds of prey were screaming as they flew from one pile of ashes to another, looking for something to eat. In the course of two years they had cleaned things up rather well. Now pickings were slim, and the birds made a weird noise as they voiced their displeasure. I thought, what a banquet they must have had, once, here in Rogatica!

As I stood there, a winter wind cleared the sky of clouds. Against the deep clear blue I counted the white minarets of five Moslem mosques. Somehow they had lived through the bombs and shells and torches of the invading armies. It was just twelve noon. I watched a white-haired muezzin climbing up the circular iron staircase which corkscrews around inside each slender minaret and leads to the little platform which runs around on the outside, near the top. Ordinarily he would have been out of sight, on the circular staircase, but this particular mosque had suffered some damage. The round wall of the minaret was almost all stripped away. Now the tiny figure was on what was left of the circular balcony. In that plaintive monotone of the East he was chanting his call to prayer. By custom he should have walked around and around as he sang, but there wasn't enough left of the balcony for that. What difference? Even the men down in the town in fezzes and the women with faces hidden by black pieces of cloth were paying no attention.

Then I noticed what looked like a church, across the Rakitnica River, so I went to investigate. I was nearly there when a gendarme came hot-footing it after me. He shouted a whole string of Serbian words at me. The only one I understood was *"legitimacija,"* so I showed him my passport and *permis de séjour.*

It's curious to watch a foreign guard or soldier inspecting an American passport. He starts with the cover. The golden eagle on the cover always impresses him. You can tell that. Also the great red seal inside, with Cordell Hull's name under it. Then he looks at the "photograph of the bearer," and that generally leads to complications, for a picture taken in the summer, four years ago in New York clothes, bears little resemblance to this character the guard is staring at so suspiciously—this man in hip boots, American army parka, fur hat, and beard and mustache grown long and shaggy through weeks of neglect.

But then the trouble really begins, for our friend the guard now starts flicking pages slowly, one by one.

"This passport is valid only for travel to the British Isles as a war correspondent and expires on March 16, 1945."

If he can read any of that he's going to be terribly confused, because unless you know his language, how can you point out to him that over on Page 21 there's a renewal and extension, making the passport good until 1948 for travel anywhere except to Germany, Japan, and Nansei Shoto and Nanpo Shoto, wherever they are.

But now he hits the visa of the Free State of Eire and gets intrigued by the harp that the people of Eire use as their symbol.

And then there's that beautiful French visa, with so many colorful stamps pasted across it.

The Swiss and Swedish visas don't interest him much. There's nothing very decorative about them. But the Italian and Greek and British are all quite nice to look at, so he lingers long over them.

He doesn't apologize for taking up so much of your time while he entertains himself. If you're wise you'll fill your pipe, sit on the rail of the bridge, and be patient and understanding. The waste of time will be worth it when you see the face of this young Yugoslav officer as he turns a page and suddenly makes a strange little noise down in his throat. It's the sort of noise *you* might make if, stranded in Timbuctoo for years with people who didn't speak a word you could understand, you suddenly came upon a man from your own home town. What's happened, of course, is that he has turned a page and come upon your Yugoslav visa.

To show his appreciation of finding something he can read, he leans back against the bridge rail and pores over every word, from the heading "VIZA" right down to the signature of the Consul General in New York.

Finally he hands the passport back to you. As he does, he bows slightly from the waist and utters a single word:

"Izvinite!" Which means, in this case,

"My humble apologies for having taken your valuable time and questioned your validity. You are free to go your way, and a pleasant trip to you!"

It's a good word, "Izvinite"!

And so I finally reached the church. It was Rogatica's Orthodox Church and in it, during the occupation, Chetniks, Ustaši, Germans, and Italians had tethered their horses, just as they had done in the Catholic church, the Jewish synagogue, and some of the mosques. Now, what was left of the structure, which wasn't much, was being used as a granary. Sacks of corn were piled to the roof. Remembering the scene on Tito Ulica, it seemed significant that the front door of the church was open and the place was unguarded, a comment either on the honesty of the peasants, or on the exaggeration of their hunger.

On the way back I passed a slight shell of a building which had been the synagogue and remembered someone telling me that there had been sixty Jews in Rogatica. Today there are none. Four are alive in Sarajevo. What happened to the others even the people of Rogatica would prefer that you not ask.

Back in the center of town I found the street packed almost as solid as Times Square on a New Year's Eve.

When I located Momock he said:

"It's hard to believe, but one year ago there were only one hundred people in Rogatica!"

Chapter Twenty-Seven

TO POULTRYMEN IT'S A DISEASE

EDHEM THE PRESIDENT said he had something special he wanted to show us. It was across the road from the County Council Building, in a vacant lot. In the center of that open space there was a small pile of rocks. Edhem pointed to them and started a long speech to Anita. She shuddered as he talked. I couldn't understand. They looked like quite ordinary rocks to me, in a quite ordinary vacant lot. But it was obvious, even from the quiet way Edhem spoke, that this really was "something."

It turned out that here, before the occupation, there was a great open well. Most of the town was in the habit of getting its water here and carrying it home in gracefully curved oriental containers which really were more like vases than buckets.

When the slaughter of Rogatica began, dead bodies were left where they fell, until finally even Nazis and Chetniks and Ustaši could stand the odor no longer. So they collected the bodies and dumped them into three wells. Some sadistic, macabre instinct made them separate the heads from the rest of the bodies. This well was the one they used exclusively for the heads. Until it was so full, it could hold no more.

Edhem said that no one knew for sure how many heads of women and children were here, below our feet. Probably hundreds. Maybe a thousand. The County Council, when it finished more pressing tasks, would place a monument at this spot.

Anita and I stood staring down at the little heap of rocks. A few feet away three Barred Rock hens were scratching in ground which so short a time ago must have been stained deep red with blood.

I raised chickens once on a farm in New Hampshire. Sometimes, in a flock of hundreds, you have a bird or two that goes "cannibalistic," as poultrymen put it; a chicken which attacks its own kind and tries to peck to death one of its roosting companions. There's no motive for it that poultrymen have ever been able to discover. It does not come from hunger, or fear, or jealousy, or fright. It happens generally among chickens raised away from grass and earth to scratch in. As soon as a good poultryman discovers a "cannibal" in his flock he either kills it quickly, or tries to cure it of the disease, which is very contagious.

Then, as I looked down, I noticed that luxuriant, rich-green grass had begun to grow among the rocks which covered the pile of skulls. There seemed to be some symbolism in that. It was too early to judge, of course, but from what we had seen so far the same thing was happening to

Yugoslavia. Or at least the attempt was being made. Out of the debris of war, on the richly fertilized ruins of cities and towns, they were trying, in their own way, to create something rich and fresh and better and new. One thing anyway. They were trying to outlaw hate and put in its place brotherly love, and they were trying to do it under conditions as adverse as if a fiend of hell had established them.

Yugoslavia, I had written, when I fled from the country six years ago, could never be reconstituted. It never should be. Here, hates were too strong ever to be reconciled. There were differences of nationality, race, creed, political ideology. Here there were too many diverse ways of life, too many kinds of culture, ever to be blended into one.

I wrote those lines even before brother began murdering brother; even before Ustaši from the Croatian plains began killing Serbs in the mountains, and Serbian Chetniks began killing Turks, and Catholics began fighting Moslems and followers of the Orthodox faith.

After such fratricide, reconciliation alone would have been called impossible by any sane observer. The idea that the survivors could co-operate, in rebuilding a country, with the families of men who had done the killing was an idea the most optimistic Pollyanna would have laughed at.

Yet here, before our eyes, all around us, it was happening.

Momock the Serb and Edhem the Moslem were standing here with us, close together, friends and working partners in an ambitious enterprise.

Green grass growing among the skulls of war!

Could it last out the season, and spread and grow?

Or would it wither and die?

Chapter Twenty-Eight

THE OLD MAN FROM SELANI

HE WAS TALL and erect, despite his obvious age. His head was wrapped in a piece of brilliant scarlet cloth, but we could see that his hair underneath was as white as the white of the five minarets against the deep blue of the sky. He carried a twisted wooden cane in one hand and in the other he held a graceful cigarette holder. His mustache was almost the color of the cloth around his head.

Mahmutević whispered, as the old man approached us on the road:

"He's a peasant, but he talks with the words of a professor. Wait until you hear his story!"

Then he introduced us to Milvoje Rasković, from the village of Selani, three kilometers away.

"Milvoje, tell these Americans the story of your life."

The old man puffed on his cigarette and looked embarrassed.

"There is nothing much to tell. What happened to me happened to many others. I am an old man. I have come in to market. I must get home before the setting of the sun. I have no story to tell, but I do have work to be done. I have come to town to get my ration and then I shall go back to Selani. I must work on the land. We had two seasons of the bad drought. Before we harvest again people will be hungry. This year we must have a crop so large that next year people will be well fed. So I must hurry now, for the sun is already in the west and back in Selani they'll be wondering what happened to Old Milvoje."

Old? How old was he?

He smiled and took the cigarette holder from his mouth.

"If you saw me at work in the fields you might guess eighty."

Then he squared his bent shoulders, stood as erect as he could, and said:

"No. Not eighty. I'm really a young man. In spite of what they tried to do to me. Last October I just turned sixty-five."

Then he waved his hand for silence.

"Don't try to be polite. I look eighty. But I am only sixty-five. We Yugoslavs all look older than we are today. I can show you boys of sixteen who look thirty. Why shouldn't they? They did a man's job in the hills when they were hardly more than babies. I can take you to Selani and show you girls of twenty-one who are as old as the Virgin Herself, for they have wisdom and understanding. They know about life, and about death too. They have buried their fathers and brothers; their mothers and sisters and aunts and grandmothers. They themselves were raped. They saw their homes burned to the ground. Yet today you should see them!"

Mahmutević bent over and whispered:

"Didn't I tell you? Just like a professor!"

Milvoje was going on.

"My generation and yours, too, young man, is finished. We may stay around for a few years more. But it is the youth that will keep the spirit inside us alive. The New Yugoslavia is youth. Youth is the New Yugoslavia. Have you heard them singing? They sing all the time. They sing at their work. They sing when the day is done and their work is finished until the morning. It keeps me from wanting to die, that singing. It keeps me from ever doubting about what is to be. You'll notice, young fellow, that nowadays they don't sing foolish songs of love. They sing of the work to be done. Last summer they went from here, and some from Selani, too, to help build a railroad. They were singing when they marched off. And they were singing when they came back a month later, with the job done.

"I go to sleep at night, I tell you, forgetting all that has gone before, which was a nightmare. I sleep at night with the music of young people singing in my tired old head.

"But now . . . now the sun is in the west and Old Milvoje must be on his way. There is corn to be got, and a long walk home, with the sacks on my back. I shall . . ."

But Mahmutević put his hand on the old man's arm and said:

"First, tell these Americans what happened to you."

And so finally the old man did. Many times he had to be prompted to continue. Several times he tried to get away and hurry into town. He seemed afraid the co-operative would close before he got his sack of corn. But finally we pieced together, from his broken sentences and the disjointed facts which came tumbling from his lips, the tale of Old Milvoje from Selani.

In that village, before the war, he lived quite happily with his wife, who was fifty-five, his only daughter, who was twelve, and his four sons. His sons were the pride of his life. They were tall, he said, "as tall as the spruces of The Romanija." And each one of them had the strength, Milvoje insisted, of "a dozen great oxen."

His favorite was the boy named Beco. One of the other three was married to a girl from a neighboring village. She was twenty-five and Milvoje said she was "pretty to look upon." She had borne two babies and everyone in the village said you could tell that Old Milvoje Rasković was their grandfather, for they had the same twinkle in the eye. They were both girls. One was four. The other was just a year and a half.

When the children's father, early in the war, went into the hills to join the Partisans, he entrusted their welfare to the old man and jokingly said:

"If anything happens to those babies or their mother, you, my father, shall pay in hell for it!"

And then the other three boys went too. Beco, the favorite, was the last to go. Milvoje said:

"Of course I wanted him to go. He had to go. But I was afraid it would happen, just as it did. I knew it would happen because Beco was as fearless—well, as fearless as the wind that blows down from Romanija Mountain. I was afraid for him, because I was afraid he would try to take on the entire army of the enemy, single-handed."

The Old Man paused, looked down at the black piece of silk sewed to the arm of his coat, bit his thin lower lip, and then went on. His voice was almost a whisper now. We had to lean forward to make out the words.

"It happened. It happened to first one of them, and then the next, and the next, and the next. Beco was the last. Three of them fell in battle with the Chetniks, those same Chetniks who did so much of this."

And the Old Man waved his wooden cane in the direction of the ruins of one thousand and six buildings which lay around us.

"Beco fell in battle with the Germans, who can take the full blame for sending this curse upon us."

Now Milvoje was digging in his pocket for something. At last he found it. It was a medal issued by the Partisan army, and the paper with it was signed by Tito himself. You could tell that Milvoje had shown that paper to a thousand people, for it was worn thin at the folds and was covered with the print of peasant fingers.

"I never have understood just what it was my Beco did to be honored this way. But I can easily imagine. You see, he was my son and I knew him well. He had the cunning of an animal of the forest. He had the strength of twelve oxen. He had the wits of a hunter. And he had the courage it takes to kill an invader with the guns and bullets the invader brought a thousand kilometers to kill us. So—they gave him a medal. Only he wasn't here ever to wear it. So they sent it to me. They also give me a pension of a thousand dinar a month, because I am Beco's father.

"Now the Bible says that the sins of the father shall be visited on the children. But . . ." The Old Man was trying so hard to make a joke, to hide his emotion. "But I say that here the medals of the son shall be given to the father. And now if it is permitted, Old Milvoje shall go down into town for . . ."

But Mahmutević stopped him again.

"You still haven't told them what happened to you."

The Old Man sighed and looked nervously at the sun. Then finally, seeing no escape, he told his own story.

He was past his sixtieth birthday when a force of Italian soldiers came to the village of Selani and rounded up all the male inhabitants and turned them over to the Germans. They shipped Milvoje, along with many others, to a Nazi prison camp in the industrial city of Zemun, across the Sava River from Belgrade. They kept him there until early in '43. Then they decided to save on food and prison space by setting free all the men too old to be of any danger to them.

Milvoje seemed as hurt by this insult to his strength and his wits as by anything else. But anyway, he made straight for the village of Selani, for he had worried, all the while he was in prison, about his family; about his wife, of course, who was so dependent on him, and his young daughter, but more especially about the wife of his son and her two babies, whom he had so faithfully promised to look after.

It's a long trek from Zemun on the Sava to the village of Selani in the hills of The Romanija, in the heart of Bosnia. It takes from eleven o'clock one night until dusk the next night by train, just to get to Sarajevo, and Selani is hours farther, by automobile, through Romanija Pass. On foot, it's a trip to make a man in the prime of his life reconsider. But Old Milvoje made it.

He got to Selani one evening, just as it was getting dark. What he saw was enough to turn a man to stone.

There was no village any more. Germans and Italians, Chetniks and Ustaši had seen to that. Where houses once stood now stood only piles of ashes, or heaps of crumbling stone.

This was where the cottage stood in which his neighbor had held such a party the night Beco said good-by to them and went off. But where was that cottage now? Could this heap of stones be all that was left of it? Or maybe his memory was failing him, after so long a time in prison. Maybe it was over . . .

No. Milvoje recognized something about what was over there. That chimney, now standing all by itself, without a wall near it! Milvoje could never mistake that chimney. He remembered every stone in it. He had laid those stones one on top of the other so carefully. That was *his* chimney!

With the cane that he carried, which he had hacked out himself from the limb of a tree to help him on his long trip home, he poked around in the ruins. Yes, this was *his* home. There was the iron hook he'd sunk in the front of the fireplace for his wife to use when she was making soap.

Why had they done this? Because he had had four sons in the Partisans? Well, if any one of his four sons could have seen this, someone would have paid.

But now he must find his people. His wife and daughter, and the daughter-in-law and her two babies. So Old Milvoje went searching through the countryside for some survivor of the obliteration of Selani to tell him where they were hiding. When he did find someone, he wished that he hadn't. What he was told gave birth to a feeling deep down inside of him that he realized he had never known before, not even when he was in prison; not even when he had been informed of his four sons' death in battle; not even when he had seen what they had done to Selani.

From that moment on he knew hate. From that moment on he felt that he had the power, in those gnarled gray hands, to wring the last drop of life out of men who commit such crimes.

He never did find the bodies. He never did learn all the details. But in the days which followed he found people who told him of hearing the screams of the two babies.

Old Milvoje doesn't remember exactly what he did in the days and the weeks and the months after that. Time lost meaning for him. But not geography. He had one fixed idea. He wanted to get as far away from Selani as his feet could carry him. He wanted to get away from The Romanija. Even from Bosnia itself. And so he pointed his face toward Serbia.

There, somewhere, he can't to this day tell you exactly where it was, a Serbian farmer befriended him, gave him a piece of land, and allowed him to stay put awhile. He was there when the final liberation occurred two years later.

That's all there is to the story. There is no surprise ending. Surprise endings occur only in fiction and films.

That's all there is to the story, except that he's back now. He's trying to forget.

He may look eighty, but he's really only sixty-five and there's no reason why he, too, shouldn't take part in the rebirth of his country. It's contagious, he says. When everyone else is active and full of hope and spirits it doesn't do for an old man to sit around on a stool with his memories.

And so, if the Americans will excuse him, he would like to go now. The sun is slanting toward the western horizon. If he doesn't hurry, the co-operative will be closed and he'll not get his sack of golden corn. And even if he does, night will overtake him on the road home to Selani. And so . . .

"*Izvinite, gospodin. Izvinite, gospodjica. Dobro veče.*"

The last we saw of him he was heading into the street called Tito Ulica, striding along with his cigarette-holder at a defiant angle, his shoulders thrown back, the scarlet cloth around his head marking him as an aristocrat among peasants.

That night we raised our small glasses of rakia and drank a toast:

"*Zivio* Milvoje Rasković, the Old Man from Selani!"

Chapter Twenty-Nine

RED, RED FLOWS THE DRINA

DRINA is a Serbian word, corrupted out of an old Turkish word, *"derin,"* which means deep.

Drina is the name that has been given to Yugoslavia's most beautiful river, as well as to one of her best cigarettes. Most of Yugoslavia's cigarettes are named after her rivers.

The Drina River has its origin in high mountains on the frontier of Montenegro and Bosnia. It winds its way, sometimes gently, sometimes wildly, for four hundred and fifty kilometers, until it flows into the Sava, which in turn flows into the Danube.

The people of Bosnia have a great love for their Drina, and some of their most beautiful songs are about it.

The Drina has always been their friend. That's what one of the songs says. From the Drina they get fish when there's no other food to be had. Fish covered with red spots which weigh up to twenty pounds apiece and have no bones to bother about.

The Drina waters their fields in the heat of the summer when there is no rain.

They use the Drina for transporting goods up and down the valley.

The women wash their clothes in the river and swear that no other kind of water can get them so clean.

Men who are daring swim in the Drina, when the July sun is so hot it exhausts them, and they say that the Drina is like a fountain of youth.

In the Drina Valley they grow apples which they claim are the largest in the world and which will keep in pristine condition for twelve months at the least. The Drina also gets credit for that.

Of course there have been spring seasons when the people of the valley have blamed the Drina for turning traitor against them. There was the spring of '96 that they still talk about, when many a village was flooded.

But that was a long time ago, and even then it didn't kill the people's love for their river.

There's one way they have always shown that love. On any suitable occasion they deck the bridges over the Drina with garlands of evergreen and flowers. Whenever they do this, they always say, as they place the decorations in place:

"For the Drina!"

At one of the gentle bends in the Drina, about eighty-six kilometers from Sarajevo, where the wild-rushing river cascades over a great many rocks and then turns to the north, there is a town called Goražde, lying half on either side of the river.

Goražde is an old town. It was founded before the start of the Turkish occupation five centuries ago. Until the last war it was home for about two thousand people, 80 per cent of them Moslems.

The people of Goražde like to compare their little part of the valley to some of the rich fruit valleys in California. Proudly they'll tell you that in 1945 they exported nearly a thousand carloads of grapes, apples, and plums to distant places. Well, if not a thousand, then seven hundred and fifty anyway. Last year not a carload went out, because for four and a half months not a drop of moisture fell from the sky. Still, they'll do it again someday, even though 40 per cent of their orchards were destroyed in the war.

What they're the proudest about today, in Goražde, is a little narrow-gauge railroad line which runs down the center of the main street of the town.

Before the war they had a railroad here. It crossed and recrossed the river at various points, the way railroads will. It ran for a while on this side, now on that. But in the war all the railroad bridges were destroyed, and someone got the idea that it would be easier to build a new railroad just on one side of the river than to rebuild all the bridges.

When it was put up to the people, they were enthusiastic about doing something, and quickly, too, because men were having to carry hundred-pound sacks of grain on their backs for a great many miles, because there was no railroad.

To do the job in a hurry and save the labor of constructing a new road-bed, they decided to lay the tracks right down the main highway, which led through the center of town. It was all volunteer work. In Goražde they are very proud that they built one bridge and eight kilometers of road in a few hours under fifty-seven days. In that time they also repaired another forty-five kilometers of tracks that was badly ripped up.

Sixteen hundred people, some as young as eighteen, some in their fifties and sixties, gave a minimum of one month of their time, without pay. The first train puffed through Goražde—the first train in years—on July twenty-seventh, which is an important day in Bosnian history for another reason. That is the day they celebrate the start of the Partisan uprising in this area.

About the war?

That's a grim chapter in Goražde's history. You may not believe it, but this little town changed hands forty-seven times. Everyone can remember when as many as three armies swapped Goražde back and forth in a single day. It worked like this:

There are steep hills leading straight up from the Drina on each side, not very far back from the river's edge, for the valley is an extremely narrow one. At the start the hills on the far side of the Drina were held, for the Axis, by the Chetniks. The hills on this side were held by the Ustaši.

Let's say, now, that the Ustaši are in occupation of the town. Their Italian masters give them an order to retire; to let the Chetniks come swarming down and across the river to slaughter Turks. The killings and looting will go on for several days, and then the Chetniks will be ordered to retire to allow the Ustaši to come in and murder Serbs and do a bit of looting, too, if there's anything left.

Yes, forty-seven times the town changed hands.

No man in Goražde likes to talk about it, but they say there was not a girl or woman here between the ages of eight and eighty who was not raped, at least once; maybe many times.

The people of Goražde still love their river. They don't blame the Drina for what happened, but from now on, until this generation which can remember has passed away, there won't be many women washing clothes in the river, and even those men who have no fear of whirlpools and undertows will be reluctant to do any swimming there.

It's all because the Nazis, the Italians, the Chetniks, and the Ustaši made a vile use of the people's river. They were all short of ammunition, and so they did most of their killing with knives. And digging graves was such a bother, so—they just used the Drina.

Down there, where that swaying suspension bridge is that the Partisans put up in nine days after they liberated the town, there used to be a great stone *most* connecting the two sides of the town. It was an old bridge and a good one too. It looked quite nice when it was decorated with evergreens and flowers. There were twenty-one stone steps leading from the bridge down to the water's edge. The steps are still there. But the bridge is gone. The Germans blew it up when they finally left. And that's probably just as well, because here in Goražde they'd just as soon forget the bridge which used to be there.

The enemy would do their killing at night, picking up people on the street, or if there was no one on the street they would go indiscriminately from house to house.

Altogether five hundred of the people of Goražde out of the two thousand met their death like this. It was an orgy, the way they did it, gathering that many people on the bridge, jabbing and slitting with their knives, and then tossing the bodies into the water.

Because most of the victims were Moslems, Moslems making up the majority of the population, the river each night ran red with Turkish fezzes. It also ran red for quite another reason. There were some nights when the people of Goražde, huddled in their homes and hearing the screams, would say:

"There will be more blood than water in the Drina tomorrow."

The stones of the bridge were now no longer white, although the enemy, with a nice interest in spotlessness, each next morning made the people still left in town go to the bridge and get down on their hands and knees and scrub away the blood.

And then we met Bećer Kosho; a Moslem. About fifty, you would say to look at him, but they all swore that he was only thirty-five.

What happened to Bećer Kosho happened on the night of December the twentieth of '41. He lived in a peasant cottage on the far side of the river. He was one of those they rounded up that night. He didn't know why. He hadn't had anything to do with the war. He didn't even have a distant relative in the Partisans.

They took him to the bridge. They jabbed their knives into seven different parts of his body. Then they slit his throat and threw him into the river to float down toward Belgrade, with the rest.

But Bećer Kosho's body didn't float down. It got caught on some logs and branches of trees sticking out into the river.

Bećer Kosho says the only way he knows how long he was unconscious is that it was just getting light when he came to. Of course it may have been dawn of some other day.

Bećer Kosho doesn't curse the Drina, as some people do today. He says it was the cold water of the Drina that stopped the flow of his blood.

The spot where the branches of trees brought him to shore was only a few hundred meters from where he lived. Somehow he managed to get to his house. His brother, who later did join the Partisans and was killed, hid Bećer in the basement for two months. It took that long for the wounds to heal because there was no doctor available, and no medicine, even.

"When the Partisans finally came, months after that, they gave me some kind of a yellow salve."

Bećer Kosho for eleven years had been a railroad worker. His great regret today is that "I can't seem to work the way I used to do."

And yet he was one of the volunteers who helped lay those narrow-gauge tracks through the center of town last year.

Bećer was not married when he had his big experience. He took a bride just last month. In a thin voice, which always seemed about to crack, he said:

"I hope that's all you want of me. I have no wish to talk to anyone. I would just like to forget everything. I'm married now and I want to be happy and forget. What happened, happened, that's all. I guess it was just what they call a miracle. I can go now, can't I?"

He was twirling a cap in his right hand and standing first on one foot and then the other.

As he left the room he was unconsciously rubbing an ugly scar on his neck.

Chapter Thirty

ALWAYS THE SAME QUESTION

It HAD been just dusk when we got into Goražde. In the railroad station we saw a poster which read:

"WINTER IS COMING. LET'S PUT A ROOF OVER OUR HEADS"

Only Anita had translated it, "Winter Is Coming. Let's Raise the Roof," until I pointed out that that didn't make sense.

We said a silent prayer, as we dragged our luggage through the dark streets, that there would be at least a second-class hotel in town: some place where we could "put a roof over our heads."

When I tell you that we finally found rooms in "the" local hotel, please don't picture the Commodore in New York, or even the Shady Rest Tourist Home in Twin Falls, North Dakota.

The Goražde Hotel consists of a first-floor *kafana* and six sleeping rooms on the second floor. Sleeping rooms is just a figure of speech. The room between Anita's and mine was occupied by the proprietor, his wife, and their numerous children, including a baby with lungs all out of proportion to the rest of its small body.

And then there was "The Witch" as we called her. If during the night either of us wandered off looking for the outside privy, which unfortunately was on the inside and on our floor, we always bumped into The Witch. She moved without a sound and was in the corridor all night. Bumping into her was almost like bumping into a cloud of dust in the shape of a woman. We never saw her during the day.

The Little Flower, as we were now calling the Sarajevo reporter because of a slight physical resemblance to New York City's former mayor, put up with the owner of the local *apoteka* because the other rooms in the hotel were rented.

The entire town was without electricity. Anita and I had one kerosene lamp between us. The hotel was unheated except for any warmth which came up, by sheer chance, from the kafana.

After dinner we went for a walk. In the dark we collided with a small peasant boy and his donkey. He was crying because, he said, he had been unable to sell the few sticks of cordwood strapped to the animal's back which he had brought down that morning from the mountain. The cordwood cost eighty cents a mule's back full.

On the County Building there was a large poster telling peasants how to control diseases of trees.

That night we talked to what reporters like to call "a man in the street."

I am sure he was a typical citizen of this typical Drina Valley town.

Bogdan Tanasković is a Serb. Fifty-seven years old. His family has lived in the Drina Valley for two hundred and fifty years. He's a tailor by profession. This is exactly the way he told his story. I still have the notes, just as I wrote them that night in a Goražde kafana. He said:

"In the old days, in these parts, a man like myself had to work very hard merely to keep alive. We had no insurance against anything. If we got sick, there wasn't any hospital here and no doctors. Often, in lean seasons, people died of hunger. Workers had no rights and our wages were miserable. There were about ten wealthy merchants in Goražde who exploited the peasants all the time. If, during a drought year, a peasant couldn't pay his taxes, the bank took over his land. Everything we had to buy was expensive. We were not allowed to purchase direct from a factory. Goods went through as many as ten hands before they got to the consumer. In those days we had no chance to send our children to school, except for two or three years. In the old days there were all-Moslem villages around here and a Serb wouldn't dare go through them. Just singing a Serb song was cause enough for attack.

"It's all different today. The change began during the war. When the Chetniks and Ustaši were taking turns killing us, the Serbs would hide their Moslem friends in their homes on the Moslem killing days. And the other way around too. Four members of my family were thrown dead into the Drina. Even my eighty-year-old mother and my niece who was a schoolteacher. My oldest son and oldest daughter were in the hills with the Partisans. I guess that was the reason.

"Anyway, now there is no more persecution, or hatred, or exploitation. Some of those ten merchants fled and never came back. But several of them are now managers of government-operated shops. Now we buy direct from co-operatives, without ten middle men. We are better off financially today, in spite of all the money the reconstruction is costing. Now I am able to send my small children to school and if they are bright they will go to the university. Now the government is eager to teach the young and make something of them. Now, if a worker is unemployed he gets insurance, and when he's ill too. We have a hospital now, and doctors, and we get free medical care.

"My home was destroyed. So was my shop. I received a loan from the government at a low rate of interest and I'm rebuilding. Since the war there hasn't been one case in this county—I don't think anywhere in Bosnia—of a Serb killing a Moslem or the other way around."

And then he pulled a greasy picture postal card from his pocket. It was of orchards in Cumberland, Maryland. It was from a Goražde man who had gone there to learn something about tree surgery. Bogdan Tanasković the Tailor of Goražde silently studied George Washington's face on the stamps. Then he looked up. He was biting his upper lip to keep back emotion. But the emotion showed in his voice.

"Why is it . . . why is it that your country and mine can't get along?"

Chapter Thirty-One

DWARFED BODIES, BUT MINDS ALIVE

THERE are five hundred and seventy-three thousand war orphans in Yugoslavia.

Exactly seventy-six of them are being cared for in Goražde, which has a population of two thousand. That's about the way it is all over the country.

The orphanage in Goražde is on that main street with the railroad tracks running down the center, but it's removed from the noise of traffic, behind a clump of trees.

The girl orphans sleep as well as eat here. The boys have cots in the classrooms of the local *gymnasium*. Relatives of the children pay what they can. If there are no relatives, which is generally the case, the government foots the entire bill.

The youngest orphan is ten; the oldest, eighteen.

The orphanage is run by two motherly women, who do all the work, even to making the beds. The children spend all their time eating, sleeping, studying.

In the kitchen closet there were, the night we paid our visit, eggs, corn bread, and, from America, chocolate, powdered milk, and marmalade.

Because there is still no electricity in town, and because of the shortage of kerosene lamps and fuel to go in them, the seventy-six children eat in the dark. But they rather like it. In between courses (there are only two) they sing songs.

There is no printing press anywhere in Goražde, but the orphans have their own newspaper. It's called a "Wall Newspaper," which means that articles are written, cartoons are drawn, and then they're pasted onto a large sheet of cardboard on the wall.

Anita and I had dinner with the seventy-six children. And then I made a little speech to them, about how they had many friends in America. It's weird, talking to a room full of human beings and not being able to see a single one of them.

Before we left that night a hot "bulletin" went up on the wall newspaper. It was written by fifteen-year-old Djebo Rayhart and it was as correct a piece of reporting as I had ever seen. It read:

"We were not acquainted with Americans before tonight, although we knew that they were a great ally and helped us with food and machinery after the war.

"But on Wednesday, the nineteenth of this month, we were visited by a writer from New York and his interpreter. The writer does not know Serbian very well, but his companion translated everything that we said.

"He asked us if we were happy in our new home and what we thought about everything. When he asked us what we all wanted to be, some comrades answered they would like to be doctors; others, engineers, etc.

"He asked us if any of us had worked on the Youth Railroad and one boy held up his hand.

"Then we asked him some questions about whether they had anything like a Youth Railroad in America, and how did orphans like us live over there, were they as happy as we are, and was America ever bombed, and did they have Chetniks and Ustaši over there who went around killing people like they killed our parents.

"We asked them to have some American children write us a letter, so we can correspond with their students. Then we danced the *kolo* and sang our songs. They wrote down the names of the individual comrades who led the kolo and the songs. There were many comrades who were fighting to have their names written down. The American promised that he would write about life in our student home. Up to now we have always lived in the hope that we might someday become better acquainted with students from our ally America and maybe now it is going to happen."

There was not one inaccuracy in that piece of reporting!

But what Djebo Rayhart could not put into his dispatch, because he had no way of knowing, was what went on inside my head as I watched the seventy-six Yugoslav orphans dancing their kolo.

They were in the back yard, under some large trees. It was pitch dark, except for a feeble light from a kerosene lamp in the kitchen, which cast a beam exactly six inches wide out across the yard, four or five feet from the ground.

Anita and I stood in the shadows, by a tree. The kolo was led by a very serious-looking youngster of thirteen, Andia Ćegić. Slowly, to the rhythm of the music, they went around and around, serpentine fashion. The shaft of light from the kitchen spotlighted every face that passed.

At that moment I wished more than anything else that I was a motion-picture photographer instead of what I was.

Most of the little faces were serious. Intense. There was no trace of self-pity. Some had eyes that were deep sunk. Some had the tragedy of their experiences written on their faces. Some of the small bodies had been dwarfed by what they had been subjected to.

But they were singing with a vigor and an enthusiasm which made me recall the words of the Old Man of Selani:

"The New Yugoslavia is youth. And Youth is the New Yugoslavia."

These children were going to be part of the future, whether they had any parents or not. That is, unless atom bombs did worse things to their bodies than had happened to the bodies of their fathers and mothers.

Thirteen of the girls sang some songs in chorus, led by a boy named

Milan Vutisivić, who said he was thirteen and kept insisting he was thirteen, although he had the body of a child of seven. One of their songs said:

"We don't want King Peter again. We want our Tito, for Tito gave life to our youth."

Then two girls, Sejda Bukvica and Milka Topalović, who were also thirteen but looked it, sang a duet. I managed to get several lines from the song:

"One brother was killing another . . ."

"That shall not happen again . . ."

"Our new battle has not lasted long, but we shall win it."

The boy Andia then started a final kolo, but halfway through it he collapsed. I think it was just that his voice gave out. It's strenuous business leading a kolo, for you have to sing as well as lead the steps. But a girl next to him took his place without losing a step or a note.

The dark hills in the distance seemed to be echoing their small voices. The night seemed full of song. We left them feeling strangely happy. Except that going out the door a small boy who looked about eight, but was probably fifteen, popped up from somewhere, blocked my path, looked up at me from deep-sunken eyes, and with the ingenuousness of the child that he was said:

"You're an American, aren't you? Well then, do you know where Ante Pavelić is? I wouldn't ask except—Ante Pavelić killed my mother and father. Someday I want to see Ante Pavelić."

Chapter Thirty-Two

"I FORGOT TO TELL YOU . . ."

ON THE west edge of Goražde, perched on a small hill, there used to be an exclusive little residential district. The homes were not large but they were attractive, and they were set among a great many tall trees. At the head of the single street there was an Orthodox church.

Today there's a pile of rubble where each house stood. The church is a shell of what it was. With a weird sense of the dramatic, fate left an elaborate hearse, turned on its side, at the head of the street.

The area is just as it was the day the street fighting up there ended. There are even strands of barbed wire, with pieces of men's clothing still caught to them.

Anita and I were browsing around this section late one afternoon when we noticed a three-story building not far away. Someone told us it was the town school, made out of the wreckage of an old army barracks of Austro-Hungarian Empire days.

So we went over and wandered through the school. We apparently had the place to ourselves. We opened the door of classroom after classroom. Anita translated the slogans on each blackboard for me.

But when we opened the last door down the hall we got a surprise. It smelled like a hospital room. And it was a hospital room, a temporary makeshift hospital room, for there, propped up in a bed, lay an old man with white hair.

Anita apologized, explained who we were, and the two of us started backing for the door. The old man almost jumped out of bed. He insisted we come back. That accent with which Anita spoke? It sounded . . . She must know Russian!

For the next fifteen minutes they talked like mad in Russian to each other.

Yes, he was a Russian. He had been a teacher in Leningrad, only that wasn't the name of the city then. He had been in the Czar's army and had been taken prisoner by the Germans. The First World War, of course. The Germans put him in a prison camp in Rumania. But he escaped, swam the Danube, and wound up in Yugoslavia. And he'd been here ever since.

Yes, he's a teacher, here in this school. Teaches Russian and nature study. Until several years ago he taught physics and mathematics. But now they want the young people to learn Russian too.

"It's the irony of destiny that I find myself in a little hole like this!

I, who once taught at the university in Russia! I could tell you more if I had the strength. It is a fantastic, unbelievable story of life.

"I have made application, finally, after thirty years, to go home. I shall at last go back to Russia in the spring to see my people, if there are any of them alive, after a revolution and two wars. And if I myself am alive by spring.

"You see me here, a man who looks eighty. Oh yes! I know. A man who looks eighty. I really am only fifty-seven. But I have pneumonia, you see. For twelve days I was unconscious. They say, now, that perhaps I am getting better. I do not know.

"The terrible thing is that I have been too weak to read while I have been in bed. It has been my books, these thirty years, that have kept me going. But now I am much too weak to read."

I whispered to Anita (for the professor understood a little English) and she told him we had to leave but we would be back in fifteen minutes.

At the hotel we dug out our alcohol stove, a package of tea, some cups, some sugar, and what food in the cardboard box that was left. And then we went back to have a tea party with a dying Russian professor. I wanted to take him a gift of some kind. There's nothing to buy in the shops of Goražde, even if they had been open. But leaving the hotel room, I noticed a soft white woolen scarf I had brought from New York, and so I took it along.

We were joined at the tea party by Fahro Bashćelia, the principal of the school, and his attractive young wife, Cornelia.

In whispers, out in the hall, they told us what I had sensed already, just looking at the old professor. He would never go back to Russia. His illness had sapped so much of his strength that the local doctor said it was a matter of days, perhaps hours. As a matter of fact, they said they had had a coffin built for him already. We could see it if we wished. It was down in the cellar. A nice coffin it was too. They liked the old professor. It wouldn't be quite the same around the school without him.

So we went back into the room and talked with him, until he finally went to sleep in the middle of a sentence. The only reason we knew he was asleep and not dead was that the bedcovers over his chest moved up and down ever so slightly.

While he slept the young principal and his wife told us about their school. They had a hundred and fifty pupils, including the orphans we had met. They said even schools are run differently under the new regime. Now there's real self-government in all the schools. The pupils have an elected council. They organize children's conferences at which all phases of schoolwork are thoroughly discussed in quite an adult manner.

Under the new system no teacher has a right to resort to corporal punishment. In fact, she can inflict no punishment at all. That's done by the student body itself, or by the council. They vote what punishment shall be meted out for infraction of rules. A mild punishment is that the offender is not allowed to go on school hikes, attend parties, or join in the singing of songs for a certain period. For graver offenses, the Council may rule that for seven days no one in the school will speak to the offender.

That's as far as we got, for then a small, black-haired boy came in to say good night to Madame Cornelia. He was introduced to us as Sjedo Sjerćić and he said he was fourteen, but like all other Yugoslav "war children" he didn't have the body to go with his years.

He sat at Madame Cornelia's feet and held tightly to one of her hands and looked up into her face for long minutes at a time, his gaze never wavering. He paid no attention to us, even though we were strangers.

Because the child didn't know English and his teacher did, she was able to tell us his story as he sat there.

He was one of the orphans. He had been forced to stand by and watch while his father and mother were killed with knives. It did something to the child which neither time nor the love Cornelia tried to give him had completely erased. For several years he wandered the hills, alone, more an animal than a human. When they found him he was literally a savage. His body, from living on berries, roots, and the bark of trees, had almost wasted away. But it was his mind they were the most worried about. His body they were trying to take care of, with a special diet. But it was a real task trying to cure his mind.

Cornelia had decided that affection was what he needed, and that's why she encouraged him to hold her hand and to snuggle into her arms like a baby.

Just last week Sjedo got a mistaken idea she was angry with him, so he ran away. They found him heading for the bridge over the Drina. He admitted that he was going to throw himself on the rocks where the river runs the swiftest.

I wanted to see the youngster's eyes, so I told Anita to ask him how he would like to go to New York someday.

He jumped to his feet, still holding his teacher's hand, his black eyes flashing. He ran his free hand through his mop of curly black hair and said what I am sure is the Serbo-Croat equivalent for:

"Gee!"

Of course he would like to go to New York someday! He knew all about New York! He had read about it! Did we think that . . .

But then a strange, rather terrible look came over his face. The look a man has when he's going under for the third time. He threw himself at Cornelia's feet and clutched desperately at her legs.

"But not without you! No! No! I don't want to go! Not without you!"

The principal's wife ran her fingers through his hair and said that of course she would be going too. Then he gradually grew calm again.

During the silence that followed I remembered that the white woolen scarf I had given the professor had a label with the words "New York" on it. I looked over at the bed. The professor was still asleep. If what they said was true, he wouldn't have use for a scarf or anything else in a few days. I talked to Cornelia about it and she agreed, so I took the scarf from the bed, showed Sjedo the words "New York" on the label, and then tied the scarf around his neck. The boy's eyes danced with fun. He went over to a mirror to look at himself. Then he took the scarf off and tied it around Cornelia's neck. They agreed that they would take turns wearing it. Except that if the professor got well he was to have it.

Before we left, the principal and his wife rounded up the seventy-six orphans and we danced a kolo up and down the length of the hall. Sjedo was between Cornelia and me. That meant we each held one of his hands. During the few minutes of dancing he was the happiest youngster I had ever seen. He looked up at first one of us and then the other with a big grin on his face. And then he would look at the scarf around his neck with the label that bore the two magic words.

Cornelia and her husband walked to the road with us. Just before we separated the wife very casually said:

"Maybe I should have told you before, but Sjedo isn't going to live either. He—he spits blood. You know what that means. The doctor says if there was some place we could send him . . . But we don't have places like you do in America to send such people. Not yet. Anyway, we promise to make him as happy as we can, as long as we have him with us. *Laku noć*. Good night."

Chapter Thirty-Three

AS YELLOW AS GLITTERING GOLD

ČAJNIČE (it's pronounced just like China with a "che" on the end) was once one of the most thriving towns of the Drina Valley. And one of the most beautiful. It's set close against a towering mountain. The woods used to come right down to the edge of the main street. The black dome of the Orthodox Cathedral was silhouetted against the green of the great spruces. Two thousand people lived in Čajniče the year round. There were twelve sawmills which employed five hundred men. In the summer the town prospered because Čajniče had a spa famous for the curative power of its water. Tourists came from France, Germany, even England. Twelve kilometers away, on the mountainside, there was a large building which used to be an Austrian military barracks. More recently it had been transformed into a six-hundred-bed sanitarium. It stood exactly on the old frontier between the Turkish and Austro-Hungarian empires.

That's the way it was before the war. During the fighting Čajniče changed hands forty-eight times. The Germans destroyed the sanitarium with bombs. They destroyed most of the houses in town. Čajniče was finally reduced to such a ghost of its former self that only eleven inhabitants of the two thousand remained.

Today Čajniče is struggling desperately to accomplish a revival. Some of the homes have been rebuilt. Two of the twelve sawmills are in operation again. But Čajniče is a tragic place to look at. The roads leading in and out of the town are still lined with the burned-out wreckage of enemy trucks and tanks. The beauty of the mountainside has been destroyed, for the Germans, in their fear that Partisans were lurking there, cut the great spruces for a quarter of a mile up the hill.

Čajniče has lost its place of honor as a county seat. It is cut off from the outside world, except for one highway. During the winter few vehicles dare move over that mountain road. A doctor appears in town just once every fifteen days.

But Čajniče has her memories and no one can take those away. Once Čajničc was not so quiet and insignificant. That was in 1942, when, as the saying goes, "the towns died and the forests came to life."

On January the twenty-seventh Partisans from the mountain came sweeping into Čajniče and liberated the town. And then, a few weeks later, great swarms of Partisans appeared from all sides, filled the town with their shouting and singing, and congregated around the local hotel.

There was sudden silence as a man appeared on the hotel balcony and began to speak. He was a dynamic-looking character, and he spoke with words that no man could misunderstand. When he finished his speech the people of Čajniče whisperingly demanded his name. His followers smiled and said:

"Why, that's . . . we call him Stari!" (It's a Serbian word. There is no exact equivalent in English. It means the "Old One" only it implies a great deal of respect.)

The man on the balcony left town that night, having taken part in the formation of what came to be known as the Second Proletarian Brigade. It was some time later before the people of Čajniče realized that they had had as their guest the man the world called "Tito."

It was just five years to the day later that Anita and I walked through the Čajniče Hotel and stood on the same balcony. The hotel has been rebuilt. Its stucco today is painted a brilliant pink. It is to be used, henceforth, as a home for two hundred orphans.

In Čajniče we went poking around on our own, opening doors of houses and looking in. We talked with old women, pregnant wives, and little children. We wanted to see exactly how they were living, and we did.

One building we entered was a temporary home for six bombed-out families. It contained six small rooms. Twenty people were somehow existing there. In each room there was a wood-burning stove with an oven on top, an iron kettle for cooking food and washing clothes, a tiny kerosene lamp, and in most of the rooms a cradle. There was just one bed in the entire building. There were some scrawny chickens in corners of five of the rooms.

We asked them to show us their larders. What were they eating these days? They showed us. Their entire diet consisted of corn and salt, which were mixed together and baked in the ovens into something they called bread.

There were ten or twelve children in the building, mostly between the ages of six and eleven. I looked at them closely and then turned to Anita and said:

"My God! Their skin is yellow!"

So we took them, one by one, out into the bright winter light. We made them take off some of their clothes. Their arms and legs were tragically thin. Their stomachs were fat, protruding, and hard. And their flesh was yellow. As yellow as the corn in a bag we had seen in each room.

Chapter Thirty-Four

THE MIRACLE OF ČAJNIČE

THE Turks swept through the Drina Valley and joined it onto their empire in 1483. It was just a few years before that that a small but beautiful church was built by those of the Orthodox faith on the edge of the town called Čajniče.

Among the treasures of priests and parishioners which they managed to keep out of the hands of the invaders for hundreds of years were a parchment Bible of great size, and a book bound in rich red leather in the handwriting of an ancient monk which told the history of the Orthodox Church.

Ninety years ago, immediately after the end of the Crimean War, they built close beside that little church what was intended to be the largest Orthodox cathedral anywhere in the Balkans. It was built expressly to house two ikons. One was of the Virgin Mary and the Christ Child. The other was of the Apostle St. John. The first was unusual, as a work of art, because the Child was being held in the Mother's right arm instead of the left. But there was something more important about it than that. The crown the Virgin wore was made of thick silver and gold. It was studded with large diamonds. It was three by four feet. It was called "The Miraculous Ikon" and praying in front of it was reputed to enable the blind to see, the deaf to hear, and barren women to become large with child. There were only three other ikons like it in the world. One was in Jerusalem, one in Kiev, the third in Ethiopia. The ikon of St. John was the same size and was also heavily encrusted with silver and gold. They did not claim, however, that it had the miraculous powers the other one had. People came from hundreds of miles around to pray before the likeness of the Virgin Mary. Pilgrimages of great crowds of people were not uncommon.

In the cathedral there was also a secret steel-lined chamber which few but the priests knew about. That was where they hid the wealth of their church from the Turks. That was where they hid the two great books in time of trouble.

As you approach that part of Čajniče today you can see the black dome of the cathedral against the blue of the sky and the green of what is left of the spruces high on the mountain. But even from a distance you can tell that something happened here. The cross at the top, made of gleaming gold, is bent so that it now points toward the ground. The small church near by is trim and neat. It looks about four months old. Not four hundred and some odd years. The cathedral is just a shell. So are all the other buildings in sight except the small church. There's a white-bearded priest wandering around the churchyard. He squints through narrow eyes because he is almost stone blind.

We thought it would be a good idea to get the story of the Miracle of Čajniče from the Rev. Jovan Jovanović himself and then there would be no question. He said he'd told it many times but he'd keep repeating it as long as he lived, which probably wouldn't be much longer because he was seventy-eight and very feeble now from the experiences he'd been through.

"I was here," he said, "when the Germans came in. Then they turned Čajniče over to the Italians. The Italians used the little old church, the cathedral, our seminary, and the county building across the road as store-places for their munitions. About ten carloads were in the little church and the county building. The Germans and Ustaši, when they were here, discovered the secret safe and stole everything that was in it. But we had already hidden the old Bible, the ancient history book, and some valuable pictures in peasant homes out in the villages. It was on April 11, 1943, that the terrible thing happened. The Italians got orders to with-draw from this area. They didn't have vehicles enough to haul the muni-tions away, so they decided to blow them up. A village woman who heard what they were going to do told me about it. There was nothing I could do to stop them, but I didn't want to see it happen, so I went and hid in a nearby village. It was two o'clock in the morning that the explosions began to go off. They shook the mountains. Yes, I tell you, they shook the mountains. Everyone ran from the city. After the Italians left and we came back . . . it was terrible to see. The little old church didn't exist any more. There wasn't a sign of it. Nor of the County Building either. My house across the road was gone too. The cathedral was—well, the dome was there, as you see it, and three of the walls. That was about all. But this is the miracle. The two ikons were just where they had always been. They hadn't moved one inch out of their places. And in front of the picture of the Virgin and Child two small candles were still burning.

"If I had just seen it myself, I would say my tired old eyes were playing tricks. But everyone in Čajniče saw it. Everyone who was still alive. The great roof had collapsed. Steel girders were twisted as if they were made of those pins the women use in their hair. Fire had destroyed most of the woodwork. But the ikons didn't move an inch, and the two candles were still burning.

"But that is only part of the miracle. On August twenty-eighth we held a festival of thanksgiving in the ruins. People came from all the villages around. That day one steel beam which was still in place came crashing down.

"It hit the wall on which the ikon of the Virgin was hung. It caused a great deal of damage. But the ikon still didn't move one inch and the candles still didn't go out.

"But really it did not surprise me, for I am a Man of God. It surprised other people. But it did not surprise me, for I have seen the blind and the deaf healed in front of that ikon. I know ten women who were barren for years. Then they prayed before the ikon and all ten of them now have children."

When the Chetniks finally came to town, they raided the cathedral, took the ikons and hid them in a large stove. They were retrieved by some townspeople who then buried them in the ground. But the Chetniks located the hiding spot, dug them up, and took them up into the mountains, to their headquarters. This was duly reported to the Partisans, who made a raid on the place, for the express purpose of recovering the two holy pictures. Which they did.

Now they hang in their original places, on one of the three walls of the cathedral which still stand. The rain beats down through the open roof. Snow drifts deeply in. But two small candles are kept constantly burning in front of the silver-and-gold likeness of the Virgin.

It was Anita who noticed that there were no diamonds in the halo. When she spoke about it, the priest said:

"Ah no! But there were. If you look closely you can see the holes. The Germans stole the diamonds the first day they came to town."

The little church next door? That's a new one. Just been completed. It's an exact copy of the one built nearly five centuries ago and destroyed because some Italians didn't have the trucks to haul away their surplus munitions. It was built, the priest tells us, entirely with voluntary labor. Men of Čajniče went up into the mountains in their spare time and cut the trees, and milled the timber, and did the job.

We asked the padre how he was making out under the new regime. He said:

"The government built me a new house. The people of my church give me food to eat. I hold services every Sunday. More people attend than ever before. You know how it is in bad times. And these have been bad times for Čajniče! Does the government interfere with religion here? No. It's just the same. People come and worship if they have a mind to. But now you must excuse me. I must see the doctor. Today he is to tell me how much longer he thinks I shall be able to see anything at all."

Chapter Thirty-Five

AN ENEMY OF THE REGIME

THE Yugoslavs make a strong *rakia* and a weak rakia. The weak variety has the alcoholic content of vodka and should be taken with great caution. The strong variety, called *rakia ljuta,* will eat the lining of your throat, set your insides on fire, and make you see pink elephants in a very limited space of time.

But in the town kafana of Čajniče they ordered glass after glass of rakia ljuta for us. Each time the glasses were filled someone proposed a toast—to President Roosevelt, to the United Nations, to the victors in the war, to "Death to Fascism; Freedom for the People."

We couldn't very well refuse to drink to such toasts and so we drank. Before long I began to hear the hoofbeats of great pink elephants, even though I couldn't see them yet. So I went for a walk by myself.

I found a carpenter shop where they had some American power tools just like some I had once used myself. The boss carpenter and I were getting along very well together when a figure appeared in the doorway. I recognized the man as one of the crowd in the kafana. He said he wanted to see me. Privately. In a mixture of three or four languages he explained that he had been a sailor once and knew some of "every language." He must talk to me. So I went with him to his home on the edge of the city. While his mother served us hot *chorba* he told me his story. He said that I had seen the good things and heard the good things but there was another side to the picture. Was I interested in that? I said of course I was. Very much. So he went on. This new regime was oppressing the people. Many didn't like it. He himself hated the government and everything it represented. He'd like to get to America. Maybe I could help him. I asked him why he didn't like the regime. He hesitated. I asked him how the government was oppressing the people. In what ways?

Finally he explained. He had been a barber before the war. A master barber. He'd had his own shop right on the main street. Late in the war he left Čajniče. When he returned he found that his shop had been confiscated by the government. Now, even though he had once been a master barber with a shop of his own, he had to work for somebody else.

I asked him in what army, if any, he served during the war. He said:

"They have told you that Čajniče changed hands forty-eight times. Well, I decided it would be the safest to be on the side of whichever army came in. When the Germans came I tried to be a friend of the

Germans. When the Italians came I was a friend of them. When the Chetniks and Ustaši came I made friends with them."

Why had he left town? Where had he gone?

"When the Germans and Ustaši left the last time I went off with them. That's all. But that isn't what I want to talk about. What I ask you is why a master barber like I am should lose his shop and work for somebody else?"

About that time Anita found me and I had my whispering friend repeat the whole story to her, just to be sure that I hadn't misunderstood him. The quotations were still the same as I had them written down.

Chapter Thirty-Six

FORGIVE THE MAN WHO KILLED YOUR MOTHER?

SINCE we first heard of the amnesty offered to Chetniks by the Yugoslav Government if they would come out of the hills and take up civilian occupations again, I have been wanting to meet one of Draža Mihailović's men who had accepted the offer. I wanted to find out what really happened in such cases.

Driving back from Čajniče to Goražde we stopped for water for the truck's radiator in a village called Miljeno. There we met a twenty three-year-old Chetnik from the town of Berkovici. Milosh Radović told us that he joined the Chetniks out of his hatred of the Croatian Ustaši and because he thought the Chetniks were going to put an end to the Ustaši for all time. He signed up early in 1943, when he was only nineteen years old. He lived in the hills for almost four years. He took part in one small fight against the Germans and one battle against the Partisans. When the war was over, because he had killed some Partisan soldiers during that battle, he was afraid to give himself up, for fear he would be executed.

For the past two years he and two fellow Chetniks had been roaming the mountainsides. They kept alive by making raids on peasant homes; stealing at gunpoint what they needed. Most recently they had been living right in these hills, and he pointed into the woods behind us.

Then in December, just the day before Christmas, some villagers whose homes they were looting told them about the amnesty offer. All three of them had grown tired of living in a hole in the ground, so they decided to "take a chance."

The authorities investigated their records and decided that none of them had done anything worse than participate in an armed struggle against the Partisans; that they had merely carried out the orders of their superiors. Therefore they were granted the full rights of citizenship and all three were given jobs.

Milosh said he was working in a sawmill. He was happy and was beginning to get his weight back. Then his bright blue eyes twinkled and he asked if anyone had a cigarette.

A man in the rear of the truck, who had the emblem over his heart which showed he had enrolled in the Partisans back in 1941, happened to be the first to produce a package of cigarettes. Someone else lighted a match for the ex-Chetnik.

We shook hands all around. Milosh pulled his green cap down over his face to keep off the snow and started back down the road. We drove on toward Goražde.

There was silence in the cab of the truck for a few minutes and then the driver, a man in his fifties, began to talk, half to himself. Just broken pieces of sentences.

"Did you see the Partisan give the Chetnik a cigarette? . . . Two years ago that boy was trying to stick a knife into that Partisan's back . . . Wish I could forget so quickly. . . . Don't see how anyone can. . . . When I see a Chetnik I see blood in front of my eyes. . . . They killed my mother . . . she was seventy . . . an old lady . . . never did anyone any harm. . . . Chetniks! . . . I know it's wrong, but my God I hate them! . . . I wouldn't give them any . . . any . . . whatever you call it! . . . And the Partisan gave him a cigarette . . . and somebody else even lighted it for him! God damn Chetniks! You can't forgive a man who killed your own mother, can you?"

Chapter Thirty-Seven

LITTLE RUBBER BALLS

IN THE days of the Turkish occupation, the small town lying at the convergence of the Ćehotina and the Drina rivers had no water supply. The women, accordingly, used to go down to one of the two rivers and carry water up to their homes in specially designed barrels which they strapped to their backs. The Turkish word for these water barrels was *fuchia*. And so the Yugoslavs today call the town Foča. (The mark over the "c" gives it the sound of "ch".)

In prewar days there were seven thousand people here. Most of the men worked for Austrian, Hungarian, and Swiss lumber interests which owned most of the timberland in the neighborhood.

During the hostilities Foča changed hands forty-six times, was 86 per cent destroyed, was bombed by British, Italian, and German planes, and fifteen hundred people were killed, almost one out of every four.

In Foča we saw the odd sight of a thickly veiled Moslem woman buying herself a ten-cent American hand mirror.

In Foča we heard the story from many lips of how most of the destruction here, and the killing and looting, had been personally directed by a Chetnik commander from Mihailović's General Staff, Zaharija Ostojić. He was here in person.

"He is now in Italy," they said. "He is now in Italy enjoying your American hospitality."

In Foča we met the president of the County Council, Captain Rajko Gagović, and from him we found out exactly how he and other officials are chosen. Some of the town and county officials with whom we had talked were peasants; others were comparatively well-educated city men. Some had been Partisan officers; but there was one who had played no part at all in the war. Rajko Gagović was a good example of a fighter turned public administrator. His father was a Serbian peasant in Foča. But he had had an uncle who was a priest and helped him get some education. In between teaching school and holding a job as a waiter he managed to get in three years' work in philosophy at Belgrade University. As soon as the Partisan Army was formed, Rajko and two older brothers joined up. The brothers were killed. Another brother who was only thirteen was imprisoned in a Chetnik concentration camp. The Gagović home was burned to the ground. The father, mother, a thirteen-year-old-sister, and a ninety-year-old grandfather fled to the woods. The little girl found a Partisan unit and became one of the youngest volunteers. Today she is a teacher in a village school. The grandfather was caught and imprisoned. But he lived, and today, although ninety-five, still works part of the time in the fields. The parents were caught, too, but the father escaped, found a gun, sought out Rajko's division, and fought by the side of his son until the end of the war.

Rajko was wounded twice. He lost 60 per cent of the unit he commanded.

Today he is a mere twenty-five, but in Belgrade they consider him a model administrator and public servant. Under him, in this most culturally backward area of all Yugoslavia, illiteracy is being wiped out, hospitals and schools are being built all over the county, the forests which were once owned by foreign interests have been nationalized, a number of woodworking factories are going up, and Foča, they all anticipate, will someday be a prosperous community, principally because of the leadership of this boy.

Rajko said he didn't think people abroad understood by what democratic methods officials in the New Yugoslavia are chosen. Then he went on to explain:

"Two or three months before the election the five parties which make up the People's Front hold a convention which anyone may attend. At that convention, by democratic means, a slate of candidates is chosen. If a man does not belong to the People's Front and wishes to run for office, he may get on the ballot by obtaining fifty signatures on a petition. Anyone can be a candidate.

"The candidates have two months to go from village to village telling people what they stand for. What their platform is. The candidates may take campaign workers with them.

"When I ran for president a year ago there were three men against me. They ranged in age from thirty-five to sixty-two. One was a former government official, one was a professor, the third was a peasant.

"They received five or six hundred votes apiece. I got seven thousand. Ninety-eight per cent of the population voted. Although this was the first time women had an opportunity to vote, fewer of them abstained than men. I told you that I am a Serb. Two of my opponents were Moslems. Yet in one almost completely Moslem village I received four hundred votes to their thirty-two.

"Our election laws should interest people in America. On election day no soldier or gendarme is allowed to appear on the streets. No firearms are allowed in evidence. No campaigning is permitted for twenty-four hours before the voting begins. No alcoholic beverages may be sold the day before election, on election day itself, or on the day after.

"Peasants come in from the countryside singing and carrying flags. It's a great holiday. The best house in town is chosen for the polling place. There is a box with a hole in the top covered by a piece of black cloth for each candidate. When a voter enters the room he is given a small rubber ball. Each voter must put his hand into each of the boxes, no matter how many there are. In one of them he drops the rubber ball. The cloth over the top of the box prevents anyone from seeing in which box he left the ball. If he is illiterate and can't read the names of the candidates on the front of the boxes, the names are read to him. On the way out of the room he must raise his open hand above his head to show that it is empty. Each candidate is permitted to have watchers to make sure that everything is fair.

"The public may attend while the balls in each box are being counted. When the count is completed, runners go from each village to the county center with the result. The grand result is known within twenty-four hours. The winner takes office the next day."

I said that that was all very interesting, but we in America had often heard that there is no way in which a Yugoslav can vote against the system. Rajko had the answer ready. He said that their system is "something like communism . . . only our own peculiar brand of it." In America, he said, the system is called "capitalistic democracy." In either country it is presumed that any officials who are elected will try to make the system work. Isn't it true, he said, that in the United States your officials must take an oath to support the Constitution, which means your way of life? If Americans consider it treason for someone to try to make a violent change in their system, why should they be surprised if Yugoslavia has the same idea? Then he answered the question more specifically. He said he had told us that a man does not have to be a member of a "machine" to win a nomination. All he needs is a few signatures on a petition to get onto the ballot. He had heard that in some parts of the United States we have the same way of doing it. But in Yugoslavia they had something else that we didn't have. His eyes sparkled as he told about it.

At every election, in every polling place, there is one ballot box more than there are candidates. If a voter dislikes all the candidates who are running for a particular office, he has the right to drop his little rubber ball in an "opposition" box. The number of rubber balls in that box means that that many people didn't like any of the candidates and wanted to vote against all of them. Did we have such a system in the United States? When our two big political machines put up two candidates for an office, say for President of the United States, and we didn't like either of them, was there any way we could say so . . . any way besides just doing the negative thing of staying away from the polls? And remember, he said, there is no way in the world that anyone can find out who put the little rubber balls in that opposition box!

I told him that in the United States we have blank spaces on our ballots which can be used by people who don't like any of the candidates and want to write in the name of a candidate of their own. He asked if people made use of those blank columns. He wanted to know, for example, how many people used the blank columns before the days of Franklin Roosevelt, say in 1920 or 1924, when, he said, the Democratic and Republican candidates were "weak characters who stood for about the same thing." I didn't know the figures, so instead of answering I asked him how he knew so much about American politics. He said I must remember that he had been in the university at Belgrade before the war. They studied all about American politics. No political system was perfect, he said, but the Yugoslav voting procedure was designed to give people as free a choice of their officials as possible.

Before we left there was one thing more the young man in the hip boots and the old leather jacket wanted to tell us. He took us to the window of his office and pointed up at the mountain called Zelan Gora, capped with snow.

"We Partisans had a hospital up there. There were two thousand wounded men in it. We heard that something had happened there, so I was sent up to investigate. I can tell you this story, because I saw it with my own eyes. When I arrived, there were two thousand dead bodies. The Germans had killed every one of those wounded men. Even men who had lost arms and legs in battle.

"It's a good thing they didn't win the war!"

Chapter Thirty-Eight

ITS STONES WERE FLECKED WITH PINK

"IF THE Drina could only talk!"

Anita's voice had a far-off quality as she said it. We were standing on the far bank of the river at the town of Visegrad. We'd been wandering for days up and down the valley. I knew she was thinking just what I was. Of the hundreds of stories we'd gathered about the Drina. Of the half-dozen armies that had come charging in and out of the valley just in the past few years. Of a previous world war during which other things had happened along the banks of the Drina. And then of older histories. Armies of Turkish sultans and armies of Austro-Hungarian kings fighting for this narrow bit of soil on either side of a river which had so often run red instead of its natural greenish-white.

If the Drina could talk, the first story it would probably tell would be the story of the Pasha's Bridge at Visegrad, because that story would entwine in its telling the whole history of the valley.

The Pasha's Bridge at Visegrad was a lovely thing. It was built in the sixteenth century by a young man named Mahmed Sokolović, who was one of the Sultan's *vesires*. After being educated at Constantinople in the ways of Islam, he was sent, as so many Bosnians were, back to the land of his birth. He ruled over the entire Drina Valley. He had one vestigial quality which had not been educated out of him. He had the vice of an inordinate curiosity. And he was especially curious about his antecedents. Finally he discovered the place of his birth. He was from that spot in the valley where the River Rzad comes tumbling impetuously into the Drina. The spot the Bosnian people called Visegrad. And so, with the pride of a man building a memorial to himself—or maybe it was a worthier motive than this; maybe it was his desire to bestow some good on the people of his own town—he ordered a great bridge built across the Drina at Visegrad.

But the people of Bosnia are a superstitious people. That's why some of them saw in this bridge an attempt to link with great blocks of stone free people and slaves. An attempt to tie conquered Bosnia to her Turkish master with pieces of rock.

And so all day long the slaves of the vesire, Mahmed Sokolović, would labor and sweat, putting the stones in their place and cementing them firmly. And all night long other men who would never be slaves tore down the little that had been built during the day. The vesire fumed and spluttered. His soldiers finally caught one man in the act of destruction and nailed his live body to a tree just as a little warning. After that work progressed more rapidly. But still it took five years to build the bridge.

Even the most superstitious had to agree, when it was finally completed, that the Pasha's Bridge was not only quite practical but that it was also a thing of considerable beauty. It had six separate arches. The stone that had been used was flecked with pinks and reds which sparkled when the sun hit the bridge from just the right angle. There was a stone tower in the center, on one side. There were balconies where people came in the cool of the evening to sit and watch the swift water flow by underneath. On holidays the bridge was always beautifully decorated. Public speeches were made from the bridge. Processions always began and ended there. Slowly, through the centuries, the people of the Drina Valley developed an odd and illogical affection for what they finally were calling "Our Bridge." Few ever referred to it as the Pasha's Bridge any more. Artists painted it. Poets and novelists wrote about it. When the days of cameras arrived it was something professionals and amateurs from far-off places considered a prize subject for the little black boxes they pointed at it.

For better than four centuries nothing happened to harm the Pasha's Bridge. Except, of course, when blocks of ice in the springtime would sometimes knock a stone loose in the footings. Then came World War I. When the Germans and Austrians were forced to retreat from the Drina Valley they mined the bridge. The damage was not great. After peace returned the stones which had been knocked out of place were put back where they belonged again. World War II was different. In World War II the same sort of things happened here as on the bridge at Goražde. Only much worse. Not five hundred victims. Here there were three thousand five hundred. That many bodies were thrown from the Pasha's Bridge into the Drina. It was cruel irony that most of them were the bodies of Moslems. The bodies of people who had adopted the faith of the builder of the bridge under pressure from Constantinople.

And then, as they did with all bridges, no matter how beautiful and how historic, the Germans in December of '44, as they prepared for flight, put dynamite under the six spans. Their dynamite was better this time than it had been a quarter of a century ago. Or maybe it was that their demolition squads were more expert. Anyway, this time every stone of the bridge was blown to pieces. This time there was nothing left to reconstruct.

Today there's a temporary bridge farther down the river. As Anita and I crossed it we saw a small boy with only one hand staring down into the water. He was the one who showed us, by pointing with his remaining hand, where the Pasha's Bridge had once been. In the sand at the point on the far bank where the start of the bridge had been we found one small piece of stone about the size of a child's fist. We could tell that this had been part of the bridge. We could tell that this had been a piece of a block of stone which four hundred years ago had been hauled from distant places at the order of a young vesire who wanted to honor the spot where he thought he'd been born. We could tell, because the fragment was flecked with pink. It sparkled and danced when we held it at the right angle in the morning sun.

Chapter Thirty-Nine

EDUCATION—YUGOSLAV STYLE

BEFORE it all began there were seven thousand people in the town of Visegrad. When Kamila Dzvrović came back there were just twenty people here. All women. When Kamila Dzvrović came back the roads were still mined. People cautioned her that she must walk only in footprints made by someone else. If she didn't, she might get blown to kingdom come. Those were her words. "To kingdom come." It was a pleasure to meet Madame Kamila. She's a warm, motherly woman of about fifty. She has soft blue eyes. She dresses simply. Generally in a skirt and a plain blue sweater. If you saw her in America you would guess that she was the principal of a small high school somewhere. That's just what Madame Kamila was before the war. Today she is secretary of education for the county of Visegrad. She's in charge of seventeen schools, twenty-two teachers, and twenty-six hundred pupils.

Madame Kamila was the first teacher in this entire area to return to work. She and her husband, who's an Orthodox priest, had had a great many war experiences. Not very happy ones either. Once she was held in a prison which had formerly been a school. It was the very school in which her own eldest son had been educated. Only now it didn't look like a school any more. Later she and her husband were in a special concentration camp for priests and their families. It was "special" because of the especially bad treatment they received. One piece of bread the size of a yeast cake for every meal. There were nearly four hundred Bosnian priests in that single camp.

"But," she says, "let's not talk about that."

Madame Kamila would rather talk about the present and the future. She'd rather talk about education. She's opened all but five of the old schools in her county. It's been a job because only three of the thirty-eight teachers they used to have came back. Many of the others, of course, were killed. She's instituted co-education. That's something these Bosnian people used to think conflicted with their religion. Once children went to school for an average of four years. Now there's a law that they must go until they are fourteen. Of course the law won't be enforced until they're able to build more schools. There's also the illiteracy work. Two thousand older people in this one small county are attending illiteracy classes right now. Then a gay twinkle came into Madame Kamila's soft blue eyes. Would we like to see her "baby"?

So we went across the temporary bridge which takes the place of the

Pasha's Bridge to the largest school in Visegrad. In the yard small boys are making a garden, while some Red Cross women cook an iron kettle full of stew to feed one hundred and fifty orphans who have no homes to go to when mealtime arrives. In this school there are five hundred pupils. But there are only four teachers. Madame Kamila says:

"In the old days we had to beg the children to learn. Today they beg us to teach them."

Madame Kamila is proud about many things. She's proud that they have abolished corporal punishment. Here the substitute for corporal punishment is for the other children to write about the culprit in their wall newspaper.

In the hallway we met Mileva Grubać, running from a class of eighty-five boys and girls to a class of grownup women she also teaches at the same time. The superintendent said that Mileva is a typical teacher of the new regime. Mileva is thirty-eight. Her father was a clerk in a shop. She had twelve years of education herself, the last four years in a teachers' college. Before the war she was a housewife. Now her normal weekday goes like this:

Up at 6 A.M. Makes breakfast, washes dishes, cleans her apartment. Reports to school at eight. From eight to twelve does double duty teaching her class of eighty-five and the domestic-science course at the same time. She doesn't mind the fact that the two classrooms are on different floors. She says that's the way she gets her exercise and keeps from growing fat. Between twelve and one she goes home and gets her own lunch. From one until four her schedule is the same as in the morning, with two different classes going simultaneously. From four until five she teaches fifty-five pupils in a vocational school. Between five and six she has another domestic-science class. The subjects she teaches there are dairy husbandry, sewing, cooking, and how to feed, kill, dress, and cook poultry. After a quick dinner which she prepares herself she serves as town librarian. Often she takes books by truck to neighboring villages. Four evenings a week she gives up most of her dinner hour to inspect the eight illiteracy courses in town. She lives with a sister who is ill. That means she has to squeeze in a little time to play nurse and housekeeper. Week ends she's generally busy attending conferences, conventions, and meetings, sometimes at a great distance from Visegrad.

Mileva wears ski boots most of the year, woolen socks, a rough woolen dress that looks like an American department-store bargain basement. She does not use make-up of any kind. Her hair and her eyes are both deep brown. Almost black. She has never been out of Yugoslavia in her life. The idea of traveling any great distance frightens her. She says she is able to live by such an exacting schedule because "I never have time to think whether I'm tired." Also because "it's such an incentive to see how eager they all are for education." Some of the meetings she must attend are of the local school board to which she was elected by popular vote of the people. She occasionally reads a foreign newspaper. When she does, she's bothered by what she calls "some of the propaganda."

"For example," she says, "why do papers abroad keep talking about religion being abolished in our country? You know from traveling around Yugoslavia that it isn't true, don't you? You know that Madame Kamila's husband is a priest. He has the biggest church in Visegrad. You should go up and see the crowds at his church on Sunday." She also wanted to tell us about how women have found their place in the New Yugoslavia. She says women never had any maternity care here before. Women just—well, they just had babies. Now, one half our local hospital is a maternity ward.

But Madame Kamila was getting impatient to show us her "baby." So we followed her upstairs.

Chapter Forty

THIS WAS HER "BABY"!

BALKAN COUNTRIES are not celebrated for their cleanliness. Dirt and smells don't bother the Balkan people as they do us. But when we pushed open the door of that room on the second floor of the schoolhouse on the far bank of the river at Visegrad we had a pleasant surprise. The smells were of good food being cooked without benefit of stale fat. And the place looked as spotless as a model American kitchen. There were twenty girls in the room. Half Moslem. Half Christian. Some were in peasant costumes. Some were in "city clothes." But all of them had discarded their shoes and were wearing on their feet only thick knitted socks embroidered with pink, red, and yellow flowers. For hundreds of years Bosnian girls have worn socks of this design. For hundreds of years mothers have taught daughters exactly how to embroider them. If a girl is a virgin and is looking for a husband her socks have more "love flowers" on them than those worn by a woman who has found her man. I knew about Bosnian socks. Six years ago, going through this section, I bought a pair from a peasant girl because my feet were cold. I wore them for days before someone explained why I was providing the natives of the Bosnian hills with a bit of comic relief to the tragedy that was taking place all around them. I continued to wear them even after I was told that unconsciously I was advertising myself as a virgin in search of love's satisfaction.

The twenty girls were sitting around two sides of the room on plain wooden benches. They were knitting, sewing, and embroidering. The third wall was taken up with blackboards. The fourth side of the room was where the stoves and other pieces of kitchen equipment were. That's where the smells were coming from. The noon meal was being cooked in two separate kettles. That was because Christian Bosnians like their food cooked with lard which Moslems strictly avoid for religious reasons.

Madame Kamila explained that this school in the domestic arts was being sponsored by the Women's Anti-Fascist League. The pupils had come from all parts of the country. From as far away as Mioće, which is a good forty-five kilometers by donkey-back. The youngest pupil was fifteen. She had a lot of flowers on her knitted socks. Seven were married and had children back home. Neighbors were taking care of the children while the mothers were away. The course lasted for a month and the pupils had dormitory space right on the premises.

How did the husbands of the married women feel about their being away from home for so long? The seven young wives just smiled. But one of the instructors said that in most cases the husbands had come begging that their wives be allowed to take the course. The girls who had been picked as "yeast," to go back after their month of instruction and pass on the knowledge they had gained, were selected by local representatives of the league. They went to classes seven days a week from 8 A.M. until six in the afternoon. They were taught the theory and practice of such matters as child care, gardening, personal hygiene, handiwork, cooking, dairy and poultry husbandry, first aid, sewing, and even how to make soap. If any of them couldn't read or write they were required to go to illiteracy classes. They were also given some instruction in their rights and duties as citizens. Of the twenty bright-looking girls in the room it turned out that only three had been able to read and write at the start. The faculty included a local doctor, a local judge, three women from the Anti-Fascist League, the secretary of the People's County Council, and our friend the overworked professional teacher. She apparently was the real spark plug of the machine. But Madame Kamila was the driver.

Madame Kamila said that in the Old Yugoslavia there hadn't been one domestic-science school anywhere in the country that she knew about. Then she laughed and said:

"It's too bad you weren't here earlier in the course. Too bad you didn't see the girls trying to learn to operate sewing machines. It's the hardest thing to teach them. That's because the movement of the feet is so different than it is with a weaving machine. And they're all used to weaving machines."

We sat around the room with the girls for hours. We ate some of the food they had helped prepare. It was the best food we'd tasted in that part of the world. We leaned out the window with them watching a wedding party across the road doing a *kolo*. We noticed the excitement in their eyes. Especially in the eyes of the girls with many embroidered flowers on their knitted socks. Late in the afternoon one girl, a Moslem in long pantaloons of red silk fastened tightly at the ankles, made a little speech quite voluntarily. I wrote down her exact words. They didn't all make sense. But this is the way they came tumbling from her lips:

"Before, only the men could learn. We women suffered so much you would not believe. I and my young brother were in the Partisan medical corps. When Visegrad was attacked the first time my mother woke us up. We heard shooting everywhere. My brother was eleven then. I was fourteen. We got out of bed in our nightclothes. We ran out in our nightclothes. All we could see was burning houses. We ran to Rogatica. [That seemed incredible. Rogatica was a great many miles away. But we didn't interrupt.] We couldn't find out about our mother. Later we heard how our mother screamed. Then I went home without anything."

At this point the girl in the red pantaloons began crying. Her crying was contagious. Most of the other girls began crying too. Then the girl in the red pantaloons went on.

"We had a little piece of land. I left my brother in Sarajevo. I went back alone. My sister who was thirteen was killed. My sister stayed with my mother and she also was killed. But I found how good and helpful people are. The wife of a minister got me out of the camp. It was the Chetniks that did it. Then the Italians came and drove them out."

The mention of Chetniks gave Stanojka Todorović, one of the married pupils, her cue to tell us that she had been an eyewitness of the capture of Draža Mihailović, the Chetnik leader. I told Anita in a whisper that we mustn't miss any of this girl's story because American correspondents at the time had had many conflicting stories about how the capture actually took place. Stanojka said that Mihailović came to her village of Polanice with eleven of his followers. Polanice was a small village. Just fifteen or twenty houses. Mihailović and his eleven men were fed by two or three families in the village. After a few days some other men with long hair and beards came and joined the Chetnik refugees. It turned out later that they were members of the Partisan secret police. When they learned all they wanted to learn by playing they were Draža's friends they took all eleven of the Chetniks prisoner. That was what the married girl named Stanojke Todorović told us. But when she finished, another girl from the same village spoke up.

"Not eleven of them, Stanojka. Only ten. Remember Dragisha Vasilević. You remember how the people of the village killed him. They killed him three days before Draža was taken away. They killed him because they knew he was the Chetnik commander in our district and had done some of the worst things. They killed him right in front of the school. I know because I was there."

Then Stanojka said:

"Out of the rest of them two more were also killed by peasants. And then three were killed while the men in the fur hats were trying to arrest them. Everyone in the village was glad when it was all over. We'd had enough shooting and all that sort of thing."

When we left we thanked the girls and their teachers for a good meal, for some good stories, and also for a miscellaneous piece of intelligence we picked up during the afternoon:

The people of Bosnia don't use toothpaste. They say that eating enough corn bread does the same thing.

Chapter Forty-One

SOME STILL LIVE IN THE HILLS

Two things happened on the train ride from Visegrad back to Sarajevo. The first was considered serious for a time by passengers and crew alike. I don't think many people noticed the second.

A few miles out of Visegrad, halfway through one of the many tunnels in that area, a car in the middle of the train jumped the tracks. There was one locomotive pushing us and one pulling. The smoke from the two engines soon filled the tunnel and also began to fill the cars. There were no lights anywhere on the train. The aisles were crowded with people and luggage. There was real danger that unless something was done quickly a few hundred people would suffocate because the tunnel was long and there was no system of ventilation. But the crowd took it in its stride. Most of them began to sing. Individually and in chorus. The only hysteria was on the part of the Little Flower. He kept opening a door of our car and demanding of the darkness outside what had happened and what was going to be done about it and when. Each time he let in volumes of additional smoke. What finally happened was that some bright railroad men unhooked the derailed car, jammed the passengers into other cars, and then pulled the two pieces of the train out of the tunnel in opposite directions. When we were in daylight again Anita looked critically at the fat reporter and whispered to me:

"After this let's not pick any flowers along the way."

The other thing that happened was that two small boys got onto the train at one of the mountain-town stops. When a gendarme came through checking *legitimacijas* the two boys, who were about ten and twelve years old, said they didn't have any identity papers. The gendarme asked them where they were going. The older boy shrugged his shoulders and said:

"Anywhere."

"Where have you come from?"

Both boys pointed up into the desolate hills beside the right of way. The gendarme looked at them sternly for a moment. Suddenly he bent down and patted their heads. Then he hurried on, as if a little ashamed of his display of emotion. When the conductor came along he found that they had no railroad tickets. An army officer standing in the aisle told the conductor to "forget it." Another man in the corridor opened a suitcase and handed each boy a chunk of black peasant bread. They grabbed at the food as if they hadn't eaten in weeks. It was gone in less than a minute. Then the train slowed down for a sharp curve. The older boy threw open the car door and they both jumped. I watched them roll over in the ditch and then get to their feet. As the train began to pick up speed the older boy waved. He seemed to be waving a thank you to the gendarme, the conductor, and the man who had given them the bread. The younger-looking didn't wave. He was staring up into the hills. I wondered what was going on inside his small mind. But maybe I had the answer from what I saw on his face.

PART FOUR

These Are the Dalmatians

Chapter Forty-Two

NIKO THE *APOTEKAR*

NIKO JEZIĆ is about sixty years old. He's a giant of a man and he boasts that he weighs one hundred and twenty kilos. He's slightly bald with wisps of white hair and he wears gold-rimmed eyeglasses. We found him standing in the door of his *apoteka* shop on the piazza inside the Old City of Dubrovnik as he does almost every day from dawn until dusk. The shop has been in the same place for generations. It's a thing of beauty, done entirely in golds and white. On the white-painted shelves there are many rows of jars and bottles. They are all milky white with the Latin letters in raised gold. Once Niko used to compound all the prescriptions himself. Today a dark-haired girl pharmacist helps him. Today he spends much of his time standing in the doorway to greet old friends and make new ones. He speaks a few words of Russian, English, French, and German. Niko is especially happy when the tourist season arrives, for his greatest delight is telling strangers about his first love. It's a love which is greater than that he bears for his wife, or for his apoteka, or for his only son who is a doctor in Switzerland. His great passion is for this city surrounded by ancient stone walls. This part of a city which people call the Old Dubrovnik. He knows every bit of its history and lore. He can tell you, for example, how here in the seventh century fugitives from a Greek colony across the bay founded the first real republic anywhere in Europe. It was called Ragusa in the early days and still is by many people. He will tell you how Ragusa survived as an independent state during long centuries when Hungarians, Turks, and other foreign people were ruling over all the rest of Dalmatia. Over much of the then civilized world. He will take you on a walk along the top of the gray-stone walls which encircle the Old City and tell you how, until the days of planes and bombs, these walls were a protection against the military and naval might of any potential invader. But then Niko will stop and say that you must understand one thing about his city. Dubrovnik, or Ragusa, was peace-loving. Always. The people never fought except in self-defense. They often kept the peace by clever diplomacy. There were periods when it had "protectors." But the people paid the "protectors" handsomely in tribute for the privilege of running their own affairs.

In the days when it was the custom to use an army to extend one's frontiers, Dubrovnik preferred to acquire additional land by purchase, or by rent agreements, rather than by conquest. Niko will tell you how for hundreds of years Dubrovnik disputed the mastery of the Adriatic with greater Venice. But it was generally a peaceful rivalry. Dubrovnik was centuries ahead of her time. She believed in democracy before the word was invented. She believed in diplomacy in the days when others believed only in the sword. As you promenade with Niko he will boast that in the days when illiterate nobles in the rest of the Balkans were eating with their fingers and signing treaties by dipping their fingers into bottles of ink, this city on the edge of the Adriatic was giving the world a literature which many great nations might have been proud to call their own. Poetry of all kinds flourished here, even in the dark days when armies of Arabs were sweeping up the coast. Even in the dark days when the Turks were oppressing most of Europe and killing off the culture of the lands they occupied. Ragusa in those periods had her own art. Her own coins. Her own diplomats in far corners of the world. Her own "most-favored-nation" treaties with sultans and kings. Her own system of democracy. The chief of state was the rector. But he was never allowed to become a dictator. They saw to that by allowing him to hold office for only one month at a time. He was just the titular head. The man who made speeches at public banquets. The real power was in the hands of fifty-one senators. Five of them were elder statesmen. They had to be more than fifty years old and they had the right of veto over the acts of the others.

Niko will tell you how African pirates, and Serbian tribes, and armies of the sultans all tried to destroy this oldest of republics. And how they all failed. It was nature rather than man that brought about the decline of Ragusa. Nature in the form of earthquakes. The first was in 1520. It caused twenty thousand deaths. But the most fatal convulsion of the earth was on Easter Day in 1667. Two thirds of the population was wiped out. On the island of Lopud in the harbor thirteen thousand six hundred of the fourteen thousand inhabitants were killed. The city was destroyed as completely as some of Europe's larger cities were destroyed by man-made devilment in the past few years. Even the great walls which had held out foreign invaders for so long a time cracked and crumbled.

Dubrovnik burned for seventeen days. But while the flames were still eating their way through the ruins, the Senate met and sent out a call for volunteers to come and settle here and help with the reconstruction. Most of those who responded were Slavs from the hills. Before many years their blood was being mixed with the blood of old Ragusa families. With ancient Greek and Latin blood. But Dubrovnik never got over the earthquake. Niko will show you invocations over many doorways today. Words carved in stone asking God to spare Dubrovnik from future violent acts of nature. He will point out the great clock tower built in 1480 and tell you how the earthquake tipped it into a weird angle, and how it remained at that angle until it was finally rebuilt in 1929. He will show you two monasteries, the Custom's House, and the Rector's Palace, which were the only buildings to survive the two quakes and a fire which swept through the city in 1706. But then he'll tell you about Napoleon. It was Napoleon who did what others had tried so hard to do and had failed. Napoleon conquered Ragusa. He declared the ancient republic at an end. Of course, after Napoleon's final defeat an attempt was made to revive the old glory of this city on the shore of the Adriatic. But then the Austrians came and hauled down the flag of Sveti Vlaho. Now Dubrovnik is just another city in one of the six republics of the New Yugoslavia.

While you're walking with Niko he'll point across the blue water to the luxuriant island of Lokrum covered with subtropical trees and flowers and tell you how it's called by some Maximilian's Island, because from there went the man who was to become emperor of Mexico and die in a civil war. Richard the Lion-Hearted was shipwrecked on that island. He had a plan to build a monastery there which might have been the greatest monastery in this part of the world. But when he heard about the earthquakes he changed his mind.

Niko isn't a man with much hate in his soul. But he hates the Germans for having disturbed the recent peace of his city. Yet he'll smile with understanding when he tells you that before the days of the Nazis the Germans called this place *Die Märchenstadt an der Adria:* the fairyland of the Adriatic.

Niko will take you through the arched doorway of the *Sponza* or medieval mint and show you words put on the wall with white chalk: *Tito nash otac; Republika nasha majka* (Tito is our father; the Republic is our mother), and he'll tell you that the mint is now a youth center and trade union headquarters.

If, as you're touring the city's churches with him, you mention that there's a story abroad that the New Yugoslavia has attempted to kill religion in the country, Niko will throw back his head and his large body will shake with laughter. Then he'll suggest that believers of such tales visit his city on February the third, which is the day of Dubrovnik's patron saint, Vlaho, whose likeness is over every gate of the city. That's the day when peasants in their native costumes come in from all the nearby Dalmatian villages for the greatest religious ceremony of the year. It begins at 6 A.M. and lasts long into the evening. Strangers are most interested in the costumes of the women from the Konavlje. That's the rich valley to the south of the walled city which, in the days of the republic, was part of Ragusa. The beauty of the peasant women and the fine features of the men of the Konavlje are reputed to stem from past indiscretions of the young blades of Ragusa who stole away to the Konavlje villages when they were in search of forbidden romance. The girls of the Konavlje have a costume peculiar to their own small area. A pale blue apron over a full-flowing white skirt which accentuates their broad hips and makes their wasplike waists look almost deformed by comparison. A white blouse with rich embroidery at the throat. A small flat cap of deep red and pale blue.

During the morning of Sveti Vlaho Day there's a great procession through the piazza to the cathedral. The bishop is followed by a dozen priests carrying the bones not only of Sveti Vlaho but also of lesser saints. Sveti Vlaho's skull is carried in a silver receptacle shaped like a skull, with a piece of glass in the top so that any unbeliever can see for himself that the petrified head is inside. The legs, arms, and torso are carried in separate containers of silver. It's a right of the people along the way, a right many take advantage of, to ask the priest carrying the skull or any other part of the body to pause while the silver container is kissed. Each priest carries a white napkin to wipe off the container before the next person kisses it.

Niko's eyes dance as he tells you how the city's ancient flags are taken to the cathedral for their annual blessing. He says former Partisan officers, now members of the People's Council, lead the Sveti Vlaho procession through the piazza.

Niko likes to take his guests past the clock tower on the dot of the hour so they'll be standing there as the doors of the belfry automatically open and two figures come parading out with hammers in their hands to strike the great bell the proper number of times. If you are tired from your tour

Niko will suggest a cup of *café mit schlag* in the Gradska Kafana. There, while an orchestra plays gypsy tunes as only an orchestra of gypsies can, Niko may tell you about himself and his apoteka.

Is the place as old as it looks?

Well, Niko will say, not so old the way things are figured here in old Dubrovnik. It was founded in 1420. But that's not old, for even then there was another apoteka in town. His shop was established by the ancient republic of Dubrovnik and was run as a State establishment until the Frenchmen came, under Napoleon, and took this city for their own. The Frenchmen were hungry for money, so they sold the old apoteka to a family named Sharić. Four generations of the Sharićs ran it. In 1922 Niko himself came down from the city of Fiume and took over. In his day such famous people as the Duke of York and his wife, and Mrs. Wallis Simpson and the Duke of Windsor, have been his patrons. Niko showed them all around the city, and he likes to tell how Edward and Mrs. Simpson danced, one night, "right in this place we're now in; right in the Gradska Kafana."

It was toward the end of 1942 that Niko and his wife, whose grandfather was one of Yugoslavia's greatest poets, began to play their part in helping the Partisans.

They were receiving shipments of medicine from Germany. They knew that off in the hills and forests the Partisans were badly in need of such supplies. So, at night, when no one was around, Niko and his wife used to make up assortments of drugs, wrap them in stout packages, and send them by secret couriers through German lines to the front.

Niko laughs as he tells about it.

"The Nazis shipped the drugs to us from Germany, and as fast as they came, we would ship them off to the Germans' worst enemies."

Only once were Niko and his wife caught in the act. It was in 1943. They prepared an extra large shipment. A friendly truck driver was to see that it got through German lines and started on its way. But he was stopped by Gestapo agents who demanded an explanation of the large package. The driver admitted it contained drugs but said they were going to Montenegro to be shipped on to Albania. The Germans were suspicious and took him back to Niko's shop to check his story. When Niko said the same thing, having rehearsed the story for an hour with the driver before he set out, the package of pills and liquids was allowed to go through.

It was just five months before the end of the war that Niko decided he could stay home no longer. So he talked it over with his wife and they agreed to take the big step together. They closed and bolted their shop, drew the iron shutters, sneaked through German lines, and enlisted in the Partisans. Niko was made a medical officer and was given a fine uniform. His wife carries a picture with her, wherever she goes, of Niko in that uniform. She herself became a nurse.

What does Niko think of the New Yugoslavia?

Before he can answer, his wife says quickly:

"You know, of course, that the apoteka is being nationalized by the government? Soon it will no longer be ours!"

And then Niko explains.

For many years the right to run a pharmacy in Yugoslavia has been a concession granted to an individual by the government. Now, the government policy is that the people must have access to good medicines at the lowest possible price. So the government is going to withdraw the licenses one by one and operate all the large pharmacies in the country. His is one of the first being nationalized, by the simple process of the government taking an inventory of his stock and giving him a check.

Mrs. Niko quickly adds:

"But don't forget, my dear, they say you will also get a pension from the government for as long as you live."

How does he feel about losing his place of business? Won't he miss standing in the door of the glittering white shop, with its rows of gold-decorated bottles?

Niko smiles a bit sadly.

"My welfare is secondary to the welfare of the people. I am not bitter about it. You see, I really believe in the aims of this new regime. If I must suffer a little so that great masses of people may benefit, wouldn't I be selfish to object? After all, I am still young. Not sixty yet. Not quite. I'm still capable of working."

Then the two bronze figures on the clock pop out and begin to pound out the hour of eight. Niko looks at his wife and she nods. They're sorry. They must go now. Won't we come and see them in Fiume sometime? Only be sure to remember, it isn't Fiume any more; it's a Yugoslav city now and it's called Rijeka. He's going back to the city of his birth. He'll miss his Dubrovnik. But it will be better for him not to be around when a manager takes over on behalf of the State.

Chapter Forty-Three

MORE "ENEMIES OF THE REGIME"

DUBROVNIK is the most cosmopolitan city in all Yugoslavia. There was much wealth here before the war, and the inhabitants have many blood strains mixed in with their own. In the shops of Dubrovnik you can buy books in foreign languages and such items as soft toilet tissue, cleansing cream for a lady's face, ribbons for a typewriter, and even eight and a half by eleven bond paper for the manuscript of a book. Violets were blooming in Dubrovnik in March when we got there. And forsythia too. The apple trees were full of blossoms. After so long a time in the frosty mountains of Bosnia, Dubrovnik looked like paradise. It was a temptation to stay longer than just long enough to get bathed, haircutted, and supplied with medicines and food for more journeying. The fact that we had each collected a great many fleas, all of them possessed with a deeply rooted maternal instinct, and our discovery that DDT is to a flea what sugar is to a bee, made "civilized" Dubrovnik even more attractive. The first night in the Argentina Hotel on a hill on the edge of the city Anita snapped on a radio. An orchestra was playing American jazz. The Czech announcer said it was a record by "Duka Ellingtown." Anita said, "Maybe it doesn't make any sense, but it sounds awfully good, doesn't it?"

On the great mountain behind the city called Srgj someone had painted in white letters at least twenty feet high the words:

"Tito Republika."

But that doesn't mean that all the people with handsome villas in and around Dubrovnik get up and cheer every time the marshal's name is mentioned. As a matter of fact Dubrovnik has the reputation of being the spot in Yugoslavia which is most out of sympathy with the present regime. That's principally because of the wealth that was once concentrated in the city. Even politicians in small American cities know that people generally "vote their pocketbooks." That they generally favor a system or a leader who promises to improve their own financial position and that they oppose a system or a leader who seems to jeopardize their financial position.

One afternoon in the Gradska Kafana Anita and I saw a tall, distinguished-looking woman having tea. The waiter said she was the sister of one of Yugoslavia's wealthiest men before the war, by virtue of his ownership of a large fleet of ocean-going ships, most of them named after kings. The government nationalized all of his property it could get its hands on. But his sister still has a large villa on the edge of Dubrovnik. She still dresses extremely well. And as she sits having her afternoon tea she does not look tragically unhappy. But no one has ever seen her get up and cheer when Tito's name is mentioned.

Although life does somehow flow on for those who once were so rich in the possession of worldly goods, the lack of spirit and enthusiasm for the present regime is everywhere apparent in Dubrovnik. Yet it's difficult to find anyone to voice any specific complaints. That's because the really violent enemies of the administration have nearly all left Dubrovnik for places of refuge abroad. Those who have remained are mostly people who are reconciled to changing, somewhat, their way of life. When they do talk, their stories are all about the same. It boils down to the fact that they resent it, if they had four houses and six motorcars, having had three houses and five of the motorcars confiscated. It's a resentment which is quite understandable.

In Dubrovnik we met the owner of one of the city's finest villas. Madame Vladamira Petraki is also one of the most beautiful women in a city which boasts of having the most beautiful women in all Europe. Not even eliminating the women of Budapest. We rented a motorboat and Madame Petraki went with us to the island of Lokrum to see a hundred war orphans living in what used to be a monastery before it became the hideout of a broken-hearted Hapsburg princess.

The director of the orphanage introduced us to children of Chetnik commanders and men of the Ustaši who had killed the parents of other children in that same orphanage. She explained that the motto of the institution is:

"Children are not to be blamed for the sins of their fathers."

One small boy, with a tragic hunger for affection, held onto our hands every minute we were on the island and he cried real tears when we left. When we noticed one small child with both hands cut off at the wrists tears came into Madame Petraki's eyes and she said:

"Is it really possible that there are human beings who could do such things? I still can hardly believe it!"

At the end of the island we saw another kind of wreckage of war. Three smashed German cannon. An Italian soup kitchen. And a former German naval barracks with some brilliant murals on the shell-torn walls done by some member of the garrison force who showed how homesick he was by painting scenes of beaches along the Elbe River.

On the way back Vladamira Petraki and I sat alone at one end of the boat. She asked if anyone had told me about what the Dubrovnik people call "The Miracle of Sveti Vlaho." During the occupation, she said, at a time when the people of the walled city were beginning to go hungry, two German ships hit some mines in the harbor. Both of them were loaded with sacks of wheat. As the ships sank the sacks floated ashore. And so for two years the people of Dubrovnik ate well. The city's patron saint, Sveti Vlaho, was given full credit.

On the way back I tried to get Madame Petraki to talk about herself and her attitude toward the regime. I begged her to tell me the truth. I said I knew that she had lost much. I knew she was not living in the style to which she had been accustomed. She could leave Yugoslavia, couldn't she? Wouldn't she like to leave? Why didn't she leave? How did she really feel? No one else on the boat could hear us. And if she wished I'd keep confidential anything she told me.

The lovely lady looked across the blue water for a full minute saying nothing. Then suddenly her eyes brightened. She had the answer. She pointed to a steep cliff on the shore.

"That section is called Boninovo. That cliff is named Suicide Jump because so many heartsick young people have jumped from there into the sea. I think they are all very foolish. You have to be very young or very old to do that, don't you? At my age, life is good whatever happens. Do you understand what I mean?"

Chapter Forty-Four

WOMEN WITHOUT MEN

SITTING in the rather intimate dining room of the Argentina Hotel at Dubrovnik, Anita and I worked while we ate. All the time we stayed here we took down every word of conversation we overheard at the other tables. Because we always spoke English to each other, our fellow guests were off their guard.

So what do people talk about in the dining room of a rather good hotel, in a city of Yugoslavia which has the reputation of being very "anti"?

The men at the next table talked constantly, meal after meal, about fishing.

The man and his wife beyond them talked through all one dinner about the fact that when the government called in all the old money and issued new, people of Dubrovnik turned in twenty-seven million dinar in one-thousand-dinar bills alone. That's only five hundred thousand dollars, but they thought it was a great deal.

Food was a favorite subject, as it is in all *pensions*.

Two young women complained that all the films they were getting in Dubrovnik were Russian. Why couldn't they have some American movies?

A tall, thin, sad-looking man at a far table, who always ate with his hat on and whom we labeled "The Cadaver" because he seemed on the verge of death, talked poetry, philosophy, and religion in first one and then another of the six languages he knew equally well. He talked much about Paris. He'd lived in Paris for sixteen years.

Dushanka sat alone. She read a book at every meal. It wasn't until our last day in Dubrovnik that we went on a boat trip with her and found out something about her. Dushanka was a '41 Partisan. She wore one of those glittering silver-and-gold stars over her heart. She had been a battle-front Partisan. She had used a machine gun and had taken part in a great deal of killing. She'd lived the hard life of the mountains for years with men from whom she asked no consideration because of her sex. Now Dushanka was one of the editors of the same Sarajevo newspaper whose editor had contributed the Little Flower to us for our greater pleasure while touring the mountains of Bosnia. Dushanka was as vigorous and vital a character as the Little Flower was pale. She talked in sharply bitten-off words. Her mind was as keen as a razor edge. Her fund of knowledge about any subject which came up for discussion was immense.

You couldn't use the words "lovely" or "pretty" or "beautiful" or any other really feminine expressions about Dushanka. Her life in the hills had made her hard and masculine. I couldn't imagine taking her arm to guide her across the street. I couldn't even imagine a man holding her hand, no matter how soft the moonlight. Dushanka wore slacks most of the time. And there's nothing a girl can do that's more effective in keeping men from looking a second time than wearing slacks. Her hair was not neatly curled or waved. She used a little make-up, but she used it badly. She smoked cigarettes like a man. She instinctively resisted any small masculine courtesy that came her way.

Anita saw Dushanka alone several times. After we left Dubrovnik, Anita said:

"There's a tragedy in Dushanka and in all these other Partisan girls. Out of the war there's come, here in Yugoslavia and perhaps in some other countries too, a whole race of frustrated women. In the mountains they discovered, with machine guns and rifles and hand grenades, that they were not really dependent on men at all. Also, in the mountains they learned to live almost as animals. Of course you realize that in the mountains there was no lipstick. No perfume. No pretty clothes. Men accepted them as their equals in battle and their equals in every other way. That was good. To a point. But now look what's happening. The war ends. The Partisans come home from the mountains. The men have the greatest respect for these girls they call their 'comrades.' They pay honor and tribute to them. But that isn't what they want. Not now. The men call them 'comrades' and pay honor to them. And then they take pretty little feminine things to dances and parties. You can't blame the men. They're hungry for pretty little feminine things after those years in the mountains. But what about these girls they call 'comrades'? Maybe you think they don't want love and tenderness and affection! If you do, that's because you're not a woman and you don't understand."

Chapter Forty-Five

BUT THEY DO SING

OUR LAST DAY in Dubrovnik Anita went into town shopping. She came back with a copy of the Belgrade newspaper *Borba* and a cable from New York telling her to stop all this "foolishness" and get home in a hurry. *Borba* contained a two-column article about some of the public statements being made in the United States by Ambassador Patterson who had spent much of the time since he had been sent to Yugoslavia back in America telling the people of America what he thought about Yugoslavia. The article quoted paragraph after paragraph of the Ambassador's accusations. Charges of the obliteration of religion by the new Yugoslav Government. Dictatorship over discontented masses by an evil group of tyrants. Charges of forced labor and suppression of liberties. The picture of a miserable people being driven along an unhappy path against their will. The article quoted the Chicago *Tribune,* the Baltimore *Sun,* and the Washington *Times-Herald.* It carried quotations from a U.P. story out of Houston, Texas. In an editorial statement, *Borba* (which means The Struggle) said:

"We have quoted Mr. Patterson at great length so our people may know the charges he is making and so they themselves may judge the truth or irresponsibility of such charges. We also wish to show how Mr. Patterson is fulfilling his task of creating friendly relations between our country and his."

Anita said:

"It ought to prove something that the leading Yugoslav paper with a circulation all over the country dares to print these charges. If they were as true as Mr. Patterson says they are, wouldn't . . ."

But I wasn't listening. I was looking out from the balcony across the blue Adriatic. Out there two small Yugoslav naval vessels were moving swiftly through the water. From both boats came the music of many voices. The sailors were singing some of their Partisan songs. I sat there wondering whether Ambassador Patterson had ever left that office with the dancing girls on the ceiling long enough to hear these Yugoslav people singing. Singing out loud. Singing as if they meant it.

Then, suddenly, the singing stopped. The reason was soon apparent. A cloud of black smoke went up from just behind one of the boats. Then, a split second later, there was the noise of an explosion. A shout went up from both the boats. They got it! Another mine which had broken loose from its moorings during the war and had been jeopardizing Adriatic shipping ever since had been exploded by gunfire from the patrol vessel.

I sat there remembering that we had been told there are still a great many of these escaped mines between here and the city of Split. Any one of them could send a good-sized ship to the bottom. In a few hours we would be out there on the Adriatic on a ship which wasn't even "good-sized."

Chapter Forty-Six

THEY LOVE THEIR ADRIATIC

THERE'S A SAYING in these parts that no matter how far a sailor roams, no matter what attractions he may see in distant places, he will always return home, if he's from the Dalmatian coast. They have a great affection for their sea and their land, these Dalmatians. It explains many things. It may explain some of the people of Dubrovnic. It surely explains Filip Misić and Ivusha Napica. Filip Misić is the captain of a steamer called the *Rab*. He has lived forty-seven years. Thirty of them he's spent at sea. He's been all over the world. Wherever a man can get to by water. But he never stays away from Dalmatia very long. He's learned four languages in his travels. He speaks English as well as some foreigners who have lived in Paris for twenty years speak French. And yet Filip Misić was only in the United States a few times, the last time fifteen years ago. And he rarely hit an English port.

Filip Misić has the typical sea captain's face: bronzed as an Indian's, with deep lines furrowed in it by wind and weather.

About the *Rab*. The Italians took her. And then the Germans took her away from the Italians. She was sunk at an Adriatic seaport called Crikvenica by bombs dropped from forty British or American planes while she had seven hundred Germans aboard. Misić knows all about it, because he saw it happen. He wasn't on the *Rab* then. Oh no!

"I refused to work for them. I just took my little sailboat and I fished for all of three years."

The *Rab* was raised after the war and now she's on a passenger and freight run from Dubrovnik up to Rijeka. She's an old vessel and she can't make much speed, but the bronze-faced man at the wheel loves her, and he's happy.

About the mines which he and several lookouts on the bridge keep hunting with their eyes? What would they do if they saw one? He laughs deeply and says:

"We see them every trip. We treat them just as you would if you met someone on the street who was *antipatić*. We go a bit to port or starboard and avoid them!"

Ivusha Napica is only a naval cadet on the Adriatic run, but he takes the wheel sometimes and is looking forward to the day when he passes his examinations so he can wear the uniform of a second officer. Anita and I interviewed him in his cabin. He's twenty-two years old but he looks younger, despite his war experiences. He has red cheeks which the girls probably envy, soft blue eyes, and a youthful self-importance.

Ivusha was born in Dubrovnik of a poor family, but he did have a roof over his head, a clean bed to sleep in, and food that was at least substantial. He went into the Partisan Army voluntarily, even though it did mean that for weeks, maybe years, he would at times have to go hungry, suffer the rigors of winter in the mountains without shoes and adequate clothing, and for long periods would have no contact with home and would be in ignorance of what had happened to his family. The last was the most difficult because of Ivusha's strong love for his mother and sister.

Ivusha was seventeen when he joined up. One brother who had gone in before him had already been killed. Another brother enlisted with Ivusha. The sister, who stayed at home with the mother, was then just fourteen.

At first the Partisans made the boy stay in Dubrovnik, gathering food, medicine, and weapons for them, and then sneaking through German lines with the supplies. He took back leaflets which had been printed on Partisan presses up in the mountains.

He became a fighter in 1944. That was the year his sister and mother had to flee from Dubrovnik because of threats by the Ustaši. Both of them then joined the Partisan Army as nurses.

Late in the war he heard that his mother was in a town fifty or sixty miles from where he was stationed. He got a short leave to visit her. It meant working his way through two German lines. He did it, only to find that one hour before he completed his journey his mother had been sent somewhere else.

He didn't see his mother and sister until after the war. Then, he says:

"We all met, my mother, my sister, and my older brother, as comrades. As fellow Partisans."

After the war Ivusha heard that it was the Chetniks who had killed his other brother and that it had happened at a town called Slivnica. The mother was eager to find the body because she wanted a "proper funeral," so the two of them went to Slivnica. Villagers told them what had happened. Hundreds of men had been killed here. Women slit the throats of the victims, and then the men hauled the bodies to what people in the neighborhood called a "bottomless pit" and threw them in.

Ivusha and his mother saw the bones of about a hundred men on a rock ledge, partway down in the pit. They also saw something else. At the mouth of the pit there were four heads on spikes. Birds and weather had left them little more than skulls. But when she looked at the second head, the mother began screaming.

"She recognized it as my brother's head because of some gold teeth he had."

They took the head home with them and in Dubrovnik a state funeral was held, with thousands present.

"For seven days," Ivusha said, "my mother was crazy. Really out of her head. Insane. It wasn't just finding the skull. It was the stories the peasants told her, about how my brother had been tortured, because they considered him one of the Partisan ringleaders."

Some months later the Chetnik leaders responsible were brought to trial in Dubrovnik and were executed. But Ivusha's mother, he says, has never been "quite the same since."

And now this boy who has lived so much in a mere twenty-two years is on his way to being an Adriatic ship captain. He could have gone to an army college, but he doesn't like dry land. So he went to the naval academy and now . . .

His eyes danced with happiness as he said:

"In a few weeks I take my second officer examinations. And then, after two years, I shall be a captain, and after that, a master. What more could a man ask for, who loves the sea?"

But there was one more tragedy in his young life which he told Anita about privately. He had been in love, when he joined the Partisans, with a girl who, he said, "was the most beautiful girl in all Dubrovnik, which is saying a lot."

They found ways of smuggling letters back and forth to each other. The minute he got home from the army he looked for her. They told him that she was dead. She had been picked up by the Germans on suspicion, and because they found some of his letters in her possession she was executed as a Partisan spy.

"I don't think I shall ever fall in love again in my life," said Ivusha, who is just twenty-two.

And then he asked Anita for a date.

Chapter Forty-Seven

LABOR—BEFORE, DURING, AFTER

SPLIT is Yugoslavia's principal seaport and is surrounded by walls which they say are two thousand years old. The city at various times in its long history has been part of five nations, France, Austria, Venice, Italy, and now Yugoslavia.

When we arrived at Split the people were talking about the fact that a Yugoslav consul, who came from this section, had been killed by Chetnik inmates of a camp in Italy before the eyes of British guards when he went into the camp on official business with all the proper credentials.

It was a bad time for us to visit Split, because Yugoslav-Anglo-American relations were not at their best. But here, as everywhere, although they knew we were Americans they treated us well as individuals.

In Split we called at a government office on a thoroughfare called The Street of the Sacrifice of Sin. (That's how it sounds, although in Serbo-Croat there is a silent "j" on the end of the "Sin.") The street is named in memory of twenty-three young men of Split who were executed by the Italians in 1941 on the sole charge that they were members of a sports club. The Italians thought, incorrectly, that the sports club was some sort of sinister organization.

We called at the government office to get a pass to visit the Split shipyards. We had talked, up to now, with city people, with diplomats, with peasants, with sailors, but as yet we had talked with no workmen. This was our chance.

The five shipyard men we interviewed, alone, so they could talk as they wished, included a mechanic, an electric welder, a structural ironworker, a locksmith, and an unskilled laborer. They were all in their twenties or thirties.

First they told us what had happened here during the war. When the Italians took over the yards, most of the men either fled to the woods with the Partisans, or engaged in a "slow down" and sabotage. Finally the Italians were forced to bring in their own workmen. The mechanic, Lino Pavaca, told how the Italians interned him on a Sicilian island, how he worked his way to Trieste, and then walked the one thousand kilometers to Split to join the Partisans. The electric welder, Vinko Puizina, had a story of torture to tell which included everything from the castor-oil treatment to burning his eyes with cigarettes.

It was the locksmith, Marko Prokopec, who gave us a description of the life of a shipyard worker before the war. He said:

"Our yards were owned, then, by French and British interests. Our pay was low. They hired and fired us indiscriminately. Any union activity was cause for imprisonment. We worked under extremely unsanitary conditions. There was a constant speed-up. Our wages ranged from three dinar to seven dinar an hour, which meant the average skilled worker made the equivalent of thirty American dollars a month. The trouble was that much of the time we were unemployed."

The structural ironworker, Bartul Alujević, by contrast, painted the picture of conditions today. He said:

"It's all changed now. Today there is full employment the year round for anyone who wishes to work. Our rate of pay runs from eleven to seventeen dinar per hour. Now the average skilled worker draws thirty-four hundred dinar a month, or sixty-eight American dollars, which will buy about twice what the average wage would buy before the war.

"We are working mostly on boats that were sunk; repairing them. We've turned out more than one hundred ships since the liberation."

Drago Dumanić, the fifth man, said:

"You should hear about the cultural life of a shipworker today. We have our own cultural center, our own motion-picture equipment, our own orchestra which plays our music, and your—your—what do call it?"

The other four men said "Jazz" in chorus and they all thought it was funny and laughed.

"We have two dramatic groups, a library of five hundred books, a sports club which holds football and ping-pong matches, and we just received a flag for having the best wall newspaper in Split.

"We workers have formed an apprentice school for boys who work half the day and study the other half.

"On week ends, teams of us take our tools and go out into the villages to repair plows and other machinery for the peasants. We make no charge for this work. Nobody pays us."

Did they have any complaints about their new government; was there anything about it they didn't like?

At first they didn't seem to understand. Then one of them spoke up and said:

"You talk as if this was something someone had forced onto us. You foreigners must understand that this is *our* government; a people's government. If there is anything we don't like, we shall change it. All the time there are things which are not perfect here in Yugoslavia. We are new at this—this business of running ourselves. We make many mistakes. But they are our own mistakes and"—he smiled with a great deal of self-satisfaction as he said it—"they are our own mistakes and we shall not make the same mistake twice."

Chapter Forty-Eight

THEY CALL "HI, SERGE!"

ONE night in Split Anita went to bed early with a headache, so I went to bed with an American newspaper which someone at the British Consulate had given me. I was enjoying being home again, synthetically, until on page five I saw a three-column picture from Fort Fairfield, Maine, showing tons of what the caption called "surplus potatoes" that had been dumped into a valley to rot. I knew that all this foodstuff might be going to waste because of any one of a number of maladjustments in our complicated economic system. I knew that the potato growers of Maine weren't to blame. But I couldn't help thinking of the children we had seen in Bosnia whose bodies were turning yellow because they had nothing to eat but corn. I couldn't help thinking of the repeated appeals that had gone out from Belgrade to Washington for food of any kind. So I got up, dressed, and went out in search of something that would keep me from thinking.

It was midnight. All of Split had gone to bed. Except that from somewhere I could hear music, singing, and laughter. Those were just the things I needed. So I traced the noise and pushed open the door of a café. It looked like a private party. I started to back out. Then I heard a familiar voice and I saw a man with wild black hair coming toward me. Boris Rubenstein, a Rumanian by birth with a Canadian passport. I knew Boris as an able field worker for UNRRA but an odd character outside business hours. What he had done tonight proved it. A few days before, a new British consul had arrived in Split. Anglo-American-Yugoslav relations were in a delicate condition just then because of several unfortunate "incidents," among them the killing of the Yugoslav diplomatic official from Split in the British camp in Italy. The new consul was having hard going, so Boris arranged a party designed to put him on intimate terms with some of the "right people." At the party were Paul Le Cointre, the French consul, his wife, and his assistant, the new British consul, and three young Partisan officers who had become key figures in the government. Two of them were ministers in the Croatian cabinet. The third was assistant chief of the State Secret Police. All three were young and handsome. With them were three attractive girls who spoke odd bits of French and English.

It was midnight when Boris invited me to join the party. As yet the ice hadn't really been broken. But Boris was still working hard to get these people of three nationalities to know and to like one another. He was trying to teach the British consul to sing *"Hvala"*, a beautiful Yugoslav song which starts out:

> For each kind word
> That you spoke to me;
> For each glance,
> For each smile—thank you.

Each verse ends with the Serbian word *hvala,* which means thank you.

Then Boris tried to teach them all a Rumanian toast which requires that everyone touch his glass first to his heart, then to his forehead, then to his lips. After the toast is drunk each person is required to turn his glass upside down on top of his head to prove that he emptied it to the last drop.

The staid British consul was doing his best to show that he could, if occasion demanded, be "one of the boys." But when Boris insisted that the party try a new kissing game he had just learned, His Britannic Majesty's diplomatic representative to the once-sovereign seaport of Split tried to beg off. This, he said, was a bit out of his line. But Boris wouldn't let him off.

"First you kiss the girl on your left. Then you kiss the girl on your right. Then you change places with the man over there. But, sir, I said 'kiss' not 'peck.' A kiss is supposed to last a minimum of thirty seconds. I have a stop watch. Now begin again. No, that's . . ."

The girl on the consul's left was the partner of the assistant chief of what the Yugoslav public still calls *Osna,* the secret police. The assistant chief of Osna didn't like the game any better than the British consul did. At least not while his girl was being kissed.

The party went on until 5 A.M. It was a great effort on the part of a well-meaning young man to cement some strained diplomatic relations. I doubt whether it did much good. But the evening was a success for me because I met Serge. His last name is Katalinić, but everyone in Split calls him simply Serge. Before the war his family owned a large insurance company and was extremely wealthy. Serge himself owned fifteen houses. He was never exactly sure from one week to the next how many motorcars and launches and yachts were licensed in his name. Serge's most obvious claim to distinction was his height. Someone told me his height in meters and centimeters. I never did get it figured out in feet and inches. But he was inordinately tall, even for a Yugoslav, and he had a build that made Boris nickname him "Tarzan."

During the war some of the Katalinić property was destroyed. After the war the insurance company was nationalized and the Katalinićs lost most of their wealth. Serge, who spoke perfect English, told me the rest of the story himself. He decided to leave the country. This was no place for him. His kind were through in Yugoslavia. That was obvious. So, on the excuse that he wanted to go to Rome to collect some money that was owed to his family, he got a passport and went.

"From Rome I could have gone anywhere. To England or America even. Once in Italy I was free. But I only stayed there a short time and I didn't go to England or America or anywhere else. In a few weeks I began to get homesick for my own Dalmatian coast. I guess I missed the blue water of the Adriatic."

So he came back. And he said he had never regretted it. Today Serge Katalinić, the son of wealth, works for seventy-four dollars a month in a government office. He lives in a modest apartment and has no motorcars, launches, or yachts. But . . .

"I have the sea. And I can bathe in it whenever I choose. I have friends here. When I go down the street they all wave at me and call, 'Hi, Serge!' It hasn't been easy, of course. I won't say that I really like it. No man gives up what he has grown accustomed to without certain regrets. But I'm glad I came back. I'm happy, only in a different way now. Anyway, I'm where I belong. In Split. On the coast of the blue Adriatic."

Chapter Forty-Nine

ONE HUNDRED THOUSAND GUESTS FOR DINNER

ONE MORNING we took a small Adriatic steamer at Split for the island of Vis. There were two or three hundred peasants on board. Some of them had been sleeping on the quay all night for fear of missing the boat. They were loaded down with empty wine casks, live chickens, sacks of corn, wooden washtubs, mattresses, and even secondhand beds they'd bought on the mainland. It's thirty miles across the water to Vis and the trip takes four hours. The boat goes from Split to Vis on Mondays, Wednesdays, and Fridays. On Tuesdays, Thursdays, and Saturdays it runs in the opposite direction. The crew has Sundays off. One of the islanders on board said that once there were twenty-five thousand people on Vis. That was when she was part of the Austro-Hungarian Empire. During the three years Italy held her right after World War I the population dropped to fourteen thousand. Then she was given to Yugoslavia and at the start of this war there were only nine thousand. Today, when everyone's home, which isn't often, the population numbers about seven thousand five hundred. We could tell, when the steamer pulled in to the harbor of the town of Vis, that the ship's triweekly arrival is considered an "occasion." Most of the seven thousand five hundred seemed to be on the dock staring to see who was on board and who had brought what home with him. We could see by looking at the narrow twisting streets that the town had been built for mules and pedestrians, and not for vehicles of any kind.

Someone found us rooms in what they called a hotel on the water front. The patron was Nate Tomić. They said that Nate's son, Vjekoslav, had been one of the twenty hostages killed by the Italians. We didn't know the story of the twenty hostages, so they told us about them. Early in the war fifty or sixty of the island men went into the hills and became guerrillas. One night seven of them made a raid on Italian headquarters in a four-hundred-year-old stone fort at one end of the island. The forty Italian soldiers in the garrison were just sitting down to a spaghetti dinner and were off their guard. The seven guerrillas, armed with only five old rifles and twenty hand grenades, lined up the Italians with their faces toward the wall and their hands above their heads. They threatened to shoot the first man who moved. Then they stole a truckload of machine guns and machine-gun ammunition. They also found some maps and some highly secret military papers. They also ate the spaghetti dinner. Then they left. As they left they told the Italians they'd be back in a little while and if a single man had moved or had put down his hands they'd all be killed.

The island people liked that part of the story. They laughed a great deal over it and kept asking one another how long do you suppose those crazy Italians stayed that way, with their hands above their heads? The rest of the story they told very solemnly. The next day the Italians went to ten houses in Vis and ten houses over in the town of Komisa, on the other side of the island, and took twenty hostages away with them. They announced that if the guns and ammunition and papers weren't returned within three days the hostages would be shot. So the people held a meeting in each town. The families of the twenty hostages were all there. Nate Tomić said he attended the meeting in Vis. They argued about what to do. Finally they voted to send word to the Partisans in the mountains that they were to keep the guns and the ammunition and the papers, but they were always to remember what they had cost. And that's why the twenty hostages were killed. The son of this man who had rented us a couple of rooms was one of them. "That's his picture on the wall."

In the waiting room of the town hall we saw another picture. It was of a banquet held two years before in San Pedro, California. There was a well-thumbprinted letter in Croatian attached to the photograph by a string. Tom Vojković, a member of the County Council who had only two teeth, said there are a lot of people from Vis in San Pedro and at this banquet they raised two thousand and eighty-seven dollars to help the island.

There was also a picture on the wall of a naval battle off Vis between the Austrian and Italian fleets in 1866. Tom said there used to be a large stone monument in the town graveyard put up by the Austrians to commemorate their victory in that battle, but the Italians "on one of their recent visits to us" stole the monument and took it home with them. Tom said he wasn't sure but he'd heard it's in Bologna now, and that they have changed the wording on the stone to make it sound like an Italian victory. Tom also said that if we thought this colored picture was pretty we should have seen the one they had of the big Russian naval victory near the island. That one was three feet by four feet. They hid it in a peasant's home but the Italians found it and now it's over in Italy too.

Roko Radisić, who was tall and very blond and said he fought all through the Drina Valley with the Partisans, told us that if we were going to try to write anything about Vis we'd have to write the whole history of Europe, because Vis was settled thirty-three hundred years ago and had been part of ten different empires. The other men in the room laughed and said that was right, and did we know about all the great naval battles which had been fought around here, and about the remains of an old Greek town that was back in the hills. Then they said we'd better start at the beginning and go over and see the monks. So they took us to the Franciscan monastery, and an old monk in black robes and a white girdle who was nearly blind showed us how it was built on top of the ruins of a Roman amphitheater. He didn't think we believed him, so he took us down a long flight of steps and showed us some stone cages in which he said they kept the lions that they let loose against the Christians. The lions' dens were full of scrawny chickens. Then he showed us a vegetable garden where the monks grow onions, garlic, lettuce, and potatoes, and the place where they raise grapes to make their wine. He said these are bad times because there are only four monks now, and they're all getting too old to do much work, so they don't have much to eat. Anita said:

"Can you take us through the monastery so we can see how you live and what it's like inside?"

The old monk didn't say anything right away. He just took out a pair of spectacles very slowly and squinted through them at Anita as if she were mad. Then very solemnly he said:

"Young lady, no female has been inside that building for five hundred years!"

But if we were interested in history we could go into the entrance hall with him. In the entrance hall there was a tablet on the wall "which told everything." The only trouble was that it was in some strange script which Anita couldn't read. The monk couldn't read it himself very well either. As far as he could make out it said that the island was settled in the fourteenth century B.C. by what he called "Ilians," who were driven out by the Greeks, who were driven out by the Romans, who were driven out by the . . . Then he stopped, took off his spectacles, and said:

"But you aren't really interested in all that, are you?"

So we went back to the town hall. By that time someone had found Niko Pincetić, the president of the County Council, who had had two young sons in the Partisans. He said we must understand that life is hard on an island like this one. The soil is excellent for growing grapes, except that there isn't much soil. It all has to be sifted out from the rocks by hand, the way women sift flour, when they have any flour. Of course there used to be some fine fields on a plateau on top of the island, but the British came and made the peasants pull up all their grape "trees" and help make it into an airport. If we weren't afraid of a long walk we could go up there tomorrow and see that there's still the wreckage of a lot of planes around. Mostly American. He said that when the Austrians ran the island they sent shipload after shipload of engineers here to try to find water. But they never found it. The people of Vis just caught water in rain barrels. Then during the war British engineers with instruments of some kind came to look for water because it was taking so many ships to bring water over from Italy for all the thousands of men the British had here. Those men from England found water right away and they laid pipes, big pipes, all over the island and everyone had water. But when they left they took the pump with them. Now the pipe is still all over the island. But the people catch water in rain barrels again.

President Niko said that some people will tell you there are more mules on Vis than there are humans. But nobody knows for sure because the County Council doesn't keep any vital statistics on mules. That made everyone in the room laugh.

The people of Vis keep alive, he said, principally by growing grapes.

Each family has its own press. They carry the wine down to town in goat-skin containers which they strap to their backs. There was a time when the island shipped out more than one million gallons of wine a year. (Only he said it in hecter liters.) More than one million. But not any more. Some of the grape "trees" are two hundred years old. Now they've "got the sickness." That's the trouble with Vis. Everything's "got the sick-ness." The mules. The horses. The chickens. Even the earth. That's the reason the hills are covered with a weed with purple flowers that smells like an herb and people call St. John's Bread. It grows in places where the soil has "got the sickness." Of course many people at night, after working in their vineyards all day, go out and fish. The sardines from these waters are the best you can ask for.

Those four forts we saw? They're British. Built when the British held Vis early in the nineteenth century. They're crumbling to pieces now. Before long they'll look like the old Greek ruins.

Anita whispered to me that we ought to get some stories of what happened here during the war. President Niko said we had better get more paper to write it down on, because there's a great deal to tell. Of course we knew, didn't we, that Marshal Tito had his headquarters on the island for a long time? He had two caves up in the hills. Both were white-washed inside. He lived in one and worked in the other. But did we know about the Chinese-American pilot? No one ever did get his name. He was the one who landed the first plane on the island of Vis. It was the first plane many of the islanders had ever seen. Only no one was very happy about what happened. Some Partisan soldiers were parading down the road. The pilot was having trouble. The plane caught on fire and hit the column of Partisan soldiers. Fifteen or twenty of them were killed. The Chinese pilot died in a hospital that afternoon.

The Americans came here early in 1944 and the last of them didn't leave until September of the next year. Everyone liked the Americans and felt sorry for them when some of them cried just like babies because they wanted to go over onto the mainland and really fight. Did we know that the American password on the island was "okay"? And then there was the story maybe we'd heard about how an American pilot was shot down by a German fighter on the other side of the island. His plane sank, but he saved himself by holding onto some rocks out in the sea. Ten Partisans went out in a boat to get him. The German plane came down and killed nine of the men in the boat. But the American was finally brought back to shore all right. Alive.

Old Tom with the two teeth asked if we knew about the evacuation. The British and Americans wanted all the people on the island to go away. So they brought ships to take them down to El Chateau, in Africa. All the women and children and old people were supposed to go. But about one hundred of them refused. They wanted to stay and help.

"My wife and two daughters stayed. My wife helped do the cooking for the island. My daughters were busy building pillboxes."

About the Americans who were here, they all wanted to make it clear that the islanders had never taken any money from them. "We just gave them wine and anything else they wanted because they were our allies and we liked them."

When a man came in with a brown sack and put it down on the president's desk they said we would have to excuse them now, because the mail had come in and they would all have to get to work. The mail came just three times a week. It obviously was an important occasion.

So Anita and I went for a walk through the twisting narrow streets. That was how we met Nick Zitko, who spoke understandable English because, he said, he had spent fifteen years gum digging in New Zealand. He came home to Vis nearly thirty years ago, but during the war he got a chance to practice his English, because the Partisans used him as an interpreter at Bari, over in Italy. Now he was a farmer again. Grapes chiefly.

Nick Zitko was disappointed that we didn't know Jim Pollack of Albany, New York. It was odd, he said, the way he met Jim Pollack. One dark night, after the Americans arrived, he was walking through the town just ahead of seven of them. One of them said this was a hell of a place; we're their allies and we haven't even got a roof over our heads. So Nick turned around and said:

"What's the matter, boys?"

The seven Americans were very embarrassed. Nick finally took them home with him. One of them was Jim Pollack, who wanted some German souvenirs, so Nick found him a German soldier's belt and some other things, and . . .

"We've been corresponding ever since he got back to Albany. He sends me packages. This coat I have on."

Nick couldn't seem to understand how it was that if we really were from America we didn't know Jim Pollack. Anyway, we must look him up when we went back. Nick also wanted to know if we knew the captain of a British ship called the *Laurana*. It was too bad if we didn't because he wanted to send his thanks to the captain. That was the boat which took a thousand people from Vis to Italy. The boat was so full that people on the lower decks stood in water up to their waists. Three old people died of drowning or heart attack. Nick didn't think the captain could possibly make port. But he did. And he went right around all the islands the Germans occupied.

Then a motherly-looking woman caught up with us and said she was "Mary Vojković from Chicago." She wasn't really from Chicago. She'd just lived there a few years when she was a child. But she still spoke English like a true Chicagoan. She said she had been one of those who stayed behind and helped feed people. Once there were one hundred thousand people on the island. Just for a few days. Nick argued with her. He said never more than sixty or seventy thousand. Mary Vojković snapped back at him:

"I was here! You were over in Italy. I guess I know!"

Some were British and American soldiers. Some were Partisans being shifted around. The rest were Yugoslav refugees from the mainland, waiting for ships to take them on to Italy and Africa. One hundred thousand! Could we imagine, she asked, one hundred women on the island cooking meals for one hundred thousand? She couldn't either. Not until they had to do it. Even the small children helped. Many of the people from the mainland cried and didn't want to go any farther. When they were told they'd be killed if they stayed, they said:

"All right. But let us die on our own soil."

Nick and Mary Vojković walked with us to the top of the island where the big airport had been. The town fathers were right. We saw the wreckage of the planes and we saw that the only rich land on the island was still standing idle. On the way back Nick said that just before the war spread to Yugoslavia he'd taken a quarter of a million dinar he'd saved from his New Zealand gum-digging days and had bought a kafana in Belgrade. But the kafana had been destroyed by bombs. Now he was a farmer again. Mary wanted to know if anyone had told us that during the war they had had to eat most of their goats and mules, just to keep alive.

Nick took us home to show us a picture of Jim Pollack, hanging on the wall right beside a photograph of Tito. In his whitewashed front yard there was an outdoor privy, six skinny chickens, a lemon tree, and a grapevine which normally produced nearly five hundred pounds of grapes a year, except that now "it's got the sickness at the roots." The yard was also full of branches of rosemary for the family donkey to eat and some dead grapevine cuttings for the family goat. "His spaghetti," as Nick put it.

Mrs. Zitko served us Vis wine and small cakes. She apologized for the cakes. She said you can't bake cakes with corn flour. But corn flour was all they had. We asked her to sit down with us. That made Nick angry. When his wife left the room to get more wine he said that in Yugoslavia they don't treat women the way we do in America. The wife does the serving. She never sits down. Then he changed the subject by telling us the big joke of the war was that the only real building hit on Vis by German bombs was a sardine factory which hadn't been used for years.

Before we went to bed that night Anita and I wanted to get a little fresh air. We were walking along the water's edge directly in front of our hotel when a gendarme with a tommy gun stopped us. He admitted that all our papers were in order. But he said we would have to go inside. Was there some law about a man and a woman not walking up and down in front of their hotel? No, but he hadn't ever seen anyone do it and we must go inside. We argued for a long time with him. He was young and he was taking his patrol job very seriously. He wouldn't give in. We must go inside. When we finally did, he said good night to us quite pleasantly. He even gave us the salutation which the Partisans used during the war. It's still a favorite motto of the Yugoslavs:

"Smrt Fasizmu. Sloboda Narodu!"
It means:
"Death to Fascism. Freedom for the people."
We had heard it many times before. But it had an ironic ring this time.
The phrase beat through my head all night:
"Smrt Fasizmu. Sloboda Narodu."
"Death to Fascism. Freedom for the people."

Chapter Fifty

SUNDAY IS SUNDAY IS SUNDAY

THE DAY BEFORE, when we were in the town hall, Roko Radisić who was one of the officials, asked us to do him a favor. He said he had relatives in California who were always writing to him about what a terrible place Yugoslavia must be now, because people aren't allowed to have any religion. He kept writing back and telling them not to believe all the propaganda they read. But they seemed to think he was being forced to write that way. And so it was very fortunate that we had come. It was also very fortunate that tomorrow would be Sunday. In the morning would we please get up early and walk around town and then he would give us the address of his relatives in California and when we got to California we could tell them what we had seen.

So the next morning Anita and I got up early and went for a walk around town. What we saw was streams of people coming from the villages and from houses in the town, all on their way to one of the three churches in Vis. Someone told us there were three other churches in Komisa, on the other side of the island, which were also functioning normally. The large Catholic church was crowded to the doors, so Anita and I stood outside and watched some children playing with an ack-ack gun. They said it had been on an Italian boat which had been torpedoed and washed ashore during the war. The gun had a revolving platform which worked with a crank. It made a perfect merry-go-round. The churchyard was also still full of empty shells, a rusty anchor, and six British ammunition carts.

Then we heard that a meeting of the island's nineteen schoolteachers was about to commence in the same hall where a dance had been held last night. So we went in, took back seats, and listened to about one hour of talk. Some of the teachers were from Komisa and had started from their homes at dawn to get here for the meeting which began at 9 A.M. The superintendent criticized the teachers. Some children in the back row criticized the teachers. Then the teachers criticized each other. Some even criticized themselves.

Then we went next door to a meeting of the Trade Union Council of Vis. There were ninety-six men and six women crowded into one small room. They were dock workers, post-office employees, mechanics, members of every trade and profession represented on the island. Officers were being elected and the chairman was begging for nominations. He said he knew they were new at this sort of thing, but this was democracy. They were supposed to pick their own officers. If they didn't speak up now and make some nominations they mustn't criticize their officers later. The gathering reminded me of a town meeting in Barnstead, New Hampshire. The men looked very much like backwoods New Hampshire farmers, except that several of them had beautifully twirled black mustaches, and except that there were some teen-aged boys taking a very active part in the proceedings.

After the elections the chairman said they were now ready to discuss any problems anyone had. A man in a long blue coat said the manager of the shop where he worked refused to pay him when he was sick for four days. How does that work out? The chairman said if a man is sick for three days or less his employer pays. If for more than three days the Trade Union Council pays. "If you're ill you always get paid by someone. We know a man must live even if he's ill."

Then an argument broke out about why farmers didn't have to pay income taxes. And an old dock worker said he never paid any taxes in the old days. Why should he now? He had a job today but maybe he wouldn't have a job tomorrow. The chairman said that wasn't true any more. There was employment for everyone. If a man lost his job all he had to do was to apply to the Council and they would get him another in quick order. An Italian boy said he worked for his own father and under the law was he entitled to a vacation? The chairman said he was.

Then we went down the street to a meeting of the Winegrowers' Cooperative. There were seventy men and two women present. The people here were more prosperous-looking. The men wore neckties, city clothes, and had polished shoes. A new president was making his acceptance speech. Only it was a speech of non-acceptance. Someone else ought to be given a chance. The honor should be passed around. He'd served long enough. But they argued him into accepting anyway, on the ground that he knew more than anyone else on the island about growing grapes.

A few rods from the winegrowers' building we saw a graveyard of hundreds of American Liberators that had made emergency landings on Vis after being shot up. The sun made them glisten. Millions of dollars' worth of aluminum, wire, rubber, glass. One had "Texas" scrawled on the fuselage. Another was nicknamed "Q.P." What had happened to the men in the crews of all those planes Anita and I agreed not to discuss. Most of the planes had come down in flames. You could see that. There were marks of fire on most of the wreckage. A small Yugoslav boy was rummaging among the planes looking for something to play with. He couldn't seem to find anything to suit his fancy.

Then we walked half a mile farther to a real graveyard behind the Catholic church. The bodies of the first three Partisans from Vis to be killed in action had been brought home and were about to be interred in a tomb of white stone built with the life savings of a peasant woman, Jakobina Ivulić, the mother of one of the three.

A band played Lenin's Funeral March as the first casket was carried to the edge of the tomb. A woman in black ran hysterically from the crowd and threw herself full length on top of the coffin. Then she turned toward the pallbearers and demanded that they pry off the lid. When they shook their heads she began a wailing which must have been heard all the way down into town.

"My one and only son. My jewel. My pearl. My *Sinko*. I will not leave you now. I will lie beside you."

When the pallbearers decided this had gone on long enough they tried to carry the coffin into the tomb. But the mother clung on and nearly fell down the steps leading underground. The same thing happened with the second coffin. Several hundred people, mostly in black, began to sob and wail too. There wasn't a dry eye in the crowd. The contagion of the grief spread even to Anita and me.

But when the body of Jakobina Ivulić's son was brought in, it was different. She was a peasant woman like the others. Thin from overwork, with gnarled hands the color of the soil. But she gave no public display of what she might be feeling. She just knelt beside the plain wooden box and said a quiet prayer. We could tell that that was what she was doing because we could see the movement of her lips. Then, standing at the edge of the tomb which she had built with the money she had earned tilling the soil since her husband's death years ago, she made a simple address to the island people. Anita translated it and I wrote it down, each clearly spoken word of it. Madame Ivulić said:

"These three died for you. When they went away you asked them why they must fight. They told you they must fight for freedom. You must now continue their fight. It does no good to lie down in the tomb beside them. You have a chance, now, to fight for the future. God rest the souls of all three."

Leaving the graveyard, we bumped into our friend Nick Zitko. He said that, speaking of burials, the people of Vis were pretty angry about how some American officers were going around digging up bodies of other Americans.

"They came here to Vis with a jeep and some burlap sacks, and without telling the town officials anything they just started going around digging them up and throwing the bones and some dirt into the sacks and then driving away. The people here couldn't understand that. If they'd only let the officials know we would have had a band and a ceremony. Maybe a procession too. Anyway a ceremony. We liked those American boys. We don't think they just ought to be thrown into a sack in the back of a jeep like that."

Down in town a soccer game was going on. The Army was playing the Civilians. The townspeople who weren't up in the hills working over their grapevines were standing around watching.

It was Sunday on the island of Vis.

Chapter Fifty-One

"WHO WANTS TO WORK?"

Anita and I noticed her at the same time. We had gone into the town kafana to buy something hot to drink because we were cold after the graveyard ceremony. She was standing behind a counter selling penny candy to a stream of children who came in with aluminum dinar pieces in their small hands. She wasn't beautiful. She didn't even have a good figure. But there was something "special" about her. Her face was pale against the all-black costume she wore. She had on no make-up and no jewelry of any kind. Her voice was soft and caressing as she talked to the children. A small child of her own played at her feet.

Nick, who had come with us, said that her name was Sonia and that she owned the kafana. He said we'd be interested, probably, in how she got it. There were five of them, Father and Mother Shegević, a son Vinko, and two girls, Sonia and Zeina. Vinko went into the Partisans. The rest of the family was shipped off to El Chateau. But before they left Sonia married a young man with whom she was very much in love. His name was Jurinović. In the refugee camp at El Chateau Sonia gave birth to the child now playing at her feet. They called her Logorka, because *loger* is the Serbo-Croat word for "camp." When the family got back to Vis again Sonia was informed that her young husband, who had never seen his baby, had been killed just a few days before the end of the war. And that's how she got the kafana. The government gave it to her because her man had been killed. Her sister Zeina helped her run the place. You wouldn't think it, Nick said, but Zeina was in the mountains in the Twenty-sixth Division for two years. When she got to Italy on her way to El Chateau she signed up with the Partisans and came back to the mainland. She had a big job in the Partisans, Nick said. He was trying his best to impress us. She was a code expert at headquarters. Now she just hands out the wine and the beer.

Maybe we were invited to the Shegević home for dinner that night because the mother noticed how Anita and I kept staring at the daughter in black. Or maybe Nick said something. Anyway, we went. The meal was prepared by Logorka's great-grandmother. She was a frail-looking old lady but she drank twice as much wine as anyone else. Besides us there were three other guests. Two men in their thirties who looked somehow out of place, and a naval officer. Sonia whispered some information to us about the two men. They were the sons of two of the wealthiest families of Split. Neither one had ever done a day's work before. But now the government was compelling them to help with the reconstruction. They had been sent to a trade school and now they were working on a building project here on Vis. Neither of them liked it. We sensed that as soon as they began to talk. Anita called one of them The Prankster because he spent the first half of the meal making jokes at various people's expense. He was the more outspoken. I had some paper in my lap to take notes on anything interesting that might be said. The Prankster was doing a lot of talking to Anita that I couldn't understand. When I asked her what he was talking about she blushed and said:

"He's trying to make a date with me for after you go to bed."

Maybe it was to impress Anita that he said some of the things he did. But I took it all down. He said he didn't like the New Yugoslavia because there wasn't any fun here any more. All they talked about was work, work, work. What he liked was a fast motorcar, plenty of liquor, plenty of women, and a good time. That's the way it was before the war. But you couldn't have those things here now. If you want to work, maybe the New Yugoslavia is all right. But who wants to work? His idea of a perfect life was to work a week and loaf a month.

Sonia's father said that what he meant was to work a week and loaf six months. The Prankster said that if Mister Shegević didn't keep quiet he'd tell his wife how he'd won twenty-five thousand dinar in their poker game last night. Everyone at the table looked at the father. The father smiled. Then he nodded to his wife and tapped his pocket.

The Prankster went on. He'd like to go to America. This place was no good for him. If he wanted to work he could go on the Youth Railroad. Sure. But he wasn't interested in work. Or in railroads either. Except one that would get him out of the country. He was interested in dances and parties. Then he winked at Anita. The other man from Split seemed embarrassed and tried to turn the conversation.

"Have you heard the riddle about where is America? The answer is that America is wherever people live well."

But that didn't deviate his friend. He said he'd tell us the principal reason he hated things now. The government is going too far with this equal rights for women. Women go to illiteracy classes. They go to lectures and *gymnasiums*. Their husbands come home and find the stove cold, and when they say anything to their wives, their wives answer that this is the New Yugoslavia and everyone is everyone else's equal now. That's going too far. The first thing they knew the government would have the men out in the kitchen washing dishes. No! This was no place for him. He was going to New York. Ah, New York! Night clubs, music, fast cars, and women. That was the life! He didn't want even to think any more about Yugoslavia. Let's talk about New York. Would Anita tell him something about New York?

So Anita did. She told him that in New York there are a great many night clubs. Fancy places. And lots of fast cars and plenty of women. But in many families, she said, the husband and the wife both go to work.

The wife comes home from her office, opens a few cans, and prepares the dinner while the husband reads his evening paper. The Prankster smiled and said that sounded all right, except that he didn't like things out of cans. Anita went on. She said that in some families after dinner someone might suggest going to the movies. Of course it wouldn't always happen this way, but it might sometimes happen that the wife would leave the room to powder her nose and get ready, and while she was gone the husband—Anita was doing it very dramatically—while she was gone it was within the realm of possibility that the husband would put aside his paper and clear the dining-room table. And he might even—it was like a ghost story, the way Anita was telling it—he might even—wash and dry the dishes!

The young man from Split sank back in his chair as Anita finished. He said he didn't want to go to New York after all. He'd have to find some other place. And he also dropped the idea of having a date with Anita that night.

The next morning on the boat back to Split the naval officer who had been at the dinner party told us that both young men had "sat out the war" and that the quiet one was really the more dangerous, but he was afraid to talk.

PART FIVE

These Are the Montenegrins

Chapter Fifty-Two

IT KEEPS YOU YOUNG FOR LIFE

SIX YEARS AGO I had written that Budva was one place I wanted to visit again someday, if peace and reason ever returned to Europe. People might argue about whether "peace and reason" had returned yet to Europe. But here was Budva, several thousand feet below us glittering in the sun. The walled city with its fortress on the edge of the sea didn't look much different from this distance than it had before. The last time I had come into it by an American Legation car which refused to run in anything but low gear. This truck we were in now, which they called a bus just because it had some holes cut in the sides for windows, wasn't much better. Last time we had come here because Budva was one of the last spots in Europe the Axis hadn't yet captured. We thought maybe we could buy a boat in Budva to take us somewhere else before the Nazis arrived. We found a boat and we left the car in the custody of the mayor, old Joko Boreta, who had once been to Cleveland and remembered every word of the English he'd learned. I had in my pocket right now the receipt he pounded out so painfully on the old Oliver typewriter he had brought home with him from Cleveland. I still remembered just how he did it. With one finger of his right hand. And when the keys stuck, as they always did, he'd pull them back in place with his left hand. The document was only eight lines long, but it took him nearly an hour to type it. Then he wasted more time trying to find a rubber stamp. Nothing was ever official in Yugoslavia without a rubber stamp. The document said that he, Joko Boreta, mayor of Budva, in the name of the community had assumed full responsibility for one Sevreley and that the community of Budva would guard said Sevreley with all diligence, but the community of Budva could not be responsible if any harm came to said Sevreley at the hands of forces not now within our midst.

Of course something had happened to the Chevrolet. But I wanted to go back and see the mayor and thank him anyway, because he was a gentleman as well as a politician. He'd made our few hours in his walled city a pleasant interlude in a month which otherwise was not very pleasant. But several years ago a Yugoslav in America told me there was no use going back to Budva to see old Joko Boreta. He was dead.

Still, there were other people I wanted to see. So here we were. I told Anita that it was right here on this main street that our car with the American flag on the fender had been stopped that April day by swarms of dazed, bewildered people who wanted to know what had happened. Was the war over? Had the King really fled the country? Some of the people in the crowd had been to America, as old Joko Boreta had, and they wanted to do something for these *Amerikanskis*. So we drank many glasses of *šljivovica* with them that day in Budva. Now here we were again. It didn't look much different except that a large German mine lay on the beach. And the pier we had started out from had apparently had some war adventures. And there were no excited people in the road. So we started to look for someone to get us rooms for the night. The man we found was the present mayor. He said his name was Petar Lukać. We learned later that he was only sixty years old. But he looked eighty. His eyes were so weak he could hardly see. They watered all the time. He also had palsy or some other ailment which made it impossible for him to keep his hands from twitching. We introduced ourselves and I said I had been here once before and . . . Then he said:

"And you don't remember me?"

Then he explained that there wasn't any real reason why I should. He had just been one of the crowd of townspeople who had stood on the pier waving to us that night we pushed off in the sardine boat we bought which we christened the *Makedonka*.

Then he introduced us to a professor who was with him. By this time we knew that anyone who teaches classes past fourth grade in Yugoslavia is called "professor." But this professor spoke English. He wanted to talk about world affairs. He wanted to know is the United States going to use all the things it's found out about atoms for war or for peace? Do the farmers of America want war? And how about students and laborers and other people? He asked a lot of questions which weren't easy to answer. Then he said he didn't think there was any possibility of war again unless the United States went Fascist. And he couldn't believe that the United States could ever go Fascist. When he left he told the mayor to "take good care of these people."

Then the town secretary came along. He was tall and young, and as vigorous-looking as the mayor was feeble. He said the Germans had destroyed the pier when they left. But plans for a great new port at Budva were already being carried out. If we looked down this way we could see a hundred workmen busy on the job. Just then I saw a bareheaded man coming up the road. He had on no overcoat, even though it was a bitter winter day. He walked with a healthy stride. He had a lot of white hair and a close-cropped mustache. I asked the mayor who he was. The mayor laughed and said:

"Don't you recognize your old friend Joko Boreta?"

It was Joko. When he began to talk, in that same broken way I remembered him talking six years ago, I felt as if I were with a man back from the dead. He laughed and said he was glad to see us. Someone had told him his name had been written in a book. Why hadn't we sent the book to him? I had a copy in my musette bag. I'd brought it along to check up on names and places. So I pulled it out and we stood there in the middle of the road while Joko put on his spectacles and read every page that had anything on it about him or about Budva. In a few minutes a lot of people gathered around him. Now Budva reminded me a little of the way it was that other time. Only the people weren't quite so excited. Each time a new group came along Joko would say, Listen to what they wrote about us in America, and then he would read the pages again.

But I wanted to find out about what had happened to him in the last six years and why he wasn't mayor any more. I was a little afraid to ask. When I did I wished that I hadn't. All the happiness went out of old Joko's face. He said:

"Well, I'll tell you, but it's a long story. You remember that Sevreley you left with me?" [He pronounced it just as he'd written it on the piece of paper in my pocket.] "It was that Sevreley that started it all. The night after you left the Italians occupied our city. The next day some Quisling here in Budva said he could tell them where they could find a nice American car. So he led them to where I'd hidden it. I knew the man probably also told them that I had had something to do with it, so I packed up some food and went into the mountains. It was a good thing I did, in a way, because the man had told them about me all right. I thought that if they couldn't find me they wouldn't be able to do anything. But I didn't know them very well. Not then. What they did was to . . ." Joko pulled a handkerchief with a black border from his pocket and pretended to blow his nose very hard. Then he asked for a cigarette. Finally he went on. "What they did was to burn down my house and kill my wife. I loved my wife and I loved my home too. It was the first house in all Montenegro they destroyed. When I heard about it I had to do something. I couldn't just sit in the woods and try to forget. So when I heard about the new Partisan Army I went to one of their headquarters in the woods and said I wanted to sign up. They laughed at me at first. They asked me how old I was. When I told them I was nearly sixty they said I could help but I couldn't fight."

Joko blinked his eyes and straightened his shoulders. We could see he was very proud of the rest of the story. He said he not only became a fighter but he wound up with the rank of group commander. He thought that was pretty good for a man of sixty. We said that we did too. When Italy gave up and the Partisans established headquarters at Bari they sent Joko over there as an interpreter. Later he took one thousand Yugoslav soldiers down to some place in Africa to attend a tank school.

While Joko talked to me in English someone in the crowd whispered to Anita in Serbo-Croat that Joko was the biggest man in town. He was their greatest hero. What I kept wondering about was why he wasn't mayor again. At first I'd thought it was because he was dead. And then when I saw him coming up the road I thought maybe he had been against the Partisans. But now it didn't make any sense. He and the present mayor were both about sixty. The other one looked eighty, while Joko seemed to have dropped off a dozen years, in spite of all the experiences he'd had lately. I said something about how young he looked. Joko laughed and said had I forgotten he was a miner for fifteen years out in Arizona? If you breathe enough of that Arizona air it keeps you young the rest of your life. Then I remembered that Mike had been just about sixty too. Little Milan Francisikovic who changed his name to Mike Francisco when he went to the United States to work in a shipyard around Philadelphia and then back to Milan Francisikovic when he returned to his home on the edge of Petrovac na More, the next village to Budva. Had the mayor ever known Mike? Joko said certainly he had. Did he know that Mike had fixed our boat when it got wrecked at Petrovac na More, and then in return for a hundred dollars in American money that we sent to his wife agreed to go with us and help guide the *Makedonka* to some safe port in Greece? Joko nodded his head. Then I told him that Mike had been killed by a bomb on the way and I wanted to go down to Petrovac na More tomorrow to see if I could find his wife. Joko said to forget it. It was impossible to get to Petrovac by land because of the roads, and there were no boats around to take us there. Besides, Mrs. Francisikovic had heard the whole story. Joko didn't know how. But she had. And maybe it would be just as well for everybody concerned to forget it.

Then Joko asked about the others in the boat. What had happened to the two young men? I told him that Russell Hill of the New York *Herald Tribune* had become one of the best foreign correspondents in all Europe. And I told him how Leigh White had been shot in Greece and had had a great many operations, but was all right now. I waited for Joko to ask about Terence Atherton, the London *Daily Mail* correspondent. Atherton had been with us when we got the receipt for the Sevreley. He and Joko had talked together. Finally I mentioned his name. Joko gave me a queer look and said he had seen Atherton since I had. I didn't understand what he meant. The last time I saw Terence was in Cairo. We went to a hospital together to have some bullet wounds dressed and then he bought a silver cigarette lighter and had them engrave the word *Makedonka* on it. When he gave it to me he said:

"I know you won't ever forget our boat. But whenever you look at this gadget remember that life isn't all Continental Hotels, and bowing doormen, and clean sheets on the bed."

I carried the lighter every day until I heard that Terence had been killed. How he was killed had always been a mystery. We finally did establish that the British sent him in a submarine from Alexandria up into the Adriatic on a secret mission. After he was put ashore he was killed. That's all we ever knew for certain. The Fotić people in America circulated stories that he had been killed by Partisans. The Partisans said he was killed by the Chetniks. But it was all third- or fourth-hand information. Propaganda. Anyway, I put the *Makedonka* cigarette lighter in a safety-deposit box so I wouldn't ever lose it and so I wouldn't think too much about those days and nights in the boat. I didn't want to think too much about two friends who both were killed before the end of that trip.

But now I could get some firsthand information. What did Joko know? He said he was there when Atherton and his party came ashore. It was in 1942 and Joko was already a Partisan. He was there and talked to Atherton. They recognized each other. Atherton told him he had two short-wave radio sending sets, some secret messages, and a great deal of gold strapped in belts around his body for Draža Mihailović. Would Joko please take him to the Mihailović headquarters? The mayor laughed as he got to this part of the story. He said British Intelligence had gotten its wires crossed. They'd landed Atherton in Partisan-held territory. Mihailović and his men were a hundred miles away. So Atherton said all right, he'd go to Partisan headquarters, and Joko guided him there. On the way Atherton told him all about our boat trip and what had happened to everybody, including Mike. Joko said he'd forgotten that part of it. Of course that was how Mrs. Francisikovic found out. It was Atherton who brought the news.

But I still didn't know the end of the story. Wouldn't Joko please tell me the rest? How had Atherton been killed? Joko shook his head. He'd rather we got it firsthand. He'd told me all he knew for sure himself. But General Velebit, back in Belgrade, knew the rest. He's in the Foreign Ministry now. But he was there at headquarters when Atherton arrived. So I made a note to see the general when we got back to Belgrade.

Every few minutes while he was talking to us Joko interrupted himself and said:

"Imagine your coming back! I never expected to see you again!"

Finally he said we would have to excuse him. He'd been planting some trees when he heard we were in town. He'd have to go back now and finish the job. But if we would like to meet him in the kafana tonight— the one inside the walled city.

Chapter Fifty-Three

YUGOSLAVIA UNDER A MICROSCOPE

Budva is so small you can put your finger on it. That's why we decided to find out everything we could about its past, its present, and its plans for the future. Budva multiplied by ten, a hundred, or a thousand was probably any other community in the New Yugoslavia. And so we went to work, walking the streets, talking to people, asking questions.

Like most other spots in this part of the world, Budva had known many masters. It started out four centuries before Christ as a Greek trading post. Then the Romans came. In 840 it was destroyed by Arabs. Fifty years after the discovery of America the Venetians took over. It had quite a democratic constitution of its own way back in 1569. It was attacked frequently by Turks. It was wiped out once by an earthquake. A century ago the French fought for it. It was Austrian until after World War I. That's enough of its history to show that it has had a history. Its ancient stone walls also prove it.

Budva itself is all within those walls. It covers an area not nearly so large as a medium-sized American cemetery. Inside the walls four hundred and seventy-six people were living the day the Axis struck. Another two thousand lived scattered in villages around the county. Inside the walls there are three twisting streets running north and south, crossed by four going east and west. There are two barbershops, a kafana, a drygoods and general store, one *trafika* where they sell stamps, cigarettes, and newspapers, one Catholic church, and one Orthodox church. No one in town had ever seen a motion picture unless he'd been to some distant city, and few had. There were several telephones but they were used exclusively by officials. Being right on the Adriatic they never saw snow except on the peaks of the distant mountains, Lovćen and Konjsko. There was one primary school, which meant just four grades. There was no playground. There was no hospital. If anyone became seriously ill he generally died, unless some way could be found to get him to a hospital in Dubrovnik or Cetinje. But both those cities are quite a distance away. The people of Budva are Montenegrins, which means they are accustomed to living a hard life. They can bear pain without whimpering. They rarely experienced what you or I would call great happiness. They did have certain simple pleasures. But they were very simple pleasures. Budva had produced one literary figure all Yugoslavia knew about. Stephan Mitro Ljubisha. He was a poet. There was a monument to him at the edge of the water. It was a statue of a girl about to leap into the sea to escape an enemy. If you looked at it from the proper angle she really did seem to be jumping into the sea. There was a bronze plaque fastened to it with Ljubisha's name and dates. Some of the men of Budva made their living out on the water. The others worked the soil. Their fields were outside the walls, but some of them kept their animals in town.

Joko Boreta was looked upon as the prosperous man of Budva. And one of the brightest too. That's why they made him mayor. He lived in town. Had an office there where he sold insurance in an American company. But he spent his spare time out on his farm. He had three hundred orange trees, some cherries, some figs, and of course grapes. He had five cows and two horses. That made him a big farmer. Out of the class of the others.

Budva people were proud of their long history and they liked to have tourists tell them that they had the most picturesque town on the Adriatic. But that had nothing to do with their standard of living. It didn't change the fact that their life was grim most of the time.

That's the way it all was on April 17, 1941, the last time I saw Budva.

One of the first things the Italians did was to tear the bronze plaque from the statue of Stephan Mitro Ljubisha. Then they went from house to house stealing food and doing minor looting. Three months later there were battles between Italians and Partisans within a mile of the city gates. Joko Boreta likes to tell about the one on the eighteenth of July because he was the commander of the Partisan unit. There were only forty-eight of them. But they killed one hundred and twenty-six Italians and captured a tank, a staff car, twenty-four motorcycles, and eighteen trucks. Then there was a battle on March twenty-fifth of the next year. It wasn't really a battle at all because thirty Partisans under Joko's direction waylaid several thousand Italian Alpine troops and mowed down two hundred of them before they knew what had happened. Twelve of the Partisans were wounded. That included their commander. But Joko says he was happy because he was beginning to get even for what they had done to his wife.

Once Joko and his men were able to encircle Budva and keep the Italian garrison cut off from the rest of the world for three whole months. They hated to think that maybe they were starving their own townspeople. But it couldn't be helped.

This is what happened to the four hundred and seventy-six people who lived within the stone walls of Budva: Sixty went into the Partisans. One hundred went into the rival Chetniks. Exactly half of the one hundred and sixty were killed. Twenty civilians were killed or died in prison. Seven civilians were killed in air raids. The rest lived under what Joko calls "fierce control." When the Italians capitulated the Germans took over Budva. Joko says the difference was that the Italians looted and burned. The Germans shot and killed. Late in the war British and American planes flew by the hundreds back and forth over Budva. Only two bombs were ever dropped inside the stone walls. They destroyed six homes. When the Germans finally retreated they mined the dock. They also blew up every bridge they passed over on the roads leading through the villages.

That's the war. Joko himself is the best authority on what's happened since. He told us that many people's minds had been poisoned by the Chetniks, the Italians, and the Germans. But today, he said, the town is as completely behind the government as any other place in Yugoslavia. Then Joko cited some proofs of progress:

Two hospitals have been built. They have two hundred beds. A third, with four hundred beds, will specialize in bone diseases. It will serve all of Montenegro. A new trade school has eighty pupils. Girls as well as boys. A children's playground has been built. Once every twenty days a movie is shown. Most of the town turns out. All the destroyed bridges have been rebuilt. Mined roads have been repaired. Burned-down schools have been reconstructed. A cultural center has been opened. Many young people from Budva worked on the Youth Railroad last year. More are going to work on this year's road. Joko thought the Youth Railroad proved more than anything else about the New Yugoslavia. He said we should just try to imagine what it was like before. To build a railroad like the young people worked on last year, the old government would have sent abroad for engineers and experts. Billions of dinar would have been appropriated. There would have been years of measuring and remeasuring. At the end of ten years the road still wouldn't be finished. Meanwhile, a few politicians would have built themselves a few fancy palaces.

Joko kept talking about America and democracy. He said what Yugoslavia wants to do is to catch up with all the other countries where there is real democracy and progress.

About his own personal reconstruction problem, the government is giving him help to build a new house out where his farm was. He now has three cows and is getting some fruit planted again. He said it's hard starting all over again at sixty, but if others can do it he can too.

I still hadn't found out why he wasn't mayor any more. I didn't want to ask him right out. So I just asked if his farm kept him busy all the time. He said no. He also had a position at the local tourist hotel. The same position Petar Lukać, the present mayor, used to have. They had really swapped jobs. The "position" turned out to be that of assistant desk clerk. I still didn't have an explanation when we drove away in the bus the next morning. But a little way down the road Anita smiled and said Joko had confided in her. He didn't want to tell me because he was afraid I might "write something."

The Italians had appointed Petar Lukać mayor after Joko ran away to the hills. They thought he was a harmless old man. The Germans thought so too. So they kept him. He was mayor all through the occupation. But all that time he was secretly working in close co-operation with the Partisans and was in communication with them from the beginning to the end. When Joko came home a hero he was more popular than ever before. The whole town wanted him to take back his old job. But Joko told them that Petar Lukać should have the honor as a reward for his loyalty. Maybe, Joko told Anita, I'll take over again when Petar dies. Anita pointed out that they were both exactly the same age. That they were both over sixty. Joko laughed and said, yes, but he had been an Arizona miner and he was going to live another sixty years.

Chapter Fifty-Four

"NEVER A RACE OF MIGHTIER MOUNTAINEERS"

THERE was a big red tomato coming up out of the sea when we caught the bus at six o'clock in the morning. That's what Anita said it looked like. It made a crazy pink light on the stone walls of Budva. The mountains which were generally deep purple were pink too. There was no place to get any breakfast, and the cold was nibbling through all the clothes we had on. But the wife of the patron had filled our thermos bottle with hot water, so I dug some aluminum cups from the musette bag and Anita made tea while we waited for the bus to start. It really wasn't as much of a bus as the other truck had been. The main difference was that this one had two holes instead of six cut in the sides. We were glad there were only two holes when the wind started to blow. We were sorry there weren't more holes a little later on.

We had to climb five thousand feet to cross over Lovćen Mountain to get to Cetinje. About one thousand feet up we started around a curve and I told Anita to get her last look of Budva. She had fallen in love with the place too. She said I was right about the people down there being the most friendly people we had met. So we both took our last look. The sun was putting spotlights on the old fortress. I said if she looked hard enough she'd probably see old Joko Boreta standing down there waving his hat at us. So we took our last look at Budva out the back of the truck and went around the curve. Ten minutes later Anita pointed and said there's a place down there that looks exactly like Budva. She was right. It did look like Budva. It was Budva. The same thing happened over and over again for an hour. We'd say good-by to it for the last time and go around a curve. Then a few minutes later there it was again. That was because we were corkscrewing around the mountain. It was funny to see the city get smaller and smaller each time we got another look at it. It was the most lingering good-by I've ever taken of an old friend. But we finally did leave it entirely.

Then the peasant women in the bus began to get sick. There were nineteen of them. I don't think they liked bus traveling very much. We didn't either. But we tried to behave. They couldn't behave. I suppose it was because of the swaying of the bus and all that corkscrewing. First a woman near one of the windows got sick. She stayed sick all the rest of the morning. That blocked one window. The same thing happened on the other side. When a third passenger got sick she couldn't push the other two out of the way. That made the woman next to her with a basket very angry. All peasant women when they go away from home carry wicker baskets over their arms. I never have found out what they put in those baskets besides a chunk of black bread, some onions or garlic, and a bottle of wine. Each basket always has a neat white towel over the top. They hang onto their baskets as if they contained everything they had in the world. The woman whose basket was ruined started screaming at the latest victim of bus-sickness. That upset the nerves of those whose nerves hadn't been upset already. So most of them also got sick. Someone yelled to the driver to stop. That was foolish. The truck was going in first gear. The driver couldn't have heard a bomb explosion. He couldn't have stopped anyway because he didn't have any brakes to speak about. If he had stopped we would have rolled five thousand feet downhill backward. So we just went on, with a truckload of sick women. In between being sick themselves they shouted at other people because they were being sick. It was worse going down the other side of the mountain because we went faster. The truck had plenty of speed going down. When we passed a car going in the other direction the fenders brushed each other gently. When our side of the road was the side next to the mountain it was all right. Nobody minded. But when our side of the road was the side with no guard rails and a drop of five thousand feet, we wondered why they hadn't ever built a railroad from Budva to Cetinje.

As we began to see more and more of the black mountains of Montenegro which give the place its name I told Anita some stories I'd picked up in various places about this section. The Yugoslavs call it Cernagora. Cernagora means the same thing in Serbo-Croat that Montenegro does in French. I told her how there's an old fable that when God went around creating the earth He had a bag full of stones over His shoulder and He placed the stones here and there to make mountain ranges. Like the Rockies and the Alps. But as He walked across what was to be Cernagora His bag broke and all the stones fell out. Anita said she could believe it, just looking down at where we were going. Then I told her that the men of Montenegro have always been fighters. That's partly because there's always been someone trying to fight them. It's the custom in Montenegro for the men to fight and the women to do all the work. Anita didn't like that. And she didn't like the expression they have here which men use to curse each other. It's the worst thing you can say to a man when you say, "May you die in bed like a woman!" Then there's a Montenegrin poem with a line in it about how no one but God could ever subdue our land, and even He might get tired of the job. The Turks tried it and they got tired of it. They tried for five hundred years and they still hadn't succeeded. I kept telling Anita stories because I was afraid she would get the female trouble all the other females in the truck had. I told her that when the Montenegrins can't find anything else to fight with they use rocks. They never have to look far for a rock. They have always had a great love of the Russians. In the days of the Czars they used to say, we and the Russians number two hundred million. Any time the Russians declared war on somebody Montenegro would, too, even if she didn't know what the war was all about, which was often the case. Anita was beginning to get a little pale, I thought, so I went on. Did she know Stoyan Pribitćević's story about an Austrian officer who, while questioning a captured mountaineer during the last war, asked him why the Montenegrins were fighting the Austrians. The mountaineer answered that they were fighting for bread, but would the officer tell him why the Austrians were fighting the Montenegrins? The officer snapped back, "For honor." The mountaineer said he guessed he understood. We are each fighting for what we haven't got.

And did Anita know about the Bogumils. They were members of a religious sect that had many followers in these parts back in the fifteenth century. Their rules and regulations forbade laughter, liquor, meat, and marriage. Their greatest hate was of children. They fought against serfdom and against all other established religions. The Byzantine Empress Theodora killed a hundred thousand of them, but there was one brief period when Bogumilism was the state religion of Bosnia. Anita said how did they ever expect to grow as a religious body if they forbade procreation? The truck sideswiped a jeep coming up the mountain just then so I didn't have to answer. When we got back on all four wheels again I noticed that the faces of most of the nineteen peasant women were literally green. Anita's was just a pasty white. She said the stories were very interesting and please tell some more. Quickly! So I told her that in Montenegro if a father dies in battle the mother always tries to get his bloodstained shirt to give to her son. Then I told her that by an ancient custom the Orthodox bishop of Cetinje was automatically the king, the head of the church, and the commander in chief of the army. All at the same time. But in those days an Orthodox bishop couldn't get married. So he always passed the crown on to his nephew. It went on like that until just about a hundred years ago. We were still going round and round. The other women were still being sick. But Anita had her mind on Montenegro now. She said she knew a little something about this section too. She knew that one of the rulers was also a famous poet. Bishop Negosh. He wrote one poem called *The Mountain Wreath* which was translated into forty-eight different languages. I asked her to name the forty-eight. But just then we came to the edge of Cetinje. Most of the peasant women got out, even though it meant walking several miles to the center of town. They'd had enough. They preferred to walk. We'd had enough too. But we weren't going to admit it.

All over Yugoslavia people had been wanting to show us museums and art galleries. I suppose they thought all foreigners are like tourists. We'd escaped the ordeal everywhere else. But we didn't escape it in Cetinje. Someone said we had to go to see the museum because once it was the

palace of King Nicholas. I didn't see that that made any difference. But
I was glad we went. Otherwise we wouldn't have met George Rasović
and that would have been a pity. He was the curator. Maybe someone else
had the title. But George was really "it." He was a little man with a limp
that he got fighting in some war. He wasn't sure himself which war it
was because he'd fought in so many. He wore a large fur cap and kept
rubbing his hands together. It was no wonder. There hadn't been any heat
in the museum for weeks. Maybe years. You have to have a lot of interest
in history to appreciate old flags and the other things they keep in museums under those conditions. But we tried to pretend that we did because
old George was so eager to have us appreciate everything.

In between rooms of old coins and costumes that royalty used to wear
I found out that he lived in Seattle once and six of his children were born
there. The way he said it I got the idea that that was a small percentage
of his total family. George had long twirling mustachios that made him
look just like the bust he showed us of Bishop-Poet Negosh. He even
opened the glass cases which he said he seldom did for anyone and let us
touch the original manuscript of *The Mountain Wreath*. It felt like any
other paper. Then we saw copies of all forty-eight editions. Anita wanted
to make a list of the forty-eight languages but I said we didn't have time.
So George closed the glass case and said did we know that the bishop had
been two meters eight tall? While I was trying to figure that out in feet
and inches he showed us the bishop's favorite chair. They had added two
inches to each leg so the bishop's feet wouldn't trail on the floor.

I asked George if the Germans stole anything from the museum. He
acted as if I had insulted all the two hundred thousand people of Cernagora. He said that if they had dared touch a single one of these historic
relics the children of Cernagora would have torn out their eyes. Another
reason there wasn't much looting in Cetinje was because the Partisans
had this valley surrounded most of the time. While he was showing us
sixty captured Turkish flags and the coat in which his favorite prince had
been assassinated I found out that he spoke four languages, had been in
the museum for twenty-two years, lived in the building all during the
occupation to protect the contents, and had once been a Yukon gold
digger. By that time we had reached George's prize piece. It was a death
mask of a Turkish pasha whose head had been cut off by some Montenegrins in 1796. George wanted to be sure we knew what a death mask
was. So he explained that first they cut off the man's head while he was
still alive. Then they poured plaster over it. And then from that form they
made this statue. Anita said it must be a very good likeness then. George
nodded solemnly and said he thought it was.

George was full of other miscellaneous pieces of information he thought
we ought to have. Pierre Loti. Of course we knew who he was, didn't
we? He got the inspiration for one of his best books in those mountains
we had just come through. And didn't we think what Tennyson wrote
about Cernagora was good? Anita made the mistake of saying she'd

never heard what Tennyson wrote about Cernagora. So George recited the whole thing. He gave it a lot of feeling when he came to the lines:

"Great Cernagora! Never since thine own
Black ridges drew the cloud and brake the storm
Has breathed a race of mightier mountaineers."

The old curator said it was a job, trying to have a museum in this country because the Cernagora people all through their history have been burying things against some enemy. The government is still digging up books and old documents and museum pieces the people buried against the Turks, and the Austrians, and in World War I, and now in this one. George said it harms things a bit to have them stay buried in the ground for hundreds of years. Some of the things have been buried four or five times. They just get them dug up and then they have to bury them against some new enemy. When we congratulated him on his collection and tried to get away he laughed and said, yes, we have just about everything in this museum. Just about everything but the atom bomb. Then he laughed again when he saw that we weren't offended. When we were going out the door he said we couldn't leave town without seeing the largest bas-relief map in the world. Sixty by sixty feet. He pointed down the road to the building it was in. We'd had enough of exhibits for one day but George was watching us. So we saw "the largest bas-relief map in the world." It was sixty by sixty feet. It convinced Anita that maybe there was some basis to the story of the bags of rocks that broke. The map was just of Cernagora. It looked like a thousand old-fashioned orange reamers of different sizes scattered around on the floor.

Then we went to the Capital Building to pay our respects to Blažo Jovanović, the President of the Republic, and to see what he was like. His *chef de cabinet,* Vojo Vushorović, was very sorry but the President was busy. He had an important appointment with an old friend. The old friend came in while we were still there. He was the Bishop of Cetinje. By the right of tradition he should also have been king, if they had a king. He wore a heavy gold chain around his important-looking middle and he had a miter on his head. He was tall without the miter. With the miter on, he had to bend going through the President's door, even though all the doors in Cetinje are inches taller than ordinary doors. He had a rosary in his hands and was counting the beads as he walked. His white beard was handsome against his black robes. The archbishop followed him carrying a five-foot mace. The chef de cabinet said the archbishop had been in the hills with the Partisans. They were both still locked with the President in his private office when we left. But we didn't leave right away. The chef de cabinet had some things he wanted to tell us. He wore a '41 star over his heart. He said Cetinje, being high up in the mountains, was always of strategic importance to any enemy. But Cetinje was also always economically poor. Sometimes enemies did get in across the mountains. But they always regretted it. Napoleon got only as far as Kotor. The mountain men went down to the seacoast to meet him. And he got only as far as Kotor.

The chef de cabinet was a very efficient person except that he had a telephone he had to ring by hand. No one ever answered it when he rang. That made him angry. So he'd ring until Anita said she was afraid he was going to break the phone. Anita was doing the interpreting from the other side of the room because that's where the radiator was. She was sitting on the radiator trying to get thawed out. Vushorović said many people from here had been to America and had come back saying they liked it. But if we wanted to know why they felt more kindly toward Russia than the United States right now we should go to Titograd. I told him we would like to go to Titograd but we had plans to go to Podgorica in the afternoon. He laughed and said then we'd see Titograd anyway because Titograd is what they call Podgorica now. He said that when the Germans retreated from Cetinje they headed for Titograd, which is in a deep valley. Partisan Headquarters asked the British at Bari, Italy, to annihilate them from the air. Seventeen thousand men in a little valley were a good target for anybody's planes. He said the British bombed Titograd three or four times before the Germans got there. They killed only Yugoslavs. Thousands of them. So the Germans got suspicious and didn't go into Titograd after all. They just stayed in the hills. He said the Partisans told Bari. But then sixty more raids were made on Titograd. Mostly by American planes. We could see for ourselves this afternoon what happened.

We went to lunch at the Grand Hotel. This was where six years ago we found out one night that King Peter and his generals and his ministers were going to surrender the Yugoslav Army and fly out of the country. Anita noticed that the plates in the dining room were stamped with the name of the Avala Hotel of Budva. She said we didn't seem to be able to get away from Budva, did we? The waiter explained that the Avala is a summer hotel. So in the winter the Grand Hotel borrows all the Avala's equipment and then gives it back during the tourist season. That's because they haven't enough things like plates in Yugoslavia yet. At lunch I told Anita to watch the way they serve bread as we went from place to place. You can tell about the culture of a people by the way they serve bread. In America we slice it with a machine. That shows we have a mechanical culture. In Dubrovnik they serve it the way they do in London at teatime. So thin you can see through it. Here in Montenegro the slices are almost an inch thick. In South Bosnia and Macedonia they serve it in big chunks. That is, when they have enough to serve it any way at all. Every time we ate in a restaurant we took all the bread that was left on the table and spread it with butter from a can in the musette bag and then sprinkled it with some of the raisins Jake had given us and put it away for future reference. That was in case there wasn't any food in the next town we hit. Which was often the case.

After lunch we met Alecj Obradović. He said he'd been a writer once himself. He didn't think he was related to Obrad Obradović. But I told him anyway about how Obrad Obradović was the chef de cabinet to General Simović who pulled off the coup d'état in 1941, and how Obradović met us in a small town close to here when we were trying to get out of Yugoslavia and promised us a boat and some machine guns and some sailors if we would meet him at a certain bridge in Podgorica at midnight. We went to the bridge at midnight but Obradović wasn't there. We never knew what happened to him until several years later. Then I got a letter from him. He was in London. He said what right did I have mentioning his name in a book? His friends had told him that if I mentioned his name in a book he was entitled to some of the proceeds of the book and would I send him a check right away. I wrote back that I was glad he got out safely and I hoped he was glad that we did, too, even though he didn't meet us at the bridge at midnight. Obradović the writer said he was sure they weren't related.

We got a jeep to take us to Podgorica and Obradović wanted to go along. He said he could tell us a great many things. On the way he told us principally about himself. He had been in a Chetnik prison camp. He showed us some scars on his wrists where the chains had been. He spent one year in prison. Then they decided to shoot him. But he escaped during the death march. Six or eight hundred others weren't so lucky. Now his teeth were falling out because of the way they fed him. Or the way they didn't feed him. He opened his mouth to show us. His teeth *were* falling out. He said did we know about General Alexander P. Biroli, who carries on his soul the lives of thousands of Yugoslav women and children? It was this Italian general who burned down so many Yugoslav villages and towns. If the jeep driver would go past his house he'd get a picture album that was found on an Italian prisoner and prove it. There were pictures in it showing the general watching the torturing of women and children. Would we like to know where the general was now? Today, two years after the end of the war, he's in an American camp in Italy.

As we were driving through the center of Cetinje to go back to get the picture album we heard band music coming from three or four places. It was rather bad band music. Obradović said before the war there wasn't a single music school in Cetinje. Now there's one on almost every street. We said we believed him. He also told us there was only one X-ray machine in all Cernagora before the war. Now they have fourteen. Before, there were only one hundred and thirty-four hospital beds. Now there are one thousand three hundred. There were no children's homes. Now every county has one. Then he told us about a rally of workers of all kinds that had just been held. At the meeting one worker suggested that everyone give up his vacation this year to make the reconstruction go faster. They all agreed. Anita asked Obradović if he was giving up his. He said he was. But he didn't act as if he were very happy about it. Anita said we had noticed that about every third man wore a '41 star. Obradović said that was right. More 41-ers from Cernagora than anywhere else. And had we noticed the picture of Marshal Tito in the Grand Hotel dining

room? We had to admit that we hadn't. He said this one was done by
one of the Božovic boys. There were nine Božovic boys. All of them went
into the Partisans. Six of them are wearing '41 medals today.

On the edge of Cetinje we passed a monument. It was of a woman with
a sword held above her head. Anita liked it so well she made the driver
stop while she took a picture of it. That's how we found out, from a
plaque on the base, that it was put up in 1939 by people from Cernagora
in the United States. It was supposed to honor a shipload of Cernagora-
Americans who were torpedoed the day before Christmas in '15 on their
way over here to help fight the Austrians. The statue was put up just in
time to be damaged in World War II. But the maiden with the sword
held above her head was still there. In her other hand she held a wreath
which was labeled "peace." The wreath was a little damaged.

Obradović said there was a lot more to his story. But I made him wait
to tell it because I was getting the story of the driver of the jeep, Vojeslav
Vujanović. He was just eighteen years old. The way he drove the jeep
around curves I said he must have been in the Partisans. I said it as a joke
because I knew he was too young to have been in the Partisans. He
laughed when I said it. He said he was one of the first "men" in the
Partisans. I said he couldn't have been much of a man. He couldn't have
been more than thirteen years old when the war began in Yugoslavia. He
said that was right. He was thirteen. He was living in the village of
Lubotin-Ceklin. We'd be passing through it in a few minutes. The first
battle of the war in Yugoslavia between the enemy and the guerrillas took
place on the edge of that village. One of the first, anyway. Vojeslav had
run away from home to take part in it. They didn't have any real weapons
so they used some old guns the Russians gave Cernagora in the nineteenth century in reward for declaring war on somebody. The boy slowed
down to something under fifty miles an hour as we passed through the
valley where he said the first battle took place. But a little farther along
he pulled on the brake and said he wanted to show us something. It was
an Italian graveyard with the names of the soldiers and the names of their
outfits written in their own language. This was where the second battle
of the war had been. Vojeslav walked up and down the rows of stones.
Then he came over to where we were and said he wondered how many of
these men he had killed himself. He said it just like that. It sounded as if
he were wondering how many slices of toast he'd had for breakfast the
day before yesterday.

After we got started again the boy said he was now a mechanic and
chauffeur by trade. He worked at that until five o'clock every day except
when he had special jobs. Did he consider what he was doing today a
special job? No, this wasn't much. But last week he had a real one. Last
week he drove the Bulgarian Ambassador to Albania fifty or sixty miles
through the mountains. His father used to own a garage in Podgorica.
Now his father was dead. Vojeslav supported the family. That meant his
mother, two sisters, and two brothers. He said all four of them were

"young." He was in the Partisans for seven months before the Italians captured him and sent him to a prison camp. Finally he escaped. Then he went back into the Partisans. But it was different after that. By that time the Partisans were well organized and they didn't give men his age a gun. He was fourteen then. So they made him a courier. He didn't want to talk about that part of the war. He'd rather talk about what he did in the hills with one of those old Russian muskets. Or about his life now. He was excited about his life now. He worked until five o'clock and then he went to school for two hours. Then he studied music until 9 P.M. He was studying the violin, the piano, the cello, and the harmonica. But what he really would like to play would be the drums. In his spare time he used a typewriter for the Trade Union Council, or he worked on his motorcycle. A jeep's all right, but you can have more fun with a motorcycle.

Vojeslav refused a cigarette every time one was offered him. Finally he said we should know by now that he didn't smoke or drink either. He said driving a car was his only vice. Now we were doing the corkscrewing act again. Anita whispered that she thought Vojeslav's vice was getting the better of him. We went around most of the curves on two wheels. Vojeslav said it was all right though, because this was the best jeep in Cernagora. It never used a drop of oil.

Then Vojeslav concentrated on the curves and Obradović told us the rest of his story. We understood, did we, that he was a writer? He had written poems, novels, and "serious books." By the time the war started he hadn't had anything published. But he had a room full of manuscripts in his home in Cetinje. Even his mother, who didn't know much about such things, thought some of them were good. But he gave his best things to a Russian girl in Scolpje to keep for him. They were in love and were going to be married someday. He left her on April the fifth. She was killed on April the sixth. He never did find out what happened to the manuscripts he had given her for safekeeping. Then, when the Germans came to Cetinje, his mother thought that it was best for his sake that she burn all the manuscripts she was keeping for him. If the Germans found them they might get him into trouble. So she burned them. Obradović said he hadn't been able to write a single word since then. Not a single word. It was psychological, he supposed. Did we understand? He couldn't sit down to a typewriter any more. Something had happened to him inside. Right here. And he pointed to his head. The rest of the way to Titograd he kept rubbing his head or the scars on his wrists. He didn't say anything more for nearly an hour.

Chapter Fifty-Five

WANTED—MORE TRUCKS, FEWER DIPLOMATS

As WE went through the town of Zeto, which is now called Obod, we were told that this was where the first printing press in the Balkans had been set up. It was also on the edge of Obod that we met Mrs. Kalog. Of course that wasn't her real name. That was just the way she spelled it when she got to America. When she returned to Yugoslavia she changed it back again to Marsha Kalujerović. We met her quite by accident. We had to slow down because there were seventy-five or a hundred women with shovels and pickaxes over their shoulders marching down the road. Most of them were singing. One of them told us this was part of an International Women's Day competition. Prizes were going to be given at the ceremonies to the women who won the voluntary work competition. So they were going off today to help build an electric plant for the next village. Their own village had electricity. But the next village still used kerosene lamps. So each day they gave a few hours of their time to help build a power plant so the next village wouldn't have to use kerosene lamps any more either. They hauled rocks and shoveled sand. Sometimes they worked as much as five or six hours a day.

We asked which was the youngest of them. They said probably Jasna. She was twelve. The oldest? That caused an argument. Marsha Kalujerović thought she was the oldest. The rest of them laughed at her and said she was only sixty-two. Plenty of them were older than that. Four of them said they were seventy. We never did get the final answer because when Marsha Kalujerović heard Anita translating to me she came over and started talking to us in a pure Bronx dialect. She said she was the mother of Dan Kalog of New York. Of course we must know Dan. It was a pity if we didn't because he was a fine lad.

Then there was her brother Blajo in Hazelton, Pennsylvania. His name's Kalog too. They all changed it to Kalog because Americans don't seem to be able to pronounce words that have many syllables to them. Blajo didn't change his first name but everyone in Hazelton calls him Billy. She'd been twenty years in New York. But when her husband died she came back. How did she like it here? Okay! Of course it wasn't like New York, but it was okay. Yes, this really was voluntary labor. No one forced them to do it. You don't have to force people, she said, to do things for themselves. Things that make life better for themselves. They help the next village get some electric lights. And then next month maybe the other village will help them get something. That's the way it is around here. Everybody helps everybody else.

No, she hadn't heard any stories from America about slave labor and dictatorship in Yugoslavia. Dictatorship was what the Germans had had, wasn't it? She didn't know about things like that. She didn't know what they were saying in New York or Hazelton either. She hadn't heard from her brother in years. Hadn't seen him since '34. Dan wrote sometimes. If we saw Dan we should tell him that she needed a new winter coat. It got cold working on the road this time of the year. Even if you were only sixty-two.

Alecj Obradović made the driver stop just before we went down the last hill into Titograd, or Podgorica as I couldn't help calling it. We parked the jeep by the side of the road, which was near the left bank of the Moracca River. Obradović said those caves we could see over on the far bank of the river were clawed out of the sand by the people of Podgorica who left the city when the British and American bombs began to drop. There were seventeen thousand people living in Podgorica at that time. A lot of them are alive today because they took shelter in the caves. Some of them still live there, summer and winter, because their homes were destroyed. That rowboat coming up the river now. That's full of some of them. Watch it and you'll see which cave they live in. All the bridges across the river into the city were destroyed, of course. But there's one new suspension bridge now. Those men working on the road are German prisoners. This is one place they're repairing damage they didn't make themselves.

Down in the center of Titograd, Obradović told us that this was the most modern city in all Cernagora before it was destroyed. Every street was paved with cement and there were some good modern buildings here. They called it the most beautiful city in Cernagora too. The first bombs dropped on May 1, 1944. The next morning twelve hundred bodies were dug out of the ruins. That was only the beginning. The worst raids were the ones the Americans made later. But not so many people were killed because everyone went out into the hills where the Germans were also hiding. Only they didn't go into the same hills. Nobody knows how many people were killed in the sixty American raids because they're still finding bodies today. If we looked at the round places in the cement roads which were filled with black asphalt we could tell where every bomb landed. Anita wanted to measure them, so we paced them off. They were all either exactly fifty feet or exactly seventy-five feet across.

Titograd was like Rogatica. Except that we were seeing this city by broad daylight. It was like the financial district of London around St. Paul's after the big blitz. Any buildings which were left standing were just skeletons of what they had been. Obradović said it was going to take a lot of work to make Titograd as beautiful a city as Podgorica had been. But the women and children had cleared away the worst of the debris and reconstruction had already begun. Only there wouldn't be any new houses for people to live in here. Titograd was being rebuilt across the river. An industrial city. If we would like to see the latest word in workers' housing . . .

So we drove across the river. By our standards they were just neat little bungalows which you wouldn't have looked at a second time in America. But here, in this land of mud huts and houses held together with bits of old straw, they were something to gasp at. We went through five of them. They had hot and cold running water, electricity, shower baths, American-looking kitchens, flower gardens in front, vegetable gardens in back. And the rent was going to be only four hundred dinar a month. That's eight dollars. Anita said she wouldn't mind living in one of them herself.

Back in the center of town I wandered away from the other three and found a truck parking lot. There were several British trucks, three Italian, six of a French make I had never heard of before, and the rest were ours. The French trucks were the newest. The engine was in the rear. The cabs were upholstered like a limousine. They had heaters and more gadgets than Goering's armored car. There were fifteen or twenty Yugoslavs standing around. Obradović had warned me not to wander off on my own. He was afraid someone would recognize me as an American and he wasn't sure what the reaction would be. After all, the people here knew whose bombs had destroyed their city. But I took a chance. I asked the men who were eying me what they thought of the French machines. *"Strašno!"* they said. And they said it as if they meant it. When you ask a Yugoslav how he likes something he either says *"dobro"* or *"strašno."* Serbo-Croat is a language of extremes. And the Yugoslavs are people of extremes. No happy middle ground. Things are either "wonderful, fine, lovely, perfect," or they're "strašno," which means horrible, dreadful, terrible, worthless.

Then I went over and pointed to the name plates on the Italian trucks. "Strašno." But this time they said it without any exclamation mark. Without quite so much feeling. The British lorries? "Dobro." But not with much enthusiasm. Finally I got to the corner of the lot where the American trucks were parked. I had thirty or forty men following me by this time. I went from machine to machine patting the words Dodge, Chevrolet, GMT. Then I turned to them for their reaction. I got a chorus of "dobros" and this time there was no question what they meant. Even if I hadn't ever heard that word for "good, wonderful," I would have known how they felt. Several men caressed the name plates as if they were stroking a kitten. They had the American trucks all classified. Some were better than others. This Dodge was better than the one beside it. They liked the Chevrolet for this reason. The GMT for some other reason. It went on for half an hour. We got into the trucks. We got under the trucks. We climbed on top of them. And all the while they were chattering a mile a minute about how much they liked them. They treated me as if I had invented every one of those machines and had personally presented them to them as gifts. Then some of the truck drivers took me into a kafana and insisted that I be their guest while we had little glasses of rakia and drank toasts to "Gospodin Chevrolet" and "Gospodin GMT," as if they were men. As I sat there drinking with them I kept thinking that the automobiles we send abroad are really our best ambassadors of good will.

And then we did the errand I had come here purposely to do. Once before I had taken time out to go to a field on the edge of this city and lay some wild flowers on the grave of someone I knew. Sonia and I were alone that other time. She picked the flowers while I took photographs of the six white crosses. Five were for the five British fliers in the crew of the plane and the sixth for War Correspondent Ralph Barnes of the New York *Herald Tribune.* Ralph was the first American war correspondent killed in World War II. One night in 1940 we had a party for him at the Athenee Palace Hotel in Bucharest, Rumania. The next thing we knew he was dead. He'd gone on a bombing mission in a British plane which got lost in a storm and hit the side of a mountain behind Podgorica.

It was just as well that I had more company on this visit, because Titograd looked so much different than Podgorica six years ago that I couldn't even find the right road. We finally did locate a high school boy who said his uncle had been at the funeral of the six men back in 1940. His uncle knew where the graves were. We asked him if he could go and get his uncle to act as a guide for us. But Anita had noticed a button on his coat lapel and now the boy was telling her what that button stood for. It meant that he was going to work on the Youth Railroad this year. There were two hundred and fifty-six boys and girls in his class at school. Only those with passing grades could go. Twenty-five didn't have passing grades. So the rest of them were taking turns tutoring the twenty-five. Maybe their class would have a 100 per cent record after all. That was what they were trying for. Wouldn't it be great if . . .

But I interrupted him. Where was his uncle? Oh, his uncle. He was sorry but his uncle was dead. He was killed when the British started dropping their bombs.

Half an hour later we found two men who not only remembered the British plane hitting the side of Garać Mountain, but they even helped bring down the bodies. They helped dig the graves. They both attended the funeral services. So Sherif Krnić and Tahir Jgećević took us to where the graves were.

It didn't look like the same place at all. I was sure they had made a mistake and I said so. I remembered very well the six white crosses with the English wording on them. There were no crosses at all on the spot the two men pointed out to us. The two men laughed bitterly and said no, nothing around here looks the way it used to look. We'd have to get used to that. If we got down on our hands and knees we could see the stumps of the crosses. We could see how the Germans had hacked them down with axes. They'd probably used the wood of the crosses to make fires to keep warm.

Anita saw how I felt so she said:

"If it's any consolation, look how they treated the graves of their own allies!"

There were hundreds of Italian graves that hadn't been here before. Maybe thousands. They stretched as far across the field as we could see. There was an iron cross over each grave. There had been a metal name plate fastened to each cross. The Germans must have worked hard to get those name plates off because they were all bent and twisted. They lay in a pile on top of the graves of Ralph Barnes and the five British fliers. They made quite a sizable pile. I picked one up and put it in my pocket. It was from the grave of Dante Lupi. He had been in the 383d Regiment of the 217th Division. He was killed on the seventeenth of June, 1943, according to the grave tag. Anita said:

"What on earth do you want that for?"

I told her it was going to be a little souvenir to remind me of something someday when I might have forgotten a lot of other things.

On the way back to the jeep Obradović promised that he would see to it that the American grave was cared for by someone.

And then we went over to look at a big Catholic cemetery behind a stone wall. An American bomb had landed right in the center of the place. It looked like no graveyard I had ever seen before. Most of the crosses had been used to fill in the crater the bomb had left. It was not a sight to increase one's affection for the business of war.

PART SIX

These Are the Croatians

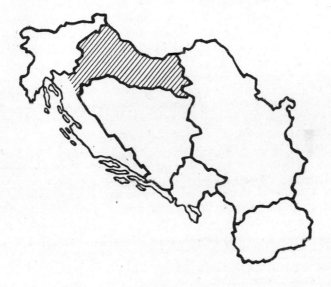

Chapter Fifty-Six

CULTURE AND THIN BREAD

FOR WEEKS we had been wandering around some of the most culturally backward parts of Yugoslavia. Now we were on our way to Zagreb, capital of the republic of Croatia, where the people do not like to think of themselves as part of the Balkans. Zagreb was founded before the birth of Christ by the Romans. For centuries it was part of the Austro-Hungarian Empire and it reflected the culture of the north. In the early days of the monarchy, Croat-hating Serbs would say with a sneer to tourists:

"You're looking for antiques, are you? Then skip Serbia. We have no antiques in our homes. Every generation, at least, we have had to fight for our freedom and our liberty and our independence. Every generation, at least, some foreign power has tried to take those things away from us. They never succeeded in taking from us our love of those things. But they did take our antiques each time they looted our homes. So you'll find no antiques in Serbia. But go up to Croatia. You'll find plenty of antiques up there. The Croats never have fought for their freedom and liberty and independence. Their homes are full of antiques."

The bitterest hatreds in Old Yugoslavia were between Croats and Serbs. It worked both ways. The Italians capitalized on these deep-rooted animosities. Even before the war started they sponsored the Ustaši of Ante Pavelić, who had been implicated in the murder of King Alexander at Marseilles in 1934. Hundreds of thousands of Serbs were massacred by the Croatian Ustaši. But before it was over there was as great a percentage of Croats in the Partisan Army as there were people of any other section of Yugoslavia. Many Croatian families lost their antiques. Many lost their homes. Many lost their lives.

In the weeks that Anita and I had been working our way through Bosnia, Dalmatia, and Montenegro we hadn't encountered a bathtub and hot water anywhere at the same time. But now we were headed for the cultured city of Zagreb where there would be good hotels, food in the Western manner, and some other things we had missed in our travels. We had been in sections where the rate of illiteracy was almost 90 per cent. Around Zagreb it isn't any higher than it is in many parts of the United States. Zagreb would mean bread cut in thin slices. It would mean saying a person had education if he had gone to a university and not just finished four years of primary school. It would mean calling a man a professor if he taught at least in some kind of college. It might mean the end of fleas for a while.

Zagreb was having a fierce rainstorm the night we arrived. But we hadn't seen bright lights for so long that we went into the public square anyway. Thousands of people were there ahead of us. They were standing in the downpour watching a free movie. The screen was on the far side of the square on the front of a three-story building. The films were of sports contests, railroad building, harvesting, parades, and celebrations in various parts of Yugoslavia. There were also some newsreels from Moscow. There were no pictures from America of baseball games, bathing-beauty contests, or anything else. Anita said that that was too bad. While the movies were being shown a loud-speaker filled the square with music. Maybe it was the music that kept the crowd there. Or maybe it was what they saw on the screen. Anyway thousands of people stood there oblivious to the soaking they were getting.

The next day we watched a long line of people of all ages signing up to start work the first of April on a concrete road which was to be built from Zagreb to Belgrade. It was all to be voluntary work. No pay. It was to be named The Road of Unity and Brotherhood. As we watched the people in line Anita said, just to think that four or five years ago Croatian terrorists were killing Serbs by the thousands, and God only knows how many Croats the Serbian Chetniks killed. Yet today they're standing in line to volunteer to build a road to tie Croatia and Serbia closer together.

That afternoon we paid a call on the Tito-Partisan Lyceum. Franjo Hrabak, who ran the school, had been a mathematics professor before the war. During the occupation he did underground work for the Partisans until he was caught and sent to prison. He had seven hundred pupils now. Some were children of fourteen. Some were adult men and women. The idea of the school was to do something about the education of Tito's former soldiers who had lost out on their schooling while they were substituting guns for books in the mountains. Orphans of Partisans were also admitted. It was a speedup course. They covered a year's work in four months. As we were going down the hall Anita asked if I had seen two boys talking together in the doorway. One was totally blind. The other had no feet. The headmaster said the boy without feet had had them amputated because they got frozen while he was in the mountains. We asked the headmaster to let us pick several children at random as they went down the hall and take them into his office for a talk. So we did.

Ilja Raletić sat on the edge of his chair while he told us what had happened to him. He was fifteen. He had on ski boots and a brown mackinaw because there was no heat in the building. After the Germans seized his village of Broćnac they turned it over to the Ustaši to occupy. One morning at 3 A.M. the Ustaši went around the village rounding up people whom they took to a hill and beat with hammers and stones. That's how his father was killed. Eighty were killed that way. The next day a carload of Ustaši stopped in the village and the people killed them all with axes. Ilja helped do it. With axes and sickles. It wasn't nice, he said, but we were awfully mad. I guess I was a little crazy. After what they did to my father. Then everyone in the village went to the woods. I went with my mother and aunt, and my six brothers and sisters. The Ustaši burned down our whole village. We went to the only village that wasn't burned in that whole part of Yugoslavia. One day the Ustaši came there, too, and said not to worry. They were through burning villages. That's what they said. Then they burned that one too. My sister was burned alive. They threw my mother's body and my brothers' bodies into a big pit. The others were wounded. But one brother and I ran into the woods. In the woods the Partisans saw that I had no shoes and was naked. So they took me to their headquarters. I was with them two months. I saw Croatian people joining the Partisans with forks and spades. I worked for the Partisans as a courier. Then, when the war was over, they sent me here. I won a contest last year and was supposed to go to the Soviet Union for a visit. But the trip was canceled because some of the boys got sick. School isn't easy for me. I guess it's because I forgot everything I'd learned. But I've done four years of school in one year and maybe everything will be all right now.

The next one we picked was Branko Zrakić from the village of Klasnić. He picked him because he had no hands and only one eye. He didn't seem a bit unhappy. He grinned every time we looked at him. Ilja had cried once. That was when he was telling us what had happened to his mother and sisters. But Branko didn't break down at all. He said he remembered very well, just like it was yesterday, how his mother and two brothers were killed. It was on a Sunday and they were all going to church in the next village in their best costumes. The girls and women were all dressed in white. There were eight hundred people in the church in the village of Glina because it was some special religious day. They were all killed with knives. All except two of them who ran up into the steeple and pulled up the ladder. They were shot from the ground after they had been up there three days. Branko hadn't gone to church that day. He was feeling sick. He was glad he had been feeling sick that day. He ran into the woods and found the Partisans. Most of the time he was a courier. He was eleven years old then. It was while he was a courier that he lost his eye and his hands. He wasn't sure exactly what happened. Someone told him he probably stepped on a mine. Anita asked Branko what he was studying to be. He said he didn't know for sure. He'd have to wait and see how he made out. Then he said would we like to see how he wrote. So I gave him my fountain pen. He unscrewed the cap with the stubs of his arms, which had been cut off just below the elbow. Then he took the pen in the two stubs and wrote his name on a piece of paper. I put the paper in my pocket with the Italian grave marker to keep. I told him he wrote better without any hands than Anita did. That made him smile and say *"hvala."*

Sveto Slight was from the village of Slunj. He didn't look as if anything much had ever happened to him. But a great deal had. He went into the Partisans when he was twelve. He learned to operate a typewriter at headquarters. The next year he was wounded in the stomach. It happened during an attack on headquarters. The German who shot him was only ten feet away. It was the next day before anyone found him. Sveto said it didn't hurt much except that he couldn't walk. He was in a Partisan hospital for three months. Then an American plane came and took him to Bari, Italy. Then to Naples. Then to Rome. Then to a hospital in Africa. Then to the British Clinic at Manchester, England. Then back to Rome. Then back to Bari. Then to Belgrade. Then to Zagreb. He thought he had had about nine operations on his stomach in all those places, but he was afraid he'd lost count. What he would do after he graduated from this school would be to go to the university and study engineering and philosophy. Then he could decide what he wanted to be.

The last of them was Presjna Treursić. She was only nineteen but she'd been a Partisan officer. She said her big worry all the time she was in the mountains was about what had happened to her mother and two sisters whom she'd left in the city of Split. She found out when she finally got home after the end of the war. An allied radio broadcast had warned the civilians in Split that their city might be bombed at any time. If they lived near military objectives they were to move at once. Presjna's mother and two sisters lived near the shipyard, so they moved way out to the edge of the city. A few nights later there was an allied air raid. One bomb fell right on the house they'd moved to. Thirty-two people who lived there were killed. Her mother and sisters were among those killed. The house near the shipyard wasn't hit at all. No bombs fell that night anywhere near the shipyard. Presjna's voice was cold and hard when she got to this part of the story. Anita and I didn't say anything except to thank her and tell her we hoped she would have a successful career after her graduation.

Then we went to the Zagreb University Student Home. It was like a dormitory in any American college. On the door of one of the student rooms there were signs that said:

"Sorry, We Have No Cigarettes."

"Please Don't Waste Our Valuable Time."

"Don't Enter Without a Reason."

"Visiting Hours, 12–2; 6–8."

They wanted us to see the student home so they could explain the difference between education yesterday and today. Before the war, they said, only 5 per cent of the students in Zagreb University were children of peasants or working people. Now most of the ten thousand students are from such families. One quarter of them pay the full fees. Fifty per cent pay half fees. The other quarter pay nothing at all. It costs two dollars a month to live in the student home. Food is twelve dollars a month. The students go into the forest and cut their own fuel. The lazy ones go cold because each room has its own stove. The room which is used as a cafeteria was once the Ustaši political prison. The president of the student council said some of the students' parents had been killed in this very room. In the cafeteria there were special tables for students with various diseases. One table was for ulcer patients. I noticed that the longest table was labeled "T.B."

Chapter Fifty-Seven

RANKIN, PENNSYLVANIA

WE POSTPONED going back to Belgrade when we heard about Vojnić. They said Vojnić had been a Serbian "island" in the heart of Croatia. After the Ustaši got through there was no Vojnić any more. Maybe a few people had come out of the woods alive, but for all intents and purposes Vojnić was dead. What was happening now at the spot where Vojnić once stood was proof, they said, of the new feeling between various nationalities in Yugoslavia. A fund had been raised to rebuild this once Serbian town. People in Zagreb, Croatians all of them, had stood in line to give money, watches, jewelry, anything they had for the rebuilding of Vojnić. We must see it for ourselves, they said.

Ratko Brzić was the one who talked the most to us about Vojnić. We met him the first day we were in Zagreb. We thought he was British. Even after he told us his name we thought he must be British. He talked with a pure Oxfordian accent. It was never the Germans. It was always "the Jerries." It was "old chappie." And "old boy." When he said "schedule" he pronounced it as if it started out with a "shed" instead of a "sked." He said he picked up his accent working with British troops during the war as a liaison officer for the Partisans. Apparently all his contacts had been with the old-school-tie boys. At least there was no trace of Cockney in the way he talked. But Ratko Brzić knew this part of Croatia so we took him along.

We went by train as far as the district capital of Karlovac. On the way Ratko asked whether we liked Shelley. He was translating Shelley into Serbo-Croat. I said the question wasn't how *we* liked Shelley but how the Yugoslavs would like him. Then Ratko said it was strange about language. Before the war the Yugoslavs adopted many English words such as radio, telegraph, telephone, and automobile because we originated the inventions and the words to go with them. But when the Ustaši took over Croatia during the occupation they decided to purify the language of all foreign "contaminations." So they invented new words for many things. Telegraph became *brzoglas,* or "speedy voice." For automobile or motorcar the people were ordered to say *samovoz,* which means "self-driving vehicle." For the nice little word radio they were forced to substitute *krugoval,* which is a very technical term meaning "circular wave." One reason intellectuals such as Ratko were glad about the defeat of the Ustaši was so they could forget those unnatural words and go back to radio, car, and telegraph.

At Karlovac we called on the district president, Marko Polović. He had seven all-gold teeth. While we were stumbling around in Serbo-Croat saying *dobar dan* and telling him who we were and why we were here he suddenly said good morning. Just like that. "Good morning." And those weren't the only words he knew. He spoke perfect English. So I told Anita she could take a vacation today. But it turned out that he and Anita had once lived in the same town in Pennsylvania so I wasn't so well off as I thought I was. They kept asking each other if So-And-So was still alive and what had happened to What's-His-Name. From 1912 until 1921 Mr. Polović had been an American coal miner and steelworker. He was also an active labor leader. He said he was in Rankin, Pennsylvania, at the time of the big fire. The way he said it I decided that when I got near the New York Public Library again I'd better read up about the Big Fire at Rankin.

While he sat behind his desk talking to us I studied him. He was still just what he had been from 1912 until 1921. A member of the hard-working class. His hands were large and calloused. He was dressed in city clothes but he wore no necktie. His skin was as brown as an American Indian's. His eyes were soft. They looked like kind eyes. I told Anita that he looked as if he had a great deal of humanity inside him.

When he came back from America he returned to being a peasant in the village of Brig. All the people of Brig were related. They were all members of seven families with many cross ties. The president's farm was sixty acres. That's a big farm in Yugoslavia. But he said the land was bad. He'd tell us later more about that. But how about America? This was the first time in the twenty-six years he'd been back he'd met anyone from Pennsylvania. How was Pennsylvania now? Was it true that Brisbane was dead? He used to read the fellow's stuff every day. I couldn't tell from the way he said "stuff" how he meant it. Did either of us know Louis Adamic? Had we read any of those wonderful books by Jack London? There was a writer! So we were interested in Croatia, were we? Well, you're looking at a Croat now. This district has nearly three hundred thousand people in it. The Ustaši recruited about eight thousand members here. The Partisans recruited ten thousand. What did he do? Well, those Partisan divisions they raised kept getting wiped out. So more and more men had to be recruited. His job was to go from village to village organizing the uprising. It wasn't hard after the Germans and Chetniks and Ustaši started burning houses and killing people. They made better propaganda for the Partisans than the Partisans could make for themselves.

I decided that this was a good time to get something straightened out. So I told the president we'd been over a lot of Yugoslavia and had seen thousands, maybe tens of thousands of houses that had been destroyed by the Germans or Chetniks or Ustaši. We'd heard many stories of the atrocities they'd committed. We'd talked to some of their victims who had lived. We'd seen photographs. But now the war was over and we were interested in the plain, unvarnished truth. Even if the Partisans were better disciplined than the others, surely they must have done some burning and looting and killing of civilians too. Why didn't we ever hear about that? The president laughed and said apparently we didn't understand. The Germans started the war with a big army. The Ustaši were organized long before the fighting began. The Chetniks dated way back to the Turkish occupation. But the Partisans started from nothing. They had to win recruits. They had to get volunteers into their army. And they had to get the people of the villages to support them behind the lines. You don't win that kind of support, he said, by going around killing people and burning their houses. I said that that was good as far as it went. But there was something else. Our evidence showed that most of the homes destroyed by the others were homes of Partisans. It was revenge. It was an attempt to discourage people from helping Tito and his men. Didn't the Partisans do the same thing the other way? Didn't they take revenge on the homes and families of their internal enemies? The president shook his head of gray-black hair and said, no. The answer was still the same. He could tell us about hundreds, yes, thousands of cases of families of men off in the Chetniks and Ustaši who finally supported the Partisans because of the way the Partisans treated them. Even if we hadn't been humanitarians, the president said, it was good business.

His own family was typical of what happened around here, if we were interested. His family had been here three hundred years, living in the village of Brig. While he was organizing the other villages his wife did what she could to help the men in the hills. So the Ustaši took care of her. The president was going to let it go at that, but we asked him what they did to her. He hesitated a moment. Then he said quickly, "They hung her." He didn't say anything more for a full minute. He just looked down at the floor. Then he went on. All the four hundred people in the village of Brig, except those who were killed, were put in a concentration camp at Jasonovać. People called it the camp of death. Some say seven hundred thousand were killed there. Some say nine hundred thousand. Mostly Serbs, of course. One of his daughters got so sick being taken to the camp that the Ustaši dropped her out of a truck right here in Karlovac. She hasn't been right since. One son was killed fighting with the Partisans. His youngest child was just a baby then. Now he's in a trade school. He's going to get a real education. They didn't have any trade schools around here before the war. Nobody cared whether a peasant's children got any education or not. Most schools were private, and if you couldn't pay you couldn't go. Life is different now in many ways for the people of Brig. For those who lived and came back. Now, the president said, there's more unity. People participate in meetings and conferences. They take part in the community life. That's because they've got some rights. Men from the cities used to come in whenever an election was held and see that the people they wanted won. They used the police and the army. Now the people conduct their own elections in an orderly way. And the women take part too. Then the president talked about America. He said it was all right if the people of America wanted to make propaganda against Yugoslavia. The way they live is different from the way people are now living in Yugoslavia. He knew, because he had lived in both places. The systems are different. Time will tell which is better. But what was wrong was people criticizing something they didn't know anything about. He said he wished some of those people in America could just see his village of Brig. Then, if they didn't like it and thought it was all wrong, they'd have a right to criticize. They'd have a right to their own opinion. But the people of Brig ought to have the privilege of living the way they wanted to live, the same way the people of Rankin or any other place in America ought to have the privilege of living the way they wanted to live.

Chapter Fifty-Eight

LIDICE WITH A SERBIAN NAME

IT's TWENTY HOURS from New York to Paris by plane. Thirty-five hours from Paris to Zagreb by Simplon-Orient Express. One and a half hours from Zagreb to Karlovac by train. And from one to three hours from Karlovac to Vojnić by jeep, depending on the condition of the road and the condition of the jeep. When we got to Vojnić we found someone with a photograph taken from a hill showing the whole town in the old days. It looked a little like Pittsfield, New Hampshire, only not so large. There were three roads leading in, from the north, the east, and the west. The buildings scattered along these three roads, as they blended together, were mostly painted white. The church steeple was the highest point in town. The priest's home was right across the street. The school was only one story tall but it was a substantial building. There were several two-story residences but most of the houses were what we call the bungalow type. There was a kafana and there were several stores. The hospital was a rambling structure. The county building was old and covered with moss. The local capitalist was Milić Zivković, who went to America in 1913 and spent thirteen years working for the Westinghouse Electric Company at Turtle Creek, near East Pittsburgh. When he came home he bought the largest house in town. He rented part of it to the government for the post office. He had a drugstore on the rest of the first floor. Vojnić was the county seat. On market days it was filled with peasants from the villages. The population of Vojnić itself was only four or five hundred. But there were twenty thousand people in the nearby villages. The Vojnić people were all Serbs. All except one family. They were Croats. How they got into this Serbian "island" no one ever knew. But they'd lived here for generations and no one bothered them.

The Ustaši did the occupying of the town for the Germans. Nothing happened for the first nine months. Then the Partisans began gathering in the mountain to the south called Petrova Gora. That's when the Ustaši began their killings. They used the church with the tall steeple as their place of execution. That was in January of '42. They didn't kill just Vojnić people. They brought in truckloads of women and children from the outlying villages. When the Partisans heard about it they attacked. They weren't ready for a battle yet because they had hardly any weapons. But when they heard about what was happening in the church they attacked anyway. Peasants from the villages and the Vojnić people helped them. Even though some of them fought with shovels and spades. When the Ustaši saw that they were going to lose the town they set fire to the church to get rid of that much of the evidence of their crimes. The fire was put out. But all that remained of the church was the four bare walls.

The Partisans held Vojnić that first time for less than three months. Then the Ustaši came back with Italian help and recaptured the town. Another two months went by and the Partisans came down from the mountain again. This time the Ustaši did a thorough job. First they burned Vojnić to the ground. Then they took every man, woman, and child in town and hundreds more from the villages and drove them ahead of them down the road to Karlovac. There were twenty-seven hundred civilians in the line of march. Some eventually were sent to camps in Germany. Some died in camps without ever leaving Yugoslavia. But none of them ever came back. Vojnić now was Lidice with a Serbian name. There was no Vojnić any more. The place where the town had stood was fought over until the end of the war. First one side held it and then another. But it wasn't Vojnić any more. It was just a place people remembered as the place where a town had once been. In the winter the snow covered all traces of what had been there, except the four gray walls of the roofless church.

When we drove in from the north Vojnić wasn't anything like the picture they showed us. There were no neat white-painted houses. No flower beds or well-trimmed grass. Vojnić was *bloto*. Bloto is one of the best words in the Serbian language. It means mud. But it says it a lot better than "mud." It makes it sound deeper. Maybe that's because the mud generally *is* deeper in Yugoslavia. You sink in it until your ankles are out of sight. Anyway, Vojnić was bloto that day. The roads of Vojnić were churned up and so were the fields. Things were happening in the fields. Teams of oxen were bringing logs down from Petrova Mountain. Thirty-five German prisoners of war with nothing but hand tools were taking the logs and working them up into wagon wheels, ax handles, tongues for oxcarts, and even pieces of furniture. Peasant women in red and black costumes were pushing wheelbarrow loads of sand and rocks. Two young surveyors were making measurements for something. Hundreds of people were building a new town where an old one had been.

We stood in the mud of what they called a street and talked to a dozen town officials and workmen. Not one of them was a Vojnić native. Most of them came from the villages. They had escaped the big roundup in various ways. One had been sick in a hospital. One had hid in the woods for three years. I told Anita we ought to get the past straightened out before we went into the present or the future. Let's see if we could find out how many people had been killed in the church. The men looked at each other dumbly. A man in a fur cap said nobody counted them. How did we expect them to know? They killed people every night in the church. No one was standing around keeping score. The Ustaši themselves buried a lot of them secretly. He was quite belligerent about it. We'd have to ask God if we wanted the figure. Another peasant said he'd guess five hundred. He was immediately jumped on by all the others. The Man

in the Fur Hat said he knew where there were one hundred and forty-
five pieces. All buried in a single spot. I asked Anita what he meant by
"pieces." She said she didn't know. That's what he'd said. One hundred
and forty-five pieces. Another man pointed toward the northwest and said
if we felt like walking he'd take us up there and show us a place where
hundreds of bodies had been dumped into a hole. We could still see the
bones if we wanted to. The man beside him said he knew one family that
lost twenty-six. Just the one family. That started them talking about individual stories. There was the family with the four daughters who all died.
There was the family that lost seventeen. One of the men pointed to the
west and said there was a coal mine in that direction which they used for
a graveyard to save digging. Now no one will ever want to mine coal
around there again. The Fur Hat said how could anyone tell about numbers when the Ustaši had burned most of the bodies? Then what about
Voisnića? Hadn't anyone told us about Voisnića? It was one kilometer
from here. They burned everything and killed everybody. Just like here
in Vojnić. We asked them if they had ever heard of Lidice. Nobody had.
They said where was it? We said it really didn't matter.

So we stopped trying to get statistics and walked over to where the
church had been. It looked like an ancient Roman ruins. The inside was
deep to the knees in rubble and debris. While Anita tried to count the
bullet holes in the walls I poked around with a stick and found a small
red-and-green knitted glove made for a child. For a child of about five. I
wondered what else I'd find under that blackened mess if I kept digging.
But I didn't. Then they showed us the priest's home. Or at least where it
had been. And the old County Building. And the hospital. And the
school. But they all looked the same. Just piles of gray stones, or a cellar
hole, or a few wheelbarrow loads of bricks. I said we'd seen enough ruins.
Let's see the new Vojnić. On the way they told us they were building a
town now for two thousand people. Not for just four or five hundred. It
was going to be one of the best county seats in all Yugoslavia. They might
even be able, later, to have water pumped in so people could have toilets.
Real toilets. Inside the house. This was going to be a planned community.
They were starting from scratch. Everything was going to be better than
it had been before. It was a pity that the people who had lived here
wouldn't be able to enjoy it. But the name Vojnić would live. Even if all
the people of Vojnić were dead.

First they showed us a line of sixteen stores. The buildings were all
finished and some of the stores were open already. Outside, the buildings
were all the same except that they were painted different colors, from
blushing pink to deep green. It looked like a suburban subdivision. The
Family Co-operative was selling men's suits for twenty-six dollars and
seventy-nine cents. Not very fancy suits, but all right for the country. A
woman's rough wool dress for four dollars and eighty-one cents. Secondhand shoes. Pots and pans. In the Farmers' Co-operative there were work
pants for nine dollars and twenty-six cents. There was a grain store and a

post office. The town pharmacy was the neatest place of all. Fourteen houses were finished. The school was still only one story tall but it would have seven grades instead of just four. Work had started on a two-story dormitory for government employees. The County Building was already two stories high, and it looked as if it might wind up being three. The foundation was in for a trade school.

On the way out of town Anita noticed that a family of two women and three children were living in a lean-to they'd built of corn shocks around a chimney which was all that remained of somebody's house. It was like an Indian tepee. We both wondered what happened when it rained or snowed.

Chapter Fifty-Nine

"BLOTO" IS PERFECT

It was exactly 3:17 P.M. when the jeep broke down in the center of the village of Knezević Kosa. Knezević Kosa was a general store and three houses. It sounded to me as if there was water in the gas line. But the boy who was driving thought he'd better take the engine apart. He started with the carburetor.

The man who designed the jeep tried to think of everything to make the operation and repair of the machine simple for soldiers who might have trouble under fire. You can change a wheel on a jeep in one fifth the time it takes to change a wheel on any other American car. But the makers of the jeep apparently didn't contemplate that thousands of their vehicles eventually would be driven by young Yugoslavs, Bulgarians, Rumanians, Greeks, Egyptians, and other people. They did include with each jeep a paper-covered book explaining everything. The two difficulties in this case were that the book was in English and the driver insisted he knew everything that was in the book anyway.

He got the carburetor apart all right. There was nothing wrong with it. Now he had to get it together again. And he did. An audience of villagers looked on with considerable admiration. But while he had all the pieces of the carburetor laid out on top of the hood the gasket fell into the *bloto*. The bloto was about eighteen inches deep. The villagers were churning it up with their feet. It wasn't until we started the engine again that the driver realized he'd put the carburetor back without any gasket. A gasket is a washer. A gasket is used in an automobile engine wherever two pieces of metal come together. It prevents any leakage of fuel or power. It's like a piece of cardboard, only it's made of a special kind of material. When the driver realized he'd lost the gasket he took the carburetor off again and tried to make a gasket. First he used newspaper. Then pieces of a poster he tore down from the window of the general store. It went on for a long time. The crowd around the jeep kept getting larger and larger. Peasants up in the hills heard about it and came down to the village for a look. The driver seemed to be enjoying it. He probably had never had so much limelight in his life.

When Anita discovered that this was the village from which he had come, the place where he'd been born, and that several of the audience were relatives, she was sure he had done it on purpose. I didn't think so. If he'd really wanted to make an impression he surely would have succeeded in fixing the jeep. But that never happened. When we left him at

7 P.M. he had already cleaned all the sparkplugs, taken the distributor apart three times, and was starting in on the differential. About the only thing he hadn't done was to check the air in the tires. Once, when he couldn't get the distributor together again, Anita tried to translate a chapter from the book entitled "What to Do if the Distributor Fails to Function." She didn't get far. She knew Serbo-Croat all right. But not the Serbo-Croat words for things like "distributor plate thumb screw."

Anyway, we started walking at 7 P.M. It was only twenty-two kilometers back to Karlovac and we figured we could make it by morning if we could only keep our feet moving up and down in the bloto. Anita and I set the pace. We were followed by the man who was translating Shelley and a member of the County Council who'd joined the party along the way somewhere. We did five kilometers the first hour and were beginning to like it. But then the poet and the politician stopped us. They said it was dangerous to go through the next valley. It was full of wolves who attacked people from hunger at this time of the year. I didn't believe them. Anita was on the fence. That made things uneven. Three to one. So we stopped in a peasant home where we saw a light. The only consolation was that dropping in on some peasants this way we might see how they lived and perhaps hear what was on their minds. So I told Anita to keep her ears open. We wouldn't try to interview them. But I wanted to know every word that was spoken while we were there.

The cottage was new. The old one had been burned down by the Ustaši because the man of the house had been in the Partisans. It was as neat a home as many American farmhouses I've been in. There was one bedroom for the two daughters and then "The Room." In "The Room" there was a fireplace, a kitchen table, a bed for husband and wife covered with a fancy hand-embroidered spread, two wooden benches, one chair, a kitchen cabinet, a bicycle, and four bolts of cloth Anita said was homespun linen. I doubted it, because the material was the color of muddy water. I'd always been told linen was white.

The peasant wife gave us glasses of *rakia*. What we really wanted was food. We hadn't had a decent meal all day. But we drank rakia. The husband had been wounded. One leg was exactly eleven centimeters shorter than the other. That was his figure. He couldn't bend his knee. The conversation the first hour was about his injury and whether he ever would be able to bend his knee.

The mother and two daughters were doing something I couldn't understand. They each had a flat board with a handle, like the paddles sophomores at college whittle out to use on freshmen at hazing time. Tied to those paddles were a few handfuls of flax just as it came from the fields. The paddles were held in the left hand at shoulder height. In their right hands they held slender sticks like the sticks drummers use. The drumstick was twirled between thumb and forefinger. Some of the flax was placed on the drumstick and the twirling made a piece of thread out of the flax as it came from the paddle. Anita said there were names for all these things, even in English. But she didn't know them. Anyway, they were making thread. We finally figured that out. Then we found why the cloth we had seen in the corner was such a strange color. The women kept wetting the flax with their lips as they twisted it into a thread. They said saliva was important. It made the fibers of flax stick together. It also gathered dirt from their hands. But they said that after several washings the saliva and dirt came out and the cloth became pure white.

But I wanted to hear what they were saying to each other. The mother and the two daughters were joined by several other village women who came in with drumsticks and paddles full of flax in their hands. They all stood in a corner on Anita's side of the room talking in whispers. The poet said it wasn't because we were there. It's the way women do in these parts. They know their place. They never interfere with the important conversation of men. The important conversation was still about the leg injury. Then the peasant husband assured us that the story about the wolves was true. He spent half an hour telling about all his friends who had been attacked. Some had been killed. During the war the Partisans around here had to fight wolves nearly as much as they fought Germans. Wolves got very hungry this time of the year.

Anita said the conversation in her corner was about cotton and flax and how to make soap and would the crops be any better this year and did they know that the children in the Ovanović family were all sick again? In other words, life was rolling along in a normal way in the village of Knezević Kosa. Except that the husband couldn't bend his leg any more. So Anita and I went to sleep with our heads on our arms on the table, while the member of the County Council walked somewhere to telephone to Karlovac to send a car for us. It was 3 A.M. when we got to bed in Karlovac.

The next morning we told the president who had lived in Pennsylvania that we wanted to see how the families of the Ustaši were being treated. He offered to drive us to the village of Belaj, which had been a Ustaši center. His car was an old 1936 seven-passenger De Soto, but it looked very fancy with his official red-and-blue flag flying from the fender. It was the first "luxury" traveling we had done anywhere in the country. As we drove along I wondered what this former steelworker would have said if someone had told him thirty years ago in Rankin or even ten years ago here in Yugoslavia that someday he would be a big official and have a car with a flag on the fender and a chauffeur to take him where he wanted to go. Now that he had them he acted as if he had always been accustomed to such things. He spoke in a quiet voice to the chauffeur and they lit cigarettes for each other. On the way the president said there were some things about this kind of democracy we ought to know. A county or district council in the old days was called an *općina*. Any decisions an općina made could always be countermanded from above. It was like the army. All authority stemmed from the top. Now it's just the opposite. All authority rests with the people. Each village selects its own candidates for the town, county, and district councils. Each two thousand people have a representative. If there are less than two thousand people in a village they get a representative anyway. And no higher body can countermand the decisions of a lower body unless the lower body has violated the Constitution. That's the big difference, he said. Don't forget that no higher body can stop a lower body from doing what it pleases.

By that time we were in Belaj. Population, three hundred. We could see only six or seven houses. The rest were scattered around the countryside. There was a school and a small town hall. We went into the school. There were eighty-seven pupils in the class run by Sofia Salamon. When we opened the door two children were kneeling on the edge of the raised platform where the teacher's desk was. Miss Salamon said she was punishing them for something wrong they had done. We could see that the president was angry. He talked quietly to the teacher so the children couldn't hear. But Anita heard. She said the teacher got a devil of a bawling out. In a quiet way. Didn't she know that in the New Yugoslavia there's no such thing as corporal punishment? Yes, this was corporal punishment. She had been strictly forbidden to punish children physically in any way. So the two children went back to their seats. Miss Salamon looked embarrassed.

We asked the children how many of their fathers had been killed during the war. A great many hands went up. A small blond child who said her name was Anka Bolsolović bubbled out the information that her father was killed in that fort right behind the school when the Partisans attacked it. How many fathers had been in the Ustaši? Most of the hands in the room went up. How many had been in the Partisans? Not a single hand. Then all the children turned around and stared at a small girl in the back row. Finally she raised her hand. In the yard the children of another class were playing hop skip and jump. Anita said:

"Obviously an international game."

Then we went down the road to the Bosiljević home. The father had been one of the Ustaši leaders responsible for killing close to a million Serbs. He was killed himself in a battle in '45 not far from here. The mother, Bara, was left with three children. Her home had not been damaged. There was a porcelain statue of the Virgin Mary on the family dressing table. In the front yard there were two oxen, five chickens, and one pig. The mother and her oldest son, Ivan, got their living by working a two-acre plot of land. Ivan was eighteen and had learned some English in school. I took him into the front yard and questioned him alone. Did he have all the privileges of the sons of Partisans? Yes. Was he ever discriminated against? He hesitated. Finally he said he was everyone's equal in every way but sometimes the other boys reminded him about what his father had done. But never his teachers or older people. Back in the house the mother said the government was making it possible for Ivan to continue his studies at the *gymnasium*. She had no complaints but she did miss her husband.

On the way back to Karlovac the president said Ivan hadn't told us the whole truth. During the war he had been a member of the Ustaši Youth Organization and had done a few things that were pretty bad. That was overlooked. But about a year ago the local authorities discovered some counterrevolutionary activity going on in this section. It was being organized by the Ustaši and was aimed at stirring Croats and Serbs up against one another again. Ivan was one of those involved. He was questioned and admitted it. He was not arrested but he was given a lecture and then the school authorities expelled him. The president himself thought the boy should be given another chance so he persuaded the people of Belaj to allow Ivan to continue his studies at another school.

I asked the president about every house we passed. We stopped and checked up on a few. In most cases homes of Partisans were in ruins. We didn't find one Ustaši home that had even been damaged.

We got back to Zagreb that night, bought some salami in a delicatessen store, got the waiter at the Esplanade Hotel to give us some bread, and took a second-class day coach to Belgrade. We shared a compartment with six doctors, four men, and two women. They were on the faculty of Zagreb University but were going to Scolpje to establish a medical college in the new University of Macedonia. Their chief had studied eight years in America. We told him about the children of the Drina Valley whose flesh was turning yellow. We asked him if a prolonged diet of corn could do that. He said it not only could change the pigmentation of the skin but eventually would cause death from malnutrition. Corn lacks caloric value and is deficient in most of the vitamins. Corn is a very bad diet, he said, unless people also have milk, which they don't have in many parts of Bosnia. He said the doctors of Yugoslavia were going to have plenty of trouble on their hands unless help came from somewhere soon.

Chapter Sixty

BACK TO WAGGING TONGUES

ON THE WAY BACK to Belgrade I told Anita I still had Macedonia, Slovenia, South Serbia, and the Vojvodina to cover. She said she'd like to do all of them with me. Maybe she could make a telephone call to New York when we reached Belgrade. But when we did reach Belgrade there were two cables waiting for her. I didn't see what they said. But Anita took the first train for Paris and the first plane she could get across the Atlantic. When she left I told her I hoped they would have a happy married life.

I dedicated my first evening back in the Majestic Hotel to my collection of fleas. After I'd put a daub of iodine on each of the seventy-eight bites I could have passed for a spotted leopard. A fleabite is like unrequited love. The unhappiness it causes increases in geometric ratio to the length of time that has passed since the inoculation by the virus. But you can catch a flea. That first night back in Belgrade I tried to catch mine. The accepted Balkan technique is with a cake of wet soap. You search and hunt until finally you spot one. You creep up on him silently and cautiously, taking great care not to warn him of his approaching doom. Then, with a lightning-like motion, you press the cake of soap against the spot where you hope he still is. The odds are about thirty-seven to one that he's taken a nineteen-inch broad jump and evaded you. But if not, you have him preserved for all time in the softness of the soap. After the cake of soap is well dotted with black specks you can either throw it out the hotel window or send it to a museum of natural history. It isn't advisable to keep it. Just seeing it will make the irritation of your bites last longer than the normal two or three weeks.

That first night back in Belgrade was like a night during the blitz in London in some ways. Except that there were no sirens. Every few minutes guns went off. They shook the whole city. But I had a hot bath, and the bed was soft, and the sheets were clean, so I went to sleep anyway. If World War III had started it would be atom bombs and you can't run from an atom bomb. The next morning, while I was dressing, I realized what it had been. This was the time of the year that the Danube begins to break up. Ice flows get jammed against the bases of the bridges. It takes quick work with dynamite to keep the bridges from being swept away. I'd heard dynamiting like this before. It reverberates through all of Belgrade and makes people very jittery until they know what it is. At lunch that noon Jacqueline, from the embassy, said what a funny hour of the night to be celebrating the signing of the Paris Treaty! Why hadn't they waited until morning? She'd counted the salutes. There were exactly one hundred and twenty-one of them.

That night the Lotus Bar in Belgrade was crowded until closing time. Halfway through the evening a Yugoslav at a table near ours went into the center of the dance floor and made an impromptu speech. He was very drunk. But he was very articulate. I wrote down his words while he was saying them. He said:

"I like my freedom. That's why I like America. I want to be able to say what I think. There's no freedom in Yugoslavia. That's what's wrong here. What about Osna? We can't speak our minds."

It was a longer speech than that. But the rest was mostly repetition. Several Americans sitting at a table in the corner applauded. The rest of the crowd either laughed or ignored him. A Yugoslav army captain told the man he was drunk and he'd better go home. But he didn't. He stayed and ordered another rakia. It was 3 A.M. when the Lotus Bar closed. I didn't want to stay that long. But I did want to see what happened to the speechmaker. We followed him a mile down the street. I don't know whether he got home all right or not. But nobody except us seemed a bit interested in him. When last seen he was weaving his happy way toward Zemun, across the Sava.

The next noon I had lunch at the Foreign Press Club with eight of Yugoslavia's principal newspaper and magazine editors. When the plates were cleared away and coffee arrived they asked if there were any questions I'd like to put to them. After seeing a bit of the country, was there anything that bothered me? If I would talk frankly they would too. So we talked frankly. I asked them how, under their definition of a free press, they justified the fact that it was three days after President Truman delivered his speech announcing his new Greek-Turkish policy before the speech finally was published in the Yugoslav press. There was silence for exactly twenty-five seconds. Then they all began to talk at once. Only not to me. To each other, in Serbian. After ten minutes they arrived at a consolidated, co-operative reply. If, they said, we had printed the speech without comment it would have confused our own people and the effect would have been very disturbing. We conceive our press as a medium of information for the people. We try to help them understand things that happen. So we publish a great deal of commentary. We do a lot of editorializing. In this case it took several days of discussion and conferring to figure out the meaning and implications of President Truman's speech, to pass on to the people.

Then I said that they were always talking about our American press being controlled by a small group of men. Wasn't the same thing true of their press? They were quick with the answer to that one. One of the editors who had been in America said he had an example. If a big department store has such bad elevators that one falls and kills a lot of people, will newspapers which carry that store's advertising write editorials about it and make front-page stories of the accident? Or if some widely advertised product in America is found by one of your government departments to contain something harmful, will the story get into the papers? And in 1932, when it was obviously to the best interests of the country to have a change in administrations, what percentage of the press tried to bring about the re-election of Herbert Hoover? The fact that 80 or 90 per cent of the American press was against Roosevelt all the time he was President, while a majority of the people were for him, proved how little connection there was between public interest and the American press.

My answer was that condemnation of our papers, with which many Americans might agree, was no defense of their own. It is possible in America, I said, for the press to criticize those in power in Washington. But could any sector of the Yugoslav press criticize their regime?

The editor of the satiric paper *Yez* asked me if I could tell him what the penalty is in America for advocating the overthrow of the government. He didn't wait for an answer. He said he knew. He said it's treason and it's punishable by death. You can change leaders in America as long as no one tries to get rid of the American way of life. It's the same here. We can change party leadership as long as no one tries to overthrow the system. We have five parties. There are men from all five parties in the government. But they all believe in our system. You have two or three parties. They all believe in your system. If the Communist party or any other group in America became a serious threat—if they ever tried to overthrow your system—you'd get rid of them quickly, wouldn't you?

I tried to point out again that we have the ability to criticize the acts of whichever group is in power in Washington. But they don't have that privilege in Yugoslavia.

The editor of *Yez* jumped to his feet this time. He said he was insulted. Hadn't I ever read his publication? It ran to forty or fifty pages a week. The entire contents consisted of cartoons, satirical stories, and serious articles poking fun at the regime, or exposing the mistakes of officials. And didn't I know about the Control Commissions? There was a Federal Control Commission and then each of the six republics had one. Their job was to smell out mistakes and scandals and wrongdoing. All their findings were made public. Full reports were available to anyone. Many of the reports were printed in the papers. And any citizen had a right to file a complaint against any official or against any official act. Then he quoted an example. Recently a State official was exposed by the Control Commission after a complaint had been made by a private citizen. He had profiteered in sugar. The press carried long articles. The official was removed from office after a trial. The people held a special election to choose his successor.

One of my hosts was Yugoslavia's most famous cartoonist, so I asked him if he could draw a cartoon lampooning Marshal Tito and get it published. He smiled and said the answer was no. The explanation was that they felt Marshal Tito, as the choice of a vast majority of the people, deserved respect.

Then the editor of *Tanjug,* the official news agency, said that I must realize that this is a people's government. That it represents 90 per cent of the people, not merely the will and the interests of the 10 per cent who are enemies of society. Why should the rights and privileges and freedom of the 90 per cent be jeopardized in order to give the 10 per cent the privilege of trying to overthrow the government of the 90 per cent and put back a system which would benefit only them, the 10 per cent? You in America have a great deal of freedom for the 10 per cent. Your 10 per cent had freedom to twist and distort. It has freedom to run things for its own advantage, to the disadvantage of the 90 per cent. How many of your large newspapers and radio stations represent labor, or the Negroes and share croppers in the South?

I said that even granting that Marshal Tito is the choice of the 90 per cent, what is the safety valve in case Tito should fall into evil ways and carry on in a manner which most people considered was not to the best interests of the people? What if someday he came to represent the 10 per cent, rather than the 90? Under such circumstances wouldn't the Yugoslav press be forced to continue to lend all its support to the regime?

The editor of the newspaper *Borba* answered. He said such a situation was not conceivable. I was forgetting that this was a democracy. If the government officials began catering to the interests of the 10 per cent they would quickly be voted out of office by the people. Remember, he said, that the people have the right of the vote. All of them. Women as well as men. And the color of their skin has nothing to do with it either. We have a whole colony of Africans—of Negroes—down in Bosnia. They vote just as everyone else does. Members of all our minorities vote. An evil government could not long endure unless it abrogated all the election laws and the other democratic rights we have. In that case there would be another revolution to get democracy back again.

I told them I had seen hundreds of new bookshops scattered around the country. And public reading rooms too. I knew that they had published more books in the past two years than in the twenty years before the war. I knew about the millions of people being taught to read and write. But is it possible for a bookshop owner in Yugoslavia to carry anything but books praising the present system?

The editor of the newspaper *Politika* said he would take me that very afternoon to a shop in Belgrade which carried all the books written by Slobodan Yovanović, who was a violent opponent of the theory of the present system.

But what I wanted to know was whether a bookshop could fill its windows with copies of a book entitled *The Red Menace, or the Evils of Communism in Yugoslavia*. When they all laughed I had my answer. But someone said that I was forgetting that Yugoslavia had just gone through a bloody revolution at a great cost to get rid of an evil system which had been imposed on the 90 per cent by the 10 per cent. Would it be logical or even desirable that we should promptly accord to those whom we defeated all the freedoms you talk so much about? Why? So they could try to wreck everything our government and our people have been working so hard to accomplish for the common good these past two years?

How long, I asked, did they think it might be before it would be possible for them to allow a bookshop owner to display copies of an antagonistic book in his windows?

They argued the answer among themselves. I never did get a consensus of what they thought.

Then they volunteered some miscellaneous information. Did I know that there was a wide circulation of British, French, and other foreign newspapers in Belgrade and the other cities? Nothing was ever done to stop such papers from being sold and read. There were no Bulgarian or American newspapers on sale simply because neither of those countries had yet concluded a trade agreement with Yugoslavia. But I could go right out now into Terazzia and buy all the British papers I wished. And of course I was aware, wasn't I, that nothing was done to stop people from listening to the radio stations of their own choice. More and more radio sets were being sold. All of them operate on shortwave bands. They can pick up American and British broadcasts just as well as broadcasts from Belgrade. The air is free. And a few city blocks out of Terazzia there's a British reading room run by the British Government. In the front windows, right on the street level, they put up news bulletins several times a day. The British choose what news to display. Nothing is done to stop people from standing there all day reading the British news, if they care to.

Then the editor of *Borba* said he would send to my room copies of his own paper and copies of another Belgrade paper called *Republika* which have been engaging in a running debate on the attitude Yugoslavia should take toward Russia.

And that's the way the luncheon ended.

That afternoon I dropped into UNRRA headquarters to see Dave Leff, a young man from California who had the reputation of being one of the most level-headed Americans in Yugoslavia. He said he had been assigned to make a check of tractors which UNRRA had sent up into the Vojvodina. Would I like to go along? The Vojvodina was one area I hadn't yet covered so I jumped at the invitation.

Before I left Belgrade I had an interview with General Velebit who had been on Marshal Tito's staff. I had met him once in London during the war when he was flown out from under the eyes of the Germans to the British capital to make arrangements for the delivery of medical supplies by parachute to the Partisans. Now he was assistant Foreign Minister. I asked him for the final chapter of Terence Atherton's tragic career. He confirmed the story the mayor of Budva had told us. Old Joko Boreta had guided the London *Daily Mail* correspondent and the rest of his party to Partisan headquarters. There they were put in charge of General Velebit because the general's English was perfect. This was the period when Chetniks and Partisans were in open conflict all over Yugoslavia.

The general said he told Atherton he would do anything for him except the one thing Atherton wanted him to do. He would not put him in contact with Mihailović, the Chetnik leader. He would not make it possible for Atherton to turn over to Mihailović the radio sets, the gold, the secret messages that had been brought from Egypt by submarine. Velebit said the Britishers were given a cottage to live in and every possible consideration. They were the guests of honor at a party their first night at headquarters. Atherton and the general had many long conversations about the war and the situation in Yugoslavia. They became intimate friends.

But one morning Atherton's bed was empty. On his pillow he had pinned a note to Velebit. It thanked the general for his kindness and asked him to take care of all the personal possessions Atherton had left behind. He hoped to see the general again someday and continue some of the conversations they'd had. That was all. No explanation of where he had gone or why. But it was obvious that he had sneaked off to find Mihailović and carry out the mission he had been given by British Secret Service in Egypt. The general never saw Atherton again. Not alive. His body was found some days later in the woods many miles from headquarters. Whoever killed him stripped him of all the gold he had carried in money belts strapped around his body. He'd been killed in an area which was really a battlefield. An area full of snipers. The general's theory, however, was that he had been killed for the fortune in gold he carried. I mentioned that in the United States the Yugoslav monarchists and Chetnik propagandists had accused the Partisans of killing Atherton and then dumping his body in the woods to be found later. Velebit said such a charge was ridiculous. He and Atherton had become the best of friends. Besides, he said, the Partisan leaders, whatever else people might think about them, were not stupid. At that particular time Britain and the United States were wavering over whether to throw their full support to the Chetniks or to the Partisans. What a foolish time that would have been, Velebit said, for us to have turned London and Washington against us by killing an emissary of the British Government.

I left General Velebit convinced that he had told me the truth as far as he knew it. But the mystery of who killed one of the best friends I ever had remained a mystery. It's a mystery which probably never will be solved.

The last night of my Belgrade interlude Jacqueline and I had dinner together. She was sad, she said, because there are no such things as blue tulips. I told her I'd see what could be done about it, but why did it make her sad? She said because the Serbian word for blue is *plava* and the Serbian word for tulip is *lala* and wouldn't *plava lala* make a nice-sounding combination of words?

We had dinner that night in the Drina. While I told Jacqueline some stories of the river valley which gave the restaurant its name, Paja, the gypsy orchestra leader, played some of Jacqueline's favorite songs. He played *"Da Smo Se Ranije Spreli"* twice because he knew that that was the one she liked best. From the Drina we went to a kafana on the edge of the city. It was a "people's café" where a glass of wine cost only a few dinar. It was full of ordinary people singing and making an evening of it. At the table next to ours there was a young man who had had too many glasses of wine. Intoxication bestirred in him a desire to break glasses. He began throwing glasses around the room indiscriminately. The manager ordered him to stop or go home. The young man threatened to throw the manager around the room. A few minutes later a gendarme arrived. He had a red star on his cap and a tommy gun in the crook of one arm. I suggested to Jacqueline that we watch carefully. Here we might see what happens to a simple Yugoslav who breaks the law under the New Order. The argument between the drunk and the gendarme went on for exactly thirty-two minutes by my stop watch. Then the gendarme left. He returned a little later with a second gendarme. The second one did not have a tommy gun. Other men at the drunk's table joined in a long and heated discussion about whether the glass-thrower really had disturbed the peace. We watched the proceedings for a full hour. Then the two gendarmes left and the glass-thrower ordered another drink. Jacqueline said she wished they'd arrested him. She was afraid the next glass might be thrown in our direction.

But the evening ended uneventfully. The gypsy orchestra played a whole collection of Dalmatian love songs we both liked very much. And then some of the *Sevdalinke* tunes from Bosnia.

PART SEVEN

This Is the Vojvodina

Chapter Sixty-One

LAND OF PLENTY

WE STARTED for the Vojvodina soon after dawn. Dave had a jeep and a driver who could talk three or four languages including English. He also brought along Božo Matičević who knew where all the tractors were located that Dave was supposed to inspect. He was even more valuable as a guide for me. He'd fought all over Yugoslavia as a Partisan and knew the territory as only a guerrilla fighter could. Božo was a Dalmatian with a little black mustache and a large sense of humor. He looked like a cross between a Hapsburg prince and a Medici. He had been an officer in the

Partisans and now held an important government position. But, like all Dalmatians, his heart was on the water. If Fate plays her cards right, someday she'll let Božo be a deckhand on a ship on the Adriatic.

It was Božo who explained that this road we were taking up to the Hungarian frontier was the road the Germans used in their final retreat. They destroyed every bridge they passed over. But we wouldn't see any destruction of homes or villages because all the homes and villages in this direction had been owned by Schwabs. The Schwabs had been Yugoslavia's largest minority. There were originally half a million of them. Some of the families had lived in Yugoslavia for generations. But they always talked German and were never absorbed. Their loyalty was always to Berlin. Not to Belgrade. They proved it during the war. They raised an army of their own to fight beside the Nazis. They co-operated 100 per cent with the enemy. When the Nazi army left they left too. The Nazi commanders may have realized that this was the end. But the Schwabs didn't. Some of them even left places set for dinner on their kitchen tables. They felt so sure they'd be back soon to take up life again in a Nazified Yugoslavia. Božo said it was possible to find an occasional Schwab family here and there in the Vojvodina. But most of them never returned. And Yugoslavia had never encouraged them to return.

We drove through that mountain region called Fruška Gora where they make the bubbly wine Anita liked so much. Then we came to the village of Petrovaradin. There, by the side of the road, we found a church with three crosses and a star and crescent. A white-haired peasant said maybe it was an unusual church but he didn't know. It was combination Catholic and Orthodox. He wasn't sure, but maybe the Turkish star and crescent meant they also held Moslem services here. He remembered something about the Turks being here from when he was a boy. But he didn't mix into politics much. Dave pointed out to him that we were talking about religion not politics. The old peasant said it made no difference. Politics and religion. They were all the same to him. He said the really interesting thing about Petrovaradin was that this was a spa. Yes sir, one of the best spas in these parts. Crazy people are sent here from all over the world. Cures 'em, the water does. When most of them go away they aren't crazy any more.

Dave said he knew it was a trite expression but we were now entering what people called the "Bread Basket" of Yugoslavia. If it weren't for the Vojvodina Yugoslavia would starve to death. The fields are broad and fertile. There are few trees. The soil is as black-looking as coal dust. Dave said it's as rich as it looks. The cattle they raise here have the longest horns in Europe. And the most elaborately curled. And the most delicately pointed.

Novi Sad is the capital of this area. At Novi Sad, Dave and Božo went off looking for tractors. I went off looking for information. I found some newspaper editors who liked to drink Turkish coffee and talk. So we did both. One of them was a story in himself. Sigmund Kek had been a

Protestant minister before the war. His parents were Hungarian. He'd done his studying of theology in France and Ireland. He spoke English. Now he was a Yugoslav. He came from a long line of ministers. His father was a bishop. It was just tradition that he went into the church. He had had a church of his own here in Novi Sad. But the war gave him an excuse to switch professions. He'd always had his heart set on journalism. So now he was the Hungarian editor of the Novi Sad daily newspaper. He looked as if he were happy at last. I decided that with the strange background he had he'd be a perfect person to tell me about this corner of the world where so many empires had met and where so many nationalities still lived. Besides, he was the only person in the room who could speak English. About this place called the Vojvodina, he said that before the war there were nearly half a million Schwabs, four hundred thousand Hungarians, three hundred thousand Croats, sixty thousand Slovaks, thirty thousand Rumanians, thirty-five thousand members of a Russian minority that came here from the Ukraine two hundred years ago, and then seventy-five thousand people of other nationalities. A few Moslems. Some Serbs. You could find almost anything in the Vojvodina. The land was rich. Food was plentiful. The standard of living was high. The rate of illiteracy was low. Only about 6 per cent. Life was all right for the Hungarians and the Schwabs in the old days. They ran things. But the others didn't make out so well. The Slovaks had a newspaper of their own until 1938. But then the government suppressed it. There was no Rumanian press and the Russians didn't have a paper either. Before the war the land was mostly owned by a few. The many worked as share croppers. Church and State were joined tightly together. That meant very little freedom of religion. There was no national theater and little attention was paid to education beyond teaching people to read and write.

Now, said my Hungarian-Yugoslav-French-Irish-English-speaking friend, it's all different. Take the press, which the minorities consider the most important sign of how much freedom they have. If they can read a paper in their own language they're happy. Now, in Hungarian, there's a daily, a weekly, a youth magazine, a woman's monthly, and a literary monthly. In Rumanian there's a weekly. The Russians, Slovaks, Croats all have weeklies. Church and State have been separated and there's complete freedom of worship. There's been a land reform which means everyone today owns at least a bit of the earth. Each peasant family was given from four to seven *utars,* depending on the size of the family. The minorities can send their children to schools where the teaching is done in their own language. There's a Hungarian teachers' college. There's a national theater. The Hungarians have their own cultural societies in every town and village. And the Hungarians are allowed to have all the contact they wish with the capital of their native country, Budapest.

That's the way, said my minister-journalist friend, the problems of the past are being taken care of. But the Vojvodina has some new problems now. When the Schwabs didn't come back the government took over their property. Some villages stood like ghost places for three or four years. Now they're being filled up with what are called "colonists." People from Bosnia and Montenegro. People from places where it's impossible to scratch a living from the little soil there is between the rocks. Also some people from Serbia and Croatia whose towns were destroyed. Half a million of them altogether. They're sending the illiteracy rate right up to the sky. They're used to mountain life and all that that means. Most of them had never seen a tractor in their lives. They don't know how to work the soil the way we do it here. But they're naturally intelligent and they're beginning to get their bearings. Of course some of them would rather starve to death in the black hills of Montenegro that they love so much, than live well here. But their children will be glad the change was made.

The other four or five editors gave me enough facts and figures to make me begin to understand how different this area is from any we had been in before. Now the problem was to go out and see for myself. So I pulled Dave and Božo away from their tractors and we got under way.

Chapter Sixty-Two

UNRRA AT WORK

DAVE'S FIRST STOP was at a state farm not far from Novi Sad where they grow seed for peasants. Božo said this was something new in Yugoslavia. No one ever bothered about what kind of seed the peasants used before. This one was like a state farm in the United States. Up in New England they say that if you ever see a farm with the buildings all painted, the roofs good, the fences intact, a substantial house, and stout barns, then you can be sure it's one of two things. Either a city man spending his money in the country, or a state farm. This was a state farm. It had corncribs bulging with corn, beehives, smokehouses, and half-a-dozen stout barns. But it was horses Dave was interested in. UNRRA had given the farm seventy-five mares and six stallions. We saw all eighty-one of them. They were being kept in whitewashed stalls. There was even a hospital for the invalids. Over each stall there was a sign giving the name of the present occupant. They were mostly British and American names. I copied down some of them. No News. Fury. UNRRA. Lena. Mitzi. Prince. Rudy. Sultan. Fiat 166. That's as far as I got. Dave said we had to keep moving. I told him the names surprised me. He said, what did you expect? Did you expect all the horses to be named Stalin, Molotov, and Red Square?

We were heading for Sombor, but we stopped in the village of Krnjaja. There was no war damage anywhere in this section. That was partly because this was Schwab territory and the Germans weren't destroying their own people's houses. It was also because there had been little fighting around here. Flat land with no trees, like Kansas, is not ideal territory for guerrilla fighting. But Krnjaja was in ruins anyway. In this case weather and neglect had done it. It had been 100 per cent Schwab. For years it stood forlorn and deserted. Rain, wind, and snow worked on the abandoned houses. It made you realize that a house has to be lived in to stay in decent condition. One of the main streets was called General Živković Ulica in the past. General Pera Živković was a member of the old regime who was later charged with being a war criminal. The family that lived at No. 5 General Živković Ulica must have been the most loyal Nazi family in town. They had even gone to the trouble of taking down the number on their house and making a slight alteration. In this and other Balkan countries the house number sign also bears the name of the street embossed on it. It's not a bad idea. But the people at No. 5 didn't like the name of their street. So they hammered the embossing until there was little left of the general's name. Then with white paint they inscribed on the piece of metal the new name of the street. During the occupation this was Hermann Goering Strasse. Dave climbed up and ripped the number plate from the front wall. He said it would make an interesting souvenir. The front wall was about all there was left of the house. This was one place which had been destroyed by man. We had been looking all over Yugoslavia for a home that had been wrecked by the Partisans. Maybe this was it.

Lončar Djuro lived a little farther down Hermann Goering Strasse, or General Živković Ulica, or whatever you want to call it. He was a colonist. He'd bought an UNRRA plow. Dave wanted to see if he was happy with it. There were eight in the Djuro family. They had been given one utar of land for each of them. In the yard there were three baby pigs, four geese, six hens, and the American plow with UNRRA on it in large letters. Mr. Djuro had paid thirty-six dollars and seventy-two cents for the plow. He liked it and thought it was worth the money. Mr. Djuro said he also had a horse and a cow. If colonists couldn't afford to buy animals themselves, the government gave them a few.

The Djuros were glad they had come to the Vojvodina. Everything was all right except . . . It took Dave a long time to find out what the "except" was. Then Lončar Djuro came out with it. The State had made him turn in two hundred and fifty kilos of the grain he had raised. Of course he got paid for it. But he'd expected to keep it all, or sell it on the open market. Then Božo stepped up and said he was a government official and could explain. The people in Bosnia and Montenegro were going hungry. Really hungry. The State couldn't let them starve. And so the State was trying to see that the country's food supplies were spread out evenly. The State was paying a reasonable price for grain. But the State insisted that people up here in the rich Vojvodina share what they had with less fortunate people in the mountain districts without profiteering. Mr. Djuro seemed to feel a little better after the explanation.

Then he took us into his kitchen to show us a clipping from a local newspaper he'd tacked onto the wall. It was about a Montenegrin colonist named Ilija Iković who had made a labor profit last year here in the Vojvodina of sixty-five thousand three hundred and fifty-three dinar, which figures out to nearly one hundred and ten dollars a month. That was more than many high-ranking government officials were making. He had done it all in agriculture. The paper said this was proof of what a farmer could do in the New Yugoslavia if he had a little ambition. Then Mr. Djuro took us out and proudly showed us a large chunk of wood. It was what an American farmer would call a chopping block. He said it was a souvenir he'd brought with him. You don't see any wood like that around here. You don't see any trees at all. That's what they missed. Trees. Forests. Hills. This was all so flat. You get tired looking out a window and seeing nothing but—but just land. Still, it was better than where they'd come from. So we asked him where they'd come from. He said all the people here in this town were from the same section. We probably hadn't ever heard of the place. It was near Zagreb, in Croatia. The Vojnić section. Of course we'd probably never heard of it. They weren't from Vojnić itself. There wasn't anybody any more from Vojnić itself. They all got killed. But some people had escaped from the villages. Would we like to hear about what had happened at Vojnić? So we told him we knew a little about what had happened at Vojnić and we thought he ought to be very happy in his new home. Dave said if he had any trouble with the American plow he should let UNRRA know about it. Mr. Djuro said he didn't think he would have any trouble. But thank you just the same.

In the town square there was a statue of the Virgin Mary. It had been pale blue and pink. Only someone had knocked it from its base and now it lay in a stream of dirty water. Some geese were paddling around it. It had obviously been there a long time because the water had washed most of the pink and blue away. There were some bullet holes through the body. A woman who was drawing water from the town well said she was from the town of Vrgin Most, near Vojnić. She said the statue of the Virgin Mary was there like that when they arrived. Someone told her the Schwabs had done it.

At Sombor we stopped to watch some government workmen getting at least a hundred tractors greased and oiled for the spring plowing. I sat in the jeep while Dave and Božo checked the spare-parts supply with the foreman of the garage. A boy of about six came along with a short length of steel pipe slung over his shoulder on a rope like a gun. He was playing war. I hadn't seen any Yugoslav children playing war before. I had been in shops in a number of cities and I had never seen toy tanks, toy guns, or lead soldiers. All the Yugoslav toys seemed to be trucks, tractors, building blocks, and dolls. But this child was playing war all right. He was sneaking along in search of a potential enemy. Then he saw me. He studied my beard. Slowly he unlimbered his "rifle" and took careful aim. I think the bullet hit me right over the heart. When he slung the gun back over his shoulder and went on his way he was mumbling something to himself. The jeep driver laughed and told me the boy had said:

"Well, that's another Chetnik taken care of!"

It was the first time my beard had gotten me into trouble.

Sombor is probably a very interesting city but I didn't find out much about Sombor. That was because of a toothache. In New York a dentist might have drilled a hole and done something to the nerve and saved the tooth. But I told Dave that if we could just find a dentist with a pair of forceps I'd be happy. A toothache can be more painful than a bullet over the heart or a real bullet in the leg. So we went looking for a dentist. There were two in Sombor. But one was out of town and the other was taking part in that delightful custom known in Yugoslavia as the Corso Hour. The main street of Sombor was alive with people of all ages promenading back and forth. Somewhere among them was Dr. Korćun, the only dentist left in town. Dave found him. I don't know how. The doctor said he was sorry but he had no anaesthetics. Dave said that wouldn't make any difference. All we wanted to know was whether he had a pair of forceps. If he didn't have a pair of forceps, Dave had a pair of pliers he'd brought from the jeep. The doctor said he was sorry, but there was no electricity in town. Dave said that didn't matter. He had a flashlight in his back pocket. I don't know whether they used pliers or forceps. I do know that someone poked a flashlight down my throat and a minute later the tooth was out. Dave and Božo said they had a good meal that night. I had three glasses of rakia ljuta and four aspirin tablets and went to bed. Later someone said liquor and aspirin counteract each other. Maybe they do. Anyway, I went to sleep. For the first time that week.

When we got to Subotica Dave said Subotica was the largest village in the world. Population, one hundred thousand. It looked like a city to me. How could he call it a village? So Dave explained. A village in Yugoslavia is a community of any size, from ten people to a hundred thousand, in which the majority of the population make their living tilling the soil. A community of even five hundred people might be a town, if most of the people were shopkeepers and clerks. But Subotica is a village because most of the one hundred thousand people drive from their homes each day out into the country and work in the fields. It's as simple as that.

Then we drove to Bačka Topola. We had to find an interpreter because the town is so Hungarian that hardly anyone understands even simple words of greeting in Serbo-Croat. The Magyar language is used in the Catholic churches and in the schools too.

In Bačka Topola we called at the home of Istvan Pataki. He'd bought an UNRRA electric hammer mill. He used it to grind corn for the whole village for a small fee. But we couldn't find Istvan to ask him how the mill was working. The three or four women in the family started to cry every time we mentioned his name. It took a great deal of translating from Hungarian to Serbo-Croat to English to find out what the trouble was. Finally they broke down and told all.

Istvan was in jail. He had been arrested because the Control Commission discovered that he had falsified his report on how much grain he had on hand. It was a serious offense. Božo said the government was having a lot of trouble with some of these Vojvodina people. It wasn't that they didn't love their fellow Yugoslavs down in the hills of Bosnia. It was just that they had a tradition of always holding back from the market two or three years' supply of grain. It was a custom. You always keep two or three years' supply of grain in case of illness, drought, famine. The government had tried to explain that things were different now. Rugged individualism and enterprise would not be penalized. But when people in Bosnia, who never had enough grain to lay away a reserve, were threatened with starvation, it wasn't right for the people of the Vojvodina to have their corncribs bulging full. Still, there was trouble. So Istvan was one of those who had been arrested as an example to the others. That's what Božo told the wife and mother.

Finally they dried their tears. Božo patted them both on the shoulders and said not to worry. Their man would be coming home soon. Nothing dreadful would happen to him. But maybe after this he would obey the law and not try to falsify records. Then they took us into their home. We saw things we hadn't seen anywhere else in Yugoslavia. The family Pataki had an electric radio which would have sold in America for two or three hundred dollars. They had an electric sewing machine. They had a tiled kitchen. There were rugs on all the floors. They had a fancy kitchen stove in which they used corncobs for fuel. There were religious pictures and statues in every room. Then we saw the hammer mill. The wife said it worked perfectly except—except that they hated to see all that corn meal being sent away to—to wherever the government was sending it. And when did we think her Istvan would be back?

The next stop was the village of Sekić. It had been an all-Schwab town. Now colonists were beginning to fill the empty buildings. It was the end of the working day and the townspeople stood around on street corners. They looked lost and ill at ease. The black-domed Catholic church was boarded up, because the colonists were all Orthodox or Moslems. Most of them were from Cernagora. We talked to one street-corner group. How did they like it here? They shrugged their shoulders. They were not very enthusiastic. Most of them had long twirled mustachios. Everything about them seemed out of place. Even the mustachios. We could tell by the way they looked across the open fields that they were missing their black mountains. How did they get along here? Well, we'll tell you. The man who spoke was nearly as tall as his old bishop-king had been. He said it's this way. We get along all right because we can't find any rocks to throw at anybody. Then everyone on the street corner laughed. Another man, with a knife in his belt and a gun slung over his shoulder, said he didn't mind killing Turks or Nazis, but he was damned if he liked to tend cattle. He said they had everything they needed here but one thing. They had plenty of food. Plenty of water. Plenty of air. But no fire. No fuel to make a fire. Back home if you wanted to keep warm you went out and chopped down a tree. But how can you keep warm where there are no trees?

Dave said to notice that all the houses in this part of the country are built with the narrow side facing the road. That's because in the old Austro-Hungarian Empire days the amount of tax a man paid was figured by counting the number of windows of his home that faced the road. So they all began building their houses with the narrow side and the fewest possible windows to the road.

On the way back to Belgrade we skirted the edge of a town that looked as if it might be interesting. Dave said it was. It was Sremski Karlovici, the home of Serbian culture and once the seat of the Orthodox patriarch. So we left the main road and went up into Sremski Karlovici. A gray-haired teacher who got embarrassed when we asked her how long she had been on the faculty told us the whole story.

In the days when this was part of the Austro-Hungarian Empire, Sremski Karlovici was a little Serbian island. The Austrians allowed it a certain degree of autonomy. Here the Serbs built the first lyceum in all Yugoslavia back in the eighteenth century. It had a library of twenty-five thousand books. It had a rare collection of old coins. It had some of the finest ikons in all Europe. There were portraits in the school of most of Serbia's famous men. There were busts and other pieces of good sculpture. Then the Ustaši came.

We knew about the Ustaši, did we? We knew how they hated the Serbs? Well, they hated Serbian culture like poison. They wanted to wipe it from the earth. So they burned most of the books that were in the Cyrillic language. They stole all the coins. They smashed the ikons. They slashed the oil portraits with their knives. They used axes on the pieces of sculpture. Or threw them into the river.

The bust in front of the school? That's one which escaped because it was hidden. That's a bust of the great Branko. He was Yugoslavia's finest poet. He was a Serb, of course, but he was a poet of all the Yugoslavs. He sang, always, of Yugoslav unity. There's even a Branko kolo now. He died at the age of twenty-nine. It was too bad. Why did we think all great poets die so young? He was a great poet but he was such a naughty boy with the girls. That is, in his free time when he wasn't writing great poetry. They were glad they had saved his bust, anyway.

But maybe we would be interested in what was happening now. Some of the coins and books and other things which were hauled off to Croatia as souvenirs of war were beginning to come back. Yes, every few weeks they'd get another package with no sender's name on it but inside would be a book or a box of old Serbian coins. I mustn't smile. They were priceless, those things. I didn't tell her I was smiling because I was thinking of another old lady, in Milledgeville, Georgia. This teacher in Sremski Karlovici reminded me of her. Several years ago the Georgia lady told me an almost identical story of how their library had been looted by General Sherman's troops, and how books and other souvenirs the Northern soldiers had hauled away were still coming back. Anonymously.

Anyway, the teacher said, the lyceum now has five hundred and thirty pupils and things are beginning to be like they were. There are nineteen teachers. Four of them speak English. George Jazić here is one of the four. He was a prisoner for four years in Germany. That's where he learned so many languages. He learned French, Russian, English, and American too. George nodded his head. Yes, he spoke American, too, very okay, you bet. The teacher with the white hair said, George writes poetry too. Maybe someday he'll be as great a poet as Branko. He writes very good poetry already. But he isn't like Branko that other way. He doesn't . . . Well, he just writes poetry, that's all.

PART EIGHT

These Are the Serbs

Chapter Sixty-Three

ALL IS NOT LEAVES IN A TEACUP

BACK in Belgrade I heard about Milan. Milan was a student who translated the papers for Peter Furst every morning. Peter said he knew enough English to make sense. And Peter had a jeep. So I borrowed Peter's interpreter and his jeep and set out for South Serbia. At the last minute Peter's wife June said she'd like to come along too. That made three of us not counting the Jerries. To a Britisher a Jerry is just a nice way of saying a German or a Nazi. But to a garage man a Jerry is a ten-gallon can of gasoline. We took along eight Jerry cans of gasoline. Getting that gasoline

was more difficult than getting a cabin on the *Queen Mary*. In Europe
these days you don't just drive up to a corner gasoline station and say
"fill 'er up." Things haven't been like that for about ten years. In Yugoslavia it's the government that doles out the gasoline just as it is in many
other countries over here. So I went to the government. The government
said that in the case of foreigners the gasoline is sold directly to the
Embassy and the Embassy hands it out. Peter said that was right.
Although he was an American, he got his gasoline from the British
Embassy because he was working for a British news agency. So I went
to the American Embassy. They didn't know what I was talking about.
They said we Americans bring in our own gasoline. Bring it by ship
from New York. I said fine! I'd like to buy fifty or a hundred gallons.
Oh, but they didn't sell it! The gasoline was for the Army, Embassy
employees, the Red Cross, people like that. How, I asked, is a common
garden variety of an American who isn't any of those things going to get
gas? They didn't know. They'd never had any garden varieties over here
before. I suggested that it might be well to look into the matter. Next
summer there might be some garden-variety American tourists arriving
with automobiles. They said not to worry about that. There wouldn't
be any. They were right, as it turned out. But none of us knew then that
the State Department was going to refuse visas to people who wanted to
to see Yugoslavia for themselves. Anyhow, I had no gasoline and how did
the American Embassy suggest I get some, short of stealing it or cabling
some paper in London for a job so I could get gas through the British
Embassy? The American Embassy said an investigation would be made
and I would be informed. That meant unpacking knapsacks and suitcases and putting off the trip for another few days. When the report came
it was to the effect that my information was correct. The American
Embassy could buy gasoline and resell it to me. But that raised another
problem. The State Department has appropriated no funds for such
purposes. If I could wait until an act of Congress was passed or someone
in Washington found some fund which could be made available for . . .
And so I went to an American friend who had been a soldier in Europe
during the war before he became attached to the diplomatic mission and
he telephoned to an American friend who had been a soldier in Europe
during the war before he became attached to the American garage in
Belgrade. That's how we not only got eight Jerry cans full of gas, but also
got the ten-gallon tank filled. Men in the army learn how to break
through red tape. It's too bad diplomats aren't required to spend a year
in the army as privates during their course of training.

So we set out, Milan the Interpreter, June, eight Jerry cans, Milan's
suitcase, June's two knapsacks, my musette bag, and a book which told
how to fix a jeep if it breaks down. Mladenovac was the first stop. Someone told us that Mladenovac means "The Day of the Young Married
People." In Mladenovac the town officials happened to mention Senaja
(pronounced as if it were Sinai) and I knew we had a story. The only

trouble was the road. Nobody remembered anybody coming out of Senaja in weeks. The road must be impassable. But we had a jeep. So we laughed and said we'd see them when we got back. I still think a jeep is a fine invention. But our jeep went around a curve and up part of a hill and then buried its nose in several feet of bloto. We walked the rest of the way.

We were told there were six hundred people in Senaja. Most of them gypsies. In America when somebody says "gypsy" you think of a dirty character in gaudy rags who tries to tell your fortune at the front door while his wife is stealing whatever she can find in your kitchen. Wanderers. Covered wagons. Camp fires. Music. In Europe gypsies are most of those things too. But they're something else. The men are handsome and full of fire. Passion. Rhythm. They can all play fiddles. They're born knowing how to play fiddles. They can make a fiddle talk. The language a gypsy fiddle talks is nostalgic. Sometimes wild and happy. Sometimes low and plaintive. But always nostalgic. In Europe the gypsy women have bronzed breasts. Firm and upright. Whatever they wear from the waist up always exposes their breasts. And in a very exciting way. Not like an evening gown. From the waist down they wear skirts. A great many skirts. Sometimes a dozen. Maybe more. As the weather gets warmer they shed a few. But even in the summer; many. No two skirts are the same color. That produces a rainbow effect. In Europe gypsies wander too. They also pick up cigarette butts and save them until they have enough to make a cigarette for themselves. Cigarette butts are supposed to be why they have so many diseases. More gypsies die of t.b. than anybody else. Or of anything else. In Europe gypsies have never wanted to settle on the land. They don't like farming. The Russians had more trouble with gypsies than they did with friends of the Czar. It took years to get them to help work the co-operative farms. They'd rather starve wandering than live like kings in one place. You can't play a fiddle while you work the levers of a tractor. But the gypsies of Senaja were different. They had lived on the land for hundreds of years. Branislav Mihailović was a good example. Branislav was secretary of the village board. We asked him where he was born. Right here. Where were his parents born? Right here. And his grandparents? Right here. That's as far back as he could vouch for. But he thought his people had always been here. Branislav Mihailović was as handsome as you want to imagine. His eyes were as dark as his skin. They never stayed still. When he turned them on you it was like an old friend slapping you on the back. Even if he didn't say anything. They were happy eyes. But they were like all gypsies' eyes. There was something underneath the happiness you couldn't quite get hold of. He was married. Had two children. He hoped they'd get more education than he got. He had only four years in primary school. Part of the war they made him serve in the Chetniks. He was conscripted. Yes, he realized that he and Draža Mihailović, the Chetnik leader, both had the same name. It never embarrassed him. It's a common name in Yugoslavia.

Branislav the gypsy wondered whether we knew how his race had been treated. They were treated the same as the Jews. Only worse. The idea was to wipe them out. First the Germans mobilized all gypsies between sixteen and sixty into labor battalions. Next they passed a rule that no gypsy could go to a theater, movie, or restaurant. Gypsies couldn't have their own schools. They couldn't be employed by any business firm. If any fled, their homes were confiscated. They couldn't sell property without the Germans' permission. Branislav laughed at that one. It was funny the Germans thinking that any gypsies had any property to sell. Then they were forbidden to rent a room from anyone. That made thousands of them homeless. The punishment for violating this one was death. Three days later they were ordered to be off the streets by 8 P.M. All past business transactions which gypsies had had were annulled. In May all gypsies were given yellow armbands to wear. The shops of all gypsies who were businessmen were confiscated. It was also forbidden for them to practice as doctors, lawyers, dentists, veterinarians, or chemists. That didn't bother many. Henceforth a gypsy would receive only one hundred grams of bread. In the autumn gypsies were forbidden to use trains or trolley cars. They couldn't ride bicycles either.

Branislav said all those things weren't so bad. The gypsies could have lived even under those conditions. But the object was to see that they didn't live. Those laws were just the little annoyances. The real campaign was to exterminate them. Bands of gypsy-hunters went from village to village. Sometimes they were Gestapo. Sometimes men of the Nedić State Guard. Sometimes it was the Ljotić Volunteers. They were the Serbian Fascists and they had an army of their own. They'd surround a village at night, hunt out the gypsies, and take them off to concentration camps.

Branislav pulled some printed sheets of paper from his pocket. He had a list of what they did at some places. There was a big camp at Zemun near Belgrade. There they used the gypsies first as gravediggers. In October alone they had to dig seven thousand graves. Most of them for Jews. Then a rule was passed that any gypsy who could prove that his family had been in Yugoslavia since 1850 could go home. Not many went home. How could a man prove it? Gypsies don't carry papers in their pockets proving things like that when someone gets them out of bed in the middle of the night and makes them dress in two minutes and takes them away to a camp. So then they began to make the gypsies dig graves for themselves. It was better that they died anyway, Branislav told us. He had that look in his eyes which said so much if someone could only translate it. It was probably better that they died with bullets. They were dying anyway of typhus and other diseases. Of starvation too. Even gypsies can't live for long on soup made from the bark of trees. Branislav looked at his papers. In 1941 there were eight hundred and thirty-nine gypsies taken to the camp near Belgrade. Their families never saw them again.

That was the same camp where they had kennels of mad dogs. Some nights, just for amusement, the Germans would make the gypsies run around outdoors in the snow without clothes and then turn the mad dogs on them. That was just when they wanted some amusement.

Branislav said if we wanted to take down some other figures he could read us a list of other camps. And how many were killed in each place. It was the worst in Croatia. We knew, didn't we, about what they called camp 3-C? That was at Yasenović. That was where seven or eight hundred thousand people were killed. Maybe the number of gypsies wasn't very large compared with seven or eight hundred thousand. But the number was large compared with the number of gypsies in Yugoslavia. At Yasenović they had a rule. Never waste bullets on gypsies. Gypsies were always killed with hammers or knives. Nobody knew for sure but people said forty thousand gypsies were killed at Yasenović alone. He was sorry but he didn't know how many gypsies there were here before the war. No one ever made up any figures. They never took a census of gypsies. That was too bad. But it wouldn't be hard to count them now. Not many were left. Maybe 10 per cent. Maybe only 5. The Germans succeeded in one of their war aims anyway. They didn't conquer the world. But they conquered the gypsies. They got rid of one inferior race, as they called it, almost completely.

The town council chamber was quiet all the time Branislav was talking. And the room was full of people. While he talked I kept looking into their faces. I could see that the whole town respected its gypsy secretary. The Germans had not succeeded in making everyone in Yugoslavia hate gypsies. They stood side by side in this twenty-foot-square whitewashed room they called a village hall. The skin of half of them was like yours or mine. The skin of the other half was brown. Sometimes almost black. But they stood close together listening and nodding every few minutes at what their secretary was saying.

We had a great deal of trouble with Milan the Interpreter that day. He kept translating *ciganin* as "gyps." We told him the word was "gypsies." But he said he'd heard a lot of Americans talk about "gyps" and maybe he knew our language better than we did. We didn't have time to explain to him the difference between "gyp" and "gypsies."

Branislav said Senaja had been lucky. There were six hundred and ninety-six people in town. Most of them gypsies. There were still three hundred and forty gypsies left. That was because Senaja was so far off any good road. The enemy couldn't get in here with their trucks to haul Senaja's gypsies away. Now the gypsies were really running the town. They were trying to show that they appreciated the way the new government felt about them. Before, only a few of them had any land. Since the war each one had been given land. They can use their own language but they are also learning the language of their neighbors. In the Old Yugoslavia gypsies had little chance to get any education and no gypsy could hold any official position. But Branislav said things are very different now.

He was not only village secretary but he was also a member of the District Council. That was a really important position. And there were two other gypsies on the village council.

Then an old man in the back of the room, a non-gypsy, said before the war you couldn't come into the council chambers without knocking and taking off your hat. Now look at us! We come in like this all the time. Whenever we want to. Now we can ask the president what he is doing if we want to. We can tell our troubles to him. And now we can smoke in the council chambers and nobody can stop us. He repeated the smoking part several times. That seemed very important to him. Then he said that before the war a president could put any man in jail for three days just like that. Now nobody can put a man in jail unless there's a trial.

Everyone in the room wanted us to see their school. We must understand that they never had a schoolhouse. But look down the road. There was Senaja's first school. We looked but all we saw were four partly built brick walls. In the spring it would be finished, they said. Only five professionals were working on it. All the rest was voluntary labor. They were building it without money. It was going to have two rooms for pupils and an office and two apartments for the teachers to live in. The apartments would be right here, at either end. Branislav marked them off in the mud with a stick. Most of the town was following us by this time. They stood there looking at those four bare walls the way an artist might look at a great painting he had nearly finished. Senaja was going to have a school! We must drink to the new school, they said. So a small gypsy boy who had bare feet ran down the road and came back with a large pitcher of Senaja wine. The pitcher was passed from man to man, in the order of local importance. Branislav was the first to drink, after Senaja's guests of the day.

Then a village woman who was not a gypsy came running up the road with a letter in her hand. Please would we read it to her. It came from her husband, Milan Alekčić. But she couldn't read it because it was in words she couldn't understand. No one in Senaja could read it to her. The letter had been posted months ago. It was in German. It said the husband had been captured by the enemy in 1941. He didn't tell how he got to America. He said he wanted to know how his children and brothers and sisters were. Would his wife please write to him in care of H. M. Gras at 60 Clifton Avenue, Clifton, New Jersey. When we finished translating the letter to her she began to cry. Then she began to scream. She screamed that we should tell her husband to come home. Tell him to come home and make carts for the peasants again. The peasants need carts. And his children need food. It's hard to bring up a family without a man. We must tell him to come home. So we took down his name.

All the time we had been in Senaja I'd been wondering something. So I finally asked Branislav if the Germans stole all their fiddles, or did gypsies who had been farmers for hundreds of years forget how to play. He knew what I meant. There was a large grin on his face as he whispered to two or three men in the crowd. By the time we got back to the private home they were using temporarily for a school there were ten or fifteen gypsies waiting for us. Each one had a fiddle in his right hand. One man had an extra fiddle he handed to the village secretary. We could tell right away that besides being a member of the District Council and secretary of Senaja, he also was the leader of the all-village band. Each man's fiddle was decorated with a piece of evergreen. The yard of the schoolhouse was deep bloto, but as soon as the music began the people formed a circle and started to do a kolo. The music got wilder and wilder. The dancing got faster and faster. The whole village was there, Serbs dancing with gypsies. Hand in hand. Then Branislav sang one of the Partisan fighting songs which begins:

Over the hills and through the cities we go to battle.

Then they danced another kolo. It was a half holiday in the village now. Peasants had come in from the hills, hearing the music. I noticed that Branislav's coat was patched in three places and very frayed at the wrists. Few people in the crowd were dressed warmly enough for this weather. Many had bare feet. Then I noticed the sun. It was almost ready to go over the horizon. So I said we must go. Branislav told us to follow the road out this way over the next hill. We started to say good-by but he said we'd do that later. So we started up the road with the fiddlers following us. The whole town followed the fiddlers. A quarter of a mile up the road we went through the gypsy quarter. The houses were smaller. Some of them were only shacks. I thought how in America we also make certain people live in shacks on the edge of town. The crowd had thinned out now. Only gypsies were left. The end of the gypsy quarter was the end of Senaja. That was where Branislav made his speech. It was a very formal speech. He stood with his heels together and his fiddle under his arm. He said he was speaking for all Senaja. For the gypsies especially. They wanted us to take a message back to America. We were to tell America just what we had seen and heard in Senaja. We were to tell the truth just as it was. Maybe America would believe us. They wanted America to know the truth about Yugoslavia and about Senaja and about the gypsies. So we promised we would. Then we shook hands and left.

It was dusk now. The mountain called Kosmaj was blue gray. It was that odd color all tall mountains in the distance get at this time of day. The countryside was quiet. There were no peasants in the fields plowing. Even the cattle had gone home to their barns. I asked June if she noticed the smell of fresh-turned earth that was in the air. It was a good smell. Some of that earth hadn't been turned for years. It took us half an hour to climb the first hill. When we got to the top we were out of breath. So we stopped a minute. I happened to look back. There was Senaja down below us. From this distance even the gypsy quarter looked picturesque because you couldn't see the muddy yards and the walls that needed patching and the roofs with shingles missing. Against the white of the houses we could see a lot of black dots. June said they were our friends still standing there. She said she could almost see Branislav and his fiddle. As we squinted down at them we heard a soft sound. Maybe if we had been closer it would have sounded like a cheer. From up here it was a soft sound, with all the voices blended into one. I don't know what the words were that they were shouting up to us. Maybe they were just saying *"Živeli,"* which means "good luck to you." But the words I heard were those words Branislav had spoken:

"Tell America the truth. Tell America about the gypsies of Senaja."

When we got moving again Milan said one of the songs they had sung for us was about how after the fighting is over we shall have not only peace but unity, brotherhood, and a better world.

Chapter Sixty-Four

MILAN, MILAN, MILAN

WE GOT LOST many times going over the hills from Senaja to the place where we had left the jeep. Each time we stopped in a peasant's house to ask directions we had to have a glass of wine. Several times peasants went a short distance with us to put us back on the right path again. One of them said very proudly that he'd helped hand out UNRRA food at the store in Mladenovac. Didn't know what Yugoslavia would have done without that food from America! Another one of our guides seemed to think we'd forget about being hungry and cold if he sang for us. The song he sang the best was about peasant maidens begging Comrade Tito to allow the men of their village to come home from fighting in the hills just for a few days so they could all get married. I thought of the Greek play *Lysistrata* as he sang.

When we got to where we had left the jeep we found that a peasant in a house close by had hitched a team of oxen to it and had pulled its nose out of the mud. Before we could go on he said we had to come to his home and meet his family. It wasn't often that they saw strangers in these parts.

Most of the world knows about Balkan peasants from pretty picture postal cards. Or from seeing films of the women dressed in their embroidered costumes. Or from reading books by people who like to travel in motorcars and describe the quaint customs of this section or that. It's all made very charming. It's the smell of apple blossoms in the spring. It's brocaded vests on the men. Strange headwear. The dancing of the kolo on village greens. Peasant shoes with turned-up toes. Wooden clodhoppers. Bits of the Old World. So refreshing and charming. So different and picturesque.

Those pictures of peasant life are true and accurate. Pictures don't lie. On holidays you can see the women in their embroidered costumes and the men in their brocaded vests. You can smell apple blossoms from March until June, depending on the section you're in. But it's only 4 per cent of the truth. It's what the life of the peasants is like twelve or thirteen days of the year. It's what the ministries of propaganda show the tourists. It's what the guidebooks tell you about. It's what you can see for yourself and record on pieces of celluloid film if you travel by motorcar and hit a village on exactly the right holiday.

But if you travel by a jeep that breaks down you see 96 per cent of the truth. You see how the peasants really live. You smell the stench of privies outside kitchen windows. You see the food they eat and you say to yourself that an Iowa farmer wouldn't feed a lot of it to his pigs. You see the squalor of their life. The filth of their clothes. You look around the house and realize that there isn't a receptacle large enough for a man to wash even his feet. You smell the odor of human bodies which have never been wet all over at the same time. Not unless they got caught in the rain. You smell barnyard manure which is an odor they live with even while they sleep. You see four bunks made of wood for nine people and you know that the only thing that keeps them warm in winter is their own concentrated body heat. They have fancy peasant costumes, but they keep them packed away most of the time. They're handed down from generation to generation. They're beautiful things, whatever the section is. They're worn on feast days. They photograph well, especially if you bring along some color film.

But 96 per cent of the time they wear rags. They don't have radios, refrigerators, automobiles. Not even gramophones, iceboxes, and bicycles. Their children don't get orange juice, cod-liver oil, or vitamin pills. They don't even get vaccinations and anti-typhus injections. Most of the peasants never read anything more than public notices posted in the village square. Most of them can't even read public notices because they never went to school. In the picture postal cards they all look strong and healthy. Some of them are. Those who survive. But here in Yugoslavia before the war the death rate was one of the highest in the world. The life-expectancy of the average Yugoslav was the shortest in Europe. Forty-five per cent of the deaths were of children under ten. There were only twenty-eight thousand hospital beds for fifteen million people. There was one doctor for every fifteen thousand peasants.

Anyway, we enjoyed the hospitality of the peasant who had pulled the jeep out of the mud for us. The family's name was Riznić. The old grandmother busied herself while we talked to the children who clustered around us. Finally the grandmother came forward bearing a tin tray. It might have come from Woolworth's. But she handled it as if it were of solid silver. On the tray were four small glasses of honey with a spoon upside down across the top of each glass. And four glasses of water to wash it down. And four glasses of rakia to take away the sweet taste of the honey. We got the technique by watching. One spoonful of honey. One sip of water. One swallow of rakia.

Back in Mladenovac we found the County Council in a late night session. There were eight members of the board present. They wanted to know about everything we had seen. But more than that they wanted to ask us some questions. They had been meeting to see what they could do about the summer food crisis. But they admitted that part of the time they had been thinking of questions to ask us because it wasn't often they got a chance to talk to foreigners. Especially Americans. What was America's reaction to Truman's speech on Greece? Did our people approve of what they called America's new imperialistic policy? What was America's ultimate aim? Did we want to rule the whole world? Or did we just want to control all oil and other raw materials?

We had dinner in Mladenovac's one kafana. Two lawyers came to our table to ask some of the same questions the council members had. The town's *bon vivant* also came over and sat with us. It was June who attracted him. He liked American girls. He made many amorous little speeches to June before the evening was over. Milan had to translate them all. Milan didn't like his Cyrano de Bergerac role a bit. He thought June was attractive too. So after Milan refused to translate any more the young man went away. When the three of us were alone again Milan and June had a conversation which I wrote down to prove something. I'm not sure now just what. It went like this:

MILAN: Yovanović made a very interesting speech in Parliament the other day.

JUNE: Fine. What did he say?

MILAN: I don't know. I wasn't there.

JUNE: Then how do you know it was an interesting speech?

MILAN: Because there was an article in *Borba* about it.

JUNE: What did the paper say about it?

MILAN: What paper?

JUNE: *Borba*.

MILAN: I don't know. I haven't seen a copy of *Borba* since we left Belgrade.

JUNE: Then how do you know what Yovanović said?

MILAN: I don't know.

JUNE: Let's start all over again. You went out this morning to a *trafika* to buy a postage stamp.

MILAN: Who?

JUNE: You.

MILAN: Oh yes.

JUNE: And I presume you saw a copy of today's *Borba*.

MILAN: No, I didn't. Because this is Tuesday.

JUNE: What does that have to do with it?

MILAN: *Borba* never publishes on Tuesdays.

JUNE: But you said Yovanović made an interesting speech and . . .

MILAN: He did.

JUNE: How do you know?

MILAN: There was an article in yesterday's *Borba*.

JUNE: Then what did yesterday's *Borba* say that Yovanović said?

MILAN: Who?

JUNE: Yovanović, the opposition member of Parliament.

MILAN: I don't know.

JUNE: Then how do you know that he even spoke?

MILAN: The man in the trafika told me.

JUNE: So you bought a paper.

MILAN: No.

JUNE: Why not?

MILAN: Because they'd all been sold.

JUNE: So the man in the trafika told you what Yovanović said.

MILAN: No. He hadn't read the article. Someone else told him that Yovanović made an interesting speech.

JUNE: Let's forget it all and go to bed.

The next morning we set out for Topola. By this time I thought I had been in enough towns in enough parts of Yugoslavia to do a bit of generalizing. I told June there hadn't been a single case of inhospitality anywhere. Wherever we went people opened their doors to us. Whatever facts and figures we asked for they gave us. Most of them were simple country people who weren't quick-witted enough to twist the truth into something for foreign consumption. We checked and rechecked the stories they told us. They seemed, everywhere, to be telling us the truth. Officials and ordinary citizens as well. We had seen what we wanted to see. We had gone where we wanted to go. No barriers had been put in our way. Except for a suspicious gendarme here and there, like the one on the bridge at Rogatica, we had seldom even been asked for our identity papers. Of course we hadn't made the mistake of trying to photograph military installations.

Topola was the first place it was different. They were suspicious of us in Topola. We called on the county president and his secretary. The tension in the room was something you could feel. The way they answered the questions we asked made it clear they didn't really trust us. The president was tall enough to have come from the mountains of Cernagora. He was a village peasant. He didn't look it except that he wore the fanciest embroidered vest I ever saw. He had long white mustachios which he spent all his spare time twirling between his fingers to make the ends more pointed. The ends turned up like the horns of the oxen in the Vojvodina. The mustachios made him look like just what he said he was. An old army officer. He was sixty-two years old. Went into the Army when he was a boy. He'd risen to the rank of captain. That's good for a peasant in Old Yugoslavia. In this war he was captured the first month of the fighting and spent four years in eight different prison camps in Germany. He was a member of the old Republican party of Yugoslavia long before the war. Maybe we'd think that was strange, a man living in a village in the Topola area being in the Republican party. Of course we knew, didn't we, that Topola is where Yugoslavia buried her kings. It was a shrine of the monarchists. But Captain Mihail Trifunović kept repeating that he had been a Republican long before the war. They weren't all monarchists around here, even if there were kings buried up on the hill. It wasn't difficult getting the captain to talk as long as we spoke of military matters.

Trying to talk to the secretary wasn't so easy. He wouldn't even give us his name. He was young and he kept his eyes fastened on us all the time. He didn't want to answer questions about anything. Not even simple questions about how much illiteracy there was here. Or what percentage of the population was Serb. We asked what happened to the royal wine cellars here in Topola when the Germans came in. Destroyed. Just a one-word answer. That was all. No details. Now what else did we want to know? Had the Germans stolen anything from the church? Yes. What? Things. What kind of things? Just things. We were getting nowhere, so we left. It was the first cold water anyone had thrown on us in all our months of traveling around the country. I couldn't figure it out.

We were about to drive up to the royal church on the hill when the secretary appeared with another man. The other man was young and city-looking. He turned out to be the president of the city council in Kragujevac. Later I told June I was sure the local secretary had asked him to check up on us. But the president from Kragujevac wasn't the suspicious type. He said he was on his way to a town ten miles away where there was a delegation of Americans. If we wanted to follow him he'd show us the way. We suggested he ride with us and let his limousine lead the way. It was a test of how good a sport he was. Riding in a jeep over country roads isn't anything you do for pleasure. It was a dirt road. And the limousine ahead stirred up great clouds of dust. The jeep was not one of those closed-in jobs either. We ate the dust. It got into our eyes. It filled our ears. It sifted through our clothes. But the president, who was dressed as if he were on his way to attend a bank directors' meeting, didn't seem to mind. He passed the test all right. He told us the word for what was in the air was *prashina*. I said it was almost as good as bloto. It sounded like dust. Just like bloto sounded like mud. The president explained about Topola. He laughed and said we surely could appreciate the situation. Here was Topola, the shrine of the monarchy. But the present regime had overthrown the monarchy. The Partisans and the recently dethroned king weren't even on speaking terms. It was all very embarrassing for the New Order around Topola. Foreigners who came to Topola were generally monarchophiles. Very embarrassing. Besides, we arrived in Topola right on the heels of a British investigating commission of some kind. The Topola officials didn't know who we were. They were just suspicious. We must try to understand.

Before we got to where we were going the jeep broke down. The president and June started walking into the next town for help. While they were gone a truck loaded with stone came along and towed the jeep the rest of the way.

We found the American delegation in the village of Darosava. Only the village had been renamed Partisani. And the American delegation wasn't an American delegation at all. It consisted of twelve young people from Poland, Italy, Rumania, Albania, and Bulgaria who were traveling around Yugoslavia as part of a worldwide Youth Week celebration. We had lunch with them in Partisani. The lunch was important for two reasons. I had my first taste of *gibanica*. It's a Serbian dish of eggs, cheese, and pastry. The Serbs feel that anyone who hasn't eaten gibanica hasn't really lived. And then we met Gara. Her real name was Milunka Stanojlović. Gara was just her Partisan name. She was twenty years old. Her skin was the color of well-roasted coffee. I was sure she was a gypsy but some of her friends laughed and said if we could see her brothers and sisters we wouldn't think so. They were all pale blonds. Anyway, Gara was beautiful like a gypsy. In every way. She had a medal on a red ribbon over her left breast. That meant she had been decorated for some special act of bravery. She had gone into the Partisans at sixteen. She'd fought all over Bosnia and Cernagora. With a gun? Yes, with a gun. Had she ever used it? Her face clouded a little. Of course she had used it. Many times. She'd been in some big battles. I looked at her. She was as feminine and delicate as a rose petal. Except when she talked about her life in the mountains. Or about what the Germans and Chetniks had done here in Darosava. Two hundred and fifty civilians killed. That's why the name had been changed to Partisani. It was one way to honor the town for the rest of time.

And then we met Milan Lazarović. He was exactly Gara's age. He was from Arandjelovac. That was a town not far away. He'd also gone into the Partisans at sixteen. Was wounded in an early battle near Belgrade. After the war ended he was in a hospital where Gara became a nurse, when there was no more fighting to do with a gun. She helped take care of him. Milan was bubbling over with youth and excitement which he didn't try to suppress. The Youth Delegation was going over to Arandjelovac. We must go too. There were things to see in Arandjelovac. And couldn't he ride in the jeep with us, now that it had been fixed? So we had two Milans. Milan the Interpreter and Milan the Wounded Partisan. I suggested that Gara come along too. The three youngsters sat together on top of the jerry cans. They sang all the way to Arandjelovac. They made me feel young too. There was spring in the air. There was youth in the back seat. The jeep was working again. So on to Arandjelovac and never mind the *prashina*. In between songs we found out that thirty members of Gara's family had been in the Partisan Army. Gara herself was secretary of her home-town council.

The first thing Milan the Partisan wanted us to see was what the youth of Arandjelovac were doing. They were doing one job of slum clearance. That's what the project would have been called in America. And then they were building a park where some ruins had been. The young people doing this work were called Shock Brigaders. That meant they worked at double the speed of any other volunteer laborers. The Poles, Rumanians, Italians, Bulgarians, and Albanians watched them with wonder on their faces. The picks and shovels were moving at a speed to bring wonder to anyone's face. But I was more interested in Milan the Partisan.

Milan said he was in his sixth year at the lyceum. He'd like to go to college and become an agricultural expert. He was as excited about the future as any American youngster might be. He looked like just what he was. An especially bright high school boy. He looked like that until I happened to say something about the battles he'd been in. Had he ever killed an enemy soldier? He answered without any attempt at dramatics. He just narrowed his eyes a bit and said, "Plenty!" The quiet way he said it made me realize he probably had. His eyes when he answered were no longer the eyes of a high school boy. Milan tagged close after me wherever we went. He wrote his name on a piece of paper and asked if I would send him a letter when I got back to America. And would I do one other thing for him? There was something else he wanted me to see. It was a castle here in town which had belonged to Engineer Karagić, one of Yugoslavia's wealthiest men in the old days. He owned a dozen houses. He spent three million dinar building this castle in Arandjelovac. The government confiscated some of his property including the castle. Now it was being fixed up as a home for invalid students. It was at the top of a hill. From up there we'd be able to see everything. So we tried to drive to the top of the hill. But the jeep was tired. It collapsed halfway up. Back in town the only person we could find who knew anything about automobiles was another Milan. He was exactly the age of the two Milans in the back seat. It was very confusing for the hour it took to get the jeep running again. Then we went to the top of the mountain.

I've seldom seen a boy so full of pride. It was almost as if Milan the Partisan had built the castle himself and had arranged the mountains and valleys around it. He took us into every room. Into the cellar. Up onto the roof. It was sunset time. The rolling hills were turning deep purple. Milan said the white building in the distance with the sun on it like a floodlight was the great church at Topola. Where the kings were buried. That hotel down there in the village with the two big red crosses on the roof is the Starozdanje Hotel. When the German and Chetnik armies established joint headquarters in the hotel they painted the red crosses on it hoping that that way it wouldn't get bombed. From the roof we could see the Youth Delegates down below in the courtyard washing the prashina from their hands and faces. This was a castle but there was no running water yet. Peasant girls stood down in the courtyard pouring water from pitchers over the young foreigners' hands.

At dusk the people of Arandjelovac gathered in the village hall to pay their respects to the foreign delegation. It was supposed to be only for the youth of Arandjelovac. But everyone came. One of the speakers mentioned that there were also some Americans present and the people should know that in America there are progressive youth organizations too. Just the same as in Europe. He said someday the United States will stop supporting men like Franco in Spain and Peron in Argentina and the Fascists in Greece. After it was all over we went back to the castle for dinner. There was a great deal of difficulty finding a common language. The Bulgarians, Rumanians, and Yugoslavs got along stumblingly well with their slightly similar Slav languages. One of the Italian girls knew English. Some of them spoke French. During the evening one of the delegates snapped on a portable radio he'd brought with him. The first voice was that of a BBC announcer with a very Oxfordian voice reading the news. There was a howl of protest. The man with the radio turned the dials and got a station playing American dance music. For the rest of the evening we had American jazz and no one complained.

We slept in the castle that night. It was just like sleeping anywhere else except that I never slept before in the same room with a Pole, an Italian, and an Albanian, all at the same time. The next morning we drove to the hilltop of Topola to look over the church where the bodies of the first Karageorgević king, and Alexander, and Peter, grandfather of the most recent king, all are buried.

The church custodian was a little gray-haired man, Svetozar Lukić, who had been here all during the war but looked blank every time we asked him any question which wasn't strictly ecclesiastical. He could tell us exactly how many colors there were in the mosaics inside the church. (Fifteen thousand.) But he didn't seem to understand when we asked him about the German guests he'd had in the neighborhood for a few years. He thought maybe the German soldiers took something from the royal wine cellars at the bottom of the hill but he didn't think they'd taken anything up here. He pointed to the beauty of the church dome. But when we noticed that the heroic-sized figure of Christ in the mosaic of the dome had a hole directly through the heart he couldn't seem to remember how it happened.

So we left little gray-haired Svetozar Lukić and went to the bottom of the hill where we met Vlactimir Petronijević, the manager of the royal cellars. Vlactimir was the personification of efficiency. He was a college graduate and he knew his business. His business was making wine. He told us everything we wanted to know about the royal wine cellars and he knew what had happened up on the hill too.

That hole in the dome of the church through the heart of the figure of Christ? Sure he knew about that. The hole was hacked out by some Nazi snipers. They used the dome of the church as a hideout. They poked two machine guns through the hole they cut in the body of Christ and killed a lot of Partisans. They knew that no Serbian soldier would fire a gun at the dome of Serbia's most famous church, even though the Serbian Partisans were all anti-monarchists and this was the church of the Serbian kings. The Nazis also stole a number of valuable relics from the church. They converted the wine cellars into a fortress.

The Germans had a good time in Topola. When they left they carted away every drop of wine in the cellars. Close to a hundred thousand gallons. That included twenty-five thousand bottles of aged wine. Some of it was very old. They also carted away every cask except the big ones lined with glass that hold four thousand liters apiece.

We told Vlactimir we'd like to see the cellars. So we went down flight after flight of stairs below the ground. This was where wine was once stored for the royal family. They could put away six hundred thousand liters at a time. And that's a lot of wine for any family. Even a royal family.

Now this was the room for old wine in bottles. This was where the twenty-five thousand bottles had been that the Germans stole. Would we like to taste a small sample from a bottle they'd overlooked? So we did. It was very mellow. It didn't seem to have any alcohol in it at all. No more than sweet cider.

Then we went down another story. These were the big vats. We could see that some still bore the royal crest. Now this one. Vat 104. It's full of a good wine. Just try a small sample. Yes, that's a red wine. Good, isn't it? Better have another small glass, because you'll not taste wine like this again for a long time. We're aging this.

Then down another story. On the way Vlactimir said something about how a great deal of the labor of rebuilding the damage the Germans did had been voluntary. He said something about the number of hours the peasants had contributed. But I didn't get it. I do remember him going over to one of those great casks lying on its side which was taller than two men standing on top of each other and saying that this was Vat 95. We must try this too. This was different. This was a white wine. It tasted the same to me as the red. It tasted strong. I tried to take just a little sip. But I could see that Vlactimir was going to be insulted, so I did bottoms up with the glass. The glass looked as big as two water tumblers. Then we went down another flight. But the first thing I knew we were in the out of doors again, so I guess we went up instead of down. Vlactimir was saying about how the ideal temperature for keeping wine is about twelve degrees. But I couldn't make out whether he meant Fahrenheit, Centigrade, or Celsius, and when I tried to ask him I couldn't even say the words Fahrenheit, Centigrade, and Celsius in English. I tried a great many times. Each time it came out Celsenheit, Fahremgrade, and Census. So I said to June and Milan that I thought we'd better be leaving. But Vlactimir said we ought to know how rakia is made. That was one thing I did not want to know. It was bad enough drinking it without knowing how it was made. But he showed us. You press the grapes with the feet. That makes the first and best wine. Then you press what's left of the grapes with a big machine, until there's hardly enough left from a ton of grapes to put in the palm of your hand. That makes Wine Number Two. Then you take the pulp that remains and you cook it. I distinctly remember him saying you cook it. Then you distill it and what comes off is mostly rakia and wouldn't we like a taste? I was so anxious not to hurt Vlactimir's feelings that I took the glass he held out, but it dropped on the floor somewhere between his hand and mine. After we got back into the jeep Milan said something about Vat 95 and Vat 104. I didn't know what he was talking about. I went to sleep.

Chapter Sixty-Five

MORE BEAST THAN MAN

BY THE TIME we got to Kragujevac we were well aware that wherever we went the past, the present, and the future were all tied together. To understand the hopes and fears, the dreams and aspirations of the people we must know what experiences they'd been through. That's true anywhere. It's especially true in Yugoslavia today.

And so we sat in an automobile on the edge of Kragujevac while the secretary of the District Council pointed things out to us. We were in the heart of a region known as the Shumadija, or the Wooded Place. Kragujevac was once a great industrial city. On its horizon there were many more smokestacks than church steeples.

Here beside us was a food canning factory. It used to be owned by Steva Stefanović, one of Yugoslavia's wealthiest industrialists. He understood the Germans and the Germans understood him. They'd done business before the war. They did business during the occupation. Stefanović's factory turned out tons, hundreds of tons, maybe thousands of tons of foodstuff for the Nazi Army. Cans of meat from Kragujevac kept many Nazi soldiers alive while they fought the Russians on the Eastern Front and the British and Americans on the Western Front.

During the war Steva Stefanović did better than ever financially. To show his appreciation he helped the occupiers politically too. He knew this city and he knew who the Germans' enemies were. It was no secret that he went over lists with them, making little red checks beside the names of people who should be liquidated. And who were.

Some of his old factory workers fled to the hills. But some were still on the pay roll and most of them were trying to hinder the enemy by the slow-down method. They were trying to fill as few cans with food as possible. One by one such men disappeared. Steva Stefanović would simply give their names to the Gestapo and they'd be taken care of. He had a great deal to do with the massacre of Kragujevac. Of course we knew about the massacre of Kragujevac, didn't we?

The Shumadija was one of the first centers of resistance. The Germans tried to break the back of the resistance right here. The plan was to put the fear of the Third Reich into the hearts of all Serbs for all time. That's why they themselves gave so much publicity around Yugoslavia to what they did at Kragujevac.

Marisav Petrović, a Yugoslav Quisling, was the man who directed the operation for them. He was a native of a nearby village and knew the district well.

It all happened on the night of October the twentieth and the morning of the twenty-first, in '41. The Germans threw a cordon around the whole city. Every entrance and exit, every road, was blocked. First they rounded up four thousand men who were on a special list. Then they went from door to door, street to street, neighborhood to neighborhood, passing the word around that new identity papers, new *legitimacija,* were about to be issued. Any man who didn't have a new one by morning would be subject to the supreme penalty.

So the men of Kragujevac went, voluntarily most of them, to the city square. They went without suspicion, some of them, thinking they were merely going to be handed new German identity papers. In the case of school children, the Germans showed no partiality because of sex. They took girls as well as boys if they were in the upper four grades of the lyceum. When the teachers heard about it they were suspicious. But any teachers who questioned the Germans about what was going to happen were told to come along and see. That's how such a large percentage of the lyceum faculty got liquidated too.

All in all they rounded up six hundred students, a few dozen teachers, four thousand "special cases," and several thousand miscellaneous people. The total came to more than seven thousand. They were all marched into one of the suburbs. Mass graves had already been dug. It took most of the night with machine guns to do the job.

Kragujevac still talks with pride about one of the heroes of that night. He was a young worker named Toza Drajović. At the height of the proceedings Toza went slightly mad. Somehow he managed to wrest a machine gun away from a member of the Nazi execution squad. How many Germans he killed before he himself fell dead no one ever found out. Not exactly. But the private rebellion of Toza Drajović at the height of the Kragujevac massacre is something the people have commemorated with a song, with poems, and with a kolo.

The district secretary said we should be sure to write down the name of that Yugoslav traitor who played the leading role in the killing of seven or eight thousand of his neighbors that night. Marisav Petrović. We should remember the name because we might meet the gentleman someday. Oh yes, there were some photographs in the city files showing him actually doing some of the shooting himself. We might like to see them so in case we ran across Mister Petrović someday we'd recognize him by sight. At last report he was enjoying a very happy life in Rome. If we did run across him in Italy we might tell him that the people of Kragujevac who were left would also like to see him someday, if he ever got this way.

We were still sitting in the secretary's car on the edge of the city. Now he pointed down into the valley and said we could see some of the factories which had been rebuilt already. It isn't difficult to replace walls and roofs of factories which have been demolished. The difficult thing to replace is the machinery. There were twenty thousand industrial machines of various kinds in Kragujevac's factories before the war. All twenty thousand of them were shipped up to Germany by the Nazis. Yugoslav authorities had a list of where every machine went. When the fighting ended they gave that list to the Allied military authorities and asked if it wouldn't be possible to get the machinery back again so Kragujevac could re-establish some of her industries. So far, four hundred of the twenty thousand had been returned. I asked what had happened to Steva Stefanović, the industrialist. The secretary smiled.

"Under your American laws," he said, "a man who turns traitor like that can be executed. We didn't go that far. We arrested him, put him on trial, and he was found guilty of trafficking with the enemy. Ten thousand deaths during the course of the war were blamed directly onto him. His property was ordered confiscated. And he was given a long term at hard labor."

Since the State took over the Stefanović factories they have been doubled in size, as we could see for ourselves. The new buildings had been built mostly with voluntary labor since the liberation. They were turning out food now for some of the families of some of the men Mister Stefanović had had executed.

But the secretary said he thought we could understand what had happened in the Shumadija better if we studied a smaller community. Take his own village of Grošnica. If we would drive a few kilometers out in the country with him we could get the story firsthand.

With us in the back seat were two children. Tania was not quite six. Lepa was ten. Lepa was a blonde with hair like strands of thin-spun gold. Her eyes were blue and soft and had a fairylike quality to them. Lepa was full of the wonder of life. Tania was a little firebrand. She was dark. Her complexion was almost swarthy. Her hair was black. Her eyes were deep and brown. They were happy eyes when they smiled. But sometimes they stared out the window of the car at nothing at all. They looked far off into space and seemed like very adult eyes for a child who was only five. Once while the two small girls were arguing about something they'd seen the secretary told us about them. Lepa was his brother's child. He and his brother had gone into the Partisans at the very start. The secretary had become commander of the Shumadijska Division. His brother had been killed. So had his brother's wife. That made Lepa an orphan. So he was taking care of her.

The story of Tania was a little longer. We got it in bits and pieces during the afternoon when she wasn't listening. The secretary had a sister who was pregnant at the start of the war. When her husband went into the hills she insisted on going with him. Her mother also went along to take care of the baby when it was born. Tania's first sight of the world was from a mountaintop. She was born in the woods during a battle. Her mother and grandmother took turns taking care of her. They spent the rest of their time nursing the wounded. Then the Shumadijska Division was ordered to Bosnia. There was no chance of moving the wounded. The two women stayed here in the hills of South Serbia to help nurse them. Tania stayed with them. After the Partisan fighters left, the Chetniks found the hospital camp. They systematically killed the wounded one by one. They turned the mother and grandmother over to the Germans. The Germans in cold blood executed both of them. That made Tania a half orphan. She became a complete orphan a few weeks later when her father was killed in battle. By now this child of the forests was three months old. She was sent to a Chetnik camp not far from Kragujevac. The secretary at his Bosnian headquarters received reports on everything that had happened. He said, you can imagine how I felt when I heard that my own mother and my sister had been executed. And that all those wounded men had been killed. But they told me that Tania was still alive so I organized an expedition to raid the camp where they said the child was being held. A lot of men were killed that night for the sake of a child. But Tania was kidnaped, alive. And now here she was, sitting in the back seat of the car beside me staring out the window at cows and water buffalo.

If you have children of your own you may think it was my imagination. Maybe you know from experience that a child of five has no memory. Or that eyes of the young don't talk. But Tania's did. They didn't say things that can be put into words. They didn't tell a consecutive story. They didn't talk history. But they said something. And it wasn't a very happy something, either.

By this time we were in the village of Grošnica where Tania should have been born. Grošnica was a peaceful place on the afternoon of Saturday, March 29, 1947. If you had been driving along on a tour you probably wouldn't have looked twice at it. You might have noticed that there was a nice park and village square in the center of the community. Also that there was a strip of woods leading up a hill from the park. Also that opposite the park there was an Orthodox church with a fat padre standing in the door. You might have noticed some villagers gathered around the well in the park taking turns drawing up buckets of water. If someone had told you that the population of Grošnica was three thousand you would have looked at the small cluster of houses and wondered where they all lived. But by the time you had thought all those things your car would have been out in the country again and you'd soon forget this small village of the Shumadija.

But let me tell you what we found in Grošnica. Things happened here, too, that day in October which Kragujevac remembers so bitterly. Things happened in many villages that day but nothing any worse than what happened here. That day in October had been an important religious holiday for members of the Orthodox faith. It was a Sunday, and people came in from the peasant huts on the hills to make special prayers. There were some Germans standing around the village green and some of the soldiers of Nedić the Quisling. That made the villagers a little suspicious. But these Nedić men were Yugoslavs and they were singing Yugoslav songs about King Peter. And being Serbs they of course knew the importance of this holy day. So the people in their brightly colored peasant costumes just eyed them suspiciously and went on about their religious affairs. But as they came from the church they were seized. One by one. Indiscriminately. Women as well as men. Some young children too. They were seized and lined up until there were three hundred of them in a frightened cluster, wondering what was going to happen next. Three hundred is apparently the number that had been decided upon. Ten per cent of the population. That was the order from higher up. Ten per cent. They were killed on those church steps right over there across the green. Since then many peasant women have gotten down on their knees, reverently, on the stone steps leading up into the church to pray and scrub at the same time. The bloodstains have been mostly washed away. But if you look closely you can still see some black spots that wouldn't come out. After all, the bullet wounds of three hundred people drip a lot of blood.

The secretary said this old man by the well is one who was here and saw it all. How old is he? He looks seventy instead of the fifty that he really is. But maybe we can understand the reason. He saw it all. He ran screaming from the village square up into the hills. He hasn't acted quite normal since then. The secretary says we won't get much additional information from the *pope,* as the Yugoslavs call an Orthodox priest. He wasn't here then. But he's a character we'll enjoy meeting. The secretary says he's very popular with the village people. The only trouble is that apparently no one has ever told him that a padre shouldn't drink. He loves wine and he drinks it all the time. That's why he has such a bright red nose. The padre says he's sixty-five but on a day like this, with the smell of spring in the air, and with apple blossoms and flowers blooming, it's cause for a fight in Grošnica if anyone reminds him of his age. He feels this afternoon as if he'd like to get married. Of course the Orthodox Church has no rule that prevents a priest from getting married. Maybe he will someday. A peasant drawing water at the well stops with the bucket half full and laughs and says:

"You're foolish, padre. Wait awhile. You aren't old enough yet."

The crowd laughs and then the man next to the padre slaps the Falstaffian character on the shoulder and repeats the joke:

"You're foolish, padre. Wait awhile. You aren't old enough yet."

The secretary laughs too. Then he becomes serious again. When Church and State were tied together, the parish in this village owned most of the good land there was. Now, under the new agrarian laws, a majority of its holdings have been given to the peasants. But the Church still retains this valuable piece of timberland which runs up the hill from the park. The secretary also says that the people of Grosnica who survived what happened on the church steps are trying to build a better life for their children. They elect their own village council now. The foundation is already laid for a cultural home. There will be a bronze marker on it engraved with the names of the three hundred. Most of the destroyed homes have been rebuilt already. There's a youth center in town now. And a new co-operative where people can buy things at prices much lower than they ever knew before. When the secretary lived here there wasn't a single book in town. Now they have a library of four hundred volumes. At this point the padre raised his hand for silence. The good secretary is wrong. Five hundred there are now.

On the way back to Kragujevac the air was full of petals from the blossoms of peach, apple, cherry, and plum trees. The roads were sticky with the caterpillar-like seedpods which willows drop at this time of the year. Tania leaned far out of the window trying to catch some of the flower petals in her small hands. Her uncle held onto one of her feet. He smiled with his soft gray eyes and said:

"I'm going to spend the rest of my life seeing that nothing ever happens to her. Nothing except good things."

Halfway back to Kragujevac the secretary suddenly ordered the driver to stop. He'd seen an old woman by the side of the road. When she caught up with the car the secretary jumped out and kissed her on each cheek. I thought maybe she was his mother. But then I remembered what had happened to his mother. When we started again he apologized for wasting that much time.

"She was the mother of two of my best fighters. They were both killed in one of our battles in Bosnia. Every time I pass this way I stop and say hello. And every time, she digs into her pockets and gives me a present."

So on the way back we chewed on some apples which the secretary said were so scrawny because of last summer's drought.

There were four mass graves on the edge of the city. The secretary said they didn't contain all seven thousand bodies because some people had been so eager to get the bones of their relatives that they dug into the mass graves at night and stole away some of the bodies. But most of them were there. Someday a memorial would be built on this spot. In the meantime, the graves were marked by hundreds of plain wooden crosses. Each cross had the name of a victim on it. Some of the crosses were constructed from the wood of UNRRA packing cases. Photographs of the victims were tacked onto some of them. A few hundred feet away a group of high school pupils with picks and shovels over their shoulders were practicing songs they were going to sing in a few months when they went off to work on the new Youth Railroad.

The town of Knić was fifty-four kilometers down the road. It wasn't quite so large as Grošnica. People all over the county knew what had happened just this past month at Knić. They'd opened a motion-picture theater. Most of the villagers had never seen a movie before. The opening night they had to have three shows to accommodate everybody. By midnight one thousand eight hundred and ten of the twenty-two hundred people in town had seen *Four Hearts*. That was the first film. It was Russian. Since then several British films had been shown. The British film the people liked best was called *The Nine of Them* and was about the war in Africa. The only people who missed the opening show were those who were ill or too old to get out. Of course there were a few who thought it was all an invention of the devil. The price of admission was four dinar (eight cents) if you were willing to sit in a back row. It was twice as much if you wanted a good seat right up front where you could nearly touch those big figures on the screen. The projectionist was Milosh Fofunka, an eighteen-year-old boy. We offered Milosh a cigarette. He looked at the cellophane-covered package from America. Then he smiled and pulled out an identical package from his own pocket. Only his package was very soiled. The cellophane was nearly worn off. The cigarettes in his package were Yugoslav. He told us he'd found the empty package in the road. Some American going through town had apparently thrown it out of a car window. He just used it as a cigarette case. He liked the colors on the package and the strange American lettering. He said the building they used as a theater had been put up by the Germans as a mess hall. But now that Knić had discovered how much the village enjoyed seeing movies they planned to spend sixteen thousand dollars building a real theater. Sixteen thousand dollars would be a lot of money for a village of two thousand people. But they figured it would be worth while.

As we were leaving Knić I saw a young man with a beard. He was the first young man I'd seen in all Yugoslavia with a beard so I went up to him and tried to make a joke about it. He pretended to smile but it wasn't a very good attempt. After we got into the jeep and were out of Knić, Milan the Interpreter said I shouldn't have mentioned it. In this town they have a custom that regardless of a man's age he grows a beard and keeps it for one year after his mother dies.

It was late in the evening when we got into Čačak. Two soccer teams had arrived just ahead of us. They'd taken all the rooms in the one good hotel. We found a room for June at the Macedonia Hotel. Milan and I shared the only vacant room at something they called the Hotel Serbia. The next morning we compared notes. The republics of Macedonia and Serbia are quite different. But the two hotels were equally bad. Except that June said nothing happened to her bed. Mine was held together with pieces of wire and rope. At eleven minutes after three in the morning it collapsed. I spent the rest of the night on the floor hoping the floor wouldn't collapse. There was no bread in Čačak and of course no butter. We were used to going without butter but not even peasants were used to going without bread. You don't miss bread if you have plenty of meat and vegetables. But when bread makes up about 90 per cent of your diet it hurts to have to go without it. For dinner we had one hard-boiled egg and one spoonful of spinach apiece. No bread. No soup. No butter. No salad. No dessert. No coffee.

The business center of Čačak reminded us of a rural Middle Western town. The public square was bleak-looking. It was Sunday and there was no one around. But we found a local lawyer who told us about Čačak. He was American-looking and had had sixteen years of schooling. That made him the best-educated man we'd met outside of Belgrade. Miodrag Marković showed us a place in the center of the market place which had a chain around it. It was about twenty feet long by ten feet wide. It was paved with cobblestones just like the rest of the square. Inside the chained-off place there were two tin cans full of wax. Lawyer Marković said they were supposed to burn all the time but the wind had apparently blown them out. Under those tin cans and the cobblestones were six hundred bodies. It happened in Čačak at Christmastime in '41. The roundup began on December the twenty-second and lasted for seven days. People were gathered from streets and from their homes. They were killed with machine guns on a hillside. But they were buried here in the public square. The Yugoslav who directed the operation for the Germans was named Marisav Petrović. Maybe we'd heard of Petrović before. He was here personally. They had some photographs of the actual executions showing Petrović with a revolver in his hand if we'd like to have them. We knew, did we, that Petrović was in Rome now? Lawyer Marković was also here when the hanging took place. He said unless we knew about things like this hanging we couldn't understand the miracle of the New Yugoslavia. The New Yugoslavia in which hate doesn't exist any more. This hanging was important because the executioner and the victim had been friends. Ratko Mitrović was a young law student. He was thirty-two. Jovan Karaklavić was an automobile mechanic. He was thirty-four. They both lived here in Čačak. Ratko went into the Partisans and became the commander of a battalion. Jovan went into the Chetniks and was always in the company of members of Mihailović's general staff. Ratko was captured. Jovan officiated at his death party. It took place right here where we were standing. Before they put the rope around his neck Ratko made a speech. Just then someone snapped a picture. It showed Ratko pleading with the crowd not to let a few killings discourage them. He begged them to keep up the resistance and to let his death and anything else that happened spur them on. Lawyer Marković said he thought the picture was taken by a German soldier. But before the war was over it fell into Partisan hands. Thousands of copies of it were made. It became one of the best pieces of Partisan propaganda. You could even see the noose dangling behind Ratko's head. The whole district knew that Jovan the executioner was now in Austria serving as a chauffeur for some American army officers. They couldn't understand why a good country like America would give protection to a man like that.

Another thing that hurt the people of Čačak was that there used to be an American grave in the public park. The words on the white cross said:

LIEUTENANT MAURICE BLOCK

The lieutenant had been shot down in June of '44 while flying an American plane over this area. The people of Čačak had prided themselves on the good care they took of the grave. They saw that there were flowers on that grave all the time. In the winter when they couldn't get any fresh flowers the women would make paper flowers for the grave. But a few months ago an American jeep drove into town and the body was taken away in a burlap sack. The people of Čačak wondered if the people of America thought the grave wasn't being properly cared for.

About the reconstruction, the big thing here the lawyer said, was the electrification program. Many mountain villages had no electricity at all. The government wanted to put electricity into every home in the next few years. But more important than that, they needed power for the industrialization of the countryside. Ten miles down the road we'd pass between two great mountains, Kablar and Ovćar. There, the people of this district were building a power dam. It would be finished by the end of next year and would supply electricity for half a million people.

We drove from Čačak to the site of the new dam. It was being guarded by soldiers armed with rifles and tommy guns. We parked the jeep at the side of the road. We were talking to each other in a language the guards must have known was the language of foreigners of some kind. We were studying a map. That might also have made a spy-conscious guard suspicious. And we had no proper number plate on the front of the car. Peter Furst, the owner of the jeep, had been lazy about getting it registered, so he'd just painted a number of his own on the front and rear bumpers. The figures were actually his own age, June's passport number, and their street address back in New York City. Besides all these causes for suspicion, we had our luggage and the cans of gasoline covered with a tarpaulin. For all the guard knew there might be a ton of bombs under that canvas covering. Yet he smiled at us, said *Dobar dan,* and went on up the road.

We made Užice that night. In Užice we found a hotel which had several bathtubs and some hot water. When we'd removed all the *prashina* we'd collected we found that we'd also collected a goodly assortment of fleas. June and Milan didn't bother to count their bites. I had seventy-nine. Each one was a welt about two inches in diameter. If any mathematician wants to figure out that there isn't that much area on a human body let it merely be stated that some of them overlapped. Anyway, we felt better after our baths so we went for a walk down the road that leads to Sarajevo. Užice had been one of our first stops after Belgrade in those days when we were chasing a king and his ministers across the country in April of '41. We'd spent a night in a kafana on the edge of town. June, Milan, and I found the kafana again. Old Milorad Radenković who ran it stared at me and then said:

"My God, I remember you!"

Then he called his wife. And his daughter. And all the neighbors. He told them how we'd offered him a lift to the edge of the sea six years ago but his wife wouldn't let him go. Now she was sorry she hadn't let him go.

"The Germans took out all my teeth."

The statement wasn't quite true. When he opened his mouth we could see two perfectly good teeth.

He remembered that we sat up in his kafana all that one night playing cards. He said in the New Yugoslavia things aren't bad. But they aren't good either. He wished that he were Aleksić. Milan explained that Aleksić was a famous prewar Yugoslav stunt flier. If he were Aleksić he'd take a plane and fly to Genoa. Why Genoa? Oh, he just thought it might be nice in Genoa. He'd rather be most anywhere than in Užice. He said he didn't "gain much" during the war. Of course he did double the size of his kafana. This large building? He built it during the occupation. Still, he'd like to be Aleksić and fly off to Genoa. Things weren't good here. Not for an up-and-coming businessman like he was. If he got too successful and did a lot of business the government would probably nationalize his kafana.

Back in the public square of Užice the evening promenade was under way. Music was coming from a loud-speaker. Occasionally the music would stop and a public announcement would be made. After one announcement Milan the Interpreter said they were holding an "academy" in Užice tonight. June wanted to go to a dance, so she asked Milan:

"What is an academy? Is it a meeting, a concert, a dance, or . . . what is it?"

Milan said didn't we know what an academy was? They were holding an academy tonight. We tried to explain that in English an academy is a school. It isn't something you hold. Would he please try to think of a better translation? What was it they were holding tonight? But we never found out. And anyway Milan had already forgotten just where the academy was being held. So we went to bed.

Chapter Sixty-Six

BROTHER AGAINST BROTHER

UŽICE has a population of only ten thousand. That makes it a small city anywhere. Even here in Yugoslavia. But for two months in 1941 Užice could boast that it was the only liberated city on the entire continent of Europe. Užice had had a bit of history even before 1941. There was the stone bridge across the Jetina River, for example. It was built by the Romans before the time of Christ. But the bridge isn't there any more because the Germans destroyed it during the war. And besides, no one cares very much about ancient history. But what happened in Užice in 1941 answers a lot of questions which American newspaper readers often asked about the Partisans and the Chetniks. Historians who wish to set the record straight about when the Partisans began fighting the Germans should go to Užice. There they can find a warehouse full of evidence to disprove the propaganda that Tito and his men didn't go into action until after the Nazis attacked Russia. There are photographs, newspapers, and old records by the ton. Historians can also find in Užice the truth about how the internal conflict, brother against brother, really commenced. There were hundreds, perhaps thousands, of eyewitnesses to the whole thing.

In the few months when Užice was a freed city it was occupied jointly by the Chetniks of Draža Mihailović and the Partisans of Marshal Tito. They were working together. They had joint headquarters here in Užice. They took over the city when the Germans began transferring troops to the Eastern Front in preparation for the attack which was soon to be made on the Soviet Union. Tito offered Mihailović five hundred rifles, half a million rounds of ammunition, and twenty-five million dinar in cash to co-operate with him. It was the first time the two men had met. And the last time. They worked out a system by which a man could volunteer into whichever of the two liberation armies he chose. But the two armies were operating on two different principles. They showed us in Užice some of the enrollment cards which were given to Chetnik volunteers. They were instructed to go home and wait to be called into action. The Mihailović theory was that this was no time to fight the Germans. They should wait until the Western Allies invaded through the Balkans. Tito's theory was different. He sent his volunteers into action immediately on various fronts in the mountains of Yugoslavia. That was one of the first causes of conflict.

When the Germans withdrew from Užice they blew up the city's munition plant. It was the largest in all Yugoslavia. Chetniks and Partisans alike were in vital need of bullets. Nearly every peasant had a gun of some sort. But no ammunition. Some of the machinery from the blown-up factory was salvaged and they fabricated some new machinery. This was divided into three parts. The old munitions plant was rebuilt and one third of the machinery was left there. The second third was taken to a kafana on a street called Ada Ulica on the edge of the city where an auxiliary munitions factory was established. The rest of the machinery was taken into the vault of the Yugoslav National Bank. The vault was in the side of a hill called Treasury Hill. It had been constructed by the government several years before the war as a storehouse for Yugoslavia's gold supply. It was made in the shape of the letter "H" and went one hundred and twenty yards into the heart of the mountain. Partisans and Chetniks decided that this was the safest place in all Yugoslavia to try to make munitions. It also would make a good air-raid shelter. The two long tunnels were used as the munitions factory. The crossbar of the "H" was the air-raid shelter. Somewhere in that cavern Tito also had his head-quarters. Every seventh day German planes came over and bombed the factory they had destroyed when they fled but which they knew from their espionage reports had been reconstructed. But the factory in the kafana on Ada Ulica and the factory in the side of the mountain were turning out guns and bullets by day and by night. At the peak of production they made four hundred rifles every twenty-four hours, besides truckloads of ammunition. It was all split fifty-fifty between Partisans and Chetniks.

When Marshal Tito received reports that the Germans were so worried about the activities of his liberation army that they were preparing to send five full divisions back from the Eastern Front to deal with Užice, he asked Mihailović for help in defending the city. That help was not forthcoming. Instead, sporadic fighting broke out between Chetniks and Partisans in some of the villages around Užice. Before long a full-scale war was going on between the two guerrilla forces. That was the signal for the Germans to attack. The five Nazi divisions were augmented by Italian and Ustaši forces which converged on Užice from the direction of Visegrad. And then the Chetniks joined in the enemy attack. Užice soon was no longer the only liberated city in Europe. Užice soon was Nazi again. Tito himself managed to escape. Thousands of his soldiers didn't. At one time a German battalion on the hunt for the Partisan leader got to within thirty feet of where he was hiding in the woods. For days Tito's own general staff didn't know whether he was alive or dead.

It was during the enemy encirclement of Užice that the incident occurred which the people of Užice will never forget. On November 24, 1941, a German plane flew low over the city at 10:30 A.M. As many as could flocked into the air-raid shelter in the side of the mountain. On the dot of 11 A.M. the whole countryside was shaken by an explosion. The theory advanced today is that the explosion was caused by a mine hidden deep inside the Treasury Hill munitions factory by the Chetniks. We asked

each person who told us the story what he thought the German plane
had to do with it. No one knew. But each one of them mentioned
that a German plane flew over exactly half an hour before the explosion.
Many hundreds of civilians in the air-raid shelter were blown to bits. How
many hundred workmen were killed at their benches no one had any
idea. The only people who knew how many men and women worked in
the cave were the officials in charge of the factory. They were all killed in
the explosion. Novak Jivković, who's the editor of the Užice newspaper
today, said if we wanted an idea of how bad an explosion it was he could
tell us that one body was blown out through the entrance of the cave and
over a two-story building. That's how bad it was.

We spent all of one day with Novak Jivković. We kept telling him we
were not writing a history of the war. He kept answering that we couldn't
understand Užice if we didn't know all these things. We couldn't understand the present-day spirit of the people. For the next four years, he said,
the territory around Užice was a battleground. All the time. Day and
night. Summer and winter. He talked quietly and calmly. Except when
he spoke of the Chetniks. Then his voice got bitter and so did the look on
his face. Maybe, he said, we'd like to know why he felt as he did. Maybe
if he told us we would at least understand him. He was a writer and law
student before the war. Not much interested in politics and surely not interested in military affairs. His instrument was the pen and not the sword.
But in his village of Godovik the Chetniks rounded up at least one person
from every home. All the members of his family were taken to concentration camps. Most of the people of Godovik never returned. His fourteen-
year-old brother was taken. So was he. He was put in a death camp to
await execution. After one hundred and eight days of waiting they took
him and two other men, lined them up on the edge of a cliff, and shot
them. All three of them toppled over the precipice. The other two fell to
the bottom, dead. Novak Jivković smiled strangely as he went on with his
story. His body was caught by the branches of a tree on the way down.

"And they hadn't shot me very well."

He lay in the branches of the tree for a long time. How long he had no
way of telling. Maybe days. He didn't know. But he did figure that it was
about three months before he was able to work his way out of the ravine.
There was water down there and he lived on wild berries. While he was
getting his strength back he lived in a cave. Finally he wandered into a
village and found some people he knew who took care of him. But he
never had any treatment for his wounds. No doctors. No medicines. After
he got well he joined the Partisans. He was wounded in a battle. Then he
was captured. Then he escaped. Later in the war he was wounded again.

Novak Jivković told us he was now twenty-eight years old. He held up
his hand to stop us from making any comment. He knew what we were
thinking. He knew that his bald head and his physical condition made him
look closer to fifty. He said:

"I'm telling you all these things because you ought to know something about the people you talk to. Then maybe you'll understand a few things."

For example, he said, what was our reaction to this photograph? And he pulled from a drawer of his desk a picture of a Yugoslav woman helping Chetniks execute a Partisan soldier. The woman was holding the head of the victim, while one of Mihailović's soldiers slit his throat with a knife. To us it might be just one more horrible picture of war. But he knew that Partisan. And he knew the woman too. Could we understand how he felt every time he looked at that photograph? But here was another picture which proved something else. It showed a dozen Chetniks in a schoolyard around the body of an old man they'd just killed. The editor pointed to one of the twelve figures and said:

"That's Milan Sredić. He was a Chetnik all through the war. He's back here in Užice now. He's working at the municipal electric plant. The only punishment they've given him is that he's lost his right to vote. Otherwise he's a free man as long as he behaves. That ought to answer the propaganda of how we Partisans treat our political enemies."

The editor thought we ought to go out and see Mr. Sredić and talk to him and take the photograph with us to be sure he was the same person. But we said we'd take his word for it. We didn't have time. But we did talk to the superintendent of the power plant by phone and he confirmed the fact that Milan Sredić worked for him.

Editor Jivković was trying to gather together material for a war museum. He would be very unhappy if we didn't go down the street with him and look at some of the things he'd accumulated already. Rather than make him unhappy we went. When we got to the barnlike place he was using as a storeroom June said she thought he had enough for a whole museum already. The editor said these banged-up pieces of steel were what was left of some of the munition-making machinery that had been in the factory in the side of the hill. Those dark spots were stains made by the blood of the workmen who had been killed as they operated the machines. Here was a cardboard box full of nice-looking fountain pens. Only please don't even touch them. If you unscrew the cap on one of them you'll blow all of us through the ceiling. No one's ever gotten around to taking the explosive out of them. The Germans dropped them from planes into the streets at night. They had English wording stamped on them. The Germans hoped that friends and relatives of people who committed involuntary suicide with them would blame the British for having dropped them.

"But our people weren't as stupid as that. They weren't stupid enough to unscrew the caps or to blame the British either. They knew who it was that wanted to wipe out the entire Yugoslav race."

Then the editor opened another box. Before he showed us what was in it he told us the story of a girl named Stojana Mićić, from the nearby village of Rećice. People said she was the most beautiful girl for miles around. One night German officers broke into her home. She tried to hide the piece of embroidery she was working on. But they seized her and took it from her. It was a cotton handkerchief with a rose embroidered in red thread. Under the rose were these words in green:

"This flower I send to a Partisan officer whom I lo . . ."

She had only two letters more to make. But the embroidering was never finished. Stojana Mićić was killed the next day. The handkerchief was later found in the pocket of a dead German officer.

And then there was a record book in which German jailers kept a list of all the people they locked in their prison here in Užice. It was started in ink. But the Germans apparently soon ran out of ink. The last half was in pencil. After each name, place, and date of birth and other vital statistics there was a column for the disposition of the case. In most cases it took just one word to tell. *Streljana*. In English that means "executed." There were two thousand eight hundred and thirty-one entries. And this book covered a period of only a few months. June took the left-hand page and I took the right as we went through the book looking for the oldest victim. Prisoner No. 672 was born in 1865. That meant eighty years old at the time of execution.

From the museum we went to call on Mirko Popović. Mirko was a type we'd never met before. He was twenty-three years old and looked like a college football player. He owned a '41 star but said he never wore it. He had been a student when he joined the Partisans at the age of seventeen. Now he was county secretary. He was six feet three inches tall, with blond wavy hair. He would have seemed less out of place in Hollywood. But when he started talking about Užice's plans for the future he was as serious as a New England banker.

Fifteen people out of every seventeen in the district had never had electricity. In six years they hoped to have electricity in every home. Many villages which were cut off from Užice during some months of the years because of the lack of good roads were going to be linked to the district capital with paved highways. That project was being done entirely with voluntary labor. Thousands of people worked on the roads on Sundays. They'd always had a turpentine industry but in the past the peasants worked the trees in a very primitive manner. Now they're going to be educated in modern methods. Years ago the Yugoslav Government started work on a railroad from Užice to Nova Varoš. In ten years twenty kilometers of the road were completed. Then the Germans came and in four years built another seven kilometers. At the time of the liberation fourteen kilometers remained to be built. It took the new regime just seven months to construct the fourteen kilometers. And it was all done with voluntary labor. Mostly youth brigades.

When we left the enthusiastic young secretary June whispered:

"Wouldn't it be wonderful, just for a change, if we found a town where they hadn't built a single new road or new school, hadn't repaired a single house, had never heard of voluntary labor, and told us the people were getting more illiterate every day?"

I admitted that it was beginning to get monotonous. But at least it proved that there was nothing sectional about what was happening in Yugoslavia.

We wanted to leave Užice that afternoon, but the jeep broke down again. We'd been making a chalk mark on the side of the car every time we had to go searching for mechanics to fix it. But that had grown monotonous too. Fortunately there were two or three expert German mechanics at the Municipal Garage who knew all about the eccentricities of American jeeps. Yugoslavia has few automobile mechanics of her own. She has few experts of any kind. But she's training experts as fast as she can. Boys are being rushed through four years of primary school and then into speed-up technical courses. In another five years Yugoslavia will have some mechanics and engineers. But for the present she's relying on her prisoners of war. If the day comes soon when treaties are signed and the Allies come to some agreement about German prisoners being sent back home, Yugoslavia is going to find herself in a difficult fix. People in jeeps that break down are also going to find themselves in a difficult fix. The boy they assigned to the Peter Furst jeep looked about seventeen. That meant he couldn't have been more than fourteen when he was taken prisoner. But he seemed to know everything about a jeep. So we left the machine with him and went back to see our friend the editor. He suggested a trip up over Surduk Mountain where he said he could show us a few things. Halfway up the mountain we saw a power station of considerable size which the editor said some workmen bought from the Germans for two liters of rakia worth about forty-eight cents. When the Germans got ready to retreat the last time they were going to blow it up. The Yugoslavs offered them the rakia in return for the dynamite they were about to use. And so the power station was saved for forty-eight cents' worth of hard liquor.

At the top of Surduk there's a drop from the edge of the road straight down for several thousand feet. The editor stood there looking down for a full minute before he said anything. Then he explained.

"This was just the sort of cliff I dropped over. Remember? My cliff wasn't quite as high as this but—almost. This place is where the Germans brought a lot of people to kill them. It saved bullets just pushing them off into space. Only one man ever escaped. He fell into a deep bank of snow part way down. He's a friend of mine, Obrem Karajičić. Today he's our chief of police in Užice."

The rest of the trip was like a Cook's tour. The editor turned out to be very multilingual. He kept up a running conversation in three languages. He talked to Milan in Serbian, to June in German, and to me in French. He reminded me of one of those chess experts who plays half-a-dozen opponents all at the same time.

We should notice how the forests have been cut back from the road everywhere. This proves how frightened the Germans were of Partisan raiding parties. The Germans got a lot of exercise in Yugoslavia. They had to cut millions of trees. Along this road there was a time when you could see a dead German body every two or three yards. That hill over there is where the Germans killed an entire Partisan battalion, to the last man. Did we know the English poem about the Lost Battalion? Well, there were many lost battalions here. This spot on the road is where Tito's car was blown up by a land mine. But the marshal somehow escaped. Almost miraculous the number of close escapes he had. And now this is the village of Zlatibor. When Tito escaped from Užice and when his own general staff thought he was dead, this is where he suddenly reappeared. He met his general staff on the steps of that villa. The Germans heard that Tito was in Zlatibor and sent a great concentration of troops up this hillside. You can see by the condition of what's left of the houses the job of shelling they did. But Tito slipped through their fingers again. And here's what's left of a Partisan hospital. There were one hundred and eighty patients when the Germans arrived. They hoped to find Tito here. When they didn't they killed all one hundred and eighty patients. They threw the bodies through the windows onto the ground. Peasants buried them in a mass grave. That cross on top of the grave was put up by the mother of one of the men. She walked twenty-eight kilometers to get here and then she made the cross herself and fastened a photograph of her son to it. And over here is where two Flying Fortresses that were in trouble made a crash landing. Six of the American fliers got out of the wreckage alive. But Chetniks killed all six with knives. Would we like to talk to an eyewitness of that event?

So we went up to a kafana on the top of the hill and talked to Slobodan Tasić. He was right here at the time. He saw it all. After the Chetniks left he helped bury the six bodies. They were dug up just fifteen days ago by an American officer who came in a jeep.

In the Tasić kafana we had tall glasses of milk. It was the first milk I'd had since I left New York. It was thin as water and it had been boiled. But it was milk.

On the way down the mountain Milan the Interpreter made another of his classic remarks. He said:

"This trip is very important for me!"

We said we were very glad. Why?

"Because nobody will get me for this trip else."

We thought we knew what he meant. June said apparently the trip was too much for him and he'd never take another job like this one. Milan looked at her blankly.

"What did you say about my translating?"

June answered that she had said nothing about his translating. She hadn't even used the word "translating." She'd just said the trip apparently was too much for him.

"What did you say about too much? That is what I am. Too much."

It took fifteen minutes to unsnarl that linguistic tangle. It turned out that the Serbian word for interpreter is *"tumach."* So from then on Milan had a new name. From then on he was "Too-Much Milan." Sometimes that's just the way we felt about him.

When we got back to Užice we found that the anatomical condition of the jeep was grave. A major operation was being performed. The German boy mechanic thought the patient might survive but it was too early to tell. June said her condition was as good as could be expected considering that she had been driven several years by American soldiers over Italian battlefields and had been in three major accidents which bent her frame, had a bad effect on her chassis, and did various damage to other parts of her anatomy. I told June I wished I'd known all that before we left Belgrade. I would have hired a mule instead. The editor said his paper required a little attention so if we would excuse him he'd leave us to our own devices. But we soon had another guide.

Nedeljko Savić had heard there were Americans in town. Could he talk to us? He'd met many American soldiers and liked them. He'd been in German prison camps for five years. His best friend was an American pilot who said he was the son of the owner of the largest paper in New York. Nedeljko said he was a very liberal man and talked a lot about democracy. He had a liberal attitude toward all Yugoslavs and liked the country. He was a lieutenant and was captured when his plane was shot down by the Germans over Yugoslavia. Then Nedeljko said there was something he couldn't understand. He'd seen with his own eyes how the Germans treated their American prisoners. They stole things right out of their baggage and once they killed some American prisoners because they were too ill to walk to another camp. What he couldn't understand was why the American Government had forgotten things like that. Why had the American Government forgotten who their friends had been and who their enemies had been? So soon.

Nedeljko said we must climb to the top of a little mountain on the edge of town while we waited for the jeep to be fixed. We must see the Old City. It was only a few miles. It was where the river and the railroad went through a narrow mountain pass. This was where the Serbs in the twelfth century built a great stone wall to keep the Turks out. But the Turks came in anyway in the fourteenth century. Up here in this fortress cut into the rock thousands of soldiers could live. In the past war the Nazis used it as a storage place for munitions. From here Užice is a city of red roofs. It's quiet up here. The only noise is the murmur of the city down below and the noise those men are making on that other mountain where they're cutting stone to build houses. And the noise of water rushing over a power dam. But we weren't alone. There were two young boys on our mountain top. They were probably students who had come up here to learn their lessons in solitude. Nedeljko didn't think it would bother them if we sang a few songs. Would we sing some of the songs the Americans sang in his prison camp? The ones he liked best were "John Brown's Body" and "Tipperary." If we didn't know all the words it wouldn't matter. It would be good for him if we would just sing the tunes.

One of the two small boys was a pacer. He walked back and forth with a book in his hand, his lips moving all the time. The other lay on his stomach on the top of a wall built seven hundred years ago. The wall was only eighteen inches wide. If he fell, his body would land two thousand feet below in the river. June said he had more faith in ancient cement than she'd dare have. Both boys ignored us. They were absorbed in their books. We'd seen this same thing before. In out-of-the-way places all over Yugoslavia. In a graveyard on the outskirts of Titograd. On the edge of rivers. In deep woods. Young people with books in their hands. It seemed to be proof of what their teachers had told us in various places about the hunger of Yugoslav youth for knowledge and education. Finally The Pacer closed his book and started down the mountain trail. I caught up with him and said *"Izvenite,"* which is much more polite than the French word *pardon.* Then I asked him if I could see the book he'd been reading. The boy looked about ten. The book was an advanced chemistry textbook. He said he was studying his lesson for tomorrow.

When we got back to Užice we found that the jeep had survived the operation and was breathing on all four cylinders again. Nedeljko insisted on riding two or three miles out of the city with us to put us on the right road. He wanted to say a few final words about America. Even if only 20 per cent of the population was progressive right now and wanted to improve our democracy it was all right. After all, he said, in Yugoslavia the Partisans started with only two or three or maybe 5 per cent of the people behind them. But today at least 90 per cent support the regime because they know that what's happening here is for the good of at least 90 per cent of the people.

When he put us on the right road he got out, shouted *"srećan put,"* which is a beautiful way of saying bon voyage, good journey, may the travel gods protect you, and then he turned around to walk the two or three miles back to town.

Chapter Sixty-Seven

HER FIRST CORSAGE

As WE APPROACHED the small city of Valjevo Milan began to get worried. This was his birthplace. His family had many friends here. So did he. He was worried about what some of them might think of his traveling companions. The friends of his father and mother were likely to be very conservative and rather anti-regime. His own friends were the other way. If we acted like enemies of the regime in front of his friends it would get him in trouble. If we acted like friends of the regime in front of the people who knew his family they might report back to his father and mother that he was in bad company. Milan was very worried. So we worked out a little scheme to calm his mind. When he introduced us to any of his family's friends he must introduce me first. That would be a signal for both June and me to talk like William Randolph Hearst or Ambassador Fotić and tell all the stories of the Terror we could think of. But if we bumped into any of his friends he was to introduce June first. Whereupon we would both talk about the new regime with the enthusiasm of fanatics. Milan sank back into the seat happy. But a few minutes later he grew nervous again. What if we got our signals mixed? Would we be sure to remember? What if he forgot and introduced the wrong one first? (As it turned out we didn't meet any friends of his or of his family either all the time we were in Valjevo.)

In Valjevo they wanted to show us the graves of three or four hundred peasants and townspeople who had been executed one day in November of '41 by the Germans. By this time we were weary of climbing hills and looking at mass graves. The grave of five hundred people or five thousand looks the same whether it's in Croatia, Bosnia, or South Serbia. Whether the people were killed by Germans, Italians, Chetniks, or Ustaši. But I was glad we did it again in Valjevo. Otherwise we wouldn't have met Negosava Ivanović.

Negosava today is twenty-two years old and holds a minor government position. She isn't pretty. There's nothing ravishing about her. She uses no cosmetics. When girls her age in other parts of the world were fussing with ribbons and bows and pleats and tucks, and thinking about making themselves look attractive to boys, Negosava was living in the mountains in rags with a gun as her only close companion. Negosava doesn't know much about dressing even today. Clothes to her are principally something to protect the body from the weather. The gray suit she wears when it's cold is made of wool. She likes it because it keeps her warm. The fact that it exaggerates the defects of her figure and does nothing to accentuate the good points probably hasn't ever occurred to her. The red woolen socks she wears under her ski boots are warm too. The small red star on her coat lapel is not a piece of jewelry or decoration. To her it's something to show that she fought too. Yet as we sloshed through the bloto and climbed the hill she seemed beautiful. Her eyes are light blue. They're kind eyes and sensitive too. She talked softly most of the time. She didn't want to talk about the one thing I wanted her to talk about. Whenever I was forcing her to talk about herself she blushed like a schoolgirl and wanted to know what difference it made what she had done and what she wanted to do.

She said it was on November the twenty-seventh that it happened. The Chetniks went from village to village rounding up people they considered enemies of the things the Chetniks believed in. They rounded up nearly four hundred people and marched them through the streets of Valjevo. Many of the peasants put on their fanciest costumes. All they knew was that they were coming to town. And coming to town meant dressing up in the best clothes they had.

The Chetniks turned the whole lot of them over to the Germans. The Germans marched them over this same route that we're taking. Over this bridge. Across the railroad tracks. And up the side of the hill. Only, of course, it was winter then and everything was deep with snow. That pile of stones over there was a four-story building then. It was the largest building in this part of Yugoslavia. It was the barracks of the Fifth Yugoslav Regiment before the war. But the day they marched the peasants up the hill the windows were full of German soldiers who had a good view of what happened. This is the way they marched them. Right up to the top of this hill. They were shot in several groups. You can tell by where the graves are because the Germans buried them right where they fell. This bit of earth in the center of the field that's slightly raised. About sixty feet by ten. This is where two hundred and sixty-nine bodies are. It says so on the cross. The cross also says they were shot by "The Fascist Invaders Who Were Helped by the Traitors of Draža Mihailović." Those Serbian words made of white stones on the ground say:

"To the Believers in Freedom Who Died Here."

They say some of them weren't dead when they were buried. Negosava didn't see the shooting. But she and everyone else in Valjevo heard the screams. Some people in Valjevo haven't forgotten the screams yet. Negosava was only sixteen years old then. But she was helping. She worked for the People's Underground Council. She was collecting medicines and packing parcels of other supplies to send off to the Partisans. Everyone was doing things like that. She even helped print pamphlets. She worked underground until the middle of 1944. That was when she finished her commercial schooling. Then she joined the Partisans as a fighter. She was a fighter until December and then they made her a youth leader. She fought against the Chetniks and the Germans too. She took part in the fighting for Belgrade. Then they sent her as a fighter up to Hungary. It was the first time she had ever been out of Yugoslavia. Twice she was stone deaf for days because hand grenades exploded so close to her. She fought with a rifle. She used it too. Many times. She didn't like to kill other human beings. Even if they were some of the soldiers who had shot all the peasants up on this hill. She didn't believe in killing. But everybody knew there wouldn't be any peace until the Germans and Chetniks were defeated. And to defeat them meant killing some of them. So she did her share.

But now we must walk over to this other grave. Here fifty more bodies are buried. And there's another hill over there with forty or fifty more. About the big barracks. Five planes flew over one day. Maybe they were American or maybe British. It was their bombs that made a pile of bricks out of the big building. No one ever did find out how many Germans were killed.

But I wasn't interested in graves. It was spring. The war was over. The fields were covered with small purple flowers. A farmer in the distance was plowing with a team of oxen. Sheep were eating grass on the edge of the graves. The earth smelled good. The air was full of the sights and sounds and smells of spring. The war was over. What of the future? What were Negosava's plans?

She avoided the question for a full minute while she picked a bunch of the purple flowers. Then she looked up at me with happy eyes and said she wanted to study economics at the University of Belgrade. In the old days in Yugoslavia it didn't do for a girl to have too many ambitions. But now it didn't make any difference that you weren't a man. And it didn't make any difference that you came from a poor peasant family either. Nobody ever heard of the Ivanović family before. They'd just been village people. But her older sister had finished secondary school since the end of the war and had even taken a bookkeeping course.

Negosava herself was taking a part in the life of the community. Mornings she worked at the District Council office. Afternoons she attended conferences. Three afternoons a week she went out of town and did voluntary labor on the land. Lately they'd been building irrigation canals to help increase the productivity of the farms. Sundays she worked as a librarian. That was a voluntary job too. Sunday evenings she was a youth leader and arranged dances, programs, and parties for the young people. Her sister's name was Vidosava. Didn't I think it was a pretty name?

Vidosava was married. Negosava was too busy to think of things like love and romance. Maybe it was my imagination but she seemed to say it a little wistfully. That made me think of the Partisan editor at Dubrovnik and what Anita had told me about frustration. Negosava didn't know how to dress for men. But she had lovely eyes and a mass of naturally curly brown hair and the figure of a girl of sixteen. It was quiet on the hill now. Sheep don't make any noise when they chew grass. And the peasant who was plowing in the distance wasn't making the noise that other peasants had once made on this same hill. A peasant woman and her daughter were watching the sheep. They were busy making thread out of some wool fastened to paddles. They were quiet too. But as we left the hill there was a sharp noise in the distance. I looked around quickly. Negosava laughed. I hadn't noticed that half a mile away there was a military parade ground. A whole regiment was drilling. An officer was shouting commands to his men. Negosava said that as soon as one war ends people always start thinking about the next one, don't they? That was wrong, wasn't it? I said I thought it was wrong too. Then I picked a bunch of the small purple flowers and put them in a buttonhole of Negosava's unattractive gray woolen suit.

Chapter Sixty-Eight

BELIEVING ISN'T SEEING

ON THE WAY BACK to Belgrade we went through the town of Ub. I told June and Milan that I liked the town of Ub. I didn't know anything about the place and we didn't stop to find out anything. I only knew that it was the first name I'd struck in Yugoslavia I was sure I could pronounce and have right.

On the way back to Belgrade we detoured a few miles down a strip of mud which the peasants along the way kept assuring us was a road. The only difference between it and the fields on either side was that the mud in the fields was undisturbed by wagon wheels or automobile tires. At the end of the bloto was Skela. What happened here was exactly what happened at Lidice. Except that no one ever heard of Skela. On this road we had just come over four German officers in a car were waylaid by Partisans and killed. Within twenty-four hours Skela was wiped from the map. Twenty-seven truckloads of German soldiers surrounded the village. They loaded everything that pleased their fancy into the trucks. They soaked the one hundred and twenty-seven houses in the village with gasoline and put dynamite in the larger ones to be sure they'd really be destroyed. Then they set them afire. The women and children were chained together. The men were forced to dig the graves. Then they were all killed. It was worse than Lidice. It was worse because when the Germans came in their trucks they brought forty-five high school boys and their teachers with them from some other place and killed them at the same time.

Where Skela used to be we saw a new village taking form. Fifty houses had been built already. This was where Negosava and other volunteers were building canals to improve the land. In Skela we talked to one old man who escaped the massacre, Nikodin Jevadjić. He owned the town kafana. His only son was among those killed. He couldn't seem to remember how it was that he escaped. The others said the old man's mind wasn't quite right any more.

When we set out from Skela for Belgrade a peasant asked us if we would take him along. His wife and son were lost somewhere in the capital. They'd gone to Belgrade days ago and he was worried. Something terrible had probably happened to them. He must go to Belgrade himself and see if he could find them. So we put him on top of the empty Jerry cans and set off. About five miles down the road we came upon a woman and boy trudging toward Skela. The peasant said to stop. He wouldn't have to go any farther. Nothing had happened to them after all. He jumped from the jeep and walked up to his wife and son about whom he had been so worried. They said *"dobar dan"* to each other and that was all. Then they started back to Skela together. There was no physical embrace. No warm word of greeting. No sign of happiness over the reunion. Just "good day," and that was all. But after we'd gone a few rods I looked back. The small boy was trying to slip his arm around his father's waist. Maybe when he grew up he'd be as cold and phlegmatic as his parents. But now he was a small boy who was glad to be back with his father again. It made me think of a backwoods New England farmer's wife I once knew. One winter day she went half a mile up the hill to see her father who was ill. On her way home again she stopped in our house to get warm. After talking about the weather awhile she said:

"Paw died last night."

Then she went back to the subject of the weather for another five or ten minutes. Finally she said it was time to be getting on. As she sniffed the winter air at the door she said:

"Reckon they'll have to use pickaxes to dig the grave."

I said something to June about the similarity of backwoods New Englanders and Serbs. At that Milan said:

"I am a Serb."

Where was he born? In Macedonia. Where had he been brought up? In Slovenia. Then why was he a Serb?

"I am a Serb because I like to be a Serb because the Serbs are the strongest people in Europe. So I live now in Serbia and I want to be a Serb so I am a Serb."

When we got into Belgrade, Milan insisted we have a cup of tea with his mother. We knew a little about Milan's background. We knew that his father had had something to do with the prewar regime. In the old days he had made out very well financially. Now his income was a small percentage of what it used to be. The family still lived considerably better than the average but the parents had no use for the present "goings on." Milan's mother was full of curiosity about where we had been and what we had seen. What were our general impressions? What had we learned? Milan gave us a dark look so we said that June had learned a lot of Serbian and Milan had learned a lot more English. It had been a very interesting trip.

"But did you see people doing anything except making those silly little red stars? That's all they spend their time doing, you know. Just making those silly red stars."

We said we had seen them building a lot of houses and schools and roads and factories and hospitals.

"Ba! Those buildings you saw were all there before the war."

Milan told her we saw people actually working on such buildings.

"Ba! It's only propaganda. They have built nothing new since the war.

That's what your father told me, Milan, and your father knows about such things."

Then she turned to June and me.

"I don't know what the younger generation is coming to. They simply will not believe anything we try to tell them any more."

PART NINE

This Is Greece

Chapter Sixty-Nine

LUXURY INTERLUDE

By the time we got back to Belgrade I had prowled around four of the six Yugoslav republics and the Vojvodina. Macedonia in the far south and Slovenia in the far north were the only ones left. But there were some loose threads of the old story I wanted to gather up, so I decided to make a side trip to Greece and hit Macedonia on the way back.

In the old days you took a train at night from Belgrade and got into Athens the next day. There was a direct line and a good train called the Taurus Express. That was in the old days. It's different now. You have to travel thousands of miles to get from Belgrade to Athens. All the way up to Zagreb, Ljubljana, Trieste, Milan, then down to Rome, then by plane or ship the rest of the way. That's because the Greeks haven't yet been able to get their trains running.

But Colonel Anderson, the American Air Attaché at Belgrade, said he was flying an Embassy plane directly from Belgrade to Rome in a few days and there'd be a vacant seat.

In Rome I waited over a couple of days for a T.W.A. New York to Athens plane with a spare seat. While I waited I solved a little more of the Sonia mystery. We had dinner together one night.

After Yugoslavia Rome seemed like a city out of the *Arabian Nights*. If you stayed close to the great boulevard called Via Vittorio Veneto. Here there was everything. White bread. American cigarettes. Luxury food. Rich black coffee. Beautiful women in expensive evening gowns. Soft lights. Glamour. Romance. Gentlemen in swallowtails kissing the finger-tips of fair ladies. Plenty of upholstered taxicabs. Here they didn't shoot a man if he engaged in Black Bourse transactions. Here the streets were full of men fighting with each other, sometimes literally, to buy anything an American had to offer. From dollar bills to half-filled tubes of shaving cream. Ten minutes later what they bought was on public sale on street-corner stands set up on slender tripods. There were five or six rates for the dollar. Legally it was worth only two hundred and twenty-five lire. But no one paid any attention to the legal rate. The top rate was around seven hundred. Prices were cheap for Americans who changed their money that way. No wonder the foreign correspondents begged their offices to transfer them to Rome. No wonder this was the place diplomatic employees all wanted to come to. No wonder Embassy planes made frequent trips in this direction and went back with the passenger space taken up with packages of all shapes and sizes filled with all manner of beautiful things.

That's all I saw of Italy. I didn't try to poke behind the curtains. Italy wasn't my "beat." All I know is that the dinner Sonia and I had in a very ordinary restaurant cost thirty-five hundred lire. That's five dollars at the black rate. It's fifteen dollars at the legal rate. In lire it's a servant's wages for a whole month. In lire it's three days' pay for the Prime Minister.

Sonia was little changed in appearance. She was still attractive in a Slav way. She still had her flashing wit and her flashing brown eyes. But her touch of fatalism was more than a "touch" now. It seemed like an obsession. Yet she had not lost that defiant tilt to her chin.

Sonia didn't want to talk about the past. All she wanted to talk about was her son. She froze when I asked her what happened after I left her on the edge of the seaport at Kotor. She didn't want to think about that chapter of her life. Or the next chapter, either, because her husband had been killed. She didn't tell me who her husband had been, how she met him, how he was killed or when. She made it clear she didn't want to discuss such matters. But her son! I must see her son. Couldn't I be in Rome for his birthday next month? He was the most intelligent child. Someday she might go back to Yugoslavia. But now she had an important job. And she had her child to think about. He wasn't old enough to do much traveling yet.

That night I walked the streets of Rome alone. I saw the ancient ruins by moonlight. These ruins were different from the ones I'd been seeing the past few months. These were made by nature as well as by man. These were covered with moss and flowers. The way to see Rome is alone by moonlight. The next night I took a plane for Athens.

Chapter Seventy

MILLIONS FOR COSMETICS; NOT A CENT FOR RECONSTRUCTION

THE stewardess on the plane said she thought that the town of Murtos ought to be right down about there. But what could anyone care about a town that small? So I told her how one day during the war Russell Hill and I and some sailors hid on the mountain which goes straight up from the edge of the sea at Murtos. That was because the captain of the Greek freighter taking us through the Ionian Sea into the Gulf of Corinth refused to operate his schooner by day for fear of bombings. He hid his vessel in that cove right down there, while we and the crew wandered over the mountain. Hill and I never forgot Murtos because up on the top of that mountain he opened his portable typewriter and tried to write a dispatch for his paper, the New York *Herald Tribune*. Hill was an optimist. Every day for four weeks he was sure that the next day we'd find communications so we could tell the story of what was happening to Yugoslavia and Greece. He'd just gotten started with his dispatch when one of the sailors who had made a trip to America once and knew about six words of English blurted out:

"Ah! New York *Times*."

Hill, who had the typical *Herald Tribune* reporter's disrespect for the rival *Times,* corrected him immediately.

"No! Not the New York *Times*. The New York *Herald Tribune*."

The sailor grinned.

"Ah! New York *Times*."

Hill shouted: "No! *Herald Tribune!*"

It went on for quite a while, with the two of them shouting at each other like two rival newsboys. Hill never did get his story written. But he'd written some good ones since then. He was the one veteran of that escape from Yugoslavia and Greece who had remained a newspaperman and had covered Europe all through the war and whatever anyone wants to call this period since the actual shooting stopped.

It was just getting light over Greece. First Murtos. Then the island of Leukas. That was where the prior of the monastery of St. Nicholas had entertained us. The rest of the passengers in the plane were sleeping. But the hostess seemed interested. So I told her about the old monk who fed us goat's cheese and plates of honey and raisins and almonds all mixed together, with a rich red wine to wash it down. And how he pointed across the water to that other island and said that was where Ulysses was born.

And now Patras. In the early morning light from this high up Patras looked still asleep. That's where we'd left the schooner. That's where we'd hopped a troop train that ran along the edge of the gulf. It was about here that the Messerschmitt came across the gulf, much lower than this plane's flying. It came across the gulf and began pumping steel into the side of the railroad coaches.

The T.W.A. plane was going fast now. It was making past events happen over again too quickly. This was Corinth which we finally reached by British lorry. From up here there didn't seem to be any sign of the hospital where a nurse said she'd look at the wounds in our legs. But there was the railroad siding where the thirty-car hospital train arrived just in time to be bombed and set on fire by a wave of Stuka planes. Even up here, so high, I could still smell the smell of those burning bodies. Even six years later. I asked the stewardess what the date was. It was April again. It was almost six years to the day. I wondered what had happened to the pretty little nurse who was in charge of the hospital. I wondered whether she lived through that day when the main street of Corinth was lined with men hauling on stretchers to her hospital pieces of things which had once been other human beings. On the railroad siding where the hospital train was set afire there were some old boxcars now. The bridge leading to Athens was still in the bottom of the Corinth canal, just as it had been six years ago when we left. And the canal still had some sunken ships in it.

But Athens when we got there blotted out memories. Athens was lush and full of sweet smells. Trees were in blossom. The day was balmy. There were fried eggs for breakfast. Coffee with thick cream, American style. Soft white rolls. Outside the Grande Bretagne Hotel the kiosk had this week's issue of *Life* and the day before yesterday's New York *Times*. Here a man could get anything. So it seemed. As long as he remembered that if he nodded his head up and down it meant no instead of yes. And if he remembered that the word *nay* means yes instead of no. And as long as he changed his dollars, as everyone did, at the black rate. At the airport I was a little frightened when the waitress handed me a check for eight thousand drachma for a simple breakfast and I felt like a plutocrat giving her a bill with the figure "1000" on it as a tip. At the hotel I was relieved to discover that the day's black rate was seven thousand to the dollar, if you had twenty-dollar bills with no yellow on them. Of course if you had gold Napoleons, as some of the Embassy people did, you could get sixteen thousand.

It was Good Friday and most of Athens was still asleep. But there were some people out strolling or sitting in sidewalk cafés. They looked extremely well dressed. Overdressed in many cases. In one café there were two Greeks trying to learn how to twist the face to make a monocle stay in place. I wondered if that was the British influence. On that Good Friday morning I wandered around under the acacia trees window-shopping. It was the acacia trees that were filling the air with such a rich, heavy odor. At the legal rate the prices I saw in shop windows were almost unbelievable. Even at the black rate a small jar of five-and-ten-cent-store cold cream cost two dollars and sixty cents. Nylon stockings, about eight dollars a pair. A tube of shaving cream, one dollar and sixty cents. A ten-cent American candy bar, fifty-five cents. A ten-cent cake of soap, sixty cents. A package of American cigarettes, sixty-five cents. Men's clothing was even worse. A cheap necktie came to five dollars. Twelve dollars for a cotton shirt. Fifteen dollars for cotton pajamas. Those prices applied only if American money was changed at the black rate. If anyone wanted to be legal and law abiding, which hardly anyone did, the prices would have been twice that much. But of greater importance was what a Greek could buy. A Greek workman, they told me, made seven thousand drachmas a day. Just one dollar. So a day's pay would get him a ten-cent candy bar and part of a package of cigarettes. Or less than two cakes of soap. He would have to work a week to buy the cheapest sort of necktie. Two weeks to buy a cotton shirt. Obviously he didn't buy such things. But he did have to buy food. I found a Greek doctor that first day who had made a study of food prices. To buy what he considered the minimum number of calories required by the average-sized family it took ten thousand drachmas per day, or more than the average workman earned. The doctor said:

"Young man, that is one reason they go into the mountains."

Chapter Seventy-One

"ME AND MY SHADOW"

IN THE DAYS before Yugoslavia threw out her pro-Axis government and thereby invited invasion by the Germans, a ubiquitous Greek character named Pappas popped up in Belgrade. He said he was an Athens journalist but had a diplomatic passport. He confided to a select list of Yugoslav officials, foreign correspondents, and Embassy people that the British had landed three hundred thousand troops in his country for a Balkan operation. Also hundreds of tanks and planes. How much this whispered information had to do with the decision to stage the Yugoslav coup d'état no one ever found out. But some of General Somović's advisers later told me that the Pappas reports had been taken very seriously. Actually, as history later proved, only a handful of British troops were in Greece at that time. And practically no tanks and planes had been landed.

Later, in Sarajevo, Pappas popped up again. He was panicky about the danger of being caught by the Nazis. Wouldn't we help get him out? He looked and acted like a cornered wildcat. He dogged us everywhere we went. We finally did wedge him into our car. We soon wished we hadn't. He went panicky every time a bomb dropped. If we stopped the car during a raid, Pappas opened the door while the wheels were still turning and pushed Sonia aside in his dash for a place of hiding. When we finally started out of Sarajevo, two men carrying a mass of broken bones and torn flesh that had once been a human being waved us down and asked us to take the bombing victim to a hospital. While Russell Hill and I were trying to get the dying man into the back of the car, Pappas went hysterical. He slid over into the driver's seat, took off the brake, and tried to start the engine. It was the only time I can remember that I really lost my head. I grabbed Pappas by the neck with one hand, pounded his face with the other, and threw him into the street. I hadn't seen him again since that day in Sarajevo and I never wanted to.

But now . . . That man coming through the door of the Grande Bretagne Hotel? I asked a British correspondent with whom I was drinking tea if he knew him. I seemed to recognize his shifty eyes. He looked squarely at me for a split second. Then I was sure.

"Why, that's Pappas. If you don't know about him yet you soon will. He was a high-ranking government official until they had a temporary economy wave here a few weeks ago. He lost his job. But he'll be back helping to run things in a few weeks. Just as soon as the economy wave blows over."

I stared at the back of the man. I recognized even the neck. I could feel my hands on that neck again.

"It's curious that you asked about him. He was here during most of the occupation. He and the Germans got along very well together. He made quite a bit of money during the occupation. And yet today he's one of the inner circle running the country."

So I told the British reporter the story. I told him I had promised the rest of our party six years ago that I'd probably engage in a little physical violence if I ever saw Mister Pappas again. And now . . . There he was standing at the bar. Every few minutes he glanced over his shoulder at me and then quickly looked away. The Englishman suggested I count ten and forget it. A row with Mister Pappas would be the quickest way to land in jail. It would embarrass everyone. So I counted ten. But I had to count ten a great many times. That night I went looking for some people to whom I had letters. I was followed across half the city by Mister Pappas. He always kept twenty or thirty yards to the rear. If I stopped, he stopped. If I turned around and walked toward him, he disappeared into some dark side street and then took up my trail again after I'd passed the side street. I didn't deliver any of those letters that night. I didn't want the names and addresses to go into any Gestapo file. Instead I took Mister Pappas for a long walk. We walked all the way to the top of the Acropolis. I enjoyed the view from up there. And I hope Mister Pappas enjoyed all the exercise he got.

PART TEN

These Are the Macedonians

Chapter Seventy-Two

"SREĆAN PUT" TO MYSELF

THE Yugoslav consul in Salonika had troubles. The Greek Government
was expelling Rumanians and Yugoslavs. They were being summoned
to the police station and relieved of their identity papers. That meant
they had to get out in a hurry. There was no Rumanian consul in
Salonika so the Yugoslav consul had to take care of all of them. That
meant he was very busy. But he said he had a jeep and he'd get me to
the frontier. There was no other method of transportation unless I wanted
to go back the way I had come, in a great circle, to Athens, Rome,

Belgrade, and down to Macedonia. Greeks apparently aren't supposed to go north and Yugoslavs aren't supposed to go south. What foreigners are supposed to do I don't know.

At the frontier town of Evzone the Greek border official was very suspicious. He had a list of the names of hundreds of people who mustn't be let out of the country. He looked through it six or seven times. Finally he let me go through. There's no way to travel the half mile from Evzone to the invisible line which separates the British-American zone of influence in Europe from the Russian zone of influence—this meeting place of two antagonistic ideologies—except to walk. You walk through a Greek gate, across a strip of no-man's land, through some barbed wire, through a Yugoslav gate, and then you yoddle to some of Marshal Tito's subjects up on the top of a hill that you have arrived, please don't shoot, and how about coming down and checking you in.

When I left Belgrade the Yugoslav press official in charge of taking care of foreign correspondents said if I would telephone or telegraph him from Salonika he would pass the word along to the Macedonian capital of Scoplje that I was coming so there would be a hotel room waiting for me. But the press officer forgot that we were living in the year of peace, nineteen hundred and forty-seven. Telephone lines between Greece and Yugoslavia are like railroad lines. They don't exist any more. So I tried telegraphing. A cable from Salonika to a Yugoslav city just a few miles north must go thousands of miles by way of London and it takes days. So the Yugoslav consul in Salonika gave me a letter. It was a simple letter addressed to the chief of the Yugoslav gendarmes at the frontier city of Gevjelia, across the invisible line from Evzone. It asked him to telephone the press officer in Belgrade that I was on my way and please would he thus inform Scoplje. The consul translated every word of the letter for me. I was sure it was going to help solve my housing problem when I got to the Macedonian capital. I presented that letter at the frontier post just across the invisible line. A guard took it up to the barracks on the top of the hill. I should wait down in the road. I waited. I waited forty-five minutes in the baking sun. Every one of the soldiers stationed there at the frontier must have read the letter two or three times. Then an officer was assigned to accompany me on the three-mile walk into town. It was hotter than hell. I had a coat. A twenty-pound bundle of Greek documents. A heavy knapsack. And the road seemed to be all uphill.

At the gendarme post in Gevjelia I was told to wait outside. There was no shade and nothing to sit on. I wanted a drink of water. I wanted the use of some plumbing facilities. I wanted something to eat. Mostly I wanted to get out of the sun and to sit down. But a guard with a tommy gun wouldn't let me move. Then I remembered that it was Saturday noon. The press office in Belgrade would be closed until Monday morning. I wanted to tell the chief of the gendarmes not to bother to try to make that telephone call to Belgrade. But the guard wouldn't let me move.

Four hours isn't long if you're sleeping. Or sitting in an air-conditioned office. Or lying on a beach. But four hours was a long time that Saturday afternoon. The more I wanted a drink of water, and some plumbing facilities, and some shade, and something to eat, and a place to sit down, the more anti-Yugoslav I grew. I wrote pages of an essay on human stupidity on the pieces of tissue paper I was using for notepaper. Then I ran out of ink. Then I remembered I had some American money in my pocket. I wouldn't be able to cash it into dinar at the national bank or to take it out of the country again unless customs officials entered in my passport the fact that I had brought it legally into the country. That was the Yugoslav law. It was now Saturday afternoon. I hadn't yet gone through any customs formalities. The customs officials might be knocking off work for the week end. So I started shouting.

The soldier with the tommy gun could keep me from moving but he couldn't keep me from shouting unless he shot me. So I took a chance and shouted. Some of the gendarme officers came running out to see what was causing all the noise. I showed them my money. They thought I was trying to bribe them. That made them very angry. Then they thought I wanted to change the dollars into dinar and they said the bank was closed. I kept saying the word *douane*. It's the French word for customs but it's used internationally. I'd seen it over the door of the customhouse right down the main street of this Yugoslav town of Gevjelia. But none of them had ever heard of the word.

One of the officers said he spoke German. Couldn't I talk German? I couldn't. But I had a French-English-Italian-German book of phrases in my knapsack. I found a phrase which said something about customhouses. But the officer who spoke German couldn't read German. He couldn't read Latin script even. So I had to try to pronounce it for him. He and I apparently didn't pronounce German the same way. But after a number of attempts he understood. So we went to the customhouse.

There was no trouble about the money. But then they wanted to examine my baggage. I had all my notes in my knapsack. Months of notes. All on small folded pieces of toilet tissue. The sheets weren't numbered but they were in order. There were thousands and thousands of those tissue-paper sheets. They made a bundle about a foot high. The Gevjelia inspector of luggage was a boy about nineteen. He couldn't speak or read a word of any language except Macedonian. Not even Serbo-Croat. But he undid the bundle of notes and started in. He examined each piece of paper, line by line, word by word. I started my stop watch. I figured that at the rate he was doing the job he'd get finished, if he didn't take time out for eating or sleeping, at 9 P.M. the following Tuesday. Then I noticed what he was doing with the sheets he'd "read." He was dropping them carelessly from his hands onto the table. They were getting all mixed up. It would take me days to get them in order again. I protested. I tried to say that if he was having fun pretending to read them, fine. But for God's sake keep them in order! He ignored me. Then he spotted five Greek newspapers in the bottom of the knapsack. He couldn't read

Greek but he went through every column of every page of every paper.

It went on for hours. It was getting dark now. I knew that the final train of the day left for the north at eight-thirty. In two hours. When we got back to the gendarme post they told me I had cleared customs all right but I wasn't yet free. I wouldn't be free until they could get the press office in Belgrade by phone. But they had decided that I could go to a kafana and have something to eat in the meantime. Except that an armed guard would have to accompany me. The armed guard was a simple peasant soldier. He was a pleasant sort, merely doing what he was told to do. I didn't mean him any harm. But I couldn't help doing what I did.

When we got to the kafana I asked for two double orders of rakia in a hurry. I needed a stimulant badly. I needed something to jog my brain into activity. I was not going to spend the week end in Gevjelia. It was watching the smile on the guard's face when the rakia came that gave me the idea. So I ordered two more double rakias right away. I poured mine into a water glass when the guard wasn't looking and then ordered two more. I asked him if he wanted food, hoping he'd say no. That's what he did say. He would eat at the barracks later. So every time his glass got half empty I asked the waiter to fill it up.

He had either nine, eleven, or thirteen double rakias. I couldn't keep exact track because I had to have one occasionally with him when he insisted on drinking a toast to the health of Marshal Tito, the Free Republic of Macedonia, or something else. And I hadn't had anything to eat since dawn, so my mathematics may not have been accurate. Even if he had only nine doubles, that's a lot of alcohol. Even for a Yugoslav.

I tried to time the operation like a split-second radio switch, or a D-Day invasion. When I saw that there were exactly twelve minutes to train-time I suggested as casually as I could that we go down to the railroad station. He wasn't drunk enough for that. He said, "Oh no!" several times. In Macedonian, of course. He made me understand that I wasn't going to be free to leave until they got Belgrade. I said I had no intention of going. I just wanted to buy a railroad ticket before the station closed for the night. He debated that in his mind for a full minute. I could see him trying to think. It was an effort. Finally he decided it was all right for me to go to the railroad station to buy a ticket. Of course under guard. So we went.

The little gods were with me again. The station had no electrical illumination. Just one feeble kerosene lamp. It was full of peasants milling around trying to buy tickets and find places on the train. We milled around with them until my watch said it was two minutes to traintime. Then I lost myself in the crowd. My guard was talking to a friend. In the darkness I ran down the platform to the last coach and locked myself in the washroom. Two minutes later the train left. I liked the guard. I hope he wasn't executed.

Chapter Seventy-Three

AND THE SOUTH PROGRESSES TOO

WHEN the sun came up, the Vardar Valley looked like a young woman in a transparent white negligee standing in the morning light rubbing the sleep out of her eyes. There were wisps of mist everywhere. The mountains in the distance were still buried in haze. The fresh-plowed fields gave off a good smell. It was Sunday but the animals didn't know it so the shepherds had to be up and about just as if it were Saturday or Monday. The orchards of the valley gave promise of the first real crop in three years. The trunks of all the trees were painted white. Morning doesn't generally seem exciting if a man has sat up all night in a dirty third-class railroad coach. Especially if the compartment is crowded with ten people instead of the six it's supposed to hold and they all have taken off their shoes and they all have a love of garlic. And especially if a man has those pains that come from not having eaten for hours. But this morning it did seem good to be alive. At the Scoplje railroad station hundreds of young volunteer laborers, even though it was so short a time after dawn of the day of rest, were clearing away piles of rubble which had once been part of the depot. Two musicians with a fife and a drum were entertaining them with that snake-charmer music which is so common in countries once part of the Ottoman Empire. This was an ancient city. Founded by a race called the Dardanians. Destroyed by an earthquake. Ruled over once by a Serbian czar called Dushan the Mighty. Occupied by the Turks until the 1912 liberation. Then burned to the ground by the Austrians. Scoplje is one more city where they say that the East and the West really meet. But it looked more Oriental than Western this Sunday morning. The Albanian men in the streets were wearing white felt skullcaps. There were women in wooden shoes and women with no shoes at all. There were Moslem women in bright-colored pantaloons. Baggy and tied at the ankles. There were men in red fezzes. There were young women in cream-colored homespun dresses partly covered with bodices of metallic cloth the color of gold, and with red embroidered aprons. There were Greeks here and Bulgarians too. And some real Turks. And Macedonian Moslems. And a great many gypsies. Here there were Catholics, Moslems, Jews, members of the Orthodox faith, and people with no religion at all.

This was Scoplje. This was where I had sent Paul Vajda, a Hungarian Jewish reporter who worked for me because I thought he would be safer here than in Belgrade when the Axis attack began. Scoplje, they'd told me, was surrounded by mountains. Twenty men, they said, with rocks or with rifles could hold any one of the passes against an enemy. The Germans never could get into Scoplje, even if they came with tanks. The passes could be blocked with boulders let loose from up above. So I sent Paul Vajda here because he was a Jew and high on the Nazis' black list. A few days later we heard that fifth-column officers in the Royal Yugoslav Army had let the Germans through one of the passes. And we heard that Paul Vajda had been captured. What had happened to him in the next four or five years I didn't know. I did know that he came out of it alive and was back now in his home town of Budapest.

Sitting on the stone wall of the embankment along the river I counted between forty and fifty minarets on the skyline. I watched crowds of Yugoslav army officers getting their high black boots polished because it was Sunday. Men with tripod stands were selling sticky slices of *halva* for five dinar apiece. A procession of gypsies led by a fiddler and an accordion player went by with a coffin carried on the shoulders of six men in filthy but gaudy attire. Occasionally a peasant came down the main street of this capital city driving a few sheep or pigs. Oxcarts contested with horse-drawn droshkies and with made-in-America automobiles for a right to the streets. In a tinsmith's shop window I saw UNRRA meat cans from Morris Plains, New Jersey, made into crude oil lamps. Scoplje was exotic even in her filth. Occasionally an army plane went by overhead and I thought of the oxcart army I had seen go out in 1941 to meet the mechanical might of the Nazis. Yugoslavia wasn't going to get caught with an oxcart army if war came again. She was training her soldiers to use planes and tanks and flame throwers. But sitting on the embankment I thought that if a new war did come it probably would be the same old story all over again. These people would try to fight atom bombs and V-2's and weapons of biological war with tanks and planes and flame throwers. They'd still be a generation behind.

The only bathtub in the only hotel in the city that had a vacant room was full of brooms and mops. When I changed my clothes I found thirty-seven fleabites and eleven bites by something worse. So I sat on the embankment most of Sunday afternoon and scratched. Then I called at the home of the British consul and was invited for tea. The consul's wife had just been reading a travel book on Yugoslavia by a British woman who had once been down this way and wrote a half-million-word volume on what she had seen. The consul's wife threw the book onto her living-room table and said:

"I wish people wouldn't write about this part of the world if they are afraid of short, ugly words."

Then she pointed out the window to the mountain called Vodno.

"See that cluster of houses up there? That's a village. It looks picturesque from here, doesn't it, with the sun lighting it up? Someone could write quite easily from down here about its charm. And its lovely setting. At night the lights of the village twinkle. I could be very lyrical about it myself. I could if I hadn't gone up there once and seen the village. The houses are shacks. Goats, sheep, and pigs live in the same rooms with humans. I have traveled a little. I have never seen such squalor in my life. The drainage from outhouses and barnyard manure piles runs down the center of the main street. Why can't people be honest when they write about this part of the world?"

Her husband wanted to talk about something else. He said that if people in London and Washington were going to try to compete in places like the Balkans with ideas from the East they'd have to stop trying to fight something with nothing. He was no Communist. There was much he didn't like about the Yugoslav system. But it was offering a new way of life to millions of people. It couldn't be dismissed with a wave of the hand. He said we had to offer people something more than the same old way of life they'd had in the past.

It was pleasant having tea with people who spoke English. It was pleasant to be a few hours in a home full of flowers and books and delicate china. It was pleasant to be talking to a diplomat who was completely loyal to his own country's system but was willing to look honestly at what people like the Yugoslavs were doing. I was embarrassed, however, about that tea party. When I got back to my hotel I discovered that I hadn't acquired a new fleabite in some hours. I wondered how the British consul and his charming wife would get rid of them and what they would think of me.

The next morning the press department in Belgrade came through with a profound telephone apology about the frontier trouble. The guards had misread the letter. They thought the consul was instructing them not to let me travel north until the press department in Belgrade gave telephonic approval. I must try to be tolerant about such official bungling. I did realize, didn't I, that there was a great lack of trained men for responsible jobs? Deaths in the war. An expanding economy. The former low standards of education. Would I please . . . et cetera, et cetera.

I said they should forget it, but if they wanted to do me a favor in compensation for what had happened to me at Gevjelia they should see that the guard who'd let me slip away didn't get executed. They said they would.

The next morning I discovered Vangel Temelkospki. I think he was the only Yugoslav in Scoplje who spoke English. Without him I would have been lost. So I persuaded Vangel Temelkospki to stay close at my side until I finished my tour of Macedonia. Vangel Temelkospki had been to America three times. He was a young man when he deserted his native village of Carev Dvor and went to New York the first time. He said he went because of "conditions." What conditions? Well, he said, Carev Dvor was half Moslem, half Macedonian. Before the sun went down you had to lock your door. The gendarmes called people names and scared them. Sometimes they arrested and killed people. They stirred up the Moslems and the Macedonians against each other. People were always nervous. Always unhappy and worried. They couldn't work. They couldn't learn anything. Vangel said he couldn't live like that. So he went to America.

After four years he got homesick, took what money he had saved, and returned home. He stayed six months. Conditions were still bad so he left again. He remained in America the second time for three years. Then he made another six-thousand-mile trip to "look things over again." Things were still the same. He didn't stay long this time. And he didn't come back again this time for eighteen years. As a matter of fact he never intended to come back again, ever. But after the liberation he heard that things really were better now and so he came home a third time on a gamble.

It worked out all right the third time. He found that things really were better and he's staying in Yugoslavia this time. Yes, he said, for the rest of his life. During the eighteen years he worked in New York City, Buffalo, Lackawanna, Detroit, and Cleveland. Most of the time for the Bethlehem Steel Company. He said his wife had remained faithful to him all the time he was gone. She lived with his father and helped take care of the old man. She had no idea he was coming home when he did. He didn't write to tell her. He just walked into the cottage in Carev Dvor after eighteen years and said hello.

Was his wife glad to see him? How did she react? What were her exact words when she saw him walk through the door? Vangel grinned. The questions embarrassed him. He hung his head like a schoolboy being asked about his first romance. Finally he said he guessed his wife was glad to see him all right. Yes, he could remember very clearly her first words. She looked up from a washtub and said: *"Zdravo."* That means "hello." Then while she was drying her hands she said, "It's been a long time, hasn't it?" Then she said, "How long do you expect to stay this time, Vangel?" That's all she said. But Vangel repeated that he guessed she was glad to see him. After she dried her hands she told him that his mother had died while he was away. But not his father. His father was feeble but he was still alive. His father said, "My boy, I've been waiting a long time. Now that I've seen you I guess it's time for me to die too." And he did. Just two weeks later.

What changes did Vangel find when he got back this time? Well, things are better now in Macedonia, he said. People are more enjoying themselves. They are more willing to work. They do much work by—what is it you call it?—the volunteer. They build the roads. They build the schools and the houses all by volunteer. Now nobody is afraid in the day or in the night. The gendarmes don't come any more and say bad things and do bad things. Nobody bothers nobody any more. It is good now and I think I stay.

Vangel's English was not exactly perfect but I could understand him. Then I found a young writer named Blajo Koneski who was the best local authority on Macedonia. A number of people told me so. Blajo said he wrote poetry, novels, serious books, songs, magazine articles, and newspaper stories, besides teaching at the university. He didn't speak English but Vangel could serve as a go-between. So the three of us set out together by automobile to explore this southernmost republic of Yugoslavia, where the rate of illiteracy used to run around 80 per cent and where the words "terrorist" and "Macedonian" used to be almost synonymous.

Most of the villages, Blajo said, were either Turkish, Macedonian, or Albanian. There were never many Serbs in the villages. But under the old regime Serbian was the only language permitted. The teachers spoke nothing but Serbian and taught nothing but Serbian. Now it's all different. The government is encouraging the use of the Macedonian language which is quite different from the language of the Serbs. There are Macedonian schools, Macedonian newspapers and magazines, a Macedonian university. They're even founding a Macedonian national theater.

We drove through the rich farm land of the valley and watched peasants transplanting small tobacco plants which seemed as delicate as pieces of a cobweb. We saw burros so small that the men who rode them down country roads couldn't help dragging their feet on the ground. I noticed that the houses, fences, and barns were all built of bricks made from common mud, unbaked. We drove up a small mountain to the town of Morani. Blajo said this was an all-Albanian community. There were about one hundred houses. The village square was covered with mud bricks that had been put there to dry. The women all wore balloon-like pantaloons and heavy black veils. They fled from sight when they saw there were men in our car. The only church was a Moslem mosque. The only other substantial building was a stone schoolhouse. It had fifty pupils. They were being taught in the Albanian language of their parents. The Albanian language had never been permitted here until two years ago. The *emam* or Moslem priest showed us the eighteen pink and red carpets used to give color and atmosphere to his mosque. He said the Albanians in Yugoslavia are happy now. They are happy because they can speak their own language again. Of course the people are still poor. He didn't have to tell us that. All of them we could see were in rags. And their homes looked unfit for animals. But the emam thought that maybe after the war damage was taken care of things might be better. Maybe they would all have a decent life someday. Maybe. If they lived long enough.

Twenty kilometers from Scoplje we found the town of Dračevo. All the men in Dračevo wore red sashes eighteen inches wide around their waists. There were only three hundred houses in the village but the school had seven teachers and four hundred and eighty pupils. They were nearly all Macedonians so here the lessons were given in the Macedonian language.

We met all seven teachers because we got there just at recess time. The schoolyard was heavy with the odor of the blossoms of fruit and acacia trees. For the moment this odor was winning the battle with those more habitual smells of garlic, privies, and barnyard manure. The oldest teacher was in her sixties. She'd been a teacher for twenty-three years. She looked like thousands of schoolmarms I'd seen at teachers' conventions in various parts of the United States. She smiled through her silver-rimmed spectacles and said it was so much easier for the children now. And the teachers too. Now the children didn't have to speak one language in their homes and another in their classrooms.

The youngest teacher was Elena Kurstef. Age, nineteen. She was as brown as a gypsy and as attractive too. Her black hair was done in braids which she twined around her head. She said her father had had a little schooling but her mother hadn't ever learned to read and write. Elena was a product of the New Generation. Her deep brown eyes were full of fun and she radiated enthusiasm. Her pupils apparently loved her. They clustered around her tugging at her skirt and begging her to dance a kolo with them. Elena said we must come into her classroom after recess and meet all the children. She'd told them everything she knew about America. She'd told them about UNRRA and where all the canned food they'd been eating these last few years had come from. The cans of UNRRA food made teaching geography more interesting. They'd learned the names of many cities in the United States from the words on the cans. She'd heard that America didn't like her country. Why was that? Wasn't this new freedom they had in Macedonia something America would understand and approve? That's what she thought from reading American history. But now they said America didn't approve. Was it because America didn't understand? Did America know about the wonderful opportunities there were for young people in Macedonia now? Did America know about how they were trying to help everyone to read and write? Here in Dračevo 70 per cent of the people had been illiterate two years ago. Now all the teachers were working to change that situation. All the old people were learning to read and to write. She taught a class herself with the funniest old ladies in it.

From Dračevo we drove up into isolated mountain settlements. We drove up and down through the Vardar Valley. We drove into all-Turkish villages. Into all-Albanian villages. Into all-Macedonian villages. Everywhere it was the same story. The people were being allowed to use their own language, whatever that language was. To them this seemed more important than anything else. Even than how much they had to eat. They said they didn't hate Belgrade any more. It was different now. Now Belgrade no longer meant Serbs who tried to force them to speak the language of the Master Race. They had what they called freedom, whatever anyone else might call it. And so we finally drove back to Scoplje. On the way Blajo asked if he'd mentioned that the various minorities now had proportional representation in their village, town, county, and district governing bodies. The people considered that important, too, because they remembered how just a few years ago all their officials were Serbs. Serbs appointed in Belgrade and sent down here to rule them.

There were two things I wanted to see in Scoplje before pushing on. One was what they called the "underground church." Its real name was the church of Sveti Spas. In the early days of the Turkish occupation no Christian churches of any kind could be built. Later, as corruption took hold of the Ottoman Empire, it was possible to obtain permission to put up a church if the local pasha was sufficiently bribed. But there was one absolute rule. No Christian church could be any taller than the tallest home of a Turk. The three brothers who planned the church of Sveti Spas wanted to make it the largest and fanciest church in this part of the world. That's why most of it had to be built underground. From the outside it looks like churches you sometimes see in America. The parish raises enough money to put in the foundation and the basement and then has to postpone further work until more funds are raised, so in the meantime the basement is used for services. That's what the church of Sveti Spas looks like from the outside. But inside it's quite large and elaborate. The legend is that the three brothers were wealthy but illiterate. All three were wood carvers. It took them twelve years, working constantly with little rest, to complete the mass of walnut carvings we saw in that partly subterranean place of worship. On one panel they did a self-portrait, right in with the carvings of deity and saints. It shows the three of them hard at work with their knives and chisels. A custodian in a blue sweater took us through the place with a portable spotlight in his hand. He had a dozen places to plug it in. He showed us two thrones the brothers had carved from wood. He said one was for the bishop. Then in a whisper he added that the other was supposed to be for the King. But of course now Yugoslavia has no king, so no one ever sits there. It was too bad, he said, the brothers hadn't known it was going to work out that way. They could have saved themselves a lot of work.

The other place I wanted to visit was the *Karsumli Han* or Leaden Inn. It had been built in the sixth century in the shape of a Roman amphitheater. Caravans with goods from Turkey, Arabia, and Persia used to come as far as Scoplje and were met here by traders from the West. Especially merchants from Dubrovnik on the Adriatic coast. The inn was built as a common meeting place. It got its name from the roof of pure lead it once had, before vandals did a bit of pillaging. The courtyard in the center was large enough to accommodate a great many caravans. It was surrounded by stone stalls and above them were balconies where the merchants sat looking down into the courtyard until they saw something arrive that pleased their fancy. That much I knew from what I had been told secondhand.

The man who answered our banging on the great oak door of the Leaden Inn heard me say something to Vangel in English. So he ran off and came back with two very Western-looking young women. They led us into the center of the gray-stone structure. As we stood in the great courtyard I could half close my eyes and see the place full of camels. I could almost smell the camels. And the spices strapped in straw containers on their backs. It didn't take much imagination to picture oriental rugs hanging down from the balconies. Or to hear the babble of voices and the noises of a marketplace. There were sixty small rooms opening on the courtyard with a fireplace in each one of them. This structure had stood here, if the historians were right, for fourteen centuries. Yet in all the wars there had been in all that time it had been little damaged. This last time the Bulgarians had seen to it that no harm was done to the Leaden Inn or to anything else in Scoplje because they were so sure that from then on Scoplje would be a city of the new and enlarged Bulgaria. As we stood in the center of the courtyard I was glad that Scoplje had been spared. This was too interesting a structure to be destroyed. Now it was what they called, even in the Yugoslav languages, a *"lapidarium."* It was full of old gravestones, pieces of ancient mosaic, and a number of headless statues which had been dug up somewhere. But they didn't spoil anything. Somehow they seemed to help in bringing back the old days when riches of the Orient were traded in this place for the riches of the West. But the spell finally was broken by a soft voice. It wasn't the voice of an Arab camel driver or a merchant prince from Dubrovnik. It was the voice of a girl. And she wasn't talking the language she should have been talking. She wasn't talking Macedonian or even Serbian. She was saying, with a little laugh in her voice:

"You like it, do you?"

I blinked a couple of times. Then the other girl said, with more of an accent:

"You are the American or are you Anglish?"

It turned out that they both knew English. Dushanka was the older and more articulate. Dushanka Voćković. She was an archaeologist and presided over these statues and other stones of antiquity. She had dark hair and eyes that were almost black. She didn't look the thirty years she said she was. She laughed all the time. With her eyes and her voice too. She laughed when she told us she had been married for just eight days. Her husband was a doctor of medicine. They lived in one of the "cells" of the Karsumli Han and it was very funny having your honeymoon with so many headless men standing around all the time. But it was all right, she supposed, because if they didn't have heads they didn't have eyes and then they couldn't see anything, could they?

"Krinkets" was her assistant. Krinkets was younger and much more serious. Krinkets was a librarian by profession but she was helping in the museum. They both wanted to know all about America. Dushanka nearly went to the United States a few months ago. She heard about a museum in Philadelphia that wanted an archaeologist. But by the time her letter of application got there the position had been filled. Had I ever been to Philadelphia? Was it as big as Scoplje? Would she have liked it? I wanted to find out more about her. Finally I did. She'd been a schoolteacher before the war. That was about all the career a girl could have in the Old Yugoslavia. But she'd studied a lot of Latin and Greek and all the archaeology she could. That's how, after the war, she got this position. It was different for a girl like her in the New Yugoslavia. Now a girl could hold any position a man could hold if she was good enough.

She and Krinkets had a lot of plans. This was just the beginning. Someday they would both be famous in their own fields. Someday . . . But then they suddenly grew silent. They said they had talked too much. What did we want to know about the Leaden Inn? Did we know that for centuries it had been a Turkish dungeon? For political prisoners. Yes, sometimes they, too, could half close their eyes and see camels. And smell spices.

In the summertime we must come back again. In the summertime there were flowers blooming around the great fountain in the center of the courtyard. Or maybe someday we would all meet in America. But now they must go. They had some cooking to attend to in the "cell." Dushanka was afraid the headless Roman men wouldn't have sense enough to keep the dinner from boiling over.

PART ELEVEN

This Is Yugoslavia's Youth

Chapter Seventy-Four

"THREE METERS TONIGHT!"

EVERY twenty feet in a line one hundred and sixty-nine miles long through the valleys and over the hills of Bosnia there were four stakes. Some of them were painted white and were as much as thirty feet high. Others were almost flush with the ground and were painted red. The two center stakes were perpendicular. The two outside stakes had crossbars on them at an angle. It didn't take an engineer to understand directions like these. The tall stakes indicated that here there was to be a "fill" up to the top of the stakes. And the angle bars indicated the slope of the sides of the "fill."

The stakes painted red which were almost flush with the ground had a white number on them. The number indicated how much of a "cut" was to be made here. Before the summer was over nearly two hundred thousand boys and girls from every corner of the six Yugoslav republics, and from some foreign countries, too, would dig out the "cuts," fill in the "fills," build some bridges, bore some tunnels, put one hundred and sixty-nine miles of ties in place, and lay the rails. And then, sometime in the autumn, the first train would run over the 1947 Samać–Sarajevo Youth Railroad. All the experts had to do was to put up the stakes. The children of Yugoslavia would do the rest. The children of Yugoslavia knew they could do it because last summer they tackled an identical job. Experts had said it would take two years of work by professional railroad builders to connect Brčko and Banovići. But last summer sixty-four thousand boys and girls did it in four months. They did it just as they were doing this Samać–Sarajevo job. They did it without bulldozers, steam shovels, trucks, or any other motorized equipment, because Yugoslavia had hardly any of those things. They did it with wheelbarrows so small that when they bent over to push them their backs made a figure like a question mark. Instead of using steam rollers they tamped the earth firm and solid with small squares of wood fastened to broomstick handles. Homemade tampers. They did it with sweat and enthusiasm. Eagerness and joy. And they did it without pay. Experts said a railroad built that way would collapse in a month. But today trains are still running the full length of the 1946 Youth Railroad and there have been no accidents. The 1947 job is a much more difficult one. The projected road is longer. It's over rougher terrain. More bridges. More miles of tunnels. Through wilder mountains. Over more rivers. More millions of cubic yards of "fill." More millions of cubic yards of "cuts."

They told me the way to see the project was to take an overnight train from Belgrade to the Slovenian city of Brod. And then another train from Brod down to Zenica. Zenica is the headquarters city, not far from the end of the line. Spring was in the Bosnian air the day I got to Brod and headed south for Zenica. The apple trees on the mountain slopes were covered with white blossoms. The smells that came through the car windows were clean and good.

You start seeing the stakes as soon as the train gets to Doboj. (Pronounced the same as doughboy.) At Doboj the new railroad will come out of the mountains to the east and parallel this line for many miles. This line is one of the old-fashioned, single-track, narrow-gauge roads built by the Austrians. The new road will be double track and wide gauge like any American road.

At every river bend, at every road junction, on the edge of every town and on the approaches to every mountain pass the Germans, when they were here, built concrete pillboxes to protect themselves from the sniping of Partisans. Most of them are still standing. The bullet holes in some of them are evidence enough that life wasn't all hearts and flowers for the one-time occupants. Some of the pillboxes have been reconverted for peacetime use. Some are now post offices, railroad stations, kafanas, workmen's dormitories, schools, or even homes. I wondered as I saw some of them in which people were living what it must be like to wake up in the morning and see the new day through a narrow slit made for a machine gun. But many of those "bunkers," as the Yugoslavs call them, are going to be torn down. We could tell that because here and there the line of stakes, the line of the new railroad, went right through a bunker.

Every few miles along the line of stakes there's a camp of freshly constructed one-story wooden buildings with tar-paper roofs. They look like the C.C.C. camps that were built in the United States in the '30's.

Looking at the young railroad workers you can tell almost to the day how long each of the boys has been on the job because they work in the hot sun stripped bare to the waist. Each day each body turns one shade browner. You can pick the city girls from the country girls by the clothes they wear. Peasants and the sons and daughters of doctors, lawyers, and merchants are all mixed together. But because they are not required to wear uniforms there's individuality in their appearance.

The girl across the aisle wanted to explain everything to me. She was about twenty-two and said she was a veteran of last summer's railroad and was going to work a month this year. She wasn't attractive. Her teeth were in very bad repair. Her clothes were sloppy-looking. When it got warm she took off her jacket. On the breast of her blouse there was a *spomenica* 1941 star. Four or five years in the Partisans. Maybe that accounted for teeth that were bad and a lot of other things. She said they were building this new railroad to haul coal out of the mountains to make steel to use in manufacturing articles to raise the standard of living of the people.

I said all those objectives could be reached a lot faster if they had some American machinery on this railroad job. The girl smiled and said yes, but then maybe they wouldn't accomplish one other objective that was just as important. She said the youth builds the railroad and at the same time the railroad builds the youth. She asked if I knew that many of the children working on the railroad are orphans. Their parents died in the fighting for—for—— Maybe it would sound funny, put this way, but among other things they died fighting for the right to build a railroad. Many of the workers had been in the Partisans themselves. In the hills they'd fought without pay because they were fighting for something they believed in. Here they were working without pay because they were working for something they believed in. For the next few minutes I sat looking out the window thinking of all the reasons people fought the recent war. I thought of Rabbi Roland Gittlesohn. He was the American chaplain from Long Island who delivered a historic address over the graves of the dead at Iwo Jima. When he got home he told me a story about a bull session he held one night on a Liberty ship crossing the Pacific. They were discussing what each one of them thought the war was all about. Finally a Negro sailor spoke up and said that down where he came from, if he and his wife waited at a street corner for a bus and were the first in line and then twenty white people got in line behind them, and when the bus came there were only twenty seats, he and his wife had to stand aside and let the twenty whites get on, and then they had to wait for the next bus. The Negro sailor said:

"Chaplain, the reason I enlisted and helped fight this war was for the right to get on a bus when my turn comes."

Now this Partisan girl was telling me about people who died so their children could have the right to build a railroad.

At the Zenica depot I was met by two young officials of the Youth Railroad. They looked like winners in a contest to pick the boy and girl who best personified the New Yugoslavia. Maybe they were. Janez Šmidovnik was a Slovene from Ljubljana. Blond. About eighteen. Clear-eyed and intelligent-looking. Zora Horvatić said she was twenty-three. She didn't look the age of a high school senior. She was a Croat from Zagreb. Even if she was a few years older than Janez, if I'd been a eugenist I would have tried to foster a romance. The two of them seemed to have all the good qualities of their two separate races. Zora was black-haired with eyes full of mischief and fun. Even when she talked statistics. She was a perambulating American flag. White blouse, red sweater, and blue slacks. Only of course red, white, and blue are Yugoslav colors too. She had a blue tam and wore tennis shoes. I thought she used lipstick, her lips were so red. Later I found it was just their natural healthy color. The chauffeur of their jeep was a German prisoner of war in his early fifties. He had fancy twirled mustachios. Almost as fancy as the mustachios they wear in Cernagora. He treated Janez and Zora as if they were his own two children. And as if he were very proud of them. But he said "Yes, sir" or "yes, ma'am" when either of them gave him an order. He kept his place. He never gave the impression that he was trying to make anyone forget that he was a prisoner of war. But if he'd been in chains he would still have seemed what he obviously was, a man of culture and breeding. He had the bearing of a gentleman. His eyes were kind and soft.

Zora and Janez were bubbling with their enthusiasm. And they were so eager to pass their enthusiasm on to me. They had all the facts and figures at their tongues' tip. Last year there had been three groups that came for a month apiece. Sixty-four thousand in all. This year there would again be three one-month periods. But this year there would be close to two hundred thousand taking part. Twenty per cent of them would be girls. They'd range in age from fifteen up to twenty-two. Because I had been a radio commentator in America the first thing I must see was the Youth Railroad Radio Station. It was on the air four hours a day. It broadcast music, news bulletins, and reports of each day's progress on each section of the road. So we went to the radio station. The studios were in Quonset huts. Most of the staff members were amateurs. Several German prisoners of war had given them expert advice. The station was built in twelve days.

The real job was putting up the antenna on the top of a mountain nearly twenty-five hundred feet high. There were no trails to the mountaintop. They couldn't even find anyone who had ever been up there. They had only four days to do the job. But that was where the experts said the tower should go. So they got it up there. The climb was at an angle of forty degrees in some places. That's quite an angle. And an antenna weighs something. Try carrying one. It's thousands of pounds of steel. They started up on March twenty-seventh. At 10 A.M., on April first, they broadcast their first program. Right on schedule.

And then to the office of the Youth Railroad's own newspaper. They put it out in three languages, Serbo-Croat, Slovenian, and Macedonian. They'd hauled in linotype machines, presses, and tons of equipment. The paper came out every day. On the staff there were seven professional journalists and nine amateurs. But the editor laughed and said, this isn't my whole staff. I have thousands of reporters. Or people who would like to be reporters. We get six or seven hundred letters a day. It's a job just to open the envelopes. They all write about what their brigades are doing. They aren't trying to get any individual names in the paper. But they do want publicity and credit for their brigades.

I sat in the newsroom and talked with all sixteen members of the staff. They were full of questions. Did the United States have a project like this? What did newspaper readers in the United States know about Yugoslavia? Did they know about the Youth Railroad? And if they didn't, why not? Was it true that Americans were interested only in sensations? Were they interested in how other people in the world live? Then the editor explained that last year there were brigades representing nearly a dozen foreign countries. This year the flags of even more nations would be flying over barracks scattered along the right of way. One of the best brigades was the Greek Brigade. But there had been no brigade from the United States last year. And none this year either. Why was that? Weren't there even one hundred young people in the United States interested in helping Yugoslavia get back on her feet? And in seeing this new country? And in working with people their own age from various parts of the world? There was no pay connected with the job, of course, but the Bosnian mountains are a wonderful place to have a vacation. Was it because the American Government didn't want people to come to Yugoslavia and see the country for themselves? If so, why was that? Was our government afraid to let Americans see the truth? Maybe someday things would be different and young people in America could come here and see for themselves. The editor hoped so. The other fifteen newspapermen hoped so too. They said that of course they didn't like the American foreign policy. But they did like Americans. They could learn a lot if they had an American brigade working with them. Maybe the Americans could learn something too. I said perhaps before the summer was over some Americans would get a chance to work on their road. I really thought so when I said it. I didn't know that a few weeks later the State

Department in Washington was going to cause headlines by refusing passports to a group of young collgee students who had even bought their tickets all the way to Zenice, Yugoslavia, so they could raise an American flag over a barracks on the Samać–Sarajevo, 1947 Yugoslav Youth Railroad.

Zora and Janez had a trip planned to the village of Vranduk. They said it was an interesting place historically. That castle up on the hill was built in the thirteenth century by some Bosnian king. Those rusty metal things in the ditch at the side of the road were soup kitchens the Germans abandoned in their final flight.

Over here were the barracks of a brigade from the city of Novi Sad up in the Vojvodina. This was one of the brigades working on the tunnel. One hundred and seventy boys and thirty-seven girls. Of course their workday was over now. But Zora said I should notice how they relaxed. Some of them were in a field practicing discus and weight throwing. Others were using picks and shovels they'd been handling all day. Now they were using them to make the grounds of their camp more attractive.

Their commandant showed us through their barracks. They slept in bunks of fresh pine. There were no mattresses. They lay on heaps of clean straw. Each boy or girl had two blankets. The straw and the pine gave the room a clean odor. The commandant said the place was disinfected every two days. "Just in case . . ."

The loud-speaker on the outside of the building made the whole valley alive with the music the radio station was playing. Each barracks had a library and each brigade had its own recreation and cultural director. Most of the recreation and cultural directors were young women studying to be teachers. Among other things they edited the wall newspapers that all the brigades put out every week. Tonight the Novi Sad brigade was going by truck to a village some distance away to put on a play for the country people. Each brigade had its own chef who cooked in the manner of the area the brigade came from. This brigade had only six illiterates at the start. Already five of them had learned to read and write.

Some nights they had movies. On Sundays they had sports contests. They learned new songs. They sang most of the time. Doctors vaccinated everyone against typhus and everyone had to have a periodic examination.

The schedule for the ordinary brigade started at 5 A.M. That's when they all got up. For fifteen minutes they did setting-up exercises. Then breakfast, a flag-raising ceremony, and by six-thirty they were on the job. There was a rest period in the middle of the morning. They were through work for the day at one-fifteen. They spent the afternoon and evening in educational, cultural, or sport activities. They went to bed at 10 P.M. There was no work on Sunday.

Each brigade picked its own leader by popular vote. Wherever I went I kept on the lookout for signs of military influence. There were none. Not even as much as in the C.C.C. camps in America. Or in the Boy

Scouts. The Yugoslav Army had nothing to do with the Youth Railroad.
No military drill. No saluting. No uniforms. No standing guard. No
bugles. No martial music. The youngsters lived in barracks as soldiers do.
But few armies provide barracks as pleasant as these. Zora said that for
many peasant youngsters this was really luxury living. Both as to food and
housing too.

In one of the camps we went to I asked the leader about discipline. He
didn't seem to understand. I asked him what powers he had. Was he a
gauleiter? Was his word supreme? Did he have the right of punishment?
But I was talking a language he didn't seem to understand, even when
what I said was translated to him in Serbo-Croat. There was no discipline.
Discipline in the New Yugoslavia comes from within. They held meetings every night. If someone did something wrong the meeting might
discuss it. They might even vote what to do about it. But that didn't
happen very often. They lived together in harmony. They had consideration for each other. They helped one another. If someone did something wrong someone else would point it out to him. Then he'd never do
it again. There was no need for discipline. That was something we foreigners couldn't seem to understand, wasn't it? He hoped that before I
left I would see what he meant. That I would see how they lived together without any need for discipline from above. There was no "above."
This was a democracy. There were no officers. There were no individual
medals. Everyone worked for the common good.

I spent most of that night inside the longest and most difficult tunnel on
the whole road. It was being bored through a mountain of solid rock.
The boss was Yovo Orlić. He'd been a tunnel expert for twenty-four
years. He said he'd built "some of the worst tunnels in Europe." Fifty or
sixty of them. This was going to be a mean one. He preferred to talk about
tunnels rather than about his own life the past few years. He didn't wear
a *spomenica* medal but it turned out that he had one at home. He'd gone
into the Partisans in 1941 and moved up to the rank of captain. After a
lifetime of building tunnels he became an expert at blowing them up so
the enemy couldn't use them. He said he worked and fought all over
Yugoslavia on foot. From one corner of the country to the other. He'd had
three sons. All of them were in the Partisans with him. Two were killed in
battle. The third came out alive. But on a reconstruction job just last week
he lost his right hand. But never mind about all that. He'd rather talk
about this youth project. Of course it was a real job, boring a tunnel with
girls and boys doing most of the work. Some of them came from places
like the Vojvodina. They'd never even seen a mountain in their lives.
But, old Yovo Orlić said, just wait until you see them at work! They all
call me The Old Man. I guess maybe I am old compared with them. They
say I look sixty. That's because of some things that happened the last few
years. Really I'm only forty-four. So they call me The Old Man and what
does it matter? But they work like mad for me. What they don't have
in the way of experience they make up for with strength and enthusiasm.

There's no leaning on shovels around here. They bite their way into that rock as if it were—as if it were a piece of Slovenian cheese.

The tunnel brigades were working in eight-hour shifts. Right around the clock. One brigade worked from each side. Someday they'd meet in the middle. They were using some dynamite but mostly the stone was being eaten away with compressed-air drills. The drillers worked in gangs of four. One of the four was a professional. But the other three drills were operated by boys. To meet the quota which had been set each gang had to chew its way one meter farther into the mountain every eight-hour shift. The afternoon gang had set a record of two and two-tenths meters. The night gang came from the ELAS Brigade. Boys of Greek origin. They were out to do three meters tonight. That would be three times their quota. It was a nasty job. Nasty any way you looked at it.

They were making the tunnel about six feet wide and five and a half feet high. When it was finished that size they'd start over again making it twice as large. But now it was only six feet wide and five and a half feet high. That meant you had to bend over to keep from bumping your head. Water dripped down through the ceiling. In some places it did more than just drip. I asked Yovo Orlić what would happen if they hit an underground river. The only answer I got was a shrug of the shoulders. They hadn't hit one yet. Nevertheless the floor of the tunnel was ankle deep in water.

The only light inside the mountain came from an occasional miner's lamp fastened to someone's head. The naked yellow flame from a carbide lamp makes a weird light. The smell of carbide and the smell of hot pneumatic drills somehow make you think of something in a book Dante once wrote.

Steel rails had been laid on the floor of the tunnel. They led from where the pneumatic drillers were working out to the mouth of the tunnel and then to the edge of a cliff.

Some of the boys of the ELAS Brigade were loading the steel wagonettes which ran over the rails. Others pushed them through the dark tunnel into the open and then dumped them over the cliff. There were about twenty wagonettes. Each one carried several tons of chipped-off pieces of rock. I tried to push one of them. It took more strength than I had even to budge it. Yet these Greek boys were making them sail along. The wagonettes when they were heaped full came almost to the ceiling of the tunnel. The boys pushing them had to bend down so as not to bump their heads. I didn't understand why, in the dark, they didn't run into each other. Someone explained. All the time their carts were in motion they yelled. That added another eerie noise to the noise of the drills. They yelled the single word *"hoo-raw."* It's a word that means more in Serbo-Croat than the similar word in English. It was a battle cry the Partisans used. The way a Yugoslav shouts the word it has a fierce sound. When the wagonettes were in motion the tunnel echoed with the war cry. It must have acted on them the same as music. It must have spurred them on, for tonight they were making their goal of three meters. They were breathing the granite dust made by the drills. They were covered with it. They looked like ghosts in the light of the occasional carbide lamp. They looked like those dead bodies I had seen one Easter morning in Terazzia. But they were grinning through their ghost make-up. Grinning and yelling *hoo-raw*.

In the dark it seemed miles from the entrance to where the drills were. Sometimes pieces of rock would fall out of a wagonette and throw the next wagonette off the tracks. Occasionally one wagonette, despite all the yelling, would run down the man pushing the wagonette ahead. At some places the water underfoot was so deep it came up to the knees. Water dripping from above ran down the necks of the boys. Sometimes a timber would give way and cause a traffic jam. The smell of carbide and hot metal was almost suffocating. But the work went on. Everyone moved on the double. They were doing three meters tonight. They kept shouting the figure at each other. "Three meters tonight!" "Three meters tonight!" "Hoo-raw, three meters tonight!"

When I left Sunday morning Zora and Janez helped me get off. Zora was as efficient as a New York businessman's secretary. By the time I was awake she had breakfast ordered. She had a bundle of food packed for the train. She had railroad tickets for me all the way back to Belgrade. She'd reserved a seat on the train. She'd noticed that I was out of cigarettes so there were two packages of Yugoslav cigarettes for the trip. She found out how late the train was going to be. She knew Americans are accustomed to drinking water on a railroad journey so there was an old rakia bottle filled with cold water. At the station she said they'd forgotten to tell me, but the young people in their spare time were helping the villages along the line in every way they could. They put on motion-picture shows for the villages. In one village four illiteracy courses were being conducted. She said that I should write down that the Youth Railroad workers are like yeast. They are trying to help and inspire the whole country. Zora was so eager for me to take away a good impression of the young people of Yugoslavia. And I wanted so much to say something or do something to make her understand how I felt about Yugoslavia's youth. I had several lipsticks in my knapsack that I'd brought from New York for gifts. They were in very smart, very Fifth Avenue looking red-and-silver containers. But Zora, when I gave one of them to her, looked at me with her dark lovely eyes and said:

"You save it for someone else. I—I—— You see I don't use things like that. I wouldn't know what to do with it."

I told her to use it as a pencil. Or maybe someday it would come in handy when they were putting on an amateur theatrical performance. Anyway, she was to keep it as a small reminder of America. When she looked at it she was to remember that in our country there are young people who also have freshness and ideals and vision. That maybe our youth dresses differently and uses lipstick and may not always understand, for one reason or another, things that go on in the rest of the world, but basically American youth is good, too, and maybe someday the youth of the world will get together. Then I said something stupid about how someday I might see both of them in New York. I realized it was stupid as soon as I'd said it. They both smiled. Janez said:

"I doubt it. We have a big job to do right here. There are great opportunities for us here. I'm going to law school. Zora has plans too. We're going to help make this country of ours as modern and progressive as yours is. We've got a lot of catching up to do. But I think we have a chance. I think we have a chance if only . . ."

He didn't finish the sentence. But I knew what he meant.

All the rest of the day I sat looking out the window of the train at thousands of young people in their camps along the right of way. Some were watching plays in natural amphitheaters in the hills. Some were taking part in sports contests. Some were lying on their backs in fields reading. It was a warm spring day. The locomotive was garlanded with evergreen branches. Every time the train stopped any length of time at a station the engineer went into the station kafana and came out with a bottle of water. The first few times I thought he and his fireman must be very thirsty. But when Yugoslavs get thirsty they drink rakia or vino or pivo. Then I solved the mystery. On the front of the locomotive there was a glass vase full of wild flowers. The water didn't stay in the vase very long because the roadbed of this narrow-gauge line was not like the roadbed of the Twentieth Century Limited. Nor even like the roadbed of this new line that was being built. But the engineer seemed determined that those flowers should remain fresh until the end of the journey. Yugoslav girls may not use lipstick. But the Yugoslavs have an appreciation of natural beauty all their own. Even grimy engineers and firemen who shovel coal for a living.

When it got too dark to see any more I talked with a boy in the same compartment with me. He was a Croat. He had voluntarily joined the German Navy after the occupation. He had fought against the British in the North Sea. Against the Americans when they were trying to land in France. And against his own countrymen in the Adriatic. Yet today he was free. He was even telling me, a complete stranger, about his record during the war. He was not working on the Youth Railroad. He was just on his way home from a visit down here in Bosnia. He didn't even seem embarrassed about what he had done. All that was past. Now he was a citizen of the New Yugoslavia and that's all there was to the story.

Then the moon came up. It made the landscape glimmer. The landscape of Bosnia is exciting and beautiful even in the daytime. But now the landscape glimmered. The moon came up round as a rubber ball. It was deep yellow when it pushed over the horizon. Slowly it turned pure white. It bathed the hills with its softness. It was a kind light. If there was any ugliness in sight the ugliness disappeared. Beauty was multiplied and accentuated. It should have had the same effect on human beings. It made me feel soft, anyway. There were no lights on the train to interfere. I went out and stood in the corridor because the corridor was on the same side of the train as the moon. There was a girl in the corridor. Maybe she wasn't even attractive in daylight. But in the light of the moon she looked beautiful. She'd been standing there alone for half an hour when a young man about her own age got on the train. He stood in the corridor beside her. In a short time they were in low conversation. I stood near them eavesdropping. I'd investigated work projects, reconstruction, illiteracy campaigns, and a lot of other things in the months I'd been wandering around Yugoslavia. Practical, material things. This might be a chance to investigate romance. This was a setting for romance all right. Even an unemotional English bank clerk would have gone soft under these conditions.

The moon was making shafts of light dance through the girl's dark hair. They were alone in the corridor except for me and I was being very careful not to make my presence inhibiting. It was three or four hours before we got to the end of the line. I understood a great deal of what they were saying to each other in excited little whispers. They got along beautifully together. They were obviously very *sympatična* to each other. They talked quite intimately. They talked exclusively for three or four hours about the Youth Railroad, the reconstruction program, how many miles of highway had been built here, how many tons of earth had been moved there, how many of this and how much of that. Figures. Facts. Statistics. Cold, unemotional things. They didn't even hold hands. Once they looked out at the moonlit landscape and the girl said *"krasan,"* which means "lovely." I thought this might be the start of something different. But it wasn't. They looked away from the moonlight and back into each other's eyes. And talked statistics. When the girl finally left the train the boy told her how much he had enjoyed the night. He didn't get her name or telephone number or address. Even though it turned out that he lived in the next town. The rest of the night I wasn't so happy as I had been during the day. Yugoslavia was rebuilding all right. Forging ahead. Doing an amazing job. But there was a terrible waste of soft moonlight in the hills of Bosnia. And surely holding hands has as much a place in life as railroads do.

PART TWELVE

This Is Strictly Personal

Chapter Seventy-Five

LOST IS FOUND

On BLOODY SUNDAY when the Germans set the Srpski Kralj Hotel on fire with their bombs we didn't have much time to sort out the accumulation of "things" we had in our rooms. Each man took one suitcase, jammed it full of whatever caught his eye or looked important at the moment, and ran. I've often laughed at myself about what I'd considered important that day. I had a sizable collection of articles from years of batting around Europe to choose from. And yet I threw some strange objects into the suitcase and left some of the most valuable things behind for the bombs and the fire. I remember that the first thing I took was a volume of journalistically important statistics about southeastern Europe. It gave such information as how many gypsies there were in Yugoslavia. I took the book because I was too excited to realize that what was happening in the sky over the Srpski Kralj at that moment and what would be happening all over the country in a matter of hours would make all statistics out of date. Especially statistics about how many gypsies there were in Yugoslavia. Then there were three suits of clothes I'd never worn. A tailor in Bucharest, Rumania, delivered them to me the day I took off from Bucharest for Belgrade to try to find out what was going on in Yugoslavia in the month of March 1941. The tailor's name was Ion Christescu. His shop was right around the corner from the Athenee Palace Hotel. He'd been King Carol's favorite costumier. But when the King and Magda Lupescu hurried off into exile *Domnul* Christescu lost his royal client. So he offered to construct suits for the foreign correspondents at bargain prices. He had some good English wool and the rate of exchange, dollar to *lei,* was favorable. So for the first time in my life (and the last) I ordered three suits as if I were ordering three glasses of lemonade. When they arrived, after weeks of fitting and trying, they became three of my most cherished possessions. Someday I would strut down Fifth Avenue, New York, and if anyone remarked, as someone surely would, "What a handsome suit you have on!" I would reply as nonchalantly as possible: "Ah yes! It is rather nice, isn't it? In fact it was made for me by King Carol's private tailor."

On top of the three suits I threw six shirts. Also tailor-made. Actually they were no better than shirts you buy in any men's shop in America, ready-made. But in Europe it's the thing for a gentleman to do to have his shirts tailor-made. And the rate of exchange, dollars to lei, was improving by the day. So I had six shirts made to measure by the master of Balkan shirtmaking, Domnul Mathias Neuvirth. But that wasn't all. Into the suitcase went many objects of less practical but more sentimental nature. There was a little religious emblem on a piece of red ribbon. The Rumanian girl who gave it to me was certain it would protect my body from any bullets or bombs which might be encountered when war did come to the Balkans. And there was a necktie of striking color and design which had been a gift from someone I'd cared for. And there was a book Ralph Barnes gave me to keep for him. The same Ralph Barnes whose plane hit the side of the mountain near Podgorica a few days later. I didn't ever want to lose that book. And then there was the start of a book of my own about life in Ruritania.

A lot of things went into that suitcase which made no sense. Pictures. Photographs. Little art objects. Some nearly worn-out clothes. My complete file of Associated Press dispatches for two or three years. Some expense-account vouchers. Bottles and bottles of aspirin tablets. When I tossed the aspirin on top of everything else I thought of the stock joke about how Hitler had sent enough aspirin down into the Balkans, in exchange for oil and grain, to cure all the headaches he was ultimately going to cause the Balkans. I also salvaged part of the finest collection of maps of the Balkans any correspondent ever accumulated. And then a copy of an almanac worth about fifty cents. And a corkscrew which I thought was the greatest single invention I'd run across in Europe. It made opening a bottle of wine a double pleasure. All these things went into a very ordinary-looking suitcase, thirty-nine inches long, eighteen inches wide by seven inches deep made of rough brown leather and fastened with a zipper.

That Palm Sunday morning we finally got our luggage to the home of the American minister. That's where we learned how difficult escape was going to be, even without any luggage at all. We'd be lucky if we could salvage a typewriter apiece. In those days we would rather have left an arm behind than a typewriter. So we stored our suitcases in the basement of the American minister's home and set out across the hills with our typewriters. Our luggage seemed perfectly safe. The American minister had had carpenters put some large oak beams in the ceiling of his cellar. I remembered someone looking up at the beams and saying that a block buster couldn't wreck this place. But a few days later in Sarajevo we got the bad news. The night after we left Belgrade a bomb hit the minister's home. It wasn't a block buster. It wasn't even a big bomb. But they told us that now the house was nothing but rubble. So it was good-by to tailor-made suits and fancy shirts and manuscripts and trinkets. We didn't have time to do much mourning about it. That was the day Sarajevo got it too. Some months later in New York I met an American colleague who had stayed behind because he wasn't on the Nazi black list as far as he knew. He said he'd been lucky. He hired some Yugoslav workmen and they dug in the rubble and found that the oak beams held, after all. The cellar underneath was undamaged. So the correspondent took his own suitcase, paid off the hired help, and went his way. After all, he said, he couldn't very well carry the whole cellarful of luggage.

For the next few years I wondered how my King Carol suits were wearing on the backs of those Serbian workmen. And whether my Rumanian charm was protecting them as it had not protected me from bullets and bombs. I even did a broadcast once about *The Tragedy of the Lost Suitcase*. Some people wrote and expressed condolences.

Then about a year ago Mrs. Leland Stowe telephoned from Bronxville, New York. She said she had just received a letter from her correspondent husband. He was in Budapest, Hungary. In the American Legation at Budapest he'd seen a room full of luggage. Among the suitcases there was one he'd left there early in the war. He wrote that there was also a suitcase in the Budapest Legation with my name on it. He thought I would like to know. It was an ordinary-looking suitcase, he said. About thirty-nine inches long, eighteen inches wide by seven inches deep, made of rough brown leather and fastened with a zipper.

Often in these past months in the mountains of Yugoslavia I'd thought of the suitcase. Now that I was back in the Balkans I ought to go up to Budapest sometime and see for myself. Then the trip to Scoplje made me want to find out about Paul Vajda. The thread of his story was still dangling. So I took a train for Budapest after my trip over the Youth Railroad.

I didn't poke into any Hungarian villages. I didn't try to talk to Hungarian people about their political situation. It would have taken months of studying to have begun to understand what was happening in this country. But I couldn't help seeing that Budapest was still a ruined city in the spring of 1947. It looked as if the last bomb had dropped at eleven o'clock last night. There were two makeshift bridges across the Danube where there had once been four or five of the most graceful combinations of steel and stone that were ever thrown from shore to shore of a river. The people in the streets looked hungry. They looked unhappy too. They moved at their work without any sign of enthusiasm. Along the street called Vatsi Utca, in the heart of all this devastation, they were selling mink coats again, and silk lingerie and cashmere sweaters. The Hungarian women still reminded me of painted dolls. They weren't any less beautiful than they had been before it all happened. The man who met me at the station said there was even a new Hungarian song everyone was singing about the pretty girls along Vatsi Utca. He said it was going to cost ten million dollars to fix up Margaret Island alone. He said the great hotels along the Corso were all gone. There wasn't even a Corso any more.

He said the Hungarian currency wasn't the *pengö* any more. The pengö had gone up to a few hundred trillion to the dollar. Then they stabilized the currency and put out some new money. The *forint* they called it. But it was still possible for foreigners to live in a style to which few kings are accustomed these days by changing dollars into forints at something much better than the legal rate. The American colony was doing all right. For breakfast we had orange juice, bacon, scrambled eggs, hot rolls made of flour that was white, marmalade, large dishes of rich yellow butter, and all the coffee you wanted with cream in it. I'd forgotten that food like that existed. At breakfast the guest of honor was Paul Vajda. Between hot rolls and dishes of scrambled eggs he caught me up on his story. The people of Scoplje had told him just what someone had told me in Belgrade. The Germans would never get through the mountain passes. Not in a hundred years.

And then, while they were still boasting to each other and to Paul, the German tanks began to roll through their streets. Paul was hidden first by the daughter of the head porter of the hotel. She hid him in a cellar. All she could find for him to eat was a bunch of two or three hundred spring onions. Paul said he's never eaten a spring onion since then.

For company in the cellar he had a millionaire publisher of a Berlin newspaper. He was a German but, like Paul, he was a Jew. He'd done a lot of running but now he was trapped. He'd converted much of his wealth into diamonds. The diamonds were in cotton bags tied around his waist.

When the tanks went by the cellar windows he wanted Paul to take some of the cotton bags and tie them around his waist. Paul said he was glad, when the Gestapo finally came to the cellar and arrested both of them, that he hadn't taken the diamonds. When Paul came to this part of his story he laughed and said:

"The Gestapo nearly got a picture of you that day."

Then he explained. One day in Belgrade Paul had given one of the other correspondents his camera to take a picture of the two of us. When he got to Scoplje Paul exposed the rest of the film. But it was still in the camera when the Gestapo confiscated it. He was afraid that if they developed the film, the shot of the two of us might get into my dossier up in Berlin. So he thought up a trick to make the Germans destroy the film themselves before they found out what was on it. He told them it was an orthocromatic film. He suggested they send it somewhere and get it developed to convince themselves there was nothing incriminating on the roll of celluloid; that the pictures were just innocent landscapes. Of course it wasn't an orthocromatic film. It was pancromatic. And it seems that if you develop a pancromatic film the way you should develop an orthocromatic you ruin it. Anyway, the Germans ruined it and the picture of Paul and me never got into any dossier.

Of course the Germans were angry about the film incident so they took Paul and some other prisoners to Salonika in Greece to execute them. Why Salonika Paul didn't know. Paul said the thing he remembered about Salonika was how angry the Germans there were because when the British left Salonika they poured cement down all the toilet bowls. At Salonika they began killing their prisoners at the rate of ten or fifteen a day.

But one day orders came that Paul Vajda was to be transported back to Budapest and turned over to Hungarian officials. Paul knew what that meant. He'd be killed anyway, but the Fascists in Budapest would do some third-degree work on him first. The only thing that saved him was the scar of a wound thirty years old. While he was waiting to be sent to Budapest an Austrian officer in the German Army came through the prison. Paul recognized him. They'd served together during World War I. They'd been in the same Austro-Hungarian artillery battery the night a shell burst nearby. Didn't the Austrian remember?

Paul stripped off his coat and his shirt and exhibited his back. There was the scar of the wound. Didn't the Austrian remember? They were soon talking intimately about their old experiences. The Austrian said he was going to Berlin that night in a military plane. He'd find some way to get Paul given into his custody. He'd get him out of the hands of the Gestapo and to Berlin. And he did. In Berlin he told Paul he was on his own from then on. The worst thing that could happen to him would be to get caught and executed. And that was going to happen to him anyway.

So Paul lived for weeks in hiding in the capital of the Nazis. A Hungarian Jew who was supposed to be shot. There was much more to the story than that. Paul Vajda was in dozens of concentration camps and prisons before it was all over. It was a long story. Paul said it was all unbelievable anyway and he'd just as soon forget it. The only important thing was that he was still alive. But what happened to everyone else? To the other American correspondents? And how about another hot roll? And let's go down to the American Legation and see if we can find that suitcase.

We did find the suitcase. It didn't look like mine. But maybe that was because of the green mold on it. No one at the legation knew where it had come from. But my name was on the baggage label. It had been in the tender care of the Germans all the time the Germans were in occupation of Budapest. Other pieces of luggage that were there hadn't made out so well as mine had. Most of them had been broken into. Leland Stowe hadn't found much left in his. But the padlock on the zipper of mine was unbroken. That wasn't because there was anything special about the padlock. We pried it open with a screwdriver. It was quite a ceremony. A lot of people had heard about The Mystery of the Missing Suitcase. They stood in a circle watching. Paul Vajda, half-a-dozen legation employees, some of the American correspondents, and the girl librarian for the United States Information Service who had a truck she drove around Budapest because that was the only way she could get from her home to her office, and now she liked driving a truck so much that when she went home maybe she'd try to get a job driving a truck. They all stood around waiting for the big moment.

I made a little speech as I pulled open the zipper. I said they were going to see a 1947 spring style show. Here, for example, was the finest suit of clothes ever constructed by man. I reached into the bottom of the suitcase while I talked. Here was a suit which King Carol's . . . That was as far as I got with the speech. When I held up the first suit for inspection it fell into small pieces on the floor. The other two were in the same condition. I thought of that trite old expression about something being as full of holes as a sieve. That didn't apply to my three Bucharest suits. The moths hadn't left that much space between the holes. There wasn't enough material left to hold the holes together. One of the legation people sent for a janitor to come with a broom and sweep away the crumbs of cloth on the floor. But the shirts hadn't been to the taste of the moths. The shirts could be worn someday if there was any way to get rid of a six-year smell of mold and decay. Nothing had happened to the book that once belonged to Ralph Barnes. Or to the collection of maps of the Balkans. The necktie of striking color and design had had some wool in it. The moths had worked some new designs in it. When I fished out all the aspirin tablets someone said why didn't I send them down to the chief of the Yugoslav press department who deals with American correspondents. He probably would appreciate them. The manuscript of the book about life in Ruritania seemed like a chapter out of some ancient history. When I showed Paul the Rumanian charm he suggested that I carry it with me from now on. He said, why don't you take a trip down to Bucharest some time and find out from the person who gave it to you whether there's any chance of it working against atom bombs? When I found the six-year-old bundle of hotel, telephone, and cable receipts I thought of the head of an accounting department in New York who argued for months about an expense account he didn't want to pay because he said the rules of the company specifically said no payment without proof. I don't think he ever did understand the connection when I told him that Hitler hadn't followed the rules either when he ordered his air force to bomb the undefended city of Belgrade. The last item we pulled from the suitcase was something that made everybody laugh. The librarian who would rather drive a truck than do anything else said this was the biggest mystery of all. She could understand how the Germans might have overlooked my suitcase when they began their looting. After all it was a moldy, uninteresting-looking piece of baggage. But here was proof that they must have opened it anyway. And instead of taking anything out they'd added something. This last object obviously hadn't been in the suitcase when I left it in the minister's basement in Belgrade. It obviously didn't even belong to me. It obviously was an object I'd never owned in my life. How long, they asked, had I had my beard? Fifteen years? Then who put the razor in the bottom of the moldy-looking suitcase? And why?

PART THIRTEEN

This Is Belgrade Again

Chapter Seventy-Six

CAPITAL POTPOURRI

AT DAWN on April 6, 1941, the public square of Belgrade called Terazzia was a noisy place. The noise was being made by explosions. The explosions were being made by what the Germans were dropping from planes that circled overhead not much higher than the chimney pots.

At dawn on April 6, 1947, Terazzia was a noisy place again. The noise this time was also being made by explosions. What was making the explosions we didn't know. We were crossing the bridge over the Sava when we began to hear them. We'd been for a long walk down the Zemun highway. From a few blocks away the noise sounded just as it had that other April the sixth. But when we got to Terazzia we found out that this time there were no dead bodies. The faces we saw in Terazzia were covered with white dust. They looked like the faces on the bodies we'd seen scattered around the street six years ago. But these figures were very much alive. One of the workmen explained it all to us. Terazzia was being remodeled. Some of the twists were being taken out of the roadway. The plaza in the center was being eliminated. The sidewalks were being made wider so the Corso crowds wouldn't overflow into the street. A whole forest of trees would be planted in two lines down each sidewalk so that promenading in the hot summer sun would be more pleasant. This was all part of the plan for a New Belgrade. The remodeling of Terazzia must all be finished by the end of the month because Yugoslavia was going to put on the biggest May Day parade in her whole history. That's why they were working twenty-four hours a day. Tonight they were blasting away some blocks of stone. That's what caused the noise. That's why the air was so full of rock dust. That's what made everybody in Terazzia look like a ghost. Some of the workmen were experts but most of the job was being done by volunteers. All sorts of people were giving a few hours a week. Even people from hundreds of miles away. As far away as Zagreb. College professors. Law students. High school boys and girls. Internes from hospitals. Clerks in government offices. Some of them had never held a shovel or pickax in their hands before. But they were having the time of their lives helping to turn an overgrown village into a modern city. That's what one of them told us.

The next night I had dinner with a Yugoslav lawyer and his family. I'd been to their home many times before. I'd cultivated their friendship because they were representatives of the dissatisfied percentage, whatever that percentage was. From them I got the opposition attitude toward what was going on. The father had been a corporation lawyer. Now there were no more private corporations. He didn't like it. He didn't like anything about the present system. Especially that there were no more private corporations. He passed his hatred on to the rest of the family. They talked very openly about it. They hated Tito. They hated his ministers. They hated the Youth Railroad. They hated everything about the New Yugoslavia, including the fact that there were no more private corporations. This night Iovanna was almost in tears at the dinner table. I didn't know why at first. But I found out as soon as I mentioned the explosions I'd heard early that morning in Terazzia. Iovanna was the oldest daughter. The students in her class at high school were giving two hours of their time tomorrow afternoon in Terazzia. They were going to shovel dirt and push wheelbarrows. Iovanna said she had never shoveled dirt or pushed a wheelbarrow before and she didn't see why she should start now. And right there in public, in front of everyone! It would be humiliating. She couldn't do it. Why did they have to start cutting up the city anyway? It was just more of this new regime foolishness. The whole family joined in the chorus. We didn't get off the subject the whole evening. I asked Iovanna what would happen if she didn't volunteer. Her mother looked at me as though I were crazy. Didn't I know what would happen? Didn't I know that the word "volunteer" was just an expression? Didn't I know that they had to do it whether they wanted to or not? What would happen? They'd tell me what would happen. It would simply mean that Iovanna would never get her high school diploma. Her teachers wouldn't give her passing grades. She'd be penalized the rest of the year in one way or another. Maybe the rest of her life. I asked Iovanna if she knew of any student who had not been graduated for that reason. She said no, because everyone always did volunteer. I said I thought she ought to make a guinea pig out of herself and stay away from Terazzia and see what would really happen. But Iovanna didn't think much of that suggestion.

The next afternoon I went around to Terazzia. The square was packed with high school students. Most of them were singing and laughing while they worked. There were a few who didn't look very happy. One of them was a tall girl with black hair who was more conspicuous than any of the others because she looked as if she would like to throw the shovel in her hands at the first person who came along. I tried to say hello to her. But she looked the other way. I felt very sorry for Iovanna.

One day Baum in the press department told me some of his experiences at the Paris Peace Conference. During the argument over Venezia Giulia and Trieste, the Italian delegate mentioned a tin mine in the area under dispute. He rattled off from a paper in his hand a lot of figures about the output, the annual revenue, the value of the ore. When he finished an assistant minister of foreign affairs for Yugoslavia by the name of Bebler said he would like to take exception to some of those figures. They weren't exactly accurate. For example, the annual output was so and so. The revenue from 1920 to 1930 had been so many million lire. He quoted a great many other figures without reference to any notes. When he sat down the Italian delegate asked him how he knew so much about the mine? How did he pull all those figures out of his head? Bebler smiled and said:

"My father was the owner of the factory which smelted the ore from, that mine."

I told Baum it might be interesting to meet the son of a wealthy industrialist who now was an important official of a state which had confiscated or nationalized most industry. So one day I had lunch with Ales Bebler, Assistant Minister of Foreign Affairs. It was a warm spring day. We drove to his home on the edge of the city in a sport car with a chauffeur and the top rolled down. A servant opened the door for us. We had cocktails on the terrace with his wife. She was young and beautiful. The luncheon was modest but excellent. The conversation was stimulating. Before we left his home Ales Bebler showed me a bicycle he'd brought back from New York in a plane with him a few months ago. It was for his son. His son had never had a bicycle. He was sure the boy was going to be very excited. And then I met his daughter, Jasna. The mother said Jasna means "clear" and "bright." The name fitted the little girl. She climbed all over her father's shoulders and reached up as if she were trying to pick stars out of the sky. In his library Ales Bebler showed me all the American books he'd brought back with him. And some paintings which had been done by two of Yugoslavia's best modern artists. On the way back to the center of the city he leaned back in the seat of his car and looked so contented with the world that I said it appeared that he had every ingredient for happiness. As soon as I said it the smile went from his face temporarily. Then very quietly, without any dramatics, he said:

"I think after twenty years I deserve some peace. I only hope it lasts a little while longer."

Then he told me in thumbnail fashion the story of his life. He was a student in the University of Ljubljana after the last war. He was, as Baum had told me, the son of a wealthy industrialist. But at the university he became interested in social problems. That led to an interest in labor unions. And in politics. And in trying to get some democracy for his own country. But the authorities got after him and he went to prison. He was in and out of prison a number of times. Finally he escaped to Russia. When the Spanish civil war started he volunteered. There was no chance to fight for democracy in his own country yet. But at least he could fight against the Fascism in Spain which threatened to spread like a sea of dirty oil over all of Europe. In Moscow he married a Russian girl. They were looking forward to the birth of their first child. But one month too soon orders came that he was to be smuggled immediately in a party of other volunteers by a devious route to the Spanish front. He left four weeks before his son was born. In Spain he was captured. For the next few years life for Ales Bebler was one prison after another. He was in prisons in Spain, Switzerland, and France. Finally he got back to his own country only to be put in prison again. When the coup d'état in Belgrade resulted in the flight of Yugoslavia's Fascist leaders, Ales Bebler was finally released. When the Partisan army was formed he went to the mountains and became one of the first officers on Marshal Tito's staff. The next five years were what those five years were for a lot of other Yugoslav patriots. Everyone knew about those years. His life was no different than the life of the others. A lot of fighting. A lot of suffering. Then in some roundabout way he heard that his Russian wife had divorced him and had married someone else. And so, just before the end of the war, Ales Bebler was married in the mountains between battles to a fellow Slovene, his present young and charming wife. Jasna, who always seems to be reaching for a star, is their baby.

Not many weeks ago the Vice Premier of Yugoslavia went to Moscow. He went there for a conference of foreign ministers, but he also held a conference with Bebler's first wife. The conference with the former Mrs. Bebler was more satisfactory than the one over the fate of Europe. They worked out an agreement by which the Bebler boy would spend his winters in Moscow and his summers in Yugoslavia. That was the explanation of the bicycle. Ales Bebler could hardly wait until he met his son for the first time. He hoped the boy would like the bicycle. He'd heard that the boy had never had a bicycle. Yes, of course he was happy. He had a lovely wife, a fairy-eyed daughter, a beautiful home, an automobile, books and pictures he loved, a government position which interested him, and now he was to have "half a son." Of course he was happy. But didn't I think that maybe he deserved a few of the rewards of the victory he had spent the best twenty years of his life fighting for?

Incidentally, he said, his home I had visited once belonged to a prominent Yugoslav who had collaborated with the Germans. When the Germans fled he fled with them. He'd never come back. So the government confiscated the place.

On the way to his office I said something about what I had seen in my tour of the country. I said that no one could deny the strides that Yugoslavia was making in a materialistic way, but that that was what bothered some people, the stress of materialism in the new Yugoslav way of life. Ales Bebler smiled. He said you can't do anything about the aesthetic, the intellectual, the cultural until you first deal with the materialistic. I must remember that this isn't the United States. I must remember that Yugoslavia has been a very backward Balkan country up to now. The first job was to rebuild what war destroyed. The second job was to raise the materialistic standards of the people. To get them well fed, well housed, well clothed. And then, he said, I'll tell you a little story to show what I mean. Members of the Federal Commission on Culture had recently told him that Yugoslavia must slow down her campaign against illiteracy. They said Yugoslavia was teaching people to read and write too rapidly. The anti-illiteracy campaign must move forward one step behind the electrification campaign. They said, if we make people literate before you give them electric lights in their homes they'll just ruin their eyes trying to read by candlelight.

When we got to his office the Assistant Minister of Foreign Affairs asked me to stay for a press conference he was about to hold. It was over the question of war criminals. He told nearly fifty assembled reporters that it had been Yugoslavia's desire to co-operate with her wartime allies in the arrest, extradition, and trial of the men responsible for the atrocities committed in Yugoslavia. But instead of co-operation, Britain and America were fostering in countries outside Yugoslavia's frontiers the formation of organizations which were openly trying to incite a new war among the old allies and trying to wreck the United Nations. Two years ago Yugoslavia had submitted to Britain and America three lists of war criminals. There were nine hundred and fifty names on the lists. After two years the Western Allies had approved the extradition to Yugoslavia for trial of only two hundred of that number. And of the two hundred only fifty-nine had been turned over to Yugoslavia.

Some of the most notorious of the war criminals were being allowed to move freely about Italy, Austria, and Germany. Some were even being allowed to organize anti-Yugoslav military units. Some had sneaked back into the country to try to foment a counterrevolution. He said the activities of these men and their terrorist organizations were not a serious danger to peace but they were a serious danger to peaceful relations among former allies. He told how in Austria one American camp commander had prohibited the circulation of newsreels of the New Yugoslavia and a newspaper which attempted to tell the truth to imprisoned Yugoslavs about what was happening in their own country. He used the expression "iron curtain."

He spoke of the killing of the Yugoslav consul who went into a British camp in Italy on a visit. Bebler said London had informed Belgrade that London was very sorry that the Chetniks who had done the killing hadn't yet been identified by the British. He said it was strange that the British guards who were present hadn't been able to catch a single one of the killers by the sleeve. He said everyone in the camp knew the names of the guilty men. In fact, Belgrade had submitted the names of the eight men to London. But there had been no action from London except "regrets." He said not one single Italian war criminal had been turned over. The British and Americans had been taking statements from the most notorious of the war criminals and then releasing them. We had also allowed many to escape overseas to places like Argentina.

One American correspondent asked if Yugoslavia considered men traitors who had merely expressed opposition to the new regime vocally. Bebler replied that the Yugoslav Government's attitude has always been that mistakes of the past made by people who were under the influence of the invader should be forgotten. Accordingly two amnesties had been announced. They covered the majority of Yugoslavs now abroad. The majority could come home without the slightest fear. But Yugoslavia did insist on trying the nine hundred and fifty ringleaders not only because of their war crimes but because now they were trying to incite thousands of other Yugoslavs abroad by telling them they would all be hanged if they went home. He said Yugoslavia was trying to make it possible for most of the Yugoslavs abroad to take up their lives again where they left them at the start of the war, but Yugoslavia's opponents were picturing the regime as vengeful, terroristic.

In Belgrade I had lunch with Harriett Scantland and Jake Hoptner. They were packing for a holiday trip around the country and then they were going home to America. Jake's work as American Red Cross representative was finished and Harriett had had enough of her U.S.I.S. library work under Belgrade conditions. Over coffee Harriett mentioned one thing that bothered her. Yugoslavia had adopted a point system. Honors, rewards, and promotions were handed out very much as the Boy Scouts hand out merit badges. One point of credit was given for attending an educational motion picture. One point for reading an educational book. Harriett thought that that was all right, except that Yugoslavia, she said, was pushing people too hard. For example, just last night she had seen a young Yugoslav sitting in a movie house reading a book by flashlight. Trying to get two points of credit at the same time.

In Belgrade I found out what had happened to one more character in the old drama of Yugoslavia. For years before the war the permanent Belgrade correspondent for the Associated Press had been Max Merzljak. Max was an Aryan Serb. His wife was Jewish. They were in their forties but Max loved his wife with the intensity and passion of a youngster of twenty. When I took over the Belgrade story for the A.P. in the spring of '41 Max served as my "tipster." He helped me chase down rumors, verify vague reports, and keep abreast of what was happening. He was a good reporter. The last time I talked to Max was about four-thirty on the morning of Bloody Sunday. The Berlin A.P. office had suggested by phone that I stay up all night listening to "some very fine music" which they said Berlin Radio would be broadcasting that night. I thought I knew what they were trying to tell me. So I did. It was at just four-thirty that I heard Ribbentrop's unpleasant voice interrupt the music. I got Max on the phone and asked him to turn on his radio and listen, too, because I didn't understand enough German to know what the Nazi foreign minister was announcing. Max was so excited that I had trouble getting his translation. His radio and mine were both making an awful din. But what I understood him to be repeating, over and over again, louder and louder each time, sounded like this:

"War! War! War is here, St. John! War, I tell you! Hitler says it. Hitler tells his army to march. Ribbentrop reads the order. They march against Yugoslavia. Against Greece. I see you at the Srpski Kralj when I dress. Maybe one hour. Maybe sooner. My God, it is awful!"

Then he hung up. A little while later the Nazi planes started coming. But Max never came. I never saw him again. I never heard his voice again. He could have made the Srpski Kralj Hotel before it began burning and we all deserted the place. He could have made it easily even if he had taken one hour to dress. But I never saw him again. Once during the war I heard from an underground source that Max had turned collaborator. I couldn't believe it. Not Max, with a Jewish wife! But in Belgrade in the spring of '47 I confirmed it. Max Merzljak was now in prison somewhere in the north, probably in Zagreb, serving a twenty-year term as a collaborator. The minute the Nazis arrived in the capital of the Serbs, the Croats, and the Slovenes, Max presented himself to them and offered his services. The Nazis welcomed his co-operation and appointed him Belgrade correspondent for one of the German news agencies. As a collaborator he was lucky the Tito government hadn't executed him. Instead he was in prison. He would probably die in prison. Twenty years is a long time for a man in middle life. The story can be dismissed with a couple of shakes of the head. Too bad. He was a nice fellow. But the story can't be dismissed with a couple shakes of the head. Max was more than a "nice fellow." Max had one consuming interest in life. He had one passion. The love of his wife. Max once told me, the day he took me home to meet Mrs. Merzljak, that he would do anything for her. Anything. He did. He made almost the supreme sacrifice. It might be the supreme sacrifice yet. He knew that as a Jew his wife would be subjected to the worst torture the Nazis had in their bag of tricks. Especially because she was the Jewish wife of the correspondent for a news agency of one of the "decadent democracies." How could he save her? So he made the deal. He would collaborate if they would let Mrs. Merzljak alone. It must have been a terrible decision for Max to have made, because I think he hated all that the Nazis stood for as much as the rest of us did. He held half-a-dozen university degrees. He'd written books in three or four languages. He couldn't have subscribed to the doctrines of Hitler. Especially not with a Jewish wife. But he had that love "which passeth human understanding." And so he collaborated. And so now he's spending twenty years behind bars. And his Jewish wife for whom he did it lives, they told me, close by the prison so she can send him food and messages of hope and love. No. The story of Max Merzljak can't be dismissed with a couple shakes of the head.

On the night of April the thirtieth thousands of workmen put the finishing touches to Terazzia. The voluntary laborers had done an amazing job. Here was the new heart of the new Belgrade which was going to rise out of the ashes of the old. Tonight it was floodlighted while a few more silk banners were put up, the last of the trees planted, the loud-speakers tested, the final preparations made for the great tomorrow. Few people were sleeping in Belgrade on the night of April the thirtieth. Around Terazzia people couldn't sleep even if they wanted to. The engineers, with a typically Balkan insensitivity to noise, had the loud-speakers turned up until the sound waves literally seemed to be pounding holes in your brain. Walking under one of them I suddenly thought of E. B. White and his story about the little hotel clerk from Uruguay who went to New York to attend a convention. As he was going through Times Square he passed a sound truck which was blaring forth music. The man at the controls had apparently gone to sleep. The volume was ten times what it should have been. Out of the loud-speaker came the voice of a young man singing a love song. "Thanks for all the lovely dee-light I found in your embrace. . . . And thanks for unforgettable nights I never can replace." As the hotel clerk passed the loud-speaker he went temporarily insane. Just for a moment. Just until he got out of the direct range of "unforgettable nights." A few minutes later, thinking over what had happened, he got an idea. He rushed back to his room, packed his grip, took the next plane for Uruguay, and sought an immediate audience with his government. He had, he explained, a foolproof idea by which Uruguay could conquer the world. Equip a squadron of radio-controlled planes with electric phonographs playing "Thanks for unforgettable nights I never can replace." Send the planes over foreign territories with their loud-speakers stepped up one hundred and fifty thousand times. Wherever they went the population would be reduced to insanity. Then Uruguay, at her leisure, could send in her armies, subdue the idiots, and annex the land. In Mr. White's story the idea worked. There were two or three short passages in the satire I thought of on the night of April the thirtieth as I went through Terazzia trying not to go crazy from the noise coming from the loud-speakers. When Uruguay decides to conquer the world by noise Mr. White says: ". . . although there was nothing in history to indicate that a large country is any happier than a small one." After it was all over, "life went on much as before, except that it was more secure, sanity being gone." And then the climax of the story. "It wasn't until years later, when the descendants of some early American idiots grew up and regained their senses, that there was a wholesale return of sanity to the world, land and sea forces were restored to fighting strength, and the avenging struggle was begun which eventually involved all the races of the world, crushed Uruguay, and destroyed mankind without a trace."

Chapter Seventy-Seven

MAY DAY ISN'T ONLY BASKETS

WHEN I met Belgrade's American correspondents on May Day morning they were all looking very unhappy. So were their wives. There'd been a party the night before and they were planning to sleep until just before the start of the parade. But on the dot of 6 A.M. there had been a rap on each of their doors. Gendarmes explained that this was May Day. The reviewing stand was within sight of their front windows. Therefore it would be necessary for them to evacuate their hotel suites. In every window in every building facing Terazzia a guard was to be stationed. A guard with a gun. The guards would remain at their posts until the parade was over and Marshal Tito and his cabinet and the foreign diplomats left the reviewing stand. The Brandels, who represented the New York *Times* and U.P., were especially embarrassed because they had been boasting for days how comfortable they were going to be watching the parade from the balcony of their hotel room. They'd even invited a few friends to share the balcony with them. Now they were going to have to stand out in the hot sun. I told them they should have remembered the story of what happened to Lovett Edwards, the British correspondent, on his wedding night. His marriage to Bosa took place in Belgrade. The Anglo-American diplomatic-journalistic colony helped them celebrate with a big party. It lasted until the small hours of the morning. Because of Lovett's journalistic duties no honeymoon was possible and so when the party finally broke up about dawn the gray-haired bridegroom and his fair young bride went to their new home, a suite of hotel rooms facing Terazzia. They were just getting to bed when a gendarme appeared at their door and informed them that he had instructions to station himself at their front bedroom window for the next five or six hours. Later in the morning a parade was to pass through Terazzia. The reviewing stand was just under their windows. The government didn't suspect Mr. Edwards. Guards were being stationed at all windows facing on Terazzia. It would not be necessary for Mr. and Mrs. Edwards to leave their suite. But they must not approach the windows. Lovett argued. He explained that this was his bride. He explained that they had just been married. This was their wedding night, even if it was morning. The guard said he understood perfectly. He was very sympathetic. He couldn't disobey orders, but he would promise to keep his back turned.

On the stroke of 9 A.M. on May Day Marshal Tito arrived in Terazzia in a limousine which had been presented to him during the war by the

American Government. The parade started exactly on time. It lasted until two-forty. Nearly six hours. I don't know if any of the correspondents found out how many people marched by the reviewing stand in those six hours. But there were tens of thousands of them anyway. The parade didn't make much sense from the American point of view because there were many times the number participating than witnessing the event. But eastern Europeans are like that. We Americans pack ten thousand people into a stadium to watch eighteen men play baseball, or twenty-two men wrestle with one another in a football match. But in eastern Europe there are generally more people taking part in a sports program than there are spectators. And the same with parades. Anyway, this parade lasted six hours and that was five hours too long for most of the ambassadors and ministers who had to stand in the reviewing box with Marshal Tito. Unless they wanted to violate protocol and insult the Yugoslav Government. The word "stand" isn't a figure of speech. There were no chairs that I could see on the platform. Marshal Tito obviously didn't want one. He was too interested in the procession going by to sit down. But not many of the diplomats seemed that interested. Most of them looked as if they very much wanted to sit down. Or, better yet, to escape from this ordeal and get home to a shower bath and a glass of something cool and refreshing. I didn't blame them. I felt sorry for them every time I sneaked off from the press box with the Fursts or the Brandels and went down a side street and sat in a kafana drinking cold beer before going back and watching some more. The diplomats couldn't do that. That's the price they were paying today for the prestige of being diplomats instead of foreign correspondents. The only one of them who had been smart was the British Ambassador, Charles Peck. He'd brought along one of those canes you can sit on which the English call a "shooting stick."

I think I was the first foreign correspondent who had arrived in Yugoslavia during or after the war without immediately pulling strings to obtain a personal, exclusive interview with Marshal Tito. Most of the others had obtained personal, exclusive interviews. As with Franklin Delano Roosevelt, Tito had impressed and charmed most of the men and women who interviewed him. Even those who thought that everything he stood for was anathema. I didn't pass up the opportunity to interview Tito just to be different. I did it as a matter of principle. I hadn't come to find out what Tito thought, or how he lived, or what his hopes, fears, dreams, and aspirations were. I'd come to find out those things about the fifteen million people who called Tito *druge,* comrade. But now I was leaving Belgrade. My work in this part of the country was over. I still had the republic of Slovenia to cover. But I wouldn't be coming back to Belgrade. It was in accordance with all the rules of dramaturgy that I leave now. My story of Belgrade had begun with the coup d'état when crowds jammed Terazzia to celebrate the overthrow of their native Fascist rulers. And then that other day when the story again centered around Terazzia and its dead bodies. My story of the New Yugoslavia should end here. Just as those

other scenes were symbolic and symptomatic, so was this May Day celebration. Out there in the street people from all six of the Yugoslav republics and the two semi-autonomous states were parading by. They were
showing the world a preview of the New Yugoslavia of 1952. If the world
would only open its eyes and look. As soon as the parade was over I'd pack
up and go north. But during these six hours I had a perfect opportunity
to study this man on the platform. He was just a few feet away from the
spot assigned to me for the day. This was better than any exclusive five-
minute interview with him. He was being himself here today. As I studied
him he struck me as a small boy, watching a circus parading by. His eyes
were that bright. He was that excited about everything he saw. He waved
to groups of factory workers and men doing gymnastics on top of a truck
and peasants doing their Bosnian dances. He waved at them with the excitement of a youngster waving to clowns and circus elephants. Someday
someone might want a physical description of him so I wrote in my notebook: "About five feet ten inches tall. Broad shoulders. Much fatter than
the one hundred and seventy pounds they said he weighed during the
war. Considerable of a 'corporation,' as we sometimes call it in America,
even though corporations are things of the past, in a literal sense, here in
Yugoslavia. Firm jaw. Bright eyes. Simple uniform with one or two
decorations." This was the man who was almost worshiped by an un-
determined percentage of the fifteen million Yugoslavs. Once a Croatian
metalworker he served in the Austro-Hungarian army in World War I,
until he deserted to the side of the Russian Czar because he didn't believe
in what the Austrians were fighting for. This was the man who developed
a hatred of what the Russian Czar stood for when he saw six hundred
men executed on the Czar's orders because they had engaged in a labor-
union strike. This was the man who returned after World War I to his
own country and tried to work for the betterment of labor conditions in
Yugoslavia, only to be thrown into prison for five years and frequently
tortured. This was the man who spent some time in Russia after his release from Yugoslav prisons, but was on hand, when the Royal Yugoslav
Army collapsed, to organize a force which grew into this we were seeing
in the parade before us. No wonder his eyes sparkled and he acted like a
little boy seeing his first circus procession. This pageant of the reconstruction passing before our eyes was the culmination of all his dreams and
aspirations. The New Yugoslavia, whatever the governments of these
diplomats clustered around him might think of it, was largely his creation.
Just as the accomplishments of the Partisans in the mountains had been
largely a result of his inspiration.

Some tractors went by. Peter Furst leaned over and said I should notice
that there was an American flag painted on some of them and that all of
them bore the letters UNRRA where everyone could see them. Also that
all the trucks had their American makers' names on them. Furst said it
would have been very easy to have painted them out. For six hours, except
when I was down a side street in a kafana trying to escape the heat which

was already of summer intensity even though it was only May, I kept an eye out for signs of militarism. That's one complaint that came from abroad about this new country. It was so militaristic. But not today. This was May Day. The workers' day. The army, the navy, and the air force weren't in the picture today. There was one plane overhead. But we could see that it was there for photographic not militaristic purposes. Down in the street there was just one warlike touch in the six hours. Group Number 48 represented the youth of Yugoslavia. Each child in Group Number 48 carried a four-foot pencil the way a soldier would carry a spear and a two-foot papier-mâché book as a shield. They were called "Soldiers Against Ignorance." There were sixty-five groups in the line of march. They represented fishermen from Dalmatia, peasant cattlebreeders from South Serbia, tobacco growers from Macedonia, colonists from the Vojvodina, horsemen from the mountains of Cernagora, workers on the Youth Railroad in Bosnia, displaced persons from Venezia Giulia and Istria, opera singers from Zagreb in Croatia, shepherds from the hills of Slovenia. Husky young men and women did acrobatics on moving trucks. Peasants danced their way down the street. Choral groups sang. Bands played. It was a gay, happy celebration. As I listened and watched I thought of a dispatch from New York I had read the night before. It told how members of a large religious denomination in the United States had been asked to pray for the people of Yugoslavia and other nations "behind the Iron Curtain" who were described in the call to prayer as victims of evil persecution, living in constant terror. The tens of thousands of paraders were from every section of the country and they represented every religious group, every nationality, every way of life. But especially this was industry's day. All the principal industries, trades, and professions had delegations of marchers or floats. In five years this peasant agricultural Balkan country was going to startle the world with the results of her industrial revolution. That's what most of the posters they carried said. The Five-Year Plan. There was a five-year plan for every industry. Every industry had its goal. Double the production of tractors each year. Triple the electric-power output. Quadruple this and quintuple that. Industry was going to vie with industry to see which could stride forward the fastest. The race was on. Yugoslavia henceforth would produce her own agricultural machinery. Her own trucks and automobiles. Her own railroad locomotives and baby carriages. In five years Yugoslavia would be Balkan only geographically. She would be agricultural only partially. She would be completely industrialized like any Western nation. That's what this procession was all about. The war was over. The reconstruction was "under the belt." Now for the future! And on May Day, 1947, the world, as well as Yugoslavia, got a glimpse of the future that was being planned. Only there were those who dozed and didn't see.

PART FOURTEEN

These Are the Slovenes

Chapter Seventy-Eight

MORE WEST THAN EAST

SLOVENIA and Montenegro are the smallest of the six Yugoslav republics. But that's about all they have in common. Montenegro, in the far south, is a land of bare black mountains in which life has always been grim and the standard of living as low as anywhere in the Balkans. Slovenia, in the far north, is a land of green hills and rich, fertile valleys in which the standard of living has always been as high as anywhere in southeastern Europe. Montenegro down through the ages has always maintained her independence, even defying for five hundred years the attempts of the

Turkish sultans to subjugate her. Slovenia, until the Partisan liberation, never knew what the word "independence" really meant.

Montenegro and Slovenia each has a distinctive culture. But they're poles apart. Even though the people of both sections are Slavs. The illiteracy rate in Montenegro has always been high. People engaged in a constant struggle to keep alive have little time for things of the mind. The illiteracy rate in Slovenia has always been low, about five per cent, for Slovenia was bathed by the culture of the Austro-Hungarian Empire of which she was so long a part.

In Slovenia they have always read books by British, French, and American authors. They know about Picasso, Gertrude Stein, *Studs Lonigan,* Gershwin, Margaret Sanger, Bing Crosby, T.V.A., and the theory of relativity. They have had their own theater, music academy, and art galleries. Their intellectuals have studied abroad. They fill teeth with porcelain instead of silver or gold. The peasants think the native costumes their grandmothers handed down to them are nice, but they wear them only on national holidays and dress most of the time like Kansas farm people. Foreigners don't frighten them because foreigners have used the mountains of Slovenia as a vacation ground since there have been methods of transportation to get them here. They have their own songs and dances but they are quiet, studied, and rhythmic in the Western manner. They breathe no savage defiance.

The only time the Slovenians ever saw the Turks, during the centuries the Turks were occupying southeastern Europe, was when they made an occasional plundering raid. Antiques of great age can be found in the homes and museums of Slovenia.

The Slovenes have their own language. People from South Serbia, Bosnia, Croatia, and Macedonia can learn it in a short time, for there's a common base to all these Yugoslav tongues, but the language the Slovenes speak is softer and the vocabulary is full of a great many more nuances.

The homes of Slovenia are clean and neat. "Bathroom manners" here are better. Running water is no mystery to them. They cut their bread thin. Even though they do indulge in the all-European habit of using toothpicks at the table they try to hide the ugly operation with a napkin or the palm of the left hand.

The women of Slovenia are attractive, although they don't have the charm of the girls of the Konavlje with their wasp waists and broad hips. The men are tall, handsome, and strong, although they don't have the fire of the men of Cernagora.

For people who have never been in the Balkans before, and would be shocked by the manners and customs, Slovenia is the best place to begin to know them. It's a transition ground. There are no corner drugstores selling malted milks and no hot-dog stands, but here West begins to melt gradually into East.

In a sentence, Slovenia is different from the rest of Yugoslavia. But the experiences Slovenia had in the war were little different. Slovenia had her native Fascists and her full share of Quislings. The clerical party was of great aid to the Nazis and there were even bishops and priests who went in for 100 per cent collaboration. So much so that Hitler didn't even have to make any pretense of giving Slovenia independence as he did Croatia. He simply annexed Slovenia to the greater Third Reich. But there were many among Slovenia's million, two hundred thousand who hungered as much as the rest of the Yugoslavs for that freedom they had always been denied. They flocked to the mountains just as the Cernagorans did. Their villages supported the Partisans.

When national liberation committees were formed and elections were held under the eyes of the occupiers, 80 per cent of the total Slovenian electorate voted, in September of '43, and the next month a congress of Slovene deputies was held with nearly six hundred duly-elected delegates attending.

The price Slovenia paid for this defiance was the same as the price that was paid in the other republics. Burned villages. Hostages taken at night from their homes to be shot in cold blood. Massacres and atrocities. Next to Bosnia and Cernagora, Slovenia was the most enemy-destroyed of the Yugoslav republics. Lidice? They had four hundred Lidices in Slovenia alone. Four hundred villages wiped off the map.

Slovenia is high mountains like Triglav, which means "The Three-Headed One." Every year thousands of people try to climb to Triglav's snow-crowned peak. Some each year get killed on Triglav's treacherous sides, for Triglav doesn't welcome casual guests. She makes people prove their worth before she permits them to sit on her head and look out over the world. Some get part way up and decide it isn't worth the effort. A few each year come back exhausted but with star-shaped edelweiss flowers under their hatbands to prove that they made it. To prove that they got to the very top of this nine-thousand-three-hundred-and-seventy-three-foot peak. They come back with tales they tell in awed whispers of how, just before you reach the summit, you go through fields so covered with delicate spring flowers in July that even a man who never realized he had a soul gets a feeling deep inside him that he can't explain in words.

Slovenia is peaceful valleys like the valley of the Sava in which life is soft and pleasant compared with the life most Balkan peasants live. There are other valleys in Europe like those in Slovenia, but nowhere else in the world will you see one thing they have here. They call it a *Kozolec* or "drying rack" and that's all it really is. A rack for the drying of grain between harvesting and thrashing seasons. Just a line of wooden poles stretched between three or four uprights with a roof over them. The sheaves of wheat or oats or barley are laid across the poles so that their golden heads point to the hot afternoon sun. The peaked roof protects them from the worst of sudden summer rains. Maybe you can't imagine lines of poles twenty or thirty feet long by ten or fifteen feet high, with little roofs over them, being objects of architectural and aesthetic beauty.

But they are. They are unique because no other farmers in the world, as far as Slovenia knows, build drying racks like these. They blend in with the landscape because they are endemic. They are made from trees cut on the mountain slopes. Their architectural charm stems from the fact that no matter how stupid and cloddish you may think the peasants who put them up, their proportions are always perfect. The ratio of height to length, the angle of the roof, the pitch . . . No architect over a drawing board could improve them. They form a unit with house and barns, because they follow faithfully the angles and proportions of these other structures which dot the valleys of the countryside.

Slovenia is mountain towns like Golo, which was burned down twice by the Germans and still is a mess of charred timbers and dirty rubble.

Slovenia is hilltop castles like the one in the village of Turjak which was fought over for eight days until its walls were like that many pieces of Swiss cheese.

Slovenia is beauty and poverty often dwelling side by side without realizing what strange bedfellows they make.

Slovenia is all those things and many others. But Slovenia is principally people. One million, two hundred thousand of them, each with a story to tell of what was, and is, and maybe someday will be.

Ljubljana is the capital of Slovenia. (You ignore the first "j" and pronounce the second as if it were an "i.") In Ljubljana the Grand Union Hotel is where most people stop. The desk clerk speaks French. Some of the chambermaids understand a little English. It's probable that you'll acquire a few fleas in the Grand Union Hotel, and the cockroaches in the bedrooms may bother you. But the management will apologize profusely and explain that people from other parts of Yugoslavia bring them in, in their luggage, and then they'll sprinkle some yellow powder around your room which will seem to increase rather than decrease the number of your fellow guests.

In the restaurant of the Grand Union Hotel I had trouble figuring out the menu until a young waiter said that if I spoke English perhaps he could help me. His English was excellent. He spoke with an American rather than a British accent. At the end of the meal he asked me where I was from. When I said "New York" he drew himself up to his full five feet six inches and very proudly said he, too, had been in New York. In fact, there was little of America he didn't know. New York, California, Nevada, New Jersey, Chicago. He'd been all over America. And only two years ago too. I said how was that? He hung his head a moment and then . . . "I was one of your prisoners of war. When the Germans took over my part of Slovenia they drafted me into their army. I didn't want to go but I had to." They treated him all right in America, he said. Of course they made him work as he'd never worked before. Picking cotton in the South. Digging potatoes. Picking berries. Digging ditches. Working in a laundry. There was hardly anything he hadn't done. Then he smiled again and said, "But I learned English pretty good, didn't I?"

Did he have any trouble getting back to Yugoslavia because he'd fought for the Germans? No. No trouble at all. The Yugoslavs knew he hadn't fought because he wanted to. Of course he did have some trouble in France. In France they took away everything he'd collected while he was in America. Cigarettes. Food. Souvenirs. Everything. He didn't like the French.

When I offered him a package of American cigarettes his eyes twinkled. He couldn't smoke now that he was on duty, but later . . . "I miss your cigarettes. I guess—it'll sound funny to you maybe. But I guess I was getting to be a little bit of an American." Then he laughed to hide his embarrassment. "Funny, isn't it?"

It's four hours by slow train from Ljubljana to the railroad stop called Bohinjska Bistrica. That's counting an hour's layover at Jesenice. At Jesenice I saw a workman six feet and a few inches tall, at least two hundred and fifty pounds in weight, in greasy overalls, with hands as large as baseball gloves. He looked like a railroad laborer, or maybe a locomotive fireman, on his way home from work. In one of his tremendous hands he carried a small bunch of wild lilies of the valley.

It's only four miles from Bohinjska Bistrica to Bohinjska Bistrica Jezero. The "Jezero" part means "on the lake." It takes a full twenty minutes to make the trip by station taxi because the station taxi is a 1929 Buick touring car. It takes longer than twenty minutes if rain clouds suddenly come down from the mountains and the driver has to stop and put up the collapsible top. In 1929 they hadn't yet heard of one-man tops. All the passengers have to help. The 1929 Buick has a rubber-bulb horn. Everyone in the valley recognizes the noise it makes. They like it because it's been a familiar sound to them for nearly twenty years. It's an indication that life is flowing on, unchanged and unchangeable again, after the interruption of war. The 1929 Buick seldom breaks down. That may be because the driver has a rule he adheres to with almost religious fervor. He never drives more than fifteen miles an hour. Never has. Not even if it means someone's going to miss a train. And missing a train is serious business because only two or three trains a day disturb the peace of this valley surrounded by the peaks of the Austro-Italian-Yugoslav Alps.

The Hotel Bellevue has a sign by the road which circles the lake saying it's only a five-minute walk up the hill to the hotel. At some points the path goes up at a fifty-degree angle. No one, not even veteran mountain climbers, has ever been able to make it in anything less than seven minutes. But it's worth the climb getting there. Halfway up there's a shrine to the Virgin Mary with a light burning in it day and night. People stop to pick flowers along the path and leave them on the altar of the shrine. Or to pull a rope which rings a bell on top of the shrine. The sound of the bell bounces back and forth against the stone sides of the mountains and echoes up and down through the valley. The religious people of Bohinjska Bistrica Jezero like bells. There's a church at the head of the lake with a wood-carved head of Saint John on the altar. The bell in the tower of that church rings at frequent intervals, day and night. But a few years ago there were men here who didn't respect the religion of these country people. They took an ax to the head of the Virgin in the shrine halfway up the hill. Lately a new head has been attached so carefully that no one would ever know what happened unless the story was told.

Near the church there are a few piles of brick and mortar. It's hard to believe it when they tell you that this used to be one of the largest hotels in all Slovenia. Bohinjska Bistrica Jezero's visitors burned it when they fled home to the north. They burned a lot of other places. They'd enjoyed the valley but they didn't want anyone else to enjoy it after they left. That's another one of their ambitions that failed of realization. In the summertime, now as before, thousands of people from Ljubljana and farther parts, some even from England and America, come here to rest, or swim, or mountain climb. For city people who are soft there are plenty of little mountains with nobody to bother you but cows at pasture. Each cow has a bell around its neck. There's nothing unusual about that. Farmers everywhere put bells around the necks of cattle to keep track of where they wander. But here the bell around the neck of each cow in the herd has a different pitch. The result is a xylophone concert with no intermissions.

In May there were only a few guests at the Hotel Bellevue in Bohinjska Bistrica Jezero. Because it was still chilly we were served our meals in a small, intimate room with a porcelain stove in one corner. After four or five days I was getting a little tired of the silence which language barriers imposed. In four or five days the only words I'd spoken were *dobro jutro* to each of my fellow guests each morning, *dobar dan* to each of them at luncheon, and *dobro veče* at dinnertime.

Occasionally I met an intelligent-looking young woman in the hallways in the evening and wished her good night and a pleasant sleep with those two onomatopoeic words *laku noč*, which are common all over Yugoslavia. It was either the fourth or fifth day that two things happened simultaneously. At luncheon I noticed that the intelligent-looking young woman had a package of Chesterfields beside her plate at the table. And when I said dobar dan, instead of replying dobar dan as she always had before, she said, "And how are you this morning?" I took three or four steps while I wondered how a Slovenian girl got Chesterfields and whether she'd trade me a Chesterfield for one of my Yugoslav cigarettes, and whether I knew enough Slovenian words to ask her, before it dawned that she had spoken to me in English. Then she laughed. And then she said she was a Canadian from Winnipeg, and worked for UNRRA in Belgrade, and how did I like Bohinjska Bistrica Jezero? She hadn't broken the monosyllabic spell before because she'd been having so much fun for four or five days listening to me struggling in Serbo-Croat with the Slovenian waiter. She'd even made little bets with herself about what I'd get when I asked for water, more gravy, or plums instead of apples for dessert.

Then she told me a story about something that had happened to her in Trieste which she thought was significant. She'd been there one day when the Yugoslavs of Venezia Giulia were holding a parade of protest against the British attitude toward Yugoslav claims to that territory. After the parade was over, going down one of the main streets, she passed a demonstrator who had been carrying a large banner in the procession. Now that the parade was over he'd leaned the banner against a lamppost while he fumbled through his pockets for a match to light a cigarette. The Canadian girl saw he wasn't having any success so she stopped and offered him the use of her lighter. When the man discovered she was British he forgot all about his cigarette. He wanted to talk to her. What was London like during the blitz? Did she know any men of the RAF? Had she ever seen a Spitfire? Nice little planes, the Spits. They talked for a considerable time and he insisted on shaking hands with her when they separated. As he picked up his banner to go his way, she glanced at it for the first time. In Slovenian it said:

"DOWN WITH THE BRITISH TYRANTS!"

For many weeks I went from the rich valleys to the mountaintops looking for half-a-dozen people whose life stories and whose hopes and fears and dreams would best illustrate Slovenia. From the paved streets of Ljubljana to the muddy paths that wind between peasant cottages. From university corridors to hayfields. From antique-filled summer villas to houses in which they used the same large kettle to boil potatoes, wash the baby, do the laundry, and stew a chicken. At last I found my half-dozen. Only they were seven. Call it a Slovenian baker's half-dozen. I was glad after I found them that I had put Slovenia last on my list of republics. The stories of these seven are the story of Slovenia. Perhaps they illustrate just as well the story of all the New Yugoslavia.

Chapter Seventy-Nine

WITHOUT PORTFOLIO

AFTER World War I one of the prime aims of the so-called "peacemakers" was to break up the Austro-Hungarian Empire. An incidental objective which they were finally argued into considering was the creation of a country of the South Slavs. That's what the word Yugoslavia means. And Yugoslavia is the country they finally did create. In so doing they furthered their primary object, for this new nation they brought into being included Croatia and Slovenia which had both been parts of Austria. But when they took their pencils and drew a line across the map of Europe and said "This is it," they left outside the frontiers of their brain-child country tens of thousands of Slav people.

As the new map was drawn, Yugoslavia came to a wedge-shaped point in the northwest. At the tip of that point Italy, Austria, and the new country all met. Just inside the wedge was mighty Triglav, looking down with the inscrutable wisdom of great mountains onto these childish goings-on of man. From the lake called Bohinjska Bistrica Jezero to the invisible line on a map it's only about ten kilometers, a little over five miles. Less distance than that farther on there's a village called Soča on the banks of a river by the same name. The people are Slavs. But for the whim of green-table mapmakers they would have been Yugoslavs instead of Italians by nationality after World War I. There at Soča, just as the nineteenth century was fading into the twentieth, Albert Rejec was born, an Austrian subject although his forebears had always been Slavs and had always spoken a language called Slovenian. Of course they drafted him as a boy to fight against his Slavic blood brothers in World War I. Maybe that's when the spirit of rebellion was born in him. He believed in nothing that "his side" was supposed to be fighting for. The victory of the Allies was his victory, although they'd made him carry an Austrian gun. When the talk of the formation of a Yugoslavia began Albert Rejec and all the other Slavs of Soča saw hope for release, at last, from the rule of foreigners. Orders from Vienna. Speak our language. Follow our customs. Sing our songs. Dance our dances. You're not what you think. You're Austrians. All that would be over now. Yugoslavia! The very word held promise of a better life and freedom.

For the rest of the Slovenes the new was in some ways as bad as the old. They were still a minority. One million, two hundred thousand people in a nation of fifteen million. They were ruled from distant Belgrade, the capital of the Serbs. Now they could sing Slavic songs and dance Slavic dances, but the freedom they'd dreamed of was a comparative thing. Their new masters, the Serbs, spoke a somewhat similar Slavic tongue, but Belgrade was as far away as Vienna. Figuratively, anyway.

Many of the Slovenes didn't think they had much, under this new arrangement, for anyone to envy. But the peasants of Soča envied them, for when the mapmakers around the green tables got all through with their doodling on pieces of white paper Soča was exactly eight kilometers, as a bird flies, outside the all-important line.

But there was worse news than that for the people of Soča. To the victor belongs the spoils. And so a piece of Slovenia was to be given to the Italians. And the piece included Soča.

Maybe that's when Albert Rejec started being a rebel. Anyway, for the next twenty-six years he knew no peace. For twenty-six years the mountains were more of a home to him than any house in any village or city. He roamed the mountains of Italy, Yugoslavia, Switzerland, France, Germany, and Austria. In all those twenty-six years of crossing and recrossing frontiers he never had a passport. Not a legal one. The mapmakers had made him an Italian citizen and the Italians wouldn't give him a passport to travel. But in those years he learned a thing or two about subterfuge and forgery. He got around all right.

In 1929 he managed to get to Ljubljana. Life was comparatively good there, for he was among his own people, the Slovenes. But when the Italians heard about it they sent a formal diplomatic protest to the government of King Alexander in Belgrade. Albert Rejec, the note said, was a disturbing international influence. Ljubljana was close to the Yugoslav-Italian frontier. He was probably trying to provoke border incidents. So King Alexander's government ordered Albert Rejec to get out of Ljubljana. He went to Belgrade and there became the correspondent for a number of anti-Fascist publications in Italy and Germany.

One day a strange little piece of news came across his newspaper desk. In Rome the Mussolini government had conducted a trial of five men accused of trying to foment trouble for the Mussolini government. One of the five had been tried *in absentia*. All five had been given the death penalty. The other four had already been executed. The other four were all good friends of Albert Rejec. The one condemned to death in absentia was Albert Rejec, Italian subject by order of the little mapmakers.

When the Germans and Austrians, along with their satellites, invaded Yugoslavia, Albert Rejec went quickly to the mountains he knew so well. He talks with modesty today, as all Partisan leaders do, about his life the next four or five years. But the records show that he used his journalistic talents for all they were worth. And there were times when he also used a gun. He says, "I'd been given a gun and told to fight many times before. This was the first time I fought for something I believed in."

That's all there is to the story of Albert Rejec. But there's more to the story of the village of Soča. After each war there are new conferences around green tables. Men argue again about lines on a map. Statisticians produce figures about minorities and majorities. Frontier incidents occur. Armies take over disputed territories. Irredentists arrange demonstrations. Men, women, and children carry banners in parades. Down with this. Up with that. We want freedom from our foreign masters. Death to the tyrants. And after all the shouting is over a new map is made. It satisfies some people who cheer their approval. But then there are new minorities that wonder what the future will hold for them.

The Slovenian village of Soča is one place where there's been some cheering lately, for Soča at last is going to be Yugoslav. The peasants of Soča will be able, now, to sing their Slovenian songs, and dance their Slovenian dances, and speak their Slovenian language without fear. Henceforth Ljubljana will be their capital instead of Rome. For Albert Rejec the new line on a map will mean that he'll be able someday soon to make a trip to Soča to see his three sisters without having to travel by night over lonely mountain trails with a forged passport in his pocket in case some Italian guard crosses his path, and a revolver in another pocket, in case the guard should question the passport and want him to take a trip to Rome so executioners could carry out that death sentence that was passed on him.

Chapter Eighty

"SORTA LIKE A SON"

WHEN Albert Rejec suggested a trip to the grotto of Postojnia because he said it was one of the greatest natural wonders in this part of the world I hesitated about going. A grotto was like a museum, an old church, or an art gallery. I tried to tell him that I was much more interested in people than in stalagmites and stalactites. But when he gave me a preview of the story of Ferenz Verbić and the gasoline explosion I didn't hesitate any longer. Postojnia is halfway between Ljubljana and Trieste. Like Soča it's a Slovenian place that was given to Italy after the last war. Also like Soča it's one of the places that the 1947 mapmakers decided to let Yugoslavia have. That means it's been in Zone B since the end of World War II, occupied by Yugoslav troops. Which in turn means that a foreigner can't go there without a special visa, just as if he were going into a foreign country. Rejec's car was driven by a pleasant young man, rather nondescript in appearance. Fellow passengers were John Roman, who works for the United Press in New York but was on a leave of absence to attend an international journalists' convention, and a California girl who said we could call her "Blossom" although that wasn't really her name.

On the way Albert Rejec, who speaks English as well as he does Italian, German, Russian, and French, which is nearly as well as he speaks Slovenian and Serbo-Croat, said this boy at the wheel was a story too. He'd be glad to interpret if I wanted to talk to him when we stopped along the way for lunch. The boy's father had been a drunkard and his mother hadn't been much good either. The family was large, but home conditions were so bad that one by one all the brothers and sisters left. But somewhere in their background there must have been an excellent blood strain. All of them were making something good out of their lives. And it was part of the New Yugoslav story because before the war they wouldn't have had a chance. Albert Rejec was in his middle forties. The chauffeur, Jaka Slajpah, was just twenty-seven. But between these two men there was a spirit of camaraderie which was good to see. It was difficult to tell which cared the more for the other. The relationship should have been that between employer and employee. But they called each other by their first names and each was always seeing to it that the other had a cigarette, a light, food, and drink. Jaka treated Albert Rejec like a father, never having had a father of his own, except on paper. And Albert Rejec, bachelor, treated the boy like a son, never having had a son, not even on paper.

When we stopped for lunch Jaka told about the recent years of his life with frequent spontaneous bursts of enthusiasm. He was fourteen years old and was already working as a mechanic in Ljubljana when the Axis invaded. The Italians were suspicious of him for some reason, so they arrested him and kept him in prison camps in Italy for nearly two years. When the Italian collapse came he went into the Partisans. He served for three years, first as a fighter with a gun and later as chauffeur for a mission of Russian Army officers. He got that deep scar on his hand one night when he and some others tried to blow up a German armored train.

But what Jaka really wanted to talk about was his wartime chauffeur's job. The head of the mission he drove around Italy was a Russian colonel. I didn't find out what attitude Jaka had toward Russians in general, but the colonel was his own private little tin god. The colonel was a physician. The colonel was more than that. He was a gentleman. He was like a father. In Rome he took Jaka along with him to visit the Vatican, museums, art galleries, and ancient ruins. Whenever they stopped anywhere for meals Jaka, having learned his place as a boy in a class society, tried to sneak out to the kitchen to eat with other menials. That made the colonel angry. The colonel always insisted that Jaka sit at the table right beside him. The boy told us, as he had luncheon with us, that he never really knew what that word "comrade" meant until he started driving for the colonel. The colonel gave him clothes and money, "and he made me feel like a man." Once Jaka got confidential with the colonel and told him about Ivana. Ivana was his girl. He'd known her for eight years. Ever since she was fifteen years old. He'd been in love with her most of those eight years. When the war ended he and Ivana were going to get married. In the meantime, knowing that he had been fighting in the hills with the Partisans, she became a Partisan underground worker back home.

When Jaka got to this part of his story he suddenly smiled, looked a bit embarrassed, and then went on. He said being confidential that way with the colonel had had a result he hadn't expected. Before that the colonel had never interfered with his private life, but after that the colonel would never let him go out with any Italian girls. Whenever he found out that Jaka had a date he'd just raise his eyebrows a bit and say, "What about Ivana?" and then the date would get canceled. The last time he drove the colonel was when he went to the airport in Rome to catch a plane for Moscow. It was on the way to the airport that the colonel suddenly offered to take Jaka home with him. "I guess I was going to be sorta like his son." But Jaka, after some hesitation, turned it down. "If it hadn't been for Ivana I would have gone. But the colonel didn't say anything about taking Ivana too."

Since then Jaka had driven Bulgarians, Czechs, Americans, and a lot of other foreigners. He had his own opinion of all of them. He liked Americans the best next to Russians. He had some difficulty explaining why. Finally he said it was because Americans are intelligent. They "understand things." When he was a fighter in the mountains he'd seen American ambulance planes come to get wounded Partisans and take them to hospitals in Italy. Each time the Americans gave the wounded Partisans cigarettes and candy. Once an American flier parachuted down from a burning plane into a fighting area. Jaka and several others went out into no-man's land to save him from being shot by the Germans. Jaka has never forgotten how he got rewarded for what he did that day. The American flier gave Jaka his cap and his electrically heated flying suit. The cap made Jaka feel very important when he wore it. The flying suit kept him warm all one winter when he was driving an open jeep.

This job as a chauffeur wasn't something he expected to do all his life. Oh no! Jaka had a lot of better ambitions. He was going to school in his spare time. He was also learning to use a typewriter. Maybe someday . . . And then he looked over at Albert Rejec and smiled. Albert Rejec smiled back understandingly. Maybe someday he'd learn enough to be a journalist and write articles on sheets of square white paper.

Chapter Eighty-One

FAITHFUL TO A PHENOMENON

IN THE northwest corner of Slovenia there's an eccentric river which begins in the mountains between Fiume (which the Yugoslavs call Rijeka) and Trieste (which the Yugoslavs call Trst). It's eccentric because it goes along like an ordinary, respectable river for some miles and then suddenly disappears and runs underground for a way. Then it comes to the surface and is a conventional river for a while, until it does its disappearing act again. As if to humor the river and as if to pretend that nobody knew the tricks it's playing, the Yugoslavs give it a different name each time it comes into sight. It starts out as the Pivka. Next time it comes to the surface it's called the Unec. When it approaches Ljubljana and then winds its way through the center of the Slovenian capital it's called the Ljubljanica.

In the year 1818 a Slovene, Luka Čeč by name, while wandering through the woods a mile or so from the town of Postojnia, fell through a hole in the ground. What he saw before he clambered out into the open again sent him back to town wild-eyed and jabbering like a lunatic. That's what the rest of the townspeople must have thought he'd become, until they took lights and went back and saw for themselves. The next year, 1819, the Postojnia Grotto was opened to the public. There is no record of how many people have seen its underground wonders since then, but Ferenz Verbić will tell you that in the forty-one years he's been a guide he's taken more than two million gaping spectators through. Yes, he knows, because he's kept track. Two million. Or maybe it's eight million. Let's see. The average has been two hundred thousand a year. Forty-one years. Yes, over eight million.

Of course he's been working around the grotto for more than forty-one years. That's just the time he's been a guide. He was born in '81. That makes him sixty-six years old. He started work here when he was a boy of fifteen. At first he just helped make new roads and do exploring. In 1906 they gave him a guide's uniform. Since 1925 he's been chief guide.

Before World War I he was working for the Austrians. Between the two wars for the Italians. When the Germans took over, after Italy surrendered, he worked for the Germans. But now he's happier than he's ever been because the wording over the entrance is in his native language. Now he's working for the Slovenes. Of course all this change of ownership has been confusing in a way. For example, the picture postal cards. That's a little side line that brings in quite a bit of money. The words on the postals used to be in German. Then the German words had to be crossed out and Italian words put on. And now the Italian words have also been crossed out and the description of the pictures is in Slovenian. But it's better this way. It's the way it ought to be. After all, he'd told us, hadn't he, that it was a Slovene who found the grotto in the first place?

People of just about every nationality in the world have let him show them through. Yes, even Chinese. Ferenz Verbić tells them what they're seeing in their own language generally. He speaks Russian, German, English, French, almost every language. But not Chinese. The Chinese people who come through just have to use their eyes. He learned Russian during World War I. The Austrians had forty or fifty Russian prisoners they didn't know what else to do with, so they sent them down to the grotto to build artificial tunnels and open up some new sections of the grotto that had been inaccessible before.

There were a few years during that World War when Ferenz Verbić had to leave his grotto. The Austrians gave him a gun and sent him off to fight the Allies. They didn't make him fight his fellow-Yugoslavs but he didn't like it anyway. He missed the stalagmites and the stalactites. He didn't like hearing that the Austrian Army was using his grotto as military headquarters for its fight against the Italians. But after he got back and this whole area was given over to the Italians a lot of other things happened he didn't like. For example, the Italians made him change his name. What's wrong with Verbić? It's a perfectly good Slovene name. But the Italians said if he was going to work here he'd have to have an Italian name. So for a quarter of a century everyone called him Verbi. Foolish business! Imagine a Slovene being called Verbi!

At the start of World War II the Italians made a big military hospital near the grotto. Thousands of soldiers who were wounded in Greece were sent here. Ferenz had to take them through four or five hundred at a time. Then, when Italy collapsed, the Germans took over. There were about two thousand Nazi soldiers in the Postojnia garrison. They didn't have much to do at first so they spent all their spare time wandering around the grotto. Of course Ferenz had to explain things to them. The only good thing about that period was that the Germans didn't try to give him a German name. And they didn't care whether he changed from Verbi back to Verbić. But then Partisans began to gather in the woods around Postojnia. The Germans weren't much interested in the grotto any more. They had to stay above ground worrying about what the Partisans were up to. Several times the Partisans made attacks on Postojnia.

It was in the month of March 1944 that a good friend came around to Ferenz Verbić's house one night and whispered that he was doing underground work for the Partisans, and Ferenz was a good Slovene and he must help too. The Partisans in the woods had one thing in particular they wanted from him. Was it true that the Germans had stored a lot of high-octane gasoline down in the grotto near the entrance? Yes, it was. How much? About one thousand two hundred barrels. And was it true that they had a lot of munitions hidden down there too? Yes. Yes, Ferenz could see what they had in mind, but what did they want him to do? The friend said nothing much. All they wanted was a map of the grotto. It was true, wasn't it, that besides the main entrance that everyone went through there was a place in the woods called the *Cerna Jama* (Black Hole) through which they could get into the grotto? Ferenz said that that was right but the Cerna Jama was well hidden, and even if someone got down through the hole there was a steel door, and even if they got through the steel door there was a wall of brick and cement that stood in the way. The underground Partisan worker said that that was all right. All they wanted was a map showing where the Cerna Jama was, and also showing the layout of the grotto itself.

When the old guide got to this part of his story he leaned back in his chair and had a long drink of Slovenian beer before going on. He said maybe we could imagine how he felt after that, every time he took people down into the grotto. How did he know when the Partisans were going to blow up the place? Could we imagine what went through his mind every time he passed those piles of oil drums and all the munitions? Yes, the last couple of weeks of March and the first three weeks of April were weeks he'd never forget. He guessed he lost a little weight then. But he tried not to let the Germans see that he was nervous because that might have spoiled the whole plan. What he kept wondering was why they were waiting.

On April 22, 1944, Ferenz Verbić, chief guide of the Postojnia Grotto, worked all day taking German soldiers through the underground labyrinth. He completed his last tour at 6 P.M., locked up the case in which he kept the picture postal cards, and walked the mile to his home. He had dinner with his wife and daughter, and they all went to bed at about ten o'clock. It was the smell of burning oil rather than the noise that woke him up shortly after midnight. He knew right away what had happened. He was glad that it had happened. He was especially glad that it had happened at night when he wasn't down there. But while he was getting dressed he wondered whether he'd have a job any more. Maybe the whole grotto was destroyed. And maybe somehow the Germans would find out that he'd had something to do with it.

When he got to the grotto thick black smoke and red tongues of fire were coming out of the entrance. And then there were noises. Every few minutes it sounded as if two armies were having an artillery duel down in the grotto. It wasn't safe for anyone to get too near because occasionally an oil barrel or a large piece of rock would come flying out the entrance as if it had wings. One barrel landed three hundred feet away from the entrance. The fire burned for six days and six nights. It was a long time after that before anyone could go down below. While the fire was still burning the German investigation began. Ferenz Verbić was one of the first men they sent for. A German captain whose name was Leer questioned him. The chief guide pretended he was very unhappy about the whole affair. He said it was a terrible shame. Anyway, the Germans never did find out that he was the one who supplied the Partisans with the map. The grotto was closed for two months. After that he went back to work as chief guide. He didn't know for sure, but he guessed that the reason he always kept his job, no matter what country owned the grotto, was because no one else knew as much as he did about it.

It was some time before Ferenz heard the Partisan side of the story. The story of how it was done. After they got his map they discovered that there was no guard at the place called Cerna Jama. And so on the night of April the twenty-second thirty Partisans armed with all the tools they'd need went down through the Cerna Jama, broke through the steel door, chopped a hole through the brick-and-cement wall, and then three demolition experts went about four miles through the tunnels until they came to the place where the gasoline and munitions were stored. The other twenty-seven men were posted as guards. Each one had an electric torch to guide the three experts back the way they had gone.

The plan was to set off the explosion with a British time bomb they'd brought with them. But the bomb was defective and didn't go off. The Partisans were prepared for that contingency. They took some of their tools and made a hole in the side of one of the fifty-gallon gasoline drums. Then they took a large handkerchief, tied a stone in it, soaked it with gasoline, lighted it, and threw it from a distance of about thirty feet into the river of gasoline which was running down the grotto corridor. Then all three of them ran like mad.

The first two reached a sharp bend in the corridor before the explosion went off. They were safe. They got to the Cerna Jama exit all right. But the third man was thrown to the ground by the force of the first explosion. The fall broke his lamp and it rolled into an underground lake. He was in the dark now, except for the red-black flames from the burning oil. He was barefooted because they'd all come barefooted. He knew there were places where he'd drop hundreds of feet against jagged rocks if he made a misstep. And he knew, after a few minutes, that he was alone in the grotto because they'd made an agreement that if anything happened to any one of them the rest were to go on. No use sacrificing twenty-nine lives for one.

Ferenz said that Rudy must have been awfully frightened. That was his name. Rudy. Ferenz knew him. He was from a village called Tolmin not very far away. Yes, he must have been terrified. The grotto is sort of a spooky place even when you go down with a guide and electric lights. The limestone formations have crazy shapes. You can see devils and prehistoric animals and ghosts and anything you've got an imagination to see. But alone down there with no light except the red from the fire . . . Well, Ferenz said he'd even be a little jittery.

Anyway Rudy got as far as the rock they all call Santa Claus because that's just what it looks like. Then he was too tired to go any farther. He stayed there until the next afternoon. The next afternoon he heard noises and he knew he wasn't alone any more. But he hid behind a big stalagmite.

We knew the difference, did we, between a stalagmite and a stalactite? A stalactite hangs down from the ceiling. A stalagmite grows up from the floor. Of course it doesn't really grow. That's just the way geologists and people who know about grottoes say it.

Incidentally, this grotto, in case we were interested, was hollowed out by the river. The river with the three names. That was millions of years ago. Ferenz wasn't quite sure of the date. Then the river got tired of going this way and changed its course. That left the labyrinths and the caves. It was water dripping down from above that made the stalactites. The water was full of lime from eroded rocks. It was the lime in the dripping water that made those queer shapes on the ceiling. Stalactites "grow" in this grotto at the rate of one millimeter in thirty years. That's about one inch every hundred years. Then it's the dripping of lime water from the stalactites that forms the stalagmites on the floor. They grow a little slower.

But where had we left Rudy? Oh yes. He hid behind a stalagmite and pretty soon he saw twenty-five German soldiers coming from the hole the Partisans had made in the steel door and the brick wall. Rudy said they were pretty mad-looking. They all had torches. They'd come, Rudy figured to himself, to look over the fire from this end. But they couldn't get any farther than the big room called the Dancing Hall. They had to turn back there because of the gas fumes. Rudy waited until they started back toward the Cerna Jama and then he followed them at a distance of about a hundred and fifty feet. He was glad then that he had bare feet. That's the way he finally got out. He just followed them to the entrance. Then he waited for it to get dark and escaped into the woods.

The fire and explosions ruined the first quarter of a mile of the grotto and now when visitors go through, the lights aren't even turned on in that section. Never will be. There's no way anybody knows to get the black stains off the white limestone. Pretty ugly-looking spot. After the explosion it was dangerous going down into the grotto for quite a while. Stalactites and stones that had been knocked loose kept falling down. It was the heat that did it.

The American girl called Blossom asked if there'd ever been an accident in the grotto. Ferenz Verbić put on a very serious face as he said, yes, once there was a big rock slide. Hundreds of tons of rock came tumbling down. He'd show us when we went inside.

The American girl said when did it happen and how many people were killed? Ferenz Verbić was waiting for that question. He laughed when he said that they figured out it happened in the year 10,000 B.C. The American girl said that was a good story, but how could he tell? From then on the old guide took quite a fancy to Blossom. I said he ought to hire her as a stooge on his tours. But he didn't understand.

He said they could tell almost to the day by measuring the height of the stalagmites which had grown up in the rock slide, because they know exactly how fast a stalagmite grows. No accidents since the year 10,000 B.C. that he knew about. Not unless you want to count the earthquake that shook this region on the last day of December 1925. It knocked a few stalactites loose, but no one was hurt. That's because it happened at night, thank God.

When the guide said the temperature was eight degrees Celsius in the grotto, day and night, summer and winter, the American girl asked what that was in her language and how long was it possible for someone to stay down in the grotto and live? Ferenz Verbić, with some outside help, finally figured out that eight Celsius is about forty-seven degrees Fahrenheit and he didn't know how long a body could stay in the grotto. All he knew was that he'd spent most of the last fifty-one years down there.

But that reminded him of something that happened after the end of the war. There was one German soldier who didn't like the idea of surrendering. Ferenz said maybe he thought Adolf Hitler would come to life in a few days and save him. Anyway, he hid in the grotto. No one knew he was down there until one day he appeared at the entrance and gave himself up. He had a stub of a candle in his hand and quite a growth of beard on his face. He said he'd been down there nineteen days and he looked it. He was suffering more from what the guide called "the depression" than from hunger because he had had a few cans of food.

Ferenz said it's sort of a custom for people to visit the grotto on Whitsunday. On Whitsunday in 1926 a record was set. Twenty thousand people went through. The thing you have to worry about on a day like that is people getting lost. They wander off by themselves down some narrow corridor and the first thing they know they're all alone. Then sometimes their flashlights burn out and there they are, lost. Ferenz Verbić said many a night, after taking thousands of people through and being dead tired, he's had to go back and wander through the seventeen miles of passageways looking for some stupid fool who didn't think he was getting his money's worth and wanted to go exploring on his own.

That reminded the old guide of his daughter. She started working in the grotto when she was eight. Two or three miles in from the entrance there's a big room they call the Concert Hall. They call it that because on Whitsunday and other special occasions concerts are actually held down there. Once the famous Italian Mascagni conducted a concert there.

But about his daughter. She sold the picture postal cards at a booth in the Concert Hall. People could mail them right there. Well, one night Ferenz Verbić thought she had already gone home, so he went through on his last trip turning out all the lights. He got home before he realized what had happened. He ran all the way back. He got to the grotto just in time to see a very frightened little girl coming out through the main entrance. She'd run, alone, in the dark, the entire two or three miles. She didn't even have a candle. After that she didn't want to work down there any more.

The American girl named Blossom got a few additional pieces of intelligence from him. There's enough natural ventilation so they don't have to have any artificial system. The humidity is seventy degrees. Ferenz Verbić had heard that air like that is good for the lungs. But he couldn't be sure. All he knew was that his lungs were as good as ever at sixty-six. But it was bad for rheumatism. His rheumatism bothered him a lot these days. Around here the grotto is popular with newlyweds, just like Niagara Falls is in the United States. And one thing more we might write down. He and the grotto were in a movie once. Yes, sir, he was the star actor. People said he was good but he never did get any offers from Hollywood. And now how about seeing his "baby" ourselves?

Ferenz Verbić introduced us to the man who drives the gasoline engine that pulls the string of open cars that take visitors slowly over the first two miles of the tour. Max Laveć is one of the newer employees. He's been at the grotto for only twenty-four years. But he and Ferenz are close friends. It was Max who took Ferenz's map of the grotto to Partisan headquarters in the hills.

The amazing thing about the spiel that Ferenz gives his customers is that he suits what he says to the nationality of his audience. For Americans the stalactite that looks so much like a portly figure with a white beard is "Santa Claus." Or it's "Father Christmas" if the audience is British. Or Kris Kringle. For Americans he has an Empire State Building. An Arizona desert. A Times Square. Of course there are many international objects. A parrot. A bear. The Diamond Room. The Ballroom in which at least one real dance is held every year. The Leaning Tower of Pisa. Spaghetti Hall with a ceiling that looks as if it really was festooned with strands of the Italians' favorite food. At one point he announces that you are now one hundred and sixty meters below the ground and for the benefit of those who don't understand meters he says that's five hundred feet, which isn't accurate but it's close enough.

Halfway through the labyrinth the United Press man was so overcome by the dazzling splendor of what he saw that he sat down beside an especially handsome stalactite and pinched it and said, "Obviously it's Yugoslav propaganda put out to impress the Monarcho-Fascists. But it looks pretty even if it is all paper and cardboard."

Ferenz Verbić has two big moments on every tour. The first comes as he leads the way down a corridor between what he calls the Lace Hall and the Turkish Cemetery. He pauses dramatically, calls for complete silence, takes a pencil from his pocket, and plays a tune on half-a-dozen hollow stalactites, as if he were playing a xylophone. He tries to play a popular tune of the country from which most of his guests of the moment have come. Sometimes he errs. Once during the war he had a lapse of memory at this point and played "Tipperary." The German soldiers standing there listening didn't like it a bit.

His other big moment comes when he exhibits a pool full of what he calls "human fish." He says the proper Latin name is *proteus anguinus,* but really they're "human fish." While everyone stared down at the pure-white objects in the water which Blossom said looked like anaemic eels, Ferenz Verbić waited for the inevitable question. Finally it came. "Why do you call them human fish?" Then he smiled and explained. They're the only fish in the world with skin exactly like the skin of humans. Normally they live in the dark. The grotto's underground streams are full of them. Normally they reach a ripe old age of fifty or sixty years. Of course here in this pool with the floodlight on them they don't live to be more than about ten. There's one though—and he points it out with his walking stick—that will be sixty next March. Sometimes he throws a piece of liver to them, but if he forgets it doesn't matter because scientists have told him they can live four or five years with nothing to eat at all. Then, if his guests are American or British, he adds, "Lucky fish!" Oh yes, and one thing more that's important. They're born blind and they never do learn to see. Maybe that's lucky too. Some of the people who wander through the grotto are mighty funny looking, Ferenz Verbić confides.

After we got back to the surface we bought Ferenz Verbić a sizable glass of *šljivovica*. In return he told us something I'd never known before. He said the American army, in the official Serbo-Croat language guide it gave soldiers during the war, made one grave error. It spelled the word for plum brandy šljivovice. That was bad. The word ends in an "a" because it's feminine. It's feminine because šljivovica is like a woman. Warm. Pleasant. Exciting. Stimulating. But also very treacherous if you aren't careful.

Chapter Eighty-Two

GOLD IS NOT GOLO

THE village of Ig is in a rich valley of hay and grain fields to the south of Ljubljana. Ig has one thing in common with the Serbian village of Ub. Anyone can pronounce it. From Ig to the village of Golo is a good day's walk on foot because you're climbing all the way. Golo is an isolated mountaintop community. Life has never been easy there, any more than in any mountain village. Except in the winter months, when Golo's isolated, the people worked from sunup until sundown, just to keep body and soul together. Seventy people lived there, which meant about twenty houses because there's a lot of doubling up in poor communities. Sometimes the village people found an excuse to go down to Ig and visit friends. On rare occasions someone went to Ljubljana and came back with enough tales to provide conversation for a fortnight at least. But what they talked about the most was the men who had gone to Canada. It wasn't every village that could boast that three of its respected citizens had crossed most of Europe, and then the Atlantic Ocean, and then had gone way up into the north of that country called Canada. Most Slovene peasants didn't even know where Canada was until you explained it to them. When the villagers talked about why the men had gone they talked in whispers. And they didn't use the Slovene word either. They liked the word "gold." It was better than saying *zlato,* the Slovenian way, because "gold" sounds so much like Golo. Besides, "gold" sounds so much more glittery. Yes, all three of them were in the north of Canada hunting for gold. Someday they would come back rich men. Rich enough to buy out the whole village. Rich as kings. Rich enough to go to Ljubljana every day and buy anything that pleased their fancy. Rich enough so that none of them would ever have to work again.

They went off together in 1928, the three of them. Joe and Vinko Ponikvar, and Tony Lenč. Joe and Tony were married. Tony had two baby boys. He told his wife to take good care of them. He didn't know when he'd be back, but whenever it was she wasn't to be surprised if he drove right up the hill from Ig in one of those wagons that goes without any horse pulling it; all you have to do is to pour water in both ends. Vinko was the youngest. He hadn't even thought about taking himself a wife yet.

Once across the Atlantic they separated. Joe said he'd heard that there was a place called Colorado which wasn't so far away as the place they were planning to go in Canada. He guessed he'd go to Colorado to do his hunting for gold. But even though Joe was the eldest the other two didn't listen to him. They went to Canada. To a place called Kerkilac. It was a long time before anyone in Golo heard from the three men. Joe's wife kept saying they'd probably all been drowned in the big lake on the way over. But Tony's wife said she was going to wait a year before she began to fret.

Then bright-colored picture postal cards began to arrive. Everyone in Golo saw them before they were finally tacked up on a kitchen wall. There was great excitement in the village each time a new one came. The pride of the two wives was dampened somewhat about a year after their men had gone. It happened the day one of the cards was being passed around and an old woman in the crowd said it was odd, wasn't it, that the men never wrote about how much gold they'd found? No one said anything for nearly a minute. They all just looked at Mrs. Ponikvar and Mrs. Lenć, expecting them to say something. It was Tony's wife who finally thought of an answer. She said if she knew her man he was waiting to surprise her. It was probably the same with the other two.

Several years went by and then one day someone looking down the hill toward Ig saw a once familiar figure coming up the road. As he got closer everyone knew it was Joe. The whole village ran out to meet him. No one asked him where the automobile was that Tony had talked about. They just stared at his city clothes. And at the cardboard suitcase painted yellow he carried in his right hand. Then they began to ask him a million questions. Tony's wife asked where her man was. Joe explained that he hadn't seen the other two since they separated in the United States. They'd gone up into Canada. He'd been in Colorado. There wasn't much gold in Colorado. He didn't have anything much in the yellow suitcase but a dress for his wife. He'd used all the money he'd earned to get home. He didn't know for sure what he was going to do. Maybe he'd go back to farming. Or maybe . . . Maybe he'd go to a place called Minnesota. That was also in the United States. He'd met some men on the ship coming back who said Minnesota was the place to go.

Joe didn't stay home in Golo very long. The more he thought about what the men on the ship had told him the more he thought Minnesota was where he'd find what he was looking for.

A great many years passed before anything else happened. Except that sometimes a letter would come from one man or the other, sometimes from Canada, sometimes from Minnesota, with pieces of green paper in it. When that happened someone had to walk to Ig and then take a motor bus in to Ljubljana and go to a bank and change those pieces of green paper for Slovenian money. Each time an envelope with something in it arrived, Tony's wife would search out the old woman who had made the sarcastic remark about the men not finding any gold and she'd wave the pieces of green paper in the woman's face and say, "See!" And each time the old woman would snort, "Neh gold!"

It was in 1937 that Vinko the youngest came walking up the road from Ig one hot summer's day. He didn't come in an automobile either, but he did have a suitcase and there were a lot of things for a woman in it. They made him open the suitcase in the village square. When someone saw two or three dresses and a pair of women's shoes they all asked Vinko why he hadn't brought his wife with him. What was she like? Was she one of those Canadian girls? Was she as nice as a Slovene girl? Vinko was very much embarrassed. Finally he said he had no wife. But maybe he'd have one pretty soon. That was one reason he'd come home. He was going to find himself a wife. Nobody said anything but they all looked at Annie. Annie didn't say anything either. She just hung her head. But hanging her head didn't keep her from looking at all the things on the ground that had come out of the suitcase. Vinko didn't know who Annie was at first. After all, maybe she was twenty-two now, but she'd been a little girl of thirteen when he left. Now she was a woman. She was pretty to look at too.

That night her father told Vinko he should notice her hands. They were large hands. Annie was a great help in the fields. She could do as much work as any man. Of course her father would be sorry to lose her. But Vinko would make a better husband for her than the one from Ig who walked up every Sunday to see her. And then he asked Vinko how much gold he'd found in Canada? A few days later Vinko married Annie.

Vinko stayed in Golo until the baby was born. Then, when the little girl was one month old, he told Annie that he'd better get back to Canada now. Tony would be missing him. He wanted to be with Tony when they made their "strike." Annie wouldn't understand about that. It was an English word. But if he went now he'd be back before long. And if he and Tony found gold she and the baby could have everything they wanted. And Annie wouldn't ever have to work in the fields again.

So, eleven months after he came trudging up the road with his suitcase of women's things, Vinko went back down the road, a husband, a father, and an explorer for gold again. Maybe it was what Vinko told Tony about Golo and how Tony's wife had built a new house while he was gone that made the older man decide he ought to pay a visit too. Anyway, the next year Tony came home. He told his wife she'd done a good job while he was gone. Let's see, it had been just ten years, hadn't it? She didn't look much different but the boys surely had grown. And the new house she'd built was all right. Maybe he'd stay awhile. But he didn't stay long. Just six months, and then he was off again for Canada and Mrs. Lenč went back to being mother, father, and farmer again.

It was about three weeks after the Axis attack on Yugoslavia that the Italians came up the road from Ig to occupy the mountain village of Golo. Nothing much happened at first except that everyone hid anything they thought was of value because they'd heard about the way soldiers generally act. They even hid their extra food. And the three wives dug a hole in a field and hid all the picture postal cards from Colorado, Minnesota, and Canada. The Italians behaved all right at the start. Annie had a little trouble with two young Italians who tried to get fresh, but Annie was big enough and strong enough to take care of herself. That first winter Partisans started gathering in the hills around Golo. One by one men of

Golo disappeared. They didn't tell anyone but their families where they were going. But everyone knew. Even the Italians knew. That's why they burned down the village of Golo the first time. The Italian commander made a speech in the village square. All the men who were left in the village were going to be shipped to concentration camps in Italy. Every house was going to be destroyed. The women and children would be taken to Ig. They might just as well forget Golo. The village of Golo wasn't going to exist any more. Maybe that would be a lesson to the men in the hills. After they burned the houses, all twenty of them, the Italians left the hilltop. There wasn't anything to occupy any more except piles of stone and rubble. Pieces of burned wood. A ghost village. But in ten days the women and children of Golo began to drift back. They came two or three at a time. They came because there is an instinct in humans just like the instinct in a homing pigeon. A home can't be destroyed just by burning down the house. The one building in Golo which had escaped the fate of the twenty peasant cottages was the firehouse. No one could understand why the Italians had left it. But it was good that they had because that's where most of the women and children lived while they took new timbers cut from the woods and tried to make individual homes for themselves on the ruins of where they had previously lived. But the war wasn't over yet. The women and children of Golo had come back too soon. In October of '43 the Germans began a big counteroffensive against the Partisans in the hills to the south of Ljubljana. In the course of the offensive they burned down Golo again. They did it because if they lost the mountaintop during the course of the fighting they didn't want to leave anything of value for the Partisans. So they destroyed each one of the houses that the women had rebuilt.

When we got to Golo the girl from California turned to Albert Rejec and asked if all the people in the village had finally been killed. It was a natural question, because there wasn't a human being in sight. But while we were walking around in the ruins a loaded hayrack came up the road. There were three men on it. They were the ones who gave us the story of what had happened. They said that after the Italian collapse the thirty-seven men who had been taken to concentration camps in Italy were released. All of them joined the Partisans as soon as they heard what had happened to Golo. But one man on the hayrack said that that wasn't right. Only thirty-one of the thirty-seven went into the Partisans. The other six died in the Italian camps. Out of the thirty-one, six more died during the fighting. That left twenty-five. Then one of the twenty-five was captured by the Germans and was shipped off to the north. No one ever heard about him again. So he's listed as dead too. That made twenty-four men left. Thirteen dead. Then fourteen women and children were either killed or died somehow before it was all over. Twenty-seven dead in this small village. Twenty-seven out of seventy. Besides all the other trouble they had, Golo got one bombing. There were eleven people crowded into that house over there when the bomb fell. Many of them were children. A piece of the bomb went right through the roof. That's how a lot of them were wounded. Now Golo was trying to rebuild again. But the trouble was getting materials. Maybe we'd heard about the Five-Year Plan? Well, most building materials were going into things like factories and schools and churches. Mostly factories. The government said Yugoslavia had to have factories to make bricks, machinery, railroad tracks, and turbines. But someday Golo would be like it was. Maybe better.

When we first started talking to the three men on the hayrack Albert Rejec acted as interpreter. But then one of the men laughed and said why didn't we talk to them in English. They all spoke good American, he said. And they did. That's how we found out about them all being gold miners. The three men on the hayrack were Joe and Vinko Ponikvar and Tony Lenč. They got back to Golo on May tenth, this year. Of course during the war they didn't hear anything from Golo and Golo didn't hear anything from them. They didn't know until it was all over what their wives and children had been going through. They didn't really know until they got back. Of course they'd heard that a lot of villages had been burned and they figured that maybe Golo had been one of them. They knew what they were coming back to. They knew that there would be a lot of hard work ahead of them. But the things they'd heard over in Canada about the New Yugoslavia made them decide to come home. They wanted to help make the new life. They'd liked America, but it wasn't Slovenia. Over there they got lonesome for Slovenia. Gold digging was just as hard work as farming and when you got all through you didn't have anything but a living. So why not live where you like it best? Where your own people are. Maybe in the New Yugoslavia, after all the factories were built and all the houses, they'd get a better living than they'd ever had before. That's what they were told and they believed it. They believed it enough to come back seven or eight thousand miles. They knew that they probably wouldn't be able to leave Yugoslavia again. At least not for a long time. But that was all right. The three of them nodded their heads. It was all right.

While we were talking to them a peasant woman in bare feet came up the road pulling a small cart loaded with lettuce. The first thing I noticed about her was how large her hands were. She was sunburned the color of a dried tobacco leaf. She had a white bandanna tied around her head. She looked quite attractive. In a peasant sort of a way. Vinko jumped down from the top of the hayrack and went up to the woman and said something quietly in Slovenian. Then he turned to us and said this was Annie. This was the wife he got when he came home from Canada. He told Annie to go into their house and get us something to drink. She came back with a bottle of amber šljivovica and we all drank to the future prosperity of this village of Golo, which was still mostly in ruins. The girl from California said that running a farm and bringing up a child and having all those war experiences hadn't left any bad marks on Annie. She didn't look nearly so old as Vinko did. Vinko was pleased by the compliment. Then we asked him how Annie felt, waiting all those years for him to come home. Hadn't she missed him? Vinko grinned. He said he guessed Annie had been too busy to worry about things like that. Anyway, she was waiting for him when he got home. Then Vinko took us into the place where they lived. It was the building where the people had been wounded in the bombing. They showed us the hole through the roof. The building was full of holes. There wasn't much to it except one room which had been fixed up. In the one room were two beds, a stove, a table, a bench instead of chairs, and on the wall colored pictures of Marshal Tito and Joseph Stalin. Tony said we had to see his place too. His house was the one his wife had built new in 1933. Only it had been destroyed twice by the enemy. Now they had one room fixed up the same as Vinko had. One room and a small kitchen. There was an old woman peeling potatoes in the kitchen. Tony said she and her daughter lived with him and helped with the work. That meant four of them lived in one room. Someday maybe he'd be able to fix up the rest of the house. Then the old woman and her daughter could have a room of their own.

We were just coming out of the house when a woman appeared with a large wicker basket in her arms. There were a few new potatoes in it and some greens for the animals. Tony introduced us to her as if he were presenting a queen. Mrs. Lenć grinned a greeting and held out a dirt-stained hand. When she grinned I noticed that she had just one tooth in her mouth. It was a front tooth and pointed at a northwest-southeast angle. But she was a jolly sort, and we held a long conversation with her, Tony doing the interpreting. She said they were poor here in Golo. They always had been, except when one of those envelopes came with green pieces of paper in it. Tony grinned when she said that. She'd lived in the firehouse with six other families while she was getting the one room of her house fixed up, after the second destruction of Golo. We asked Tony to ask his wife how she'd felt about his being away nineteen years. But Tony didn't pass the question on to her. He answered it himself. He said she had a good time. She didn't mind. Not much. Then Tony translated the question and his answer. His wife smiled so that her one tooth showed but she didn't say anything. She didn't deny his answer or confirm it either. She just smiled. By this time the other villagers were coming in from the fields. It was nearly 8 P.M. They all looked tired. Tony said most of them had been working in the fields since a little after dawn, except when they were eating their midday meal.

On the way back to where we had parked the car we noticed a large piece of aluminum across the top of a rain barrel. Tony said it was part of the wing of an American plane. The plane had fallen down in the valley one day in June of '44. Nearly everyone in the village had a piece of the plane they used for something or other. The men in the crew of the plane had parachuted down safely. The valley people took care of them so nothing more would happen to them. I copied down some figures on the piece of the plane that was being used as a lid for the rain barrel.

FORD MOTOR COMPANY
Part No. 32 W 500
Serial No. 2488 R

When we passed the firehouse Tony said it was being used now as a co-operative store where people could buy things they needed. Part of it. The rest was where three families lived that still didn't have their houses fixed up.

As we were getting into the car I asked Tony if he or Vinko or Joe ever got homesick for America. He thought a long time before he answered. Then he said it was funny, but when he was over there in Canada he was all the time lonesome for Golo. And when he was in Golo he was all the time lonesome for Canada. Then he said, how can you explain that?

Chapter Eighty-Three

IMPACT PSYCHOLOGICAL

BEFORE the war it was the thing to do, if you were one of Ljubljana's "better people," to have your portrait painted by Božidar Jakac because Božidar Jakac was acknowledged by everyone to be Yugoslavia's most fashionable artist. He'd traveled all over the world, was on speaking terms with intellectuals in Paris, New York, and other important places, had written a book on his experiences in America which he'd illustrated himself, and he made his subjects look handsome or beautiful, depending on the sex of the subject, even though sometimes they weren't handsome or beautiful by any stretch of the imagination. You could send for him to come to your home and do your portrait with the least possible inconvenience to you, or you could go to his studio in the street called Pred Škofijo, number 21, the fourth flight up. Of course if you went to his studio you had to climb those four flights, for there was no elevator. But it was worth while because the building, although it wasn't much to look at from the outside, had a history. It was several hundred years old and had once been a hotel where Austrian nobility stopped in the days of the Empire. Even the dim corridors with their arched ceilings were things of artistic and architectural beauty. Once inside the Jakac studio, you felt as if you were inside a museum. There were glass cases of Slovenian antiques, examples of the best of Slovenian peasant handicraft, paintings by many of Yugoslavia's other good artists, and then examples of Božidar Jakac's own work from the time he was hardly more than a boy, serving as a soldier in the Austrian Army of World War I. The fashionable people who came to have their portraits painted didn't understand or like a great deal of Božidar Jakac's own work they saw in his studio. Much of it struck them as "too modern." A few of those who came saw in some of his canvases a spirit of rebellion, on the artistic level. And a spirit of rebellion, even on an artistic level, rather frightened them. There was too much rebellion against the conventional all over the world these days. What would happen if the rebels had their way? And intellectual rebels were the most dangerous of all, for they always led the way. So they were suspicious of Božidar Jakac, the fashionable portrait painter. But they flocked to him to have flattering likenesses of themselves put on canvas. And they didn't argue with him when the portraits were completed as long as they were more flattering than they were likenesses.

Božidar Jakac hated his life in those days. He was a human dynamo, and he worked from early morning until late into each night doing portraits. But the fees the fashionable people paid him just about kept him going. He had to pinch a bit to save enough money to make the trips abroad which were so important to him. Abroad he studied the work and the technique of fellow artists who were more free. Someday maybe he would be free too. Free to paint people as he really saw them. Free to be a real artist instead of a flatterer of the better people. Free to paint fish-mongers if he pleased and people in the street if their faces were interesting. But there was one portrait he did in those days that he wasn't ashamed of. It was an almost life-sized likeness of his own mother. The little gray-haired lady staring out of the canvas was so real that she almost seemed to speak in her quiet way to anyone who entered the room where she hung. In her eyes anyone could read the hopes and the dreams she had for her son. In her eyes some people could also read the fears and the tragedies of the whole Slovene race. The hunger for things of the spirit they had been denied. The thirst for that intangible thing called freedom. In those days Božidar Jakac often thumbed through the sketches he did during the two years he was serving as a common soldier in World War I. They were mostly on the backs of old picture postal cards he'd picked up here and there. Or on any old scraps of paper that had fallen into his hands. They were crude and lacking in technique. He knew that. He wasn't very proud of them as pieces of art. He seldom showed them to anyone. But he was free then. He didn't really understand the war they were fighting. But he understood the emotions of men under fire. And in the faces of the men whose likenesses he drew he put their emotions. Fear. Hate. Fright. Terror. Suffering. Hope. Visions of death. He knew that going into battle was like sandpapering the fingertips to bring the raw nerves to the surface and make them more sensitive to what they touched. He didn't actually pray for war again. But if it came, as it began to look that it might, then maybe . . .

During the first part of World War II, before Yugoslavia was attacked, Božidar Jakac, who had never had more than just enough money to get along, found a way he could help some of his fellow Yugoslav artists who didn't have the reputation he had and were struggling to be free and therefore couldn't sell at any price to the fashionable people the rebellious things they did on pieces of canvas. War abroad had brought inflation at home. Slovenia's wealthy people wanted to turn their cash into tangible goods. Jewelry was bringing fantastic prices. And works of art, too, if they were conventional. It seemed that everyone wanted Božidar Jakac to come around and do a portrait. And so, with a little knowledge of the workings of the economic law of supply and demand, he raised his prices. Doubled them. Tripled them. Quadrupled them. And still people ordered portraits. For about a year the money rolled in. For the first and the last time in his life Božidar Jakac had a feeling of the power of wealth. Of course it wasn't really wealth. Just the equivalent of a few hundred dollars now and then that came in without having to go out immediately for oils, brushes, rent, food, clothing. It's significant how a man acquires his money. It's more significant what he does with it if he ever gets a surplus. Some people build monuments to themselves. Either in stone or in the form of hospitals, museums, and college-student endowments. Božidar Jakac did none of these things. He used what money came his way to help his fellow artists who were more rebellious than he was. And therefore poor. He knew they wouldn't accept cash from him as a gift. But he knew they would sell, eagerly, some of their work. And so that one lush year he bought many a young artist's best canvases. As a result many a young artist was kept going at a time when the cost of merely existing was reaching impossible levels.

When war came to Yugoslavia Božidar Jakac knew there was just one thing for him to do. His days of being fashionable were over. Off in the hills men were forming in guerrilla bands. Those soldiers were soon going to experience every emotion known to civilized man. Those emotions must be put down with brush and paint, or on wood blocks, or with pieces of charcoal, or with burned matches on the backs of postal cards if necessary. And so Božidar Jakac packed up a knapsack. He put into it only a few brushes and other tools of his profession. Then he vanished into the hills. There was only one thing that bothered him about going. He hated to leave his wife and ten-year-old son behind. The boy wasn't their own. They'd adopted him years ago. But no blood parents ever loved a child any more. At the last minute Jakac's wife found friends who said they would care for the boy and so she went too. Leaders of the new Partisan Army welcomed Božidar Jakac into their ranks. And they didn't insist that he man a gun. Not unless they got into one of those corners where doctors, nurses, cooks, and artists, too, had to turn ordinary soldier. Even at the start the Partisan Army was organized for education, propaganda, art, health, every phase of human existence, as well as for the job of fighting and killing. So they encouraged Božidar Jakac to get to work in the hills with his brushes and paints. Soon he was capturing all those human emotions he had seen on the faces of soldiers in that other war. Capturing them and putting them on wood and paper and canvas. Only now he was a skilled artist and he didn't have to be ashamed of his work. In all he did more than one thousand portraits of the men, women, and children of the Partisans. Any one of them was a superior piece of art to any one of those fashionable portraits he may have spent months fussing over.

When the men in the hills decided to form a free people's government Božidar Jakac, the artist reborn, was elected one of the deputies. The news got to London. The names were broadcast by B.B.C. The Germans were listening and writing down the names. Božidar Jakac? They couldn't do anything to him, but maybe he'd left some of his family behind. So they went around to that studio in the old hotel of Austrian Empire days on the street called Pred Škofijo. Number 21. Four flights up. But the small son, now twelve, had heard the broadcast too. So had the people who were taking care of him. They warned him what was likely to happen. The boy's one interest was in saving the paintings, antiques, and other objects in the studio he knew his father prized so highly. While German guards stood at the front door of the one-time hotel, the boy helped save the squares of canvas, the pieces of Slovenian handiwork, the curios his father had collected in America, and, most important of all, the best early works of the fashionable artist, Božidar Jakac. He helped save them by handing them through the bathroom window to friends who sneaked them out the back of the old hotel to a little museum where maybe the Nazis wouldn't bother them. But the boy was caught by the Germans just as he was finishing the job. He was confined in a monastery the Germans were using as a concentration camp. His life there was so unbearable to him that he risked being shot one night late in the war by running away during the confusion created by an American air raid. For months he beat his way through woods and over mountains to the home of an aunt.

Twenty-four hours after the final liberation Božidar Jakac and his wife came rushing home. They went right to the studio. What they saw frightened them. The lock on the door had been changed. They broke in. It looked as if they'd gotten into the wrong place. There wasn't an object inside the studio that was familiar. Not even the furniture or the rugs on the floor. And there was no trace of their son. It was a long time before the happy ending was written to the story. It was a long time before they found that the boy was with his aunt, that nearly all the Jakac possessions were safe in the out-of-the-way museum, and that the Chetniks who had taken over the studio and moved in some stolen furniture had either been killed or had gone into hiding. That was the end of the war story. But during the first days of peace a bitter anti-climax was written. A short time after the small son came home to take up life with his parents again he was killed. He had lived through years of what the Nazis hoped would be a fatal existence in one of their concentration camps. He had lived through air raids and through the hazards of escape. He was killed in front of his home by an automobile.

We met Božidar Jakac in his office in the Slovenian Academy of Fine Arts in Ljubljana, of which he is rector. Only he has no office. He's the director in chief but he spends all his time in the classrooms, helping to teach young Slovenes what he knows about art. Not just painting but sculpting and all other forms of the fine arts. Wood-block carving too. Božidar Jakac, despite his years of rugged life in the mountains, still looks like the artist he is. He's short, in his early fifties, sports a goatlike Van Dyke beard which makes you think you've suddenly run into Rex Stout six thousand miles from home, but you know that it isn't Rex Stout as soon as you notice the drooping handlebar mustachios. War has left no visible marks on him except that whenever the subject of his son comes up in conversation, which it frequently does, tears well up in his soft eyes. He can show you portraits by the hundreds of men he knew well in the mountains who were killed, and he can tell you, as he shows you the paintings he bought from his rebel colleagues during that one lush year, that most of them are dead too, and he can say with a touch of sadness that the friend who helped his son save all this furniture and all these works of art was killed for his efforts just two days before the liberation. He can talk about all those things with only a discreet show of how he feels inside. But there's no disguising what the loss of his only son meant. Jakac moves with the nervous energy of a grasshopper. One of his friends warned us that we'd be exhausted after the first fifteen minutes with him. The friend was conservative. It's perhaps this quality of a human dynamo which accounts for the amount of work he's done in the course of a relatively short career. Here is a sketch he did when fifteen hundred of them were surrounded by sixty thousand Germans and no one expected to come out alive. Here is a portrait Marshal Tito sat for just a few months ago. These boxes contain the six thousand photographs he took while he was in the Partisans. Here are the one thousand sketches he did of various Partisan leaders. Common soldiers too. The generals and the cooks. The colonels and the nurses. Here are some woodcut prints he's doing for the government in Belgrade. Printing them himself, one by one. This box is exclusively for sketches he did of hospitals, maternity homes, and headquarters in the woods where he spent varying amounts of time. These are portraits he did of wealthy Americans when he was in the United States. That glass case is full of miniatures of Slovenian peasant costumes. The reason these sketches are on pieces of air-mail paper is because that's all the paper he could get during several months in the mountains. These portraits were made by candlelight. Sometimes you can see more of a person's character when his face is lit by candlelight. This one was done while German planes were circling overhead. There were many interruptions while they went out and took shots at it with machine guns. The idea for the fine-arts academy was born in the woods. For two hundred years various Slovenes had fought for the realization of such a dream. Five months after the liberation the government in Belgrade and the government in Ljubljana helped make the dream come true. It's the first time in Slovenian history that anyone with a feeling for art can go somewhere and get instruction, training, the use of a studio, guidance, direction, paints, brushes, and the use of a sculptor's tools absolutely free, no matter who he is. Now here is something else that may interest you. And over there . . . And did I show you this sketch? And here are some canvases by France Mihelić. He's one of our best. And—don't sit down, I have other things to show you in the next room.

In a restaurant over a glass of beer we finally got the Slovenian dynamo into low gear. Just for a few minutes. Somehow someone made mention of that old Louis Adamic story about the nurse who killed her twenty patients and then jumped over a cliff to her own death. Jakac said stories like that couldn't possibly be believed by people who hadn't been through some of war's experiences. But he could confirm this particular story because his brother-in-law's son was one of the twenty who asked to be killed. And was. He said he thought civil wars like the one Yugoslavia went through during the Axis occupation make for a greater intensity of feeling than ordinary wars. Didn't our own Civil War prove it? And the French Revolution? And the Russian revolution? He'd had nine cousins. Some were in the Partisans. Some were on the other side. One was an old Royal Yugoslav Army officer. He was captured but escaped and got home. Jakac said, I talked to him. I told him that if he didn't feel and understand what the Partisans were fighting for he should stay at home and do nothing. Just sit it out. Then I lost track of him. Many months later, after a big battle, I heard that he was one of our prisoners. He'd joined the Chetniks and was fighting with the Germans against us. What should I do about him? I knew he wasn't a bad man. Someone had probably told him that he must go on fighting for the Yugoslav king. I did nothing about him. A few days later there was a big offensive. Just before it started some of the prisoners were put on trial. My own cousin was one of those convicted and executed as a traitor. Yet he had brothers and sisters who were such active Partisan leaders that they were elected deputies of the new government just as I was. The Chetniks captured one of his brothers and tortured him until he was dead. His own sister was one of the most heroic of the Partisan fighters. Then there was an old man I knew. He had five sons. Four of them were killed fighting in the Partisan Army. The fifth went the other way. He was captured and was up for trial. If nothing was done for him, if no one intervened, he'd surely be executed because his record was very bad. The old father came to me to talk about it. He said he'd been told that as the father of four dead Partisan heroes he could save the life of his fifth son if he made a plea to the military court for mercy. But the old man cried as he told me that he couldn't possibly do it. He couldn't do it and live with himself. He'd always feel a traitor to his four other sons and what they'd died fighting for. And so he did nothing. And so the fifth boy was executed.

Božidar Jakac took a long drink of his Slovenian beer. When he spoke again his voice was soft. His eyes were looking off into the distance. Looking at something we couldn't see. He said that many times in the mountains groups of Partisans would get within sight of their native villages. The places where they'd been born. Villages where their wives and mothers and children still lived. Maybe. After one big battle he remembered standing on a hill looking down through binoculars with some other Partisans. For a minute or two there was silence. Then one of the men said, almost in a whisper, "Look! There's my house!" And then, while they looked, the town disappeared. You couldn't see it with your naked eyes and you couldn't see it with the binoculars either. It just wasn't there any more. You rubbed your eyes and you squinted again. But it was gone. Sometimes it happened while you were looking down on little villages and sometimes while you were looking at big places. Cities as large as Ljubljana. Božidar Jakac said he supposed it was psychological. It was partly the weariness of war and it was partly psychological. You were so afraid that it wasn't there that—it wasn't. Sometimes the place looked twice as large as it really was. Sometimes it looked so small you couldn't recognize it. It's hard for outsiders to understand. You're so near and yet so far away. You're only a few kilometers away, really. But you're millions of miles away. Up here on the mountain it's one world. Down there it's another world. It's like sitting on Mars with a telescope looking down on this globe. Two worlds. It does things to your mind. Božidar Jakac said sometimes he wished he were a psychologist instead of an artist. Two worlds. But maybe now the two worlds have met and have been joined together. Maybe they'll stay melted into one world now.

Chapter Eighty-Four

GENTEEL DISCONTENT

BEFORE the war Valetta worked in a government office in Ljubljana as private secretary to one of the important Slovenian government officials. Her father had owned a small factory. When he died he left Valetta and his wife enough money so that when it was invested in foreign stocks and bonds it gave them ample to live on in a modest but genteel way. When Valetta's mother died the income all went to Valetta. She needn't have worked. But she did. For a specific reason. By taking her two weeks' vacation with pay and another three or four weeks without pay all at the same time she could go abroad for a month and a half each year. That's how she spent the salary she earned. Sometimes she went to England. Sometimes to France. Often to Vienna. Once she'd been to Berlin. The older she grew the better she liked London. Of course her dream was to go to America someday. Just for a visit, of course. There was nothing wrong with Slovenia. This was her home. Life was relatively inexpensive. Servants were cheap. They'd work for a few dinar a week and their food and lodging. They'd work from early morning until late at night and be grateful because however hard they worked and however few dinar you gave them they were better off than if they went back to their peasant villages where sometimes they didn't get enough to eat and they rarely saw any money. Valetta wouldn't have understood if someone had talked to her about "class consciousness" and the abuses of the system under which she lived. She found nothing wrong with the system. She worked for the government that was helping to perpetuate the system. Of course she didn't have a very important role to play. And she didn't like the idea of the King of Yugoslavia being a Serb. It would have been much better if he could have been a Slovene. But the idea of monarchy didn't bother her. After all, the British had a king, too, didn't they? She'd read Shakespeare in the language of Shakespeare. She'd read most of the English classics down to the early works of Galsworthy. The American literature she knew was mostly modern. Books like *Gone with the Wind* and the novels of Kathleen Norris and Edna Ferber. She knew nothing about Walt Whitman, Carl Sandburg, Sinclair Lewis, Upton Sinclair, Gertrude Stein, or Philip Wylie. The only thing of John Steinbeck's she'd read was *Of Mice and Men*. She got halfway through it and then stopped because she didn't understand what Steinbeck was driving at. She'd never heard of *Grapes of Wrath*. She knew Ernest Hemingway only by reputation. She didn't like books about war. One of her extravagancies in the 30's was a subscription to

Good Housekeeping. She liked the fiction, the fashion plates, the ads, and the recipes, although she didn't understand how American women could get along without a servant or two apiece.

During the early days of the war she was shocked by what the Germans were doing to Britain by air. She hoped they wouldn't destroy some of her favorite churches, cathedrals, and museums. She also hoped that America would come in soon and end it in a hurry. She missed her month and a half of travel each year. Stories of what the Nazis were doing to the Jews didn't especially impress her. She had never been brought into association with any Jews. In March of '41, when the Cvetković-Cincar-Marković government in Belgrade signed the Axis Pact she was confused. She didn't know how to feel about it. But the government official for whom she worked told her that they must all have confidence in their leaders in Belgrade. They knew what they were doing. Did she want war to come to Yugoslavia? Did she want the Nazis to do to Ljubljana what they had done to London and Warsaw? The signing of the Axis Pact simply meant that Yugoslavia would continue to stay on the side lines. The Germans might go through Yugoslavia to attack Greece, but Yugoslavia would be unharmed. After that Valetta stopped worrying.

But the next day, when Ljubljana heard about the coup d'état in Belgrade, there wasn't anyone to straighten out her thinking for her. That morning the government official she worked for telephoned that he wouldn't be in. She never saw him again. So she had to try to figure things out for herself. Prince Paul had fled the country, they said. But young King Peter had taken the oath and so they still had the monarchy and that was good. But the crowds in Terazzia in Belgrade had been shouting ugly words about Hitler and Mussolini. Berlin and Rome wouldn't like that. Everyone said that this meant war, and Valetta didn't want war. The next ten days were days of great confusion. In Ljubljana there were preparations for war. And then on April sixth it came. Ljubljana was quickly occupied by Italian soldiers. Then things settled down. Of course Valetta didn't have a job any more. She figured it was best not to wander too far away from her apartment anyway. The Italian soldiers were behaving themselves very well, her friends said, but there had been stories from other places, and Valetta figured it was best not to take a chance. She didn't collaborate with the enemy in any way, but she didn't oppose the enemy in any way either. She just wanted to be let alone and she was. She lived in Ljubljana all through the occupation. Of course there were many hardships. There were blackouts. Food was often scarce. There wasn't much in the shops any more. Several times the one servant she had left wanted to go back to her native village, but each time Valetta persuaded her to stay. She didn't get her interest money from abroad any more, but she managed to live on the ready cash she fortunately had saved up for three or four years' vacations she hadn't been able to take. Valetta spent most of the time during those occupation years catching up on her reading. She read every English book she had in the house. And she reread all the back numbers of *Good Housekeeping*. Of course *Good Housekeeping* wasn't coming any more, and as the war wore on she began to get tired of seeing the same old ads and reading the same old recipes over and over again. She wondered what women were wearing in America now. She wondered whether she'd ever be able to travel again.

When she heard about the Partisan Army in the mountains she got very nervous. Those guerrilla soldiers, people said, were attacking enemy garrisons not only in small villages but even in larger places. The woman next door said someday they might even try to liberate Ljubljana. Valetta hoped not. That would mean fighting in the streets, and no one would be safe. The woman next door whispered that her son had managed to get out of Ljubljana and had joined the Partisans. Valetta, with a genuine lack of understanding, asked why on earth he had done it. The mother tried to explain. But she didn't understand it very well herself and Valetta didn't understand at all, even after the conversation. She heard about the Serbian Chetniks too. They made more sense to her. They were fighting for the return of the monarchy and young King Peter. Valetta thought their boy king was such a nice young man. She'd seen pictures of him in the streets after General Simović put him on the throne. He was clean-cut and nice-looking. They said he was in love with a Greek princess. He was in London and so sometimes Valetta turned on her radio and listened to B.B.C., hoping she might hear something about King Peter and his romance. One day going to market she met a man who used to work in the same government office as she did. He was the one who told her things about the Partisans she could understand. They were being supported from Moscow. Some of them were actually Communists. If they had their way everything in Yugoslavia would be changed. They were against the return of the king. Many of the Partisan leaders had been in exile for years. Some of them had been in prison for trying to organize labor unions. Valetta didn't like labor unions. She thought they were troublemakers, stirring up difficulties between employers and employees. But it was the Partisans' connection with Moscow that set her against them. She'd never been to Russia and she hadn't read much about the country either. Once a friend gave her some old Russian novels. She tried to read one by a man named Dostoevski, but she found it very depressing. The things she'd been told about Communism made her hate it. She didn't want anything like that in Yugoslavia. If that's what the Partisans stood for then she was against them.

Ljubljana was not liberated until the very end of the war. That meant that Valetta lived through more than four years of Axis occupation. But except for certain disruptions of her daily life and the fact that she couldn't take her annual vacations any more, the war never really touched her. She had no brothers or other close masculine kin. No one she knew intimately was killed except the son of the woman next door. Ljubljana was bombed only once. It was a little raid, and the bombs fell on the other side of the city from where Valetta lived. When she heard over her radio one night that the Germans were surrendering and the war was about over she had a little celebration all her own. She opened a bottle of champagne she'd brought home from Paris years ago and she got out her big envelope of travel folders and started planning her first trip abroad. They said Paris was the least damaged city. Maybe she'd go there. And maybe now she could subscribe to *Good Housekeeping* again.

I met Valetta one day while I was swimming in the lake called Bohinjska Bistrica Jezero. She was about thirty-six, tall, well-dressed, rather aristocratic looking. She was well-dressed even in a bathing suit. She said she used to buy her clothes abroad but since 1939 she'd had to be content with remodeling all the old clothes she had. I saw Valetta many times. She made no secret of her hatred of the New Yugoslavia. She was perfectly willing to talk about it and answer any questions I asked her. She told me how she felt about everything. Everything she had any feelings about. One reason she was so frank with me was because she knew, she said, that all Americans hated this New Yugoslavia as much as she did. I'd understand and sympathize. She knew that. But there was another reason which didn't come out until the day she left Bohinjska Bistrica Jezero to go back to Ljubljana. She wanted to go abroad. The war had been over two years and still she hadn't been out of the country. That wasn't because of any lack of desire. She'd tried over and over again to get a passport. But the new government told her that Yugoslavs were needed at home. No traveling was permitted except on urgent business. They also said that Yugoslavia couldn't afford having her money spent abroad. Any dollar exchange or pound-sterling exchange was needed to buy food and machinery. Valetta didn't understand that excuse at all. It was her own money, wasn't it? What did the government of Yugoslavia have to do with it? What difference did it make to the Yugoslav Government whether she spent the money in Ljubljana or Paris? They told her the same thing when she tried to send a few hundred dinar to New York to renew her subscription to *Good Housekeeping*. They told her it might be three or four years before she could travel or buy things from abroad. Even magazines.

Valetta was one of the unhappiest women I'd met in postwar Europe. She said the only pleasure she got was that she could have some contact with foreigners again. That's why she'd come to Bohinjska Bistrica this summer. She hunted out foreigners with the diligence of a hound dog sniffing a trail in the woods. While she was in Ljubljana she concentrated on the British. It was principally because the British had a consulate in Ljubljana again. There was no American consulate there. The British Consulate consisted merely of a house in which the consul lived and had a small office. But Valetta soon became friends with his Slovenian secretary, who let her read all the British newspapers and magazines that came in the mail, and sometimes loaned her new English books. Going in and out of the consulate she sometimes met British people and could practice her English and learn about what was going on in the rest of the world.

Valetta didn't read the Ljubljana newspapers any more. There wasn't anything in them that interested her. News from abroad was mostly about political conferences and Valetta didn't pretend to understand international politics. The domestic news was all about youth railroads and competitions of workers and problems of the reconstruction. Valetta knew that homes had to be rebuilt and it was probably a good thing to have more railroads, but why did they have to talk about it so much? Why couldn't the papers print serial stories, and news about scandals and romance? For example, she never would have known about King Peter marrying the Greek princess if some British friend hadn't told her. As for the new regime, as people called it, she hated it. The servant she'd had for so many years had gone to a literacy class and had learned to read and write. What sense did that make? The woman probably wouldn't be nearly so happy now. And then all those pictures of Marshal Tito. Valetta thought King Peter was much nicer-looking. Maybe I'd tell her why they hadn't let him come back and be king again? They said his wife was such a nice girl.

It wasn't until I'd seen her many times that Valetta began to tell me stories about "The Terror." She used the same English word that the diplomatic people in Belgrade used. She told me a number of second- and third-hand stories she'd heard. About people disappearing. People being executed. None of them had been friends of hers. Friends of friends told her the stories. Finally she told me her own personal story of "The Terror." She said she was afraid to go around to the British Consulate very often. One night last summer, after she'd been there two or three hours talking to the consul's secretary and reading newspapers, she noticed that a man on a bicycle followed her all the way home. The next day a gendarme came to her house and asked to see her identity papers. The woman next door whose son was killed in the Partisans said the gendarme went from house to house asking to see everyone's identity papers. She said it was part of a checkup to try to find some men who had sneaked in across the frontier from Austria. But Valetta didn't believe that. She didn't believe anything the woman next door told her now. That woman's mind had been poisoned by the new regime. Valetta knew that she was being watched. It made her very nervous. That's why she'd lost so much weight the past year.

When I asked her if she held any position now her eyes flashed defiance. No, she didn't, and she wasn't going to accept any position, even if one were offered to her. About a year ago the woman next door, knowing that Valetta had once been a nurse, tried to persuade her to help run an orphanage that was being opened for several thousand children of Partisans, Chetniks, and Ustaši killed in the war. The woman had hardly spoken to her since then because Valetta told her just how she felt. If the government would give her a passport and let her go abroad for a few months she'd come back and do anything they asked her to do. But unless she got a passport she wasn't going to work again. Not ever.

The last day before she went back to Ljubljana, Valetta said she wanted to have a long talk with me. When we were alone by the side of the lake she said she had secretly sold her stocks and bonds to an Englishman and she figured she had enough money to get along the rest of her life. But she'd rather throw herself right in the lake than live any longer here in Yugoslavia. There was nothing about her own country that appealed to her any more. She wanted freedom. Freedom to read *Good Housekeeping* if she wanted to. Freedom to travel. Freedom to talk to British people without some little man on a bicycle following her. I must help her. The previous British consul took his cook with him when he left. The Yugoslav Government gave her a passport right away when the British consul asked them for it. Couldn't I take her out of Yugoslavia with me as a secretary? Or as a cook or kitchen maid? Anything. She'd pay her own way to Paris. I wouldn't ever see her again after we got to Paris. She'd pay her own way. She'd even give me a thousand dollars for my trouble. She'd die if she had to stay here. I wanted to ask her what contribution she thought she could make to France, England, or the United States in return for the welcome she expected those countries to give her. But I didn't. I was afraid she wouldn't understand.

That night I went to sleep thinking of some other women I'd met in my months in Yugoslavia. The nurse on the island opposite Dubrovnik who was taking care of an orphanage full of small victims of war. The Serbian wife of Lovett Edwards, the British journalist, who finally got her "freedom to wander." The girl who worked in the government office in Valjevo, Serbia, who took us up the hill to show us the mass graves. Negosava was her name. She was the one who picked the purple spring flowers while she told us about how she felt. I thought of Sonia who was out of Yugoslavia and obviously didn't want to come back. I thought of the Macedonian schoolteacher who was so eager that I find out all about the New Yugoslavia. Well, Valetta was part of the New Yugoslavia too. How many people she represented no statistician could tell. But Valetta is a small part of the story.

Chapter Eighty-Five

BROOKLYN IN A CASTLE

SOMETIME in the thirteenth century a German nobleman picked a hill on the edge of the Slovenian village of Turjak as an ideal place for a castle. The castle he built was made to last a thousand years. It might have stood a thousand years except for what happened in September of '43.

No one in the village of Turjak has anything to say against the family Auersperg. They remember two or three generations of Auerspergs. They were all "nice people." Aristocrats of the old school. The relationship between the castle up on the hill and the village at its feet was a benevolent feudal relationship. The occupants of the castle were not newly rich. They had money but it had been husbanded down through the generations. The income of the Auersperg fortune was spent judiciously. With no ostentation. Sometimes Count and Countess Auersperg and their only son had parties in the castle on the hill. People came from as far away as Berlin. They might stay for as long as two weeks. But they were quiet family parties. The Auerspergs had a staff of twenty-seven retainers. Four of them worked as servants inside the castle cooking, pressing grapes, keeping house, waxing floors, and making life pleasant for the count and his wife and son. The others worked in the fields and the forests which surrounded the castle. But actually the entire village depended on the Auerspergs for sustenance. Nearly everyone in Turjak owed his living directly or indirectly to the people up in the castle. For example, Josef Ahec who owned the village pub, or *gostilna* as the Slovenes call such a place, sold beer and wine by the barrel whenever the Auerspergs had guests, for it was a tradition that in the evening the guests would wander down to his place and sit around swapping stories over mugs of *pivo* or tall, thin glasses of amber-colored *vino*. Josef also ran a general store and the castle people bought many things from him. So did the families of the twenty-seven people on the Auerspergs' pay roll. Every hundred dinar that the count handed out changed hands two or three times right in the village of Turjak before it went any farther. The Auerspergs treated their hired help with consideration and kindness. If there was a birth or a death or a marriage in any of the village families the Auerspergs took due notice of the event with an appropriate gift of flowers, wine, or small gold pieces. If anyone was ill the countess herself might drive down to the peasant's cottage with a bottle of bitter-tasting medicine which she claimed would cure anything, from lumbago to pains in the head.

During the first two years of the German occupation the count often entertained high-ranking Nazi army officers. He told his servants that there was nothing wrong with Hitler annexing Slovenia to the greater Third Reich. As soon as the war was over things would be much better for everyone. Germany was going to be the master nation of the world and Slovenes should be proud that they were going to be allowed to participate in the glories of the eventual triumph.

Under the influence of the count several men from the village of Turjak volunteered to serve in the Domobranci. That was an army led by Yugoslav Quislings that was helping the Germans here in the north. When Italy capitulated early in September of '43 the Domobranci got their hands on a number of Italian tanks and guns. In the sudden emergency they were supposed to help the Germans who had to redeploy all their occupational troops in a hurry. All those sections of Yugoslavia which had been occupied by Mussolini troops had to be taken over by the Nazis. Garrisons had to be removed from relatively unimportant mountain towns like Turjak.

That gave the Partisans their chance. They moved quickly to take over any spots the Nazis left unguarded. Especially mountaintops. And the Partisans didn't deal kindly with any Domobranci units they met up with. That's how it was that on the night of September the fifteenth tanks came thundering through the road which leads past Josef's gostilna and winds its way up the hill to the castle. They were Italian tanks which had been taken over by the Domobranci. Some of them were dragging heavy guns.

That night eleven hundred men of the Domobranci barricaded themselves in the old castle out of their fear of Partisan bands which were roaming the area. The count had already fled to parts unknown. But his wife, the countess, and his son were there. They tried to argue at first that this was their private home. But they soon found that you can't argue with soldiers. Especially with soldiers who are in fear of their lives.

The next day the Partisans came over the hills from several directions and began attacking. At first the men of the Domobranci fought back from parapets and towers. But before long they began to run out of ammunition so most of them just hid in the deep, high-vaulted cellars of the castle and waited. They had a wild hope that their German friends would return in time to save them.

The third night Domobranci scouts went out reconnoitering. They came back very excited. They said the Partisans hadn't yet completed the encirclement. The scouts had found a way of escape if anyone wanted to take a chance. Four hundred men elected to take a chance. So did the countess and her son. They all got away safely.

The next day the Partisan siege began in earnest. Now there were seven hundred Domobranci in the castle, plus a few of the count's old retainers. The village priest was there, trying to tell the men that they must have faith in their Maker. Ivan Husner was there too. He was the chief housekeeper and as much a part of the castle as the turret from which the count's personal flag generally flew. He'd been born in the castle and when the countess begged him to leave with her he just shook his head. He was

born here and he'd die here if he had to. His father had been the chief
hunter for the count's father. His father had worked for the Auerspergs
for fifty years. Ivan had lived in the castle for longer than that. No. He
guessed he'd stay.

The siege lasted for eight days. There were four hundred Partisans in
the attacking party. The Partisans worked their way up the hill to the
castle very gingerly. They apparently were afraid of falling into a trap.
They didn't finally storm the place until they had done a great deal of
shelling. The shells made great holes in the castle walls, knocked in all
the roofs, and set many fires. But the four hundred men in the cellars were
relatively safe. In the eight days the total casualty list was only three dead,
twenty-eight wounded. It was hunger more than anything else that made
the Domobranci put up a white flag. And maybe the fact that on the
eighth day the hard cider ran out. There had been sixteen hundred liters
of hard cider in the great wine cellar. That figured out to about one gallon
for each of the four hundred men. But one gallon for eight days when you
haven't any food and your nerves are on edge isn't much to drink. Anyway, the Domobranci surrendered on the eighth day.

It was a hot summer afternoon when we drove into the village of Turjak. Josef the pub keeper was standing in front of his gostilna talking to
three other men. Across the road a pink pig was sunning herself. Even
from this distance we could see the shell holes in the castle walls. We told
Josef we'd be back to have some of his beer in a few minutes.

What was left of the castle was principally a few punctured stone walls
and great piles of rubble. Jaka the chauffeur went on a scavenger hunt
while we looked the place over. In the debris he found the stone head of
a cherub, which he gave to Blossom, a few unexploded Italian dumdum
bullets, pieces of exploded grenades, a Domobranci cap with a hole
through the top which explained clearly enough what had happened to its
owner. When Albert Rejec pointed out that the only part of the castle
which hadn't been reduced to heaps of stone and charred timbers was the
chapel, I thought of the Miracle of Čajniče. Rejec said the Slovenian Government was very eager to preserve this chapel because it was as old as
the castle itself and was one of the first Protestant churches in this part
of Europe. Later, when the Auersperg family became Catholics, the chapel
became Catholic too. In all the shelling by the Partisans not a bit of damage was done to the golden altar, the crucifix with the red light burning
before it, the ancient murals in colors which time had made soft and
mellow.

Josef and his three friends were still standing in front of the gostilna
when we drove back into the village. We ordered beer for the four of them
and for ourselves. Josef introduced us to Ivan, who had been chief housekeeper for the Auerspergs.

Ivan said, in English, that the first thing we ought to know was that he
spent two years in Brooklyn, from 1922 to 1924. He didn't like Brooklyn

very well. He made a little money at carpentering in Brooklyn but after two years he came back to the castle in which he was born and had lived there ever since. Until the castle was destroyed. Seventeen years ago his daughter Frances went to America to live. She married a Slovene over there and now she's Mrs. Henry Mikolic and lives at 1271 Tonawanda Street in Buffalo with a figure seven after it. She's written him four letters and had sent him three packages since the war.

We asked him what he did during the siege. He said he spent his time mostly feeding the rabbits. Didn't we know about the rabbits? He thought everyone knew about the rabbits. The Auerspergs were very fond of rabbits. That was one of his jobs. To take care of the rabbits. All during the battle he was busy feeding the rabbits or handing out bottles of hard cider to the Domobranci soldiers. It was a lucky thing for the rabbits that there weren't any stoves down in the cellar. Otherwise the Domobranci might have eaten all the countess's pets. Ivan didn't know what happened finally to the rabbits or to the countess and her son.

The Partisans held the castle and the village of Turjak for a short time and then the Germans drove them out. The Germans occupied this place from then on until the end of the war. Once, while the Germans were here, the count suddenly appeared one day. He didn't say much to anyone. He took one look at the castle and then he left. That was the last anyone ever heard of the family. The village missed them. Nice people they were.

At this point Ivan took off his Tyrol hat and mopped his red face with it. He said he hadn't talked so much English since he left Brooklyn twenty-five years ago. How was Brooklyn? Now that the Auerspergs were gone he wouldn't mind going back to Brooklyn. Life wasn't the same here any more. It wasn't anybody's fault except that the village lived off the castle and now there wasn't any castle any more.

Ivan himself was now what he called "an assistant to a farmer." Rejec said what he meant was that he was a farmhand for some peasant. Ivan said some people around here were content with the new way of life in Yugoslavia. Some thought there wasn't much difference between now and the way it used to be. If you got a good harvest you had something to eat, and if you didn't maybe you went hungry. Then there were other people who thought things were worse. A lot of the people of Turjak were in that last class.

Albert Rejec suggested we talk to the other three men and see if we could tell in which group each of them belonged. Ivan himself belonged in the last group. After a lifetime as the count's housekeeper, in charge of a staff of servants, being a common farmhand obviously left him discontented. Number Two was Josef the innkeeper. He was the bitterest of the lot. And he probably had the most reason. There weren't any week-end guests any more to come down the hill to his gostilna to buy beer. He admitted that some of the villagers had good jobs of various kinds now, but they didn't spend much of their money with him. Most of the business of his general store had been taken over by the government co-operative. Various villagers had told him that they would like to continue trading with him, but prices were lower at the government co-operative.

Number Three was an intelligent-looking man in his middle years. He wore a green hat with a bright red feather stuck in the band. He said that before the war he was a "worker." Now he was a forestry guard. For him personally, he said, things were better than before. He thought that for Yugoslavia in general this was a difficult period because of all the reconstruction that had to be done. So much man power and so much material had to go into repairing the damage of war. But those who had lived through other wars knew that it was always this way. He thought that in another few years things would be better.

Number Four had been one of the Count Auersperg's retainers. Now he was a road inspector. He said things had been difficult for people around here the last two years for several reasons. First, what had happened to the castle. Second, the two summers of drought. People can't be happy when they're hungry, and a lot of people had been hungry at various times in the last two years.

At that point Ivan, who had been to Brooklyn, said there was also the Colorado beetle to blame. He didn't know how it got all the way from America to the village of Turjak but it was here all right. Everyone had to spend time out in the fields trying to find the darned things. Josef said maybe Ivan had brought the beetles with him when he came back from America in 1924. That caused some good-natured banter that brought the interviews to an end.

As we drove away Albert Rejec said it looked to him as if each of the four men had his own particular attitude toward the situation and each for understandable reasons. If we listed Josef the pub keeper as a bitter enemy of the regime we probably wouldn't be far wrong. And he had a double reason. The destruction of the castle and the flight of the count had ruined his liquor business. And when the government began opening up co-operatives to decrease the price of commodities to the people his pocketbook was hit again. As for Ivan, he didn't seem bitter. He had a good sense of humor and sprinkled his whole conversation with little jokes, but there was no disguising the fact that he missed his position of importance as the count's housekeeper. The road inspector who also had worked for the Auerspergs realized that he was as well off today as he was before, and that conditions might improve. The fourth man, the forestry guard, was better off than he was before and seemed to be well aware of it.

And so, said Rejec, you see that each person's attitude toward the regime is entirely dependent on what's happened to him personally. That's true all over Yugoslavia. People all fall into one of those four groups. But of course, he said, the percentages vary from place to place. Turjak isn't quite typical. After all, Yugoslavia didn't have a benevolent German count with a castle and twenty-seven retainers in every village. And maybe that was just as well.

Chapter Eighty-Six

FROM TAXES TO SEX

ONE afternoon we sat under the trees on the shore of the lake at the mountain summer resort called Bled while Rejec answered hundreds of questions I'd accumulated in my months of wandering. I picked Rejec to "fill me in" because he spoke such excellent English, because he was the best-informed Yugoslav I had met, and because after traveling for many days with him I knew that he would tell me the whole truth. The very fact that he had suggested a visit to the village of Turjak where I would discover considerable dissatisfaction convinced me that he wasn't trying to fasten a pair of rose-colored glasses over my eyes.

Bled is Yugoslavia's number-one summer resort. In some ways it's like Atlantic City. On a miniature scale. There are expensive hotels like the Toplice and relatively inexpensive ones too. But it has always been a place primarily for the better people. Your bill for a week at the Toplice would come to about what you'd pay for a week at one of Atlantic City's boardwalk hotels. We sat for a little while at a small green table under a striped umbrella watching one-man boats take visitors out to the island in the middle of the lake on which there's a church that no tourist ever misses. Each boatman stood in the stern manipulating two slender oars with the skill of a Venetian gondolier. The boats themselves reminded us of the gondolas of Venice. There was a gay canvas awning over each one. Occasionally music came from across the water. This was a far cry from Golo. Yet Golo wasn't very many miles away. I thought of Golo when Rejec pointed out a pile of fresh earth beside the Toplice where he said a large café had stood until just a few months ago. It had been pulled down to make way for an addition which was about to be built to the hotel. I asked by what stretch of reasoning could the government allow man power and building materials to be used on such a job while some of the people of Golo didn't have roofs over their heads. Rejec said that that was an embarrassing question. It wasn't right. There had been many complaints. Perhaps it was the complaints that had brought a temporary stop to the construction job.

When Rejec mentioned that the government of Slovenia owned most of these large hotels I learned that government ownership in this section isn't something that was introduced by the Tito regime after the war. Even in the days of the monarchy there was a tradition of nationalization. These hotels, for example. They had been owned by a prominent Slovenian capitalist. Long before the war he went into bankruptcy and the

State took over his property. Nothing much had been changed by war or the new regime here in Bled. Of course many of those large villas dotting the edge of the lake were private once and are now state property. But that's just because they were owned by war criminals who fled with the Germans and when they failed to return the government confiscated their property. Rejec thought it was interesting that the son of the man who had once owned all these hotels was now manager of a government thermal bath resort at Rogaska Slatina.

Then we talked about nationalization in general. Under the Yugoslav system it's possible to nationalize an entire industry, or an entire trade or profession. All large hotels, for example, have been nationalized. That means the owners have been paid what an investigating commission decided was a fair price for their property, and now the hotels are owned, operated, and managed by the State. In some cases ownership is in the name of a town, a city, or one of the six republics. As with the post-office department in the United States, an attempt is made to charge the public enough to pay for all operating costs and return the State a nominal profit on its investment. Prices charged by government-owned establishments, or by co-operatives, are generally 10 to 30 per cent lower than they would be in privately owned establishments. Already in Yugoslavia all heavy industry, most large hotels and restaurants, some chemists' shops, and a few miscellaneous business establishments are being run by the government. In many cases the managers are the former owners. They're generally given the job if they wish it. There are no collective farms in Yugoslavia. Land has not been nationalized. The only thing that has been done about land is that the large holdings of collaborators and war criminals confiscated by court order have been divided among peasants with little land. But land has not been a serious problem because even in prewar Yugoslavia the ownership of land was on a broad, relatively even basis.

When a trade or profession is nationalized it means that those affected may no longer practice their trade or profession privately. Henceforth they are government employees. All newspapers, radio stations, theaters, and concert halls are owned by the State. Most of them have been, since long before the war. Of course it is still possible for a violinist to accept a position in a privately owned kafana or for a writer to give up his job on a newspaper and take to free-lance writing or representing an American news agency or paper in Belgrade. Among the hundreds of trades and professions not nationalized are those of carpenters, masons, farmers, bricklayers, photographers, doctors, lawyers, small innkeepers, waiters, chambermaids, small shopowners, taxi drivers, cooks, and tailors. I pointed out to Rejec that it was curious that in Yugoslavia there has been no socialization of medicine, while in England, one of the Western capitalistic democracies, there is almost complete socialization, and even in the United States a constant campaign goes on for some degree of socialization. He said it may come in Yugoslavia later.

Rejec said that it was important to note that there had been no nationalization of artisans. In these postwar years Yugoslavia has great need of the labor and talents of her relatively few artisans, such as carpenters and masons. And so they have complete economic freedom. There isn't even any control over the prices they charge. The result began to get a little fantastic. In postwar Yugoslavia the monthly salary of the head of an important state department is one hundred to one hundred and twenty dollars. But a year ago a carpenter was making as much as one thousand dollars a month. Something had to be done. And yet the government didn't want to discourage artisans by controlling their wages. And so the surplus income was absorbed quietly in income taxes but the artisan was still left enough to make it more profitable for him to pursue his own trade than to drop it for something else.

That brought up the subject of taxation in general. In the New Yugoslavia there is no set tax rate. A physician with an annual income of five thousand dollars may pay a much smaller tax than a lawyer living next door with exactly the same income. But it goes even further than that. One doctor with a five-thousand-dollar income may be assessed twice the tax of his neighbor, who is also a doctor with a five-thousand-dollar income. The assessment in every case is fixed by local government officials on the basis of how the man earned his money, what contributions he's making to the society in which he lives, and other personal considerations. I said that this seemed a dangerous system. If the local officials happened to have a personal dislike for Lawyer Jones they could tax him to death. It opened the way for the use of taxation as a political weapon. Rejec said there were two answers. First, any action by local officials is subject to review. If a man thinks he is being unjustly taxed he can file a complaint and his complaint will be publicly heard. Often such complaints lead to a revision of the assessment. But more important than that, we must realize that Yugoslavia is a brand-new state, trying to feel her way slowly. Yugoslavia as yet has no civil and criminal code. There is one now in the process of being drafted. Until it is approved by the people, Yugoslavia is actually operating without any laws. As soon as the code is completed there will probably be tax laws for everyone just as we have in the United States. Only Yugoslavia is determined that there will be no loopholes through which tax evaders can crawl with the help of good lawyers, as in some countries.

We went from taxes to sex in one large jump. Rejec said there's a lot of foolish talk among foreigners about the so-called New Morality in Yugoslavia. It is true that in the mountains during the war the Partisans discouraged any attention to sex. Immediately after the end of the fighting the barriers went down with a bang. Men and women lived together with little attention to former custom, the laws of the State, or decrees of the Church. When the government set out to discourage such indiscretions the phrase "the New Morality" sprang up.

Today Yugoslavia is trying to give importance to the institution of the family. Birth control is discouraged but not forbidden. There are no government birth-control clinics. No "planned parenthood." Maybe that will come later. Because of the great loss of life during the war, Yugoslavia is trying to encourage large families, but Yugoslavia had not adopted the Hitler-Mussolini technique of offering bonuses for babies. Instead, a man's wage or salary is based partially on need. Larger food rations are given to people with large families.

Every factory has what's called a "cradle." We would call it a day nursery. There women workers can leave their children to be cared for by trained personnel while they work.

In the Old Yugoslavia abortions were not illegal. They were frowned on by the Church but no doctor was ever prosecuted for causing the death of a woman in the course of performing an abortion. Today it's a serious offense.

Few people in Yugoslavia have ever heard of Lucy Stone, but there is widespread approval of the idea of a woman keeping her own name after marriage. Many do. A woman has a chance to carve out an independent career for herself without being tied to her husband in the public eye. Rejec knew two good examples. The Slovenian Minister of Culture and the Chief of the Slovenian Control Commission are both extremely bright women. They are both married but both use their own names. No one has any idea who their husbands are. And no one cares.

And then Albert Rejec told us about his brother. His brother was one of Ljubljana's prominent lawyers. He was also one of the earliest Partisan volunteers. He was killed in action in 1943.

His wife was young and beautiful. They had been deeply in love. She had become, in spite of the handicaps thrown in the way of a woman in the old days, an able physician. A specialist in venereal diseases. She and her husband had no secret pact. She didn't make the oath until she learned of his death. She didn't tell many people about it. She did tell her brother-in-law, Albert Rejec. She said that she could never marry again. She could never dwell in the same house with another man. The memory of her husband was too poignant. Too deep and powerful. But she had always wanted children. She and her husband had talked about it before he went to war. After the war was over they were going to raise a family. The wife knew, as a physician, that she was physically well qualified to bring children into the world. Now with the war over, Yugoslavia needed healthy children. And she still wanted them herself. So she went very seriously and very coldly about the business of having a "eugenic baby." She picked the father among her acquaintances. Maybe among her patients. Albert Rejec wasn't quite sure about that. She explained the situation to the man and he agreed to be the father of her child.

The baby is now more than a year old. The father sees him as often as he pleases and is very much in love with the child. It worked out so well that she's planning a second child. Her friends all know what she's done and there are no raised eyebrows. No one has stopped speaking to her.

She's one of the leading women in her field in the New Yugoslavia. And her case is not unique.

Then we went into the matter of religion. In the Old Yugoslavia it was impossible to be married by a civil ceremony except in one section which had once been part of Hungary. Membership in some church was essential for other practical reasons too. The result was a large church membership but not much religion. Today if a man or a woman can produce a certificate stating that he or she has not been married before or has been legally divorced, the marriage ceremony can be performed by the proper civil officials. Church and State have been separated. It is possible for a person to be a nature worshiper or a Confucianist if he pleases. The result, Rejec said, is that those who have remained church members are really religious people. Spirituality has not suffered. The influence of the Clerical party in politics has died out. But real religion is flourishing in Yugoslavia as it has never flourished before. Of course those priests and bishops, and there were some, who tried to use their religious influence to help the Nazis and became 100 per cent collaborators have been put on trial and some of them have been punished for their war crimes. But what, Albert Rejec asked, has that to do with suppression of religion?

By this time the sun had begun to set behind the hills which encircle the summer resort of Bled. The gondola-like boats with their bright canvas roofs were being tied to their wharves for the night. Waiters in white coats and black bow ties were setting the tables for the meal called *večera*. Off in the distance an accordion was playing a soft Slovenian love song. A stream of hikers was coming in from the mountains. Albert Rejec, who had spent all his life until two years ago dodging someone, lit a cigarette and said he hoped maybe we'd come back in another five years and check up again on what they were trying to do. Yugoslavia, he said, wasn't perfect yet. No country probably ever would be perfect. But it's wonderful, he said, not to have to hide any more, just because you believe in some of those things that men like George Washington, Abraham Lincoln, Thomas Jefferson, Woodrow Wilson, and Franklin Roosevelt believed in too. The right of all men to a decent living.

Chapter Eighty-Seven

BLOOD OR STAR DUST

It's a long climb to the top of Triglav. You need ropes and those instruments shaped like pickaxes that professional mountain climbers use. When you get to the top you can easily imagine you're on the pinnacle of the world and not just on the highest point of land in Yugoslavia. The wind blows strong across the top of Triglav. The wind blows strong and fresh. There are no cobwebs on Triglav. That high up mental cobwebs disappear too. That's why I wanted to go up there before I headed home from this land of the Croats, Serbs, and Slovenes. I wanted to sit alone up there and watch a golden moon come up. I wanted to sit there in silence while the gold turned to silver. Until the moon completed her circuit and set again. I wanted to think out all I had heard and seen and smelled during the past year of roaming.

The night I reached the top was a night made for gondola riding on the canals of Venice. Or for listening to a gypsy orchestra under the trees of a softly lit café. Or for sitting on a mountaintop trying to fit together the pieces of a puzzle. I lay on my back smoking and thinking. The moon was silver now. It seemed a million miles to "down below." Down there was the world. The world of good and evil. The world of charred ruins and buildings of fresh-cut timber. The world of hate and fear. Love and brotherhood. Propaganda and truth. Conflict and co-operation. The world of atom bombs and the United Nations. The world of the two Colossi and their fawning children. I lay there looking up at the stars and down into the quiet valleys. Nature was peaceful and serene tonight. I lay there looking at—nothing—and thinking of—everything. Off in America, I'd heard, there was more talk than ever about the inevitability of war. Someone in Ljubljana had shown me a recent magazine article by a reputable American scientific writer about the potentialities of biological warfare. He wrote that even if atom bombs finally were outlawed, the United States was prepared to unloose "aerosol clouds" which would plague civilians and soldiers alike in an enemy country with such diseases as yellow fever, psittacosis, tularemia (rabbit fever), melioidosis (a rare and fatal disease of the Malay Peninsula), undulant fever, and rickettsial infections such as typhus and Rocky Mountain spotted fever. Yes, everywhere men, feeble little men, were making a mess of trying to get along. The brains of the world seemed to be unwittingly concentrated on how to wipe civilization from the map. But here on the top of Triglav, where sky and mountains merged in a blackness so subtle no eye could see the line, nature was calm and serene. Day turned to night. Night turned to day. And the moon moved in her slow, inscrutable way across the heavens. All with the rhythm of nature. Defiantly. Incontrovertibly. With the rhythm of nature. Nature has a great mystic purpose. But man founders. Man has yet to understand his place in the scheme of things. Man out of tune with nature. Man who has neither become reconciled to letting nature be the master nor has succeeded in conquering nature. Man out of rhythm. Man, the one discordant note in the Symphony of Life. Man, the violinist playing E-minor when the score calls for C-major. Man who can split an atom and make a piece of steel fly through the air faster than the speed of sound, and kill a million people a thousand miles away with clouds of bugs. But still he can't figure out how to get along with his fellow man. Man, who wants only to eat and sleep and love . . . to live and let live . . . and . . . yes, to reach occasionally for a star. But in the process he collects more blood on his fingers than he does the dust of stars.

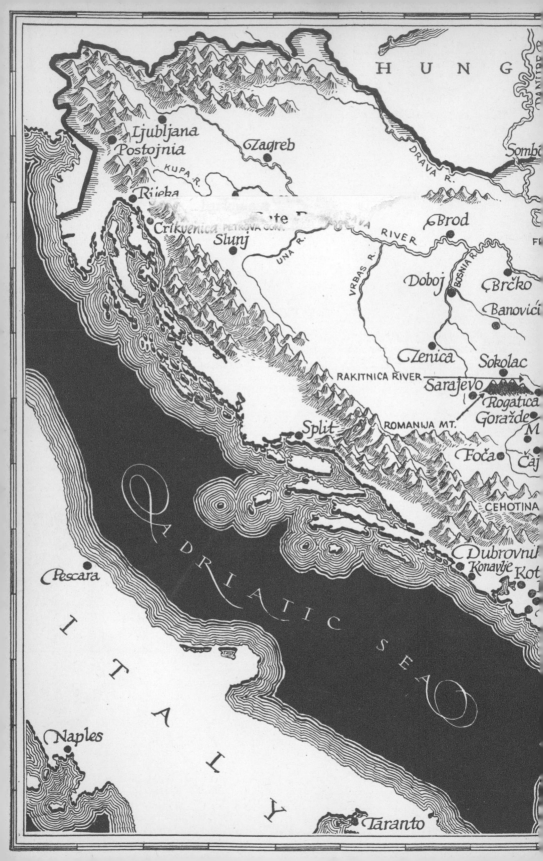